Theoretical Study on China's Political Economy

Theoretical Study on China's Political Economy

HONG Yinxing
Nanjing University, China

Translated by
HE Chengzhou
Nanjing University, China

World Scientific

NEW JERSEY • LONDON • SINGAPORE • BEIJING • SHANGHAI • HONG KONG • TAIPEI • CHENNAI • TOKYO

Published by

World Scientific Publishing Co. Pte. Ltd.

5 Toh Tuck Link, Singapore 596224

USA office: 27 Warren Street, Suite 401-402, Hackensack, NJ 07601

UK office: 57 Shelton Street, Covent Garden, London WC2H 9HE

Library of Congress Cataloging-in-Publication Data
Names: Hong, Yinxing, 1950– author.
Title: Theoretical Study on China's Political Economy / Yinxing Hong, Nanjing University, China ; translated by Chengzhou He, Nanjing University, China.
Other titles: Zhongguo te se she hui zhu yi zheng zhi jing ji xue li lun ti xi gou jian. English
Description: Hackensack, NJ : World Scientific, 2022. | Includes bibliographical references and index.
Identifiers: LCCN 2021035000 | ISBN 9789811241529 (hardcover) | ISBN 9789811241536 (ebook) | ISBN 9789811241543 (ebook other)
Subjects: LCSH: China--Economic policy--2000- | Marxian economics--China. | Capitalism--China. | Globalization--China.
Classification: LCC HC427.95 H6613 2022 | DDC 338.951--dc23
LC record available at https://lccn.loc.gov/2021035000

British Library Cataloguing-in-Publication Data
A catalogue record for this book is available from the British Library.

Sponsored by Chinese Fund for the Humanities and Social Sciences

《中国特色社会主义政治经济学理论体系构建》
Originally published in Chinese by Economic Science Press

For any available supplementary material, please visit
https://www.worldscientific.com/worldscibooks/10.1142/12403#t=suppl

Desk Editors: Nimal Koliyat/Lixi Dong

Typeset by Stallion Press
Email: enquiries@stallionpress.com

About the Author

Hong Yinxing (PhD, Renmin University of China, 1987) is a Distinguished Professor of Economics, Nanjing University. He is also the Vice-Chair of the Social Science Commission of the Ministry of Education, China. He visited the United States as Fulbright Distinguished Scholar in 2000 and was awarded an honorary Doctorate of Law by the University of Waterloo in Canada in 2009. He was selected one of the "Top 100 Most Influential Economists on China's Sixty-Year Economic Development" in 2009. He is also the Editor-in-Chief of the *Journal of China Political Economy*.

About the Translator

He Chengzhou obtained his PhD from the University of Oslo and is Yangtze River Distinguished Professor of English and Drama, School of Foreign Studies and School of Arts, at Nanjing University, China. He has published more than 10 books in Chinese and English with publishing houses both in China and in Europe. His articles have appeared in both Chinese and international journals, such as *New Theatre Quarterly*, *European Review*, *Modern Fiction Studies*, *Comparative Literature Studies*, *Gender, Place and Culture*, *Differences: A Journal of Feminist Studies*, *Modern Language Quarterly*, *Neohelicon*, and *Comparative Drama*. He is Foreign Member of Academia Europaea (the Academy of Europe) and was former President of International Ibsen Committee.

Notes on Translation

The Chinese-to-English translation of Hong Yinxing's monograph *Theoretical Study on China's Political Economy* is a collaborative work by a group of scholars from both China and the United States. The first draft of translation is completed by the following translators: Yang Ting (Preface), Guo Jiabin (Chapters 1 and 9), Zhang Ying (Chapter 2), Xu Yanfeng (Chapter 3), Wei Zheyu (Chapter 4), Zhang Qiumei (Chapter 5), Yang Yi (Chapters 6 and 19), Hao Zhiqin (Chapters 7 and 8), Zhang Yihan (Chapters 10 and 11), Chen Xu (Chapters 12 and 13), Wan Jin (Chapter 14), Wu Yikun (Chapter 15), Jiang Xianping (Chapter 16), Huang Fukui (Chapter 17), and Yuan Jiali (Chapter 18). The whole draft has been thoroughly revised by myself and then proofread by Dr. Megan Ammirati from the University of California at Davis, and Teeana Cotangco from the Johns Hopkins University.

He Chengzhou
Yangtze River Distinguished Professor of English
Nanjing University
September 26, 2020

Contents

Introduction: A Few Questions Regarding the Construction of Socialist Political Economy with Chinese Characteristics

On May 17, 2016, General Secretary Xi Jinping delivered speech at the Symposium of the Work of Philosophy and Social Sciences and commented on the construction of philosophy and social sciences with Chinese characteristics: The work of philosophy and social sciences in our nation should be centered around our current tasks and should try to excavate new materials, identify new problems, make new proposals, and generate new theories based on our practices of reform and development. Socialist political economy with Chinese characteristics then constitutes an important part of philosophy and social sciences with Chinese characteristics. While chairing the Political Bureau of the Communist Party of China (CPC) Central Committee's 28th group study of Marxist political economics, General Secretary Xi Jinping demanded specifically that, in order to construct socialist political economy with Chinese characteristics, we should proceed from national situations and practices of development in our country, reveal new characteristics and patterns, extract and summarize the regular results of national economic development practices, upgrade those practical experiences into systematic economic theories, and thus broaden the scope of contemporary Chinese Marxist political economy.

Constructing Socialist Political Economy with Chinese Characteristics is the Mission of Our Time

Political economy has a socialist aspect. Is socialist political economy with Chinese characteristics a replica of political economy? In spite of the connections, the two cannot be directly equated. The concept of socialist political economy with Chinese characteristics has specific meanings: first, it is a systemic political theory that theoretically summarizes socialist economic system and economic development path with Chinese characteristics; second, it is a theoretical summary of the state governance of the CPC Central Committee with General Secretary Xi Jinping at its core since the 18th National Congress. The construction of socialist political economy with Chinese characteristics needs to be guided by major issues of reform and development. We must not only adhere to the basic principles and methodologies of Marxism, but also combine them with the actual situation of China's economic development, and continuously form economic theory that fully reflects Chinese characteristics, Chinese style, and Chinese glamor.

As our country enters a new historical period, our contemporary mission of constructing socialist political economy with Chinese characteristics consists of the following components: strengthening our systematic summary of the practical experiences gathered during the period of reform and opening up and the process of socialist modernization, strengthening the analysis and study of the development of socialist market economy, and strengthening the research and interpretation of the CPC Central Committee's new concepts, new ideas, and new strategies of the governance of China in order to refine novel, academically grounded theories and summarize new practices with rules to follow.

The task of constructing socialist political economy has been raised by economic development practices of our nation. The founding of the People's Republic of China (PRC) in 1949 marks the inception of the construction of socialism with Chinese characteristics. Since the reform and opening up, we have realized the historical transformation from a planned economy to a socialist market economy, from a closed and semi-closed economy to an open economy, and we have achieved the transformation from a large agrarian country to a newly industrialized country. The seven decades of constructing the PRC as well as the four decades of reform and opening up are nothing but a "snapshot" in the long history of human society. However, in this "snapshot" we have managed to accomplish the modernization process that took the Western world 100–150 years. The socialist China has leaped from an extremely backward half-colonial and half-feudal society to the second largest economy in the world. Close to 1.4 billion people are about to enter a moderately prosperous society in an all-round way and the country is becoming the powerhouse of world economy. This is a great miracle of human society. The success of China's economy demonstrates the superiority of socialist economic system and development path with Chinese characteristics, and it is worthy of a scientific theoretical recapitulation with Marxist positions, viewpoints, and methods. The resulting socialist political economy with Chinese characteristics will be a contribution to the world.

Socialism with Chinese characteristics is Marxism in contemporary China. From a temporal-spatial perspective, Marx researched capitalism in a capitalist society when socialist nations had not yet been formed. He predicted that socialist and capitalist economies were two societies, the latter leading to the former in due time. Nowadays socialism and capitalism coexist in the same space. Socialist and capitalist countries exist internationally side by side, and China's mainstream socialist economy coexists domestically with diverse forms of ownership economies. The difficulty of task of Sinicization of Marxist economics with Chinese characteristics not only lies in expounding on the superiority of the socialist economic system but also in finding methods to strengthen its competitive power and influence in order to eventually overcome capitalism. In terms of material foundations, Marx believed that a developed form of capitalism would lead to socialism. Before the founding of the People's Republic of China, the country grew out of a semi-colonial and semi-feudal society. The material foundations for socialism are still not fully built; therefore the development of socialism needs to go through a primary stage which does not completely eliminate private ownership. During this time, it is necessary that a variety of forms of ownership develop their productive forces under the premise of public ownership as the main body. The history of exploring and constructing socialism with Chinese characteristics includes a series of successful practices dating from the founding of the people's republic, especially during the 40 years of reform and opening up.

China has grown from a poor and backward agrarian country to the world's second largest economic entity. The Chinese model of economic reform and Chinese path to economic development have withstood practical tests. Therefore, the socialist political economy with Chinese characteristics is a generalized theory that applies to successful practices of socialist economic construction with Chinese characteristics. To put it another way, it is telling Chinese stories with Chinese theories.

The construction of socialist political economy with Chinese characteristics should insist on following the guiding principles of Marxism. Marxism insightfully reveals the universal laws of nature, human society, and the development of humanity's ways of thinking, pointing out the direction for the development and progression of human society. In order to construct the socialist political economy with Chinese characteristics that uses Marxism as a guiding principle, we should primarily inherit the basic paradigms of Marxist political economy and make innovations in the following ways that accord with the socialist economic construction with Chinese characteristics and the practices of reform and opening up.

First, we should ask a question: For whom? For the minority or for the majority? Political economies have a distinctive class nature. The basic position of the Marxist economy is that it represents the fundamental interests of the proletariat. After the proletarians seize power, their class interests then represent the fundamental interests of the general population. Therefore, socialist political economy with Chinese characteristics puts people first. Putting people first differs from the so-called universal values in that the former complies with the well-being and common prosperity of the people. It is the political economy that aims at developing productive forces and enhancing people's well-being, that pursues common prosperity, and that strives for the all-around development of human beings.

The second question to ask is: What is the basic task? The fundamental task of Marxist political economy is to expound upon the inevitable replacement of capitalism with socialism. In socialist society, the fundamental task of the political economy then changes from critiquing the old society to constructing a new one. The political economy in the primary stage of socialism should study the economic system and development path with Chinese characteristics, elaborate on the economic laws of the primary stage of socialism, and provide theoretical guidance for building a new society.

Third, being problem-oriented is a distinct feature of Marxism. Problems are the starting point and driving force of innovation. Only by listening to the voice of the times, responding to the call of the times, and then seriously studying and solving significant and urgent problems can we truly grasp the historical context, find the laws of development, and promote theoretical innovation. After entering the middle-income stage, China's economy has encountered a series of developmental issues such as: the balance between the resource allocation determining by market and the role of government, the problem of sustaining growth of medium and high speeds, the problem of overcoming the "middle income trap", etc. Socialist political economy with Chinese characteristics needs to focus on the major issues of China's development and strive to propose theories and concepts of reform and development that can reflect China's position, wisdom, and values.

The theory and successful practices of socialism with Chinese characteristics have answered important questions about how large socialist developing nations can realize national affluence and people's prosperity, such as: What kind of socialism can be built in the economically backward countries of the East and can they go through the socialist road to prosperity? Is it possible for socialism and a market economy to coexist with each other? If so, how? How can agrarian countries with strong dual structures achieve modernization? How can countries whose resources are relatively scarce achieve sustainable development? These are the world's most difficult theoretical problems that need to be confronted directly, and Marx could not possibly fathom or scientifically predict such questions in his own time. Under the guidance of socialist political economy with Chinese characteristics, the China's economy has made great achievements and answered those questions correctly, which constitutes a significant development in Marxism and makes a great contribution to the economic and scientific prosperity of mankind.

Productive Forces and Relations of Production Constitute the Objects of Study

The contradiction between productive forces and relations of production is the basic methodology of Marxist political economy. In fact, it can be said to be the basic paradigm of Marxist economics. Socialist political economy with Chinese characteristics should adhere to this paradigm.

The task of the Marxist economic analysis of capitalism is to reveal the objective law that capitalism will be replaced by socialism. Its object of study is the relations of production, i.e., the inhibitive influence of capitalist relations of production on the development of productive forces. According to *The Communist Manifesto*, after the proletariat seizes power, their mission is to "increase the total productive forces as rapidly as possible", because the material condition for the replacement of capitalism by socialism is that socialist productive forces should equal, or even surpass, that of capitalism. Poverty is not socialism. When becoming a socialist society, China did not equal or surpass capitalist nations in terms of productive forces. One of the major breakthroughs of political economy with Chinese characteristics is to clarify that China is still at the primary stage of socialism and that the essence of socialism at this stage is to liberate and develop productive forces, get rid of exploitation, eliminate polarization, and gradually achieve common prosperity. Above all, socialism with Chinese characteristics is not only concerned with the reform and adjustment of the relations of production, but also focused on the successful development of productive forces. That means that socialist political economy with Chinese characteristics at the primary stage of socialism should put the study of productive forces at an important place.

Practices have proven that under socialist conditions, if the research object of political economy lies only in the relations of production but does not venture into the area of productive forces, the scope and domain of research would become narrower and narrower and its power of interpretation and guidance for the Chinese economy will also diminish. Meanwhile, various forms of economics are competing for legitimacy in terms of the development of productive forces. Therefore, if socialist political economy with Chinese characteristics does not take over this field, it will lose its voice as well as its right to offer guidance.

If socialist political economy with Chinese characteristics regards productive forces and relations of production together as the objects of its research, it will achieve a series of theoretical breakthroughs.

What should we research in terms of productive forces? According to Deng Xiaoping, "in the past, we only stressed expansion of the productive forces under socialism, without mentioning the need to liberate them through reform. That conception was incomplete. Both the liberation and the expansion of the productive forces are essential".[1] According to Xi Jinping, we should "bear in mind that protecting the environment equates

---

[1]Deng Xiaoping. *Selected Works of Deng Xiaoping*. Vol. 3 (Beijing: Foreign Languages Press, 1994), p. 358.

to protecting productivity and that improving the environment also equates to developing productivity".[2] In this way, establishing the theoretical system of socialist political economy with Chinese characteristics means founding a systematized economics that focuses on emancipation, development, and protection of productive forces.

Emancipating productive forces means that we should promote reform and opening up in order to fundamentally change an economic system that constrains the development of productive forces, in accordance with our current features of the developmental stage of socialism. The emancipation of productivity means reforming and improving the relations of production. The emancipation of productive forces is the driving force while the development of productive forces is the final goal. It covers reforming and improving the basic economic system, reforming the means of resource allocation, reforming state-owned enterprises, reforming and refining the basic distribution system, reforming and improving the macro control system, etc. In this respect, a series of achievements have already been made.

Developing and protecting productive forces relates to two aspects of economic development: the former aims at increasing material wealth, while the latter focuses on increasing ecological wealth. Even though emancipating productive forces is the driving force in the development of productive forces, research on the emancipation of productive forces cannot replace inquiries into the development of productive forces and subsequent economic progress, because the development of productive forces has its own laws as well as its own theoretical system. As Marx has noted, the development of social productive forces comes from three aspects: "the social nature of the working labor, the division of labor within a society, and the development of intellectual labor, especially that of natural sciences". Those aspects are the important theoretical underpinnings for research on the development of productive forces. In addition, the "China Miracle" created in the socialist modernization practices of China also needs to be summarized and generalized by the economic development theory with Chinese characteristics.

---

[2] Xi Jinping. *The Governance of China*. Vol. 1 (Beijing: Foreign Languages Press, 2014), p. 231.

The Disciplinary Positioning of Socialist Political Economy with Chinese Characteristics

Socialist political economy with Chinese characteristics is the Marxist political economy of contemporary China. As the theoretical basis of the guiding ideology, it guides China's economic reform and development and maintains its mainstream status in economics. This is related to its status as a discipline.

We need to first address the nature of the discipline. It is the Marxist political economy of contemporary China. Socialist political economy with Chinese characteristics belongs to Marxist political economy of contemporary China for it adopts the political economic paradigm of Marxism, which manifests in the following aspects. First, it is a political economy that puts people first. The basic position of Marxist political economy represents the fundamental interests of the proletariat. After the proletariat has seized power, its class interests become the fundamental interests of the entire people. Therefore, the socialist political economy with Chinese characteristics puts people first and serves people's well-being and common prosperity. This is reflected in the following goals: developing productive forces and enhancing people's well-being, achieving common prosperity, and reaching all-round development of human beings. Second, the object of study consists of the productive forces and the production relations that are interrelated in a certain society; its basic task is to elaborate the laws of economy, especially the inevitable replacement of capitalism with socialism. Embodying the requirements of "contemporary China", socialist political economy with Chinese characteristics is more concerned with the study of the development of productive forces. Only when the productive forces of socialism surpass those of capitalism can the ultimate triumph of socialism be claimed. Third, the basic methods of research are materialist dialectics and historical materialism, although some other economical methods are also used. However, we should not simply equate Marxist political economy of contemporary China with socialist political economy with Chinese characteristics. Marxist political economy of contemporary China includes the scientific analysis of contemporary capitalist economy, while socialist political economy with Chinese characteristics has its definite object of study: it is only directed at a Marxist economic analysis of the socialist economy with Chinese characteristics, although comparisons with the coexisting contemporary capitalism are also made when deemed necessary.

Second, we need to address the stage-wise positioning of the discipline. The current development stage of China has to be defined on two levels: the development of production relations and the development of productive forces. Correspondingly, the development of socialist political economy with Chinese characteristics should also be defined from two aspects. On the one hand, in terms of production relations, it belongs to the political economy of socialism at its primary stage; on the other hand, in terms of the development level of productive forces, China has already bid farewell to the low-income stage and entered the middle-income stage according to the per capita GDP standard. Therefore, the socialist political economy with Chinese characteristics belongs to the political economy of the middle-income stage. Based on this positioning, socialist political economy with Chinese characteristics is then a political economy well-suited to the conditions of contemporary China and the features of the times. Combining the basic principles of Marxist political economy with the new practices of reform and opening up, the important theoretical results of the socialist political economy with Chinese characteristics have withstood the test of practices. Therefore, it can be said that socialist political economy with Chinese characteristics not only provides a powerful guidance to practice of economic development of our country but also broadens the horizon of Marxist political economy.

Third, we need to address the positioning of the discipline in terms of its functions. As a political economy, it not only provides an ideology to distinguish socialism from capitalism but also provides basic economic theories; it not only provides ideological education textbooks to cultivate self-confidence in socialist institution, path, and theory, but also provides economic theoretical guidance for China's economic decision-making and policy making; it will not only criticize various non-Marxist economic theories, but also construct socialist economy with Chinese characteristics.

The Main Line and Logical System of Socialist Political Economy with Chinese Characteristics

The construction of a discipline cannot avoid the confirmation of its main line and logical system. The main line and logical system of the socialist part of political economy has been debated for a long time. This is even more true of the main line and logical system of socialist political economy with Chinese characteristics.

There have been different opinions in the academia on the main line of socialist political economy with Chinese characteristics. Some have advocated a socialist market economy as the main line. Some advocate that the three principles of adhering to the socialist political economy with Chinese characteristics proposed by the Central Economic Work Conference in December 2015 are the main line, namely: first, adhere to the emancipation and development of social productive forces, and second, adhere to the direction of socialist market economy reform and make the market play a decisive role in the allocation of resources. The third is to persist in mobilizing the initiatives of all parties and fully motivate the people. Others think that the essence of socialism with Chinese characteristics is the main line.

It should be said that the above-mentioned propositions are the main content of socialist political economy with Chinese characteristics, but it seems insufficient to become the main line of the entire disciplinary system. This is because the key words of political economy of socialism with Chinese characteristics are Chinese characteristics and socialism. The obvious feature is socialism at the primary stage. Therefore, the main line of this discipline should be the essence of socialism in the primary stage, as pointed out by Deng Xiaoping, which is to emancipate and develop productive forces, eliminate exploitation, eliminate polarization, and gradually achieve common prosperity. The core content is as follows: First is what Deng Xiaoping asserts: "in the past, we only stressed expansion of the productive forces under socialism, without mentioning the need to liberate them through reform. That conception was incomplete. Both the liberation and the expansion of the productive forces are essential".[3] Second is what Xi Jinping states: we should "bear in mind that protecting the environment equates to protecting productivity and that improving the environment also equates to developing productivity".[4] In this way, the construction of a theoretical system of socialist political economy with Chinese characteristics is to establish a systematic economic theory of emancipating, developing, and protecting productive forces. As far as the logical system of socialist political economy with Chinese characteristics is concerned, there are also different views

[3]Deng Xiaoping. *Selected Works of Deng Xiaoping.* Vol. 3 (Beijing: Foreign Languages Press, 1994), p. 358.

[4]Xi Jinping. *The Governance of China.* Vol. 1 (Beijing: Foreign Languages Press, 2014), p. 231.

currently. Some argue that the system should be arranged according to the four links of Marx's production relations (production, exchange, distribution, and consumption). Others advocate that the system should be arranged in six parts according to Marx's original plan of *Capital* in six volumes.

It must be acknowledged that the socialist economy with Chinese characteristics is still in practice and development. Although successful experience has been obtained, it cannot be said that it has been finalized. Marx makes concrete-to-abstract research and abstract-to-concrete narratives when studying capitalism, but this is very difficult to achieve in a short term. Moreover, it is impossible to abstract a pure "all-encompassing" economic relationship in the economy of the primary stage of socialism. Therefore, the logical system of socialist political economy with Chinese characteristics is currently only problem-oriented.

The problem-orientation of the socialist political economy with Chinese characteristics mainly involves its three major principles: first, adhere to the emancipation and development of social productive forces; second, adhere to the direction of the socialist market economy reform, so that the market plays a decisive role in the allocation of resources. The third is to persist in mobilizing the initiatives of all parties and fully motivate the people. These three aspects can be said to be the core contents of contemporary Chinese Marxist political economy, and also the major principles for constructing a theoretical system of socialist political economy with Chinese characteristics.

The narrations in different chapters on the major issues of the socialist economy with Chinese characteristics still contain a logical system. At present, there are roughly three dimensions in the analysis of an actual social economy: the first is the analysis of the economic system, which is the essential dimension; the second is the analysis of resource allocation, which is the dimension of economic operation; and the third is the analysis of the development and protection of productive forces, which is the dimension of economic development. In the context of economic globalization, an additional dimension, i.e., the analysis of foreign economic relations, can be added. The major issues of the socialist political economy with Chinese characteristics can be classified respectively into these four dimensions. Among them, the dimension of economic system is guided by the basic economic system in the primary stage of socialism; the dimension of economic operation is guided by the socialist market economy; the dimension of economic development is guided by the new development concept; and the dimension of foreign economic relations is guided by the economic globalization theory. Thus, they constitute the logical system of socialist political economy with Chinese characteristics.

Theoretical Resources for the Construction of the Discourse of Socialist Political Economy with Chinese Characteristics

General Secretary Xi Jinping requires that the construction of philosophy and social sciences with Chinese characteristics should represent Chinese characteristics, Chinese style, and Chinese manner when it comes to guiding ideologies, disciplinary systems, academic systems, as well as discourse systems. In order to construct philosophy and social sciences with Chinese characteristics, three kinds of resources must be fully grasped: Marxism traditional Chinese cultures, foreign philosophy, and social sciences. To construct political economy with Chinese characteristics, as required by General Secretary Xi Jinping, we should insist on the guidance of Marxist political economics, summarize, and refine the great practical experiences of China's reform and opening up and socialist modernization, while also learning from the useful elements of Western economics. The basic economic system theory, the basic allocation system theory, as well as the socialist market economy theory formulated during the reform and opening up period are based on Chinese situations. They were innovated and developed according to basic theories of Marxist economics and by borrowing the useful elements of Western economics. I will expound on this idea with the example of the economic development theory included in the socialist political economy with Chinese characteristics.

First of all, we need to excavate systematic theories of productive forces in the theoretical treasure house that is Marxist economics, making it into the guiding principle and the methodological foundation of the construction of the discourse of economic development theory. Marx in *Capital* elaborates on the definition of the factors of labor productivity, the distinction of the modes of economic development, the role of science and technology, the proportional relations in social reproduction, the relationship between man and nature, the relationship between production and consumption, and other theoretical categories and principles.

Second, we should draw on the useful elements of Western economics. Development issues facing developing countries are a global problem. Development economics that targets the development of developing countries and growth economics (including new growth theory) have had positive results that can be utilized by us. Examples of topics investigated by such theories include the modernization of dual structure, the middle income trap, total factor productivity, sustainable development, knowledge economics, as well as national innovation system. On the one hand, once those categories and theories have been integrated with socialist political economy with Chinese characteristics, it means that the development theories that are popular around the world can be used by us so that Chinese development theories can be objectively compared with them. On the other hand, we are also confronted with the unique problems facing China, the most important of which include our large population, our recent entry into a middle-income stage of development from a low-income stage, and our demand for common prosperity.

Third, we should tell Chinese stories and showcase Chinese wisdom. China has leaped from a backward agrarian country to the world's second largest economy; 1.4 billion people are about to march together into a moderately prosperous society, which is a world economic miracle; and the path of Chinese urbanization is completely a Chinese invention. It is obvious that Chinese methods of economic development need to be summarized and then generalized by domestic theories instead of foreign ones. The Chinese theory of economics generated in this manner can contribute to the world. While chairing the Political Bureau of the 18th CPC Central Committee's group study session of the basic principles and methodologies of Marxist political economy, Xi Jinping has enumerated the original ideas that our country had proposed during the exploration of the method of constructing socialism, such as policies of overall consideration; the important vision on the balance between agriculture and industry that treats agriculture as the foundation and industry as a guiding factor; the theory of establishing and implementing development thinking that focuses on innovation, coordination, ecological thought, openness, and sharing; the theory that the economic development of our country has entered into a new normal; the theory of promoting new forms of industrialization, informatization, urbanization, and the coordination of agriculture and modernization; the theory of utilizing both international and domestic markets and resources; and the theory of promoting social fairness and justice and the gradual realization of common prosperity.

All these theoretical achievements constitute the political economy that adapts to the national conditions of contemporary China as well as the features of the times. It not only powerfully guides the practices of the economic development of our country, but also broadens the scope of Marxist political economy.

Delving into the Newest Achievements of Contemporary China's Marxist Political Economy

Founded by Marx about 150 years ago, the Marxist political economy still has great vitality in contemporary socialist economic practices. It forms the theoretical foundation of the guiding ideology of our economy, maintaining a mainstream position in the economics discipline. There are two fundamental reasons for its foundational role in the discipline: First, Marxist political economy adheres to the idea of putting people first and regards improving people's well-being as its chief mission. This is a profound reflection on the class features of the Marxist political economy. Marxist political economy of contemporary China insists on regarding the improvement of people's well-being, the promotion of people's all-around development, and the stable march toward common prosperity as both the starting point and the foothold for economic development. This is the economics that people's support. Second, it advances with the times and constantly innovates while developing its practices. The theoretical achievements of Marxist political economy contemporary China adapt to national conditions and the features of the times, provide in-depth answers to major theoretical and practical problems encountered in the economic development of our country, and serve as a powerful guide to China's economic development practices.

Looking back at the 30 years of reform and opening up of our nation, the significant innovations in the field of Marxist political economy have greatly boosted economic reform and development. Therefore, it is important, and urgent, to generalize and systemize the important theoretical achievements of Marxist political economy of contemporary China during the period of reform and opening up and then to construct and develop socialist political economy with Chinese characteristics. What's more, new developments in the Marxist political economy since the 18th National Congress of the CPC deserve special attention in research.

Now I will address the theory concerning the basic economic system in the primary stage of socialism. The Party has made the scientific judgment that China is currently and will continue to be in, the primary stage of socialism. The emancipation and development of social productive forces is the fundamental task at this stage of socialist development as well as an important principle for socialist political economy with Chinese characteristics. In this primary stage of socialism, the basic economic system that matches the development level of productive forces is the one in which public ownership is dominant and different economic sectors develop side by side. Since the 18th National Congress of the CPC, the further improvement of the basic economic system has been highlighted in three ways. First, in terms of adhering unswervingly to the dominant status of public ownership economy. We should emphasize the leading role of the state-owned economy. Of course, this leading role is achieved through reform. During the course of such reforms, a state-owned economy needs to strengthen its vitality, its controlling capability, and its influence, enhancing its management of state-owned assets mainly in the form of capital. The second issue is directly encouraging, supporting, and guiding the development of non-public economic sectors. In order to fully stimulate their vitality and creativity, we should create a market environment that ensures their equal competition with those public sectors, implementing a unified market access system on the basis of a negative list. Third, it must be made clear that the mixed-ownership economy that integrates state-owned capital, collective capital, and non-public capital is an important part of realizing the basic economic system. Thus, an ownership structure is formed within the framework of the basic economic system with various ownership systems completing and strengthening one another.

The next topic is the theory of the socialist market economy. In 1992, the 14th National Congress of the CPC clearly stated that the establishment of the socialist market economy was the goal of reform and defined the socialist market economy in the following way: the market plays a fundamental role in the allocation of resources under the macro-regulation of the socialist nation. In the Third Plenary Session of the 18th Central Committee of the CPC, the role of market in the allocation of resources was then changed from "fundamental" to "decisive" in accordance with the nature of the market economy. As General Secretary Xi Jinping has pointed out, "Both theory and practice have proved that the allocation of resources by the market is the most effective means to this end. It is a general rule of the market economy that the market decides the allocation of resources, and a market economy in essence is one in which the market determines resource allocation".[5] The so-called market's allocation of resources refers to the fact that market laws, market prices, and market competition jointly regulate the allocation of resources. This important progress of socialist market economic theory has pushed forward reform in two respects. The first concerns government decentralization. All economic activities that can be effectively regulated by the market mechanism will be spared from the monitoring of the government; all the prices that can be formulated by the market will be handed over to the market, and the government will not intervene improperly. The second aspect is building a unified, open, competitive, and orderly market system and improving its order and standards in order to make it effective. Meanwhile, it is to be noted that the word "socialist" that precedes the phrase "market economy" holds a significant connotation. It refers to the organic combination of the basic systems of socialism and the market economy, which requires the government to play a better role. On the one hand, it creates a business environment with regulatory laws for the market's allocation of resources. On the other hand, it targets defects in the market mechanism itself, complements the shortcomings associated with market regulation, solves macroeconomic equilibrium problems that cannot be solved by market regulation while overcoming its negative effects, and deters declines in efficiency because of reasons such as monopolies. In this way, both the socialist system and the advantages of the market economy can be brought into full effect.

Moving on, I will introduce the basic distribution system of socialism. During the era of reform and opening up, our nation forms whereby the basic distribution system in which distribution according to work is dominant and multiple distribution forms coexist. While this distribution system insists on distribution in accordance with work, we should establish the principle that labor, capital, technology, managerial expertise, and other production factors participate in the distribution of income in accordance with their respective contributions. The Third Plenary Session of the 18th Central Committee of the CPC further put forward, "[w]e will improve the system in which the returns for capital, knowledge, technology, managerial expertise and other production factors are determined by

[5] *Ibid.*, p. 84.

the market".[6] With the deepening of reform, the problem of a widening income gap becomes more and more prominent. The main question we are facing now is how to secure the dominant status of distribution according to work while also allowing for other production factors to participate, which relates to the question of how to deal with the relationship between fairness and efficiency in the face of this widening income disparity. This means that, in order to improve the basic distribution system, we should uphold the market's decisive role while also promoting social fairness and justice, increasing the income of workers, overcoming polarization, and achieving common prosperity step by step. More specifically, it mainly includes three aspects. First, we should uphold people's rights and equity. We should not only guard against the abuse of power in distribution, but also decrease the high incomes in some monopolized industries. Second, we should also pay attention to the relationship between fairness and efficiency in primary distribution. In particular, we should increase the proportion of labor remuneration in primary distribution to make sure that labor remuneration and labor productivity can improve simultaneously. When it comes to the redistribution of national income, we should pay even more attention to fairness and promote equality of basic public services. Third, we should target the income gap created by unfair property possession and create conditions for more people to have property income.

Responding to Significant Economic Development Problems that Occur after Entering the Middle-Income Stage

Being problem-oriented involves listening to the voice of the times, answering its call, and diligently researching ways to solve important and urgent contemporary problems. In the Marxist political economy, economic development means developing productive forces. In the different stages of development, there are discrete laws concerning the development of productive forces, which means that we should adopt different methods of development.

---

[6]Decision of the CCCPC on some major issues concerning comprehensively deepening the reform. *China.org.cn*. Jan 17, 2014. http://www.china.org.cn/chinese/2014-01/17/content_31226494_9.htm.

First of all, we should specify the current development stage we are in. Our nation has bid farewell to the low-income stage and has entered a middle-income era. While the important development problem of the former stage is poverty, issues associated with the middle-income stage include: the transformation of the means of development, the sustainability of medium-high speed growth, the "middle-income trap", the solution to weakness in development, and human development. Targeting the significant development issues under the new economic norms, General Secretary Xi Jinping has proposed five new development concepts that feature, innovative, coordinated, green, open, and shared development. These concepts then constitute the guiding principles for the economic development of our nation in its new stage.

Second, we should innovate economic development theory systematically. The economic development theory with Chinese characteristics is the generalization of the understandings toward the rules of economic development. Since the era of reform and opening up, the improvements of economic development theory have been highlighted in the following areas. We have created a modernization path with Chinese characteristics, which simultaneously promotes five new types of development, namely industrialization, informatization, urbanization, agrarian modernization, and ecological development. We have put forward the demand and goal of transforming the means of economic development. We have specified that consumption, investment, and export should be coordinated in enhancing economic growth. Presently, the economic development of our country has entered the middle-income stage and is faced with the risk of the "middle-income trap". We need to adapt to, and also guide, the new normal of economic development, and to accelerate economic transformation and upgrading. We should not only demonstrate the objectivity of the state of turning into a new normal in terms of economic laws, but also try to search for novel development ideas and perspectives to make new breakthroughs in economic development. This includes the following methods. First, when it comes to innovating the theory concerning the goal of economic development, growth should not be the only goal. Instead, the elimination of poverty, fair income distribution, as well as the enhancement of social welfare should all be considered as objectives. Second, in considering innovations to the theory of economic development means we should not only turn to the mode of intensive growth, but also innovate the modes of development. Third, we should innovate the theory of protecting productive forces.

Third, we should establish new concept for development. In the Fifth Plenary Session of the 18th Central Committee of the CPC, General Secretary Xi Jinping has systematically demonstrated concepts of development pursuing innovative, coordinated, green, open, and shared development. To better cope with new trends in global economic development and solve the prominent problems encountered in the development of our society and economy, our country needs to accelerate the transformation of the driving force of development, making innovation the primary engine of development. We also need to solve the problem of uneven development, promote coordinated development, and set a foundation for the further overall optimization and improvement of the economic structure. We need to establish the idea that lucid waters and lush mountains are invaluable assets, strengthening environmental governance and ecological protections, building eco-civilization, and promoting the harmonious coexistence of human and nature through green development. We need to construct an open, and high-level economy by means of open development, participating in global economic governance, increasing the institutional voices involved in the global economic governance, and endeavoring to realize win-win cooperation. We need to let the people share the achievements of reform and development, which will increase their inner motivations in participating in and supporting development. New ideas of economic development mean the theoretical generalization and ideological sublimation of our practices in promoting economic development, opening up new spaces for the innovative development of Marxist political economy of contemporary China.

Fourth, we should look for "engines" for economic development in the new era. The focal point of research on the economic relationships in the political economy is about the driving forces of the economy. When it comes to capitalism, the task of the Marxist political economy is to find the force to overthrow capitalist societies. When it comes to socialism, its task is to find the force for building a new society. The important function of socialist political economy with Chinese characteristics is not only to search for an engine of development through reforming the relations of production, but also to locate new driving forces for development in productive forces. Given that the former incentives that have boosted economic growth, such as material factors and low-cost labor, have diminished significantly in their supply of driving force, we must transform the engine of economic growth and find new ones in the two aspects of supply and demand. In terms of demand, we generally need joint incentives from "troika", namely consumption, investment, and exports. However, the more important thing is to cultivate purchasing power. In terms of supply, we need to stimulate three aspects of the driving forces through structural reform. First, we need innovation, which is the engine of development. Second, we should increase the total factor productivity. We should not only avoid the structural mismatch of factors, but also decrease the institutional trade cost of the allocation of production factors. Third, we should activate the vitality of the market and mobilize the initiatives of all participants, especially activating the vitality of enterprises.

To conclude, the emancipation, development, and protection of productive forces are three issues on different levels. An integrated study of all of them, forming a systematized economic theory, is the innovative and original achievement of socialist political economy with Chinese characteristics, which has significant theoretical and practical value. When we enrich and develop socialist political economy with Chinese characteristics through practices, its utility would be amplified: it would not only play a role in ideological education, but also guide economic decisions as well as the economic policy-making of the nation and its enterprises.

Chapter 1

Socialist Political Economy with Chinese Characteristics as an Innovation of Marxist Political Economy

Marxist political economy is the theoretical basis for the theory of socialism with Chinese characteristics. Socialist political economy with Chinese characteristics is an innovation of Marxist political economy under new historical, social, and economic conditions. Socialist practices, new changes to contemporary capitalism, and economic globalization all promote the contemporary development of Marxist political economy. A series of important theoretical innovations made in the course of developing the Chinese Marxist political economy have led to the construction of the theoretical system of socialist political economy with Chinese characteristics.

1.1 Innovations in the Research Objects of the Political Economy

The theoretical innovation of socialist political economy with Chinese characteristics starts from the objects of the research. As a classical economic subject, political economy has clearly confirmed the objects of its research since its very foundation. As productive forces play a decisive role in the emergence, development, and eventual extinction of the relations of production, the political economy that is representative of capital takes the relations of production as its object when analyzing the capitalist economy. Confronted with the basic social contradiction of the productive forces and the relations of production, political economy is devoted to studying the laws of how certain social relations of production emerged, developed, and grew to be extinct. This tendency has been generally recognized by the academia. However, when entering socialist society and being confronted with a series of economic problems in developing the socialist economy, there need to be breakthroughs in basic theories. Practices of economic reform and development push forward research on theories of political economy. Driven by the practice of reform and opening up, the basic theoretical problem that the research of socialist political economy with Chinese characteristics needs to tackle first is the problem of the research object. This query consists of three parts.

1.1.1. *Productive forces as an important aspect of political economy*

Marxist political economy takes the relations of production as its research object. While it also studies productive forces, such research is always related to the study of the relations of production. For a long time, when it came to studies of socialist economy, political economy limited its research to that of the relations of production and neglected the problem of productive forces. This is probably due to Stalin's ideas. In contemporaneous discussions about the research object of socialist political economy, some proposed that scientific theories regarding the organization of productive forces in social productions should be explored and developed. In *Economic Problems of Socialism in the USSR*, Stalin severely criticized this opinion: "What is the effect, in a political economy of socialism, of replacing economic problems by problems of organization of the productive forces? The effect is to abolish the political economy of socialism".[1] "To foist upon political economy problems of economic policy is to kill it as a science".[2]

Influenced by this idea, political economy textbooks both in the Soviet Union and China neglected the study of productive forces for a considerable amount of time. Practice has proven that a confined study of

[1]Joseph V. Stalin. *Economic Problems of Socialism in the USSR*. (Beijing: Foreign Languages Press, 1972), p. 74.

[2]*Ibid.*, p. 75.

political economy limited to the study of relations of production could not provide scientific inputs for China's economic development, and as a result, it has eventually marginalized itself.

The great innovation of socialist political economy with Chinese characteristics is stressing the research of productive forces and studying relations of production from the perspective of developing productive forces. This is in accordance with the task of development that Marx envisioned after a country entered socialist society. Marx and Engels point out in *The Communist Manifesto* that after seizing power, the duty of the proletariat is to "increase the total productive forces as rapidly as possible".[3] This is because the material conditions under which socialism replaces capitalism is that socialism will reach the same or higher level of productive forces than capitalism. Poverty is not socialism. After China entered socialism, more importantly, it did not complete the socialization and modernization of production that were accomplished by other countries under capitalism. Meanwhile, the productive forces did not reach the level of developed capitalist countries and the socialist material base was not built. On this condition, the essence of socialism is to develop productive forces. It also means that only by developing productive forces can we develop socialist relations of production. Therefore, socialist political economy with Chinese characteristics gives top priority to the research of productive forces in order to increase national wealth.

If socialist political economy with Chinese characteristics takes productive forces as its research object, what exactly does this consist of? In Deng Xiaoping's opinion, one is to liberate productive forces and the other to develop productive forces. Both these aspects essential. Xi Jinping recently proposed that "bear in mind that protecting the environment equates to protecting productivity and that improving the environment also equates to developing productivity".[4] Thus, socialist political economy with Chinese characteristics studies productive forces from three aspects: the first is to liberate productive forces, the second is to develop productive forces, and the third is to preserve productive forces. Combining these three aspects together is a major breakthrough of political economy both in terms of the object and content of research.

---

[3]Karl Marx and Fredrich Engels. *Manifesto of the Communist Party*. Trans. Samuel Moore (Beijing: Foreign Languages Press, 1965), p. 58.

[4]Xi Jinping. *The Governance of China*. Vol. 1 (Beijing: Foreign Languages Press, 2014), p. 231.

Constructing the theoretical system of socialist political economy with Chinese characteristics is to build a systematic economic theory that covers the liberation, development, and preservation of productive forces. In this way, the theory of economic development becomes a critical part of socialist political economy with Chinese characteristics.

1.1.2. *Political economy studies multiple relations of production and their corresponding economic systems*

An important example of the abstract method used by Marxist political economy is that, when confronting a similar society which involves multiple relations of production, economic analysis should grasp the dominant one. Just as Marx says: "In all forms of society, there is one specific kind of production which predominates over the rest, whose relations thus assign rank and influence to the others. It is a general illumination which bathes all the other colors and modifies their particularity".[5] Hence, over a long period, the socialist part of political economy only analyzes the socialist relations of production. However, the feature of the ownership structure in the primary stage of socialism is that public ownership plays a dominant role while diverse forms of ownership develop side by side. The diverse forms of non-public economics are full of vitality, and the mixture of different forms of ownership has become the form through which the basic economic system realizes itself. Against this background, the public ownership economy will not become the "general illumination" that bathes the colors of other sectors of economy. Therefore, research on the relations of production by socialist political economy with Chinese characteristics should not be confined to public ownership. Other non-public sectors and mixed-ownership should also be included in this research.

The actual economic system is the concrete form of relations of production. Therefore, as the theoretical guidance of economic reform, the socialist political economy with Chinese characteristics should not study relations of production by only coming up with a few principles but should instead focus on their concrete forms. The most typical analysis concerns the basic economic system in the primary stage of socialism, which not only studies the basic attribute of relations of production

---

[5]Karl Marx. *Grundrisse: Foundations of the Critique of Political Economy*. Trans. Martin Nicolaus (New York: Penguin, 1973), p. 106.

reflected by diverse forms of ownerships but also analyzes the forms of their realization and mutual relations. Moreover, it also includes the basic income system, land system, and related aspects. The economic system inevitably involves the issue of superstructure, and the question raised is whether the superstructure, or which part of it, should be the research object of political economy. Superstructure is not the research object of political economy. Nevertheless, based on Marx's analysis on the relationship between economic base and superstructure, when political economy studies the total relations of production, which is its economic basis, it will involve superstructure to a certain extent, especially since the economic system, as the fundamental system which reflects the nature of the society, largely belongs to the superstructure. Above all, after China has established a law-based governance of the country, the management of many economic issues cannot work without the rule of law. Political economy needs to study the legal system that influences the definition of relations of production, protects the intellectual property, and standardizes the market operation.

1.1.3. *Political economy studies economic operation and the corresponding economic system*

Marxist political economy studies the relations of production, analyzing the nature of the economy. Accordingly, the economic efficiency related to the development of productive forces is positively correlated with the quality of the relations of production. In this case, low economic efficiency is attributed to inadaptable relations of production, which need to be adjusted accordingly. But in fact, economic efficiency is not always related to relations of production; at other times, it is instead associated with the efficiency and quality of economic operations. Although the efficiency of resource allocation and the quality of economic operations do not always reflect the quality of relations of production, they are illustrated by the mode of economic operation. The mode of economic operation is neither entirely the concrete form of a certain social relations of production, nor is it entirely built around the economic system. For instance, market economies exist as a mode of economic operation in both socialist and capitalist economies as a method of resource allocation. As another example, macro control needs to take counter-cyclical control methods when confronted with high rates of unemployment and inflation. Such micro- and macroeconomic operations cannot always be illustrated by the nature of the relations of production. However, the issues of low efficiency and loss of macroeconomic control as a result of bad management will impact the development of productive forces and socialist relations of production. Hence, it is very necessary to include modes of economic operation as one of the research objects of political economy.

The mode of economic operation, namely economic systems, such as the market economy, macro control, and social security systems. The design and reform of economic systems need to not only reflect their essential demands, but also the demands of efficiency and quality of economic operation. As to the former, the economic system must be reformed according to the requirement of the basic economic system at the primary stage of socialism. The quality and efficiency of economic operation are not always simply decided by the economic system: they are also related to the mode of economic operation to a large extent. Even though the current economic system is adaptable to the development of productive forces, the economic structure in its actual form is not always suitable to the demands of the development of productive forces. For this reason, the mode of economic operation needs to be adjusted and reformed according to the laws of economic operation. As the economic structure does not operate in isolation, but rather inside a certain framework of relations of production and economic system, such research cannot be separated from this framework. For example, the research of market economy and macro control cannot be separated from the essential demands of the basic system of socialism. Under the precondition of insisting on the basic system of socialism, they are searching for the appropriate institutional arrangements in terms of the mechanism of economic operation.

The above-mentioned breakthroughs in the research objects of socialist political economy with Chinese characteristics have promoted theoretical innovations in every aspect and achieved major theoretical accomplishments, which not only provide guidance for the practice of China's economic development, but also opens up new horizons for Marxist political economy.

1.2 The Innovation of the Essential Attributes of Political Economy

Is the field of economics associated with class? Marx's response is clear: there is a Marxist political economy which represents the interests of the proletariat, and another economy which represents the interests of the bourgeoisie. However, there are disagreements on whether the field of economics that studies the socialist economy has a class feature. Some scholars are influenced by "universal values", which tone down the class features of economics and instead emphasize general dimensions that transcend them. In fact, in the primary stage of socialism where different forms of ownership exist side by side, economics obviously has a class feature as long as it concerns economic interests and relations. Some economies claim to serve the rich, and others serve the poor. Socialism with Chinese characteristics will neither "reject both the old and rigid closed-door policy and any attempt to abandon socialism and take an erroneous path".[6] Thus, socialist political economy with Chinese characteristics inherits the tradition of Marxist political economy that not only has a clear position on class but also publicly claims to put people first. This is the manner in which it is fundamentally different from Western economies.

When Marx founded Marxist political economy, he clearly identified this class feature, pointing out that it represents the interests of the bourgeoisie and "the peculiar nature of the materials it deals with, summons as foes into the field of battle the most violent, mean and malignant passions of the human breast, the Furies of private interest".[7] Marx's political economy thus publicly claims and maintains the interests of the proletariat, serving the revolutionary cause of the proletariat as well as humankind as a whole. According to the theory of labor value, Marx established the scientific theory of surplus value and discovered the secrets of capitalist exploitation. Consequently, he sought to become the gravedigger of capitalism and raised an alarm about its impending death knell. The class feature of Marxist political economy is reflected not only in its criticism of capitalism but also in its portrayal of an ideal society for the proletariat: the socialist and communist societies that Marx called "the Community of Freemen". In the process of criticizing capitalist economic relations, Marx logically deduced the basic economic characteristics of the future society, reflecting the proletariat's yearning for such a community and

[6]Hu Jintao Full text of Hu's Report at 18th Party Congress. *Chinadaily.com.cn.* Nov 18, 2012. https://www.chinadaily.com.cn/china/19thcpcnationalcongress/2012-11/18/content_29578562.htm.

[7]Karl Marx. *Capital: A Critique of Political Economy.* Vol. 1, Trans. Ben Fowkes (London: Penguin Books, 1976), p. 92.

their determination to fight for it. After the foundation of socialist society, Marxist political economics both provide theoretical weapons for building a new society and reflect the fundamental interests of the overwhelming majority of the people.

After the proletariat seizes power, how does political economy reflect this class feature? This question is related to the fundamental interests sought by the proletariat. Based on the analysis by Marx and Engels, the proletariat's interests represent the fundamental interests of the overwhelming majority of the people. Therefore, the class feature of the political economy is reflected in the following ways. When it comes to analyzing capitalist economies, it searches for the gravediggers of capitalist society — the proletariat. When it comes to analyzing the socialist economy, it searches for the builders of this society — the overwhelming majority of the people. Hence, the essential attribute of socialist political economy with Chinese characteristics is that it is centered on the people and provides services for their welfare and common prosperity. This reflects the essential requirements of socialism.

In order to be centered on the people, one needs a clear definition of "people". In different historical periods, the notion of the people has had different connotations. According to Chairman Mao's definition during the period of building socialism: "the classes, strata and social groups which favor, support and work for the cause of socialist construction all come within the category of the people".[8] By this definition, the economy that puts people first represents neither the interests of the rich nor the interests of the poor, but rather the welfare and the fundamental interests of the people as a whole. This is in accordance with the object of socialist production, which aims to meet the increasing material and cultural demands of the people as much as possible. As a result, socialist political economy with Chinese characteristics needs to make breakthroughs in the following three aspects.

1.2.1. *One must develop social productive forces*

By this, what is meant is the founding and building of the new society's economic theory with the goal of developing social productive forces. The

[8]Mao Tse-tung. *Selected Works of Mao Tse-Tung*, Vol. 5 (Oxford: Pergamon Press, 1977), p. 385.

principal contradiction of the primary stage of socialism is that the level of productive forces cannot meet the demands of the people. The solution to this contradiction is to develop productive forces. Undoubtedly, the development of productive forces necessitates the constant refinement of the relations of production and the corresponding superstructure. However, in practice, merely adjusting the relations of production is far from enough. After China transitioned from semicolonial and semifeudal conditions to become a socialist society, the reality is that the level of productive forces could not meet the demands of socialism. Therefore, the basic approach to practice the regulations of socialism established by Marx is to create and realize regulated economic conditions, particularly by laying the material foundations that are regulated by socialism through the means of developing productive forces. Thus, the political economy should turn its attention from class struggle to economic construction, becoming the theoretical guide for economic development. The mission of political economy then becomes liberating and developing productive forces, increasing national wealth, and achieving common prosperity.

People usually describe Marx's three factors of labor process as productive forces, namely the laborers, the means of labor, and the subjects of labor. These factors could not reflect the path of the current development of productive forces. To illustrate the factors within the development of productive forces, one should reference Marx's summary of the determining factors of productiveness of labor: "the average amount of skill of workmen, the state of science, and the degree of its practical application, the social organization of production, the extent and capabilities of the means of production, and by physical conditions".[9] In accordance with this summary, Marx traces the resources of social productive forces to the following three aspects: "to the social nature of the labor engaged in production; to the division of labor in society; and to the development of intellectual labor, especially in the natural sciences".[10] In the development of modern productive forces, the primary ones are science and technology while human resources become the main forces of economic development.

[9]Karl Marx. *Capital: A Critique of Political Economy*. Vol. 1, Trans. Ben Fowkes (London: Penguin Books, 1976), p. 28.
[10]*Ibid.*, p. 51.

1.2.2. *One must gradually achieve common prosperity and construct an economic theory of shared development with this end goal*

People's aspiration for a better life is the objective of socialism with Chinese characteristics. It is also the concrete embodiment of the essential attribute of socialist political economy with Chinese characteristics that puts people first. Within this theory, the overriding principles are fairness, justice, and common prosperity. On the one hand, socialist justice is based on people's subject position. On the other hand, while common prosperity is the goal, due to low productivity, it may take time to achieve. In socialist society, especially at its primary stage, labor is still a means of livelihood. The involvement of various productive factors in distribution inevitably leads to a gap between the rich and the poor. This means that there is a difference in people's share of the fruits of reform and development. Justice and people-oriented principles that are raised at the new stage of development need to guarantee that members of low-income groups can share the fruits of economic development fairly. Only in this way can the people support development.

1.2.3. *One must promote people's holistic development and construct a people-oriented economic theory with this goal*

Socialism with Chinese characteristics is a cause that is supported by hundreds of millions of people. The people are then also a motive and source of development. Their level of development directly determines the development level of the economy and society. Development should be centered on human resources. That is to say, as technology and society develop, human talents become their primary resources, just as present innovation and entrepreneurship call for the participation of the masses. The form of development that puts people first includes people's own development, more specifically that of a holistic nature. People's development involves the improvement of qualities including those that are physical, cultural, and moral. These improvements not only depend on the level of economic development, but also on the level of social development and environmental protection.

Looking back at the development over the past 30 years, every step of economic reform and development has been promoted by the significant innovation of the political economy. The theoretical evolution of Marxist political economy, along with its contributions to China's reform and development, are the major principles of socialist political economy with Chinese characteristics. In the following, I will illustrate the theoretical innovations of socialist political economy from two perspectives: the economic system and economic development.

1.3 The Innovation of Economic System Theory

The political economy founded by Marx provides guidance for how socialist countries envision or regulate the basic attributes of the future society. However, there are two reasons why China should make innovations. First, there are sharp differences between the socialist economic system imagined by Marx at the time he was writing and real-world socialist practices. Founded on the basis of semicolonial and semifeudal society, socialist China could not mechanically copy principles when practicing Marx's demands about socialism. Second, Marx only formulated some basic characteristics for the future society; he did not make concrete regulations about the economic system of the future society, which would also necessitate China's own innovation. This means that there are no existing theories or experiences for a large developing country like China to draw upon when building socialism. It is necessary to combine the basic theories from Marxism with the actual practices of China's socialist construction in order to continue to adapt Marxism to Chinese conditions and to guide the great cause of socialism with Chinese characteristics by Marxism with Chinese characteristics. China's innovations in the actual socialist economic system and structure form part of a process of combining the basic principles of Marxist socialism with Chinese practices as well as modernizing and "Sinicizing" the Marxist political economy.

The innovation of socialist economic system with Chinese characteristics starts from the confirmation of the fact that our country is still at the primary stage of socialism. To develop socialism with Chinese characteristics, one needs to adapt to the fundamental conditions of the country which dictate that it will remain at the primary stage of socialism for a long time. At this stage, the principal social contradiction is that the level of productive forces cannot meet the increasing demands of the people. The historical mission of the primary stage of socialism is to gradually get rid of underdevelopment, realize a basic level of socialist modernization, and transform China from an agricultural country (which has a significant agricultural population that depends on manual labor) into an industrial country (in which the non-agricultural population is in the majority and modern agriculture and modern service industry have been established). Constructing socialism with Chinese characteristics neither means changing the socialist system nor lowering the requirement of socialism. It rather requires adapting the present socialist system to the level of productive forces at the current stage and making it beneficial to the development of productive forces, thereby promoting the development of the socialist cause. The proposal of this theory of the primary stage of socialism not only makes it clear that the essence of socialism is to develop productive forces but also opens up a space for a series of breakthroughs in economic systems. According to the institutional analysis of Marxist political economy, the significant theoretical breakthroughs in socialist economic system with Chinese characteristics are reflected in the three dimensions of production, exchange, and distribution.

The first breakthrough is the theory of the basic economic system at the primary stage of socialism. At first, the essence of socialism is to eliminate exploitation and private ownership. The classical socialist economic system is founded on the basis of a developed capitalist society. However, for the sake of developing productive forces at the primary stage of socialism, we need to proceed from reality and find new motives and factors to promote the development of productive forces. These would in turn promote socialist development at the primary stage of socialism and fully engage all sources that can create social wealth. Therefore, the basic economic system in which public ownership plays the dominant role and diverse forms of ownership develop side by side is established at the primary stage of socialism. Within this framework of the basic economic system, a variety of non-public sectors are on equal terms with the public sectors such as the individual economy, private economy, and foreign investments. The Third Plenary Session of the 18th Central Committee of the Communist Party of China (CPC) further identified this basic economic system as an important pillar of the system of socialism with Chinese characteristics and a foundation of the socialist market economy structure. Furthermore, the mixed-ownership economy in which government, collective, and non-public capital have cross shareholdings that mix together was highlighted as the important form through which the basic economic system realizes itself. The cross-shareholding of public and non-public capital promotes diverse forms of ownership that develop together within the same enterprise. Building the basic economic system at the primary stage of socialism is an institutional innovation, sticking to the basic principles of scientific socialism and endowing it with distinctive Chinese characteristics according to the actual conditions and features of the times of our country. This process reflects the combination of the basic principles of Marxism and Sinicization of Marxism.

The second breakthrough is the socialist market economy theory. In 1992, the 14th National Congress of the CPC put forward the reform goal of building the structure of socialist market economy. It defined socialist market economy as that in which the market plays a fundamental role in resource allocation under the national macro control. Throughout the 15th, 16th, 17th, and then at the 18th National Congress of the CPC in 2012, this definition has remained the guiding ideology for the market reform of the economic system. According to the level of development of the Chinese market economy, the Third Plenary Session of the 18th Central Committee of the CPC decided to let the market play a decisive role in resource allocation. This modification returns to the original meaning of a market economy. Just as General Secretary Xi Jinping said, "Both theory and practice have proved that the allocation of resources by the market is the most effective means to this end. It is a general rule of the market economy that the market decides the allocation of resources, and a market economy in essence is one in which the market determines resource allocation".[11] The aspect that is both unique to China and has meaningful substance is the combination of the basic economic system of socialism and a market economy. Its characteristics are reflected in the function of the government: while the market plays a fundamental role the national macro control of the market is also emphasized. In other words, while the market plays a decisive role in resource allocation, the government is required to make the process work better.

The third breakthrough is the theory of the basic distribution system of socialism. After the establishment of the basic economic system at the primary stage of socialism, the basic distribution system was

[11] Xi Jinping. *The Governance of China*. Vol. 1 (Beijing: Foreign Languages Press, 2014), p. 84.

established. In this system, the main form is distribution according to work, but multiple distribution forms also coexist. This is a significant theoretical breakthrough of socialist political economy with Chinese characteristics. Multiple distribution forms indicate that similarly varied production factors participate in income distribution. During a period ranging between the 14th and the 16th National Congress of the CPC, the principle that production factors like labor, capital, technology, and management should participate in distribution according to their contributions was settled. The 17th and 18th National Congress of the CPC then proposed to refine the system in which these production factors were participating. Based on that idea, the Third Plenary Session of the 18th Central Committee of the CPC proposed that the rewards of the production factors should be determined by their respective markets. Such statements indicate that the portion of income distribution not only depends on the input of each production factor, but also its contribution to the economy and the market's supply and demand. In general, such a basic revenue system is in accordance with the essential demands of socialism to develop social productivity. Multiple production factors are brought into full play to increase social wealth and, along with it, a significant increase in workers' absolute income that accords with their interests. However, the production factors that different people possess vary significantly. Allowing some people to get rich first implies that those who have strong saving capabilities, skills, and operation abilities also have the potential to create wealth. Adding the superposition of these factors, the gap between the labor reward and the income of non-labor factors is significantly enlarged. At present, the share of the front-line workers' reward in the distribution of national income has dramatically declined. In order to realize equality and justice, we need to bridge the income gap in the following three ways: First, when it comes to the primary distribution, we need to handle the relationship between equality and efficiency according to the demands of socialism, ensuring that the rewards of labor grow in step with improvement in productivity. Second, in consideration of the fact that the gap in rewards is caused by the differences in various factors such as an individual's access to technology, approaches like educational equality need to be taken to narrow the disparity between individuals, which will create equal opportunities and narrow income inequality. Third, we need to pay more attention to equality in redistribution, especially in terms of refining the social security system that covers both urban and rural areas.

1.4 The Innovation of the Theory of Economic Development

The fact that the issue of economic development has entered the research field of contemporary Marxist political economy is a significant breakthrough. To study China's economic development, we must be clear about its stages of development. Speaking of the stage of development is not only a reference to the primary stage of socialism in terms of the relations of production, but also addresses the low-income stage or middle-income stage in terms of productive power. After our country moves from the low-income stage to the middle-income stage, there will be calls for corresponding innovations in the theory of economic development.

The basic requirement of this innovation is to follow the law of economic development. Just as General Secretary Xi Jinping claims: "To achieve the goals we have set, we must take economic development as the central task, make development the top priority of the party in governing and rejuvenating the country, and promote sustainable and sound economic development. Development must be scientific development that follows economic laws and sustainable development that follows natural laws".[12]

Since the era of reform and opening up of the economy, we can observe the following breakthroughs in the theory of economic development achieved by socialist political economy with Chinese characteristics:

The first innovation is the theory of socialist modernization with Chinese characteristics. It involves the following aspects: to holistically construct a moderately prosperous society within the process of modernization and to advance the development of theory as a specific stage; to consider science and technology as primary productive forces; and finally, to establish a path of modernization in which new industrialization, informatization, urbanization, and agricultural modernization are carried out simultaneously.

The second innovation involves the scientific outlook on development. One might describe the main points as follows: development is the top priority; putting people first is the core requirement; pursuing a comprehensive, balanced, and sustainable development is the basic

[12]From the speech that General Secretary Xi Jinping made at the Symposium on Economic Situation on July 8, 2014.

requirement; taking a holistic approach is the fundamental method; and building a resource-saving and environment-friendly society is the goal.

The third innovation is the theory of an open economy. Socialist countries need to draw on the advanced technology and managerial experience from developed capitalist countries in order to take an active part in international economic cooperation and competition, to strengthen their international competitiveness, to make use of both international and domestic resources and markets, and to build a new system of an open economy that can bring mutual benefits.

The fourth innovation is the theory of transforming economic development modes. Growth is not equivalent to development. We should improve quality and economic benefits in order to serve as a foothold for promoting development. In this way economic development will more dependably rely on domestic demands, especially consumer demands, on the promotion of the modern service industry and those that are strategically emerging, on the advance of science and technology, on improvement of the quality of the workers, on managerial innovation, on resource saving and the promotion of recycling economy, and on the coordinated development of urban and rural areas, to constantly boost sustainable development in the long run.

After the 18th National Congress of the CPC, China's economic development has proceeded to a new stage. For one, China's economy entered the middle-income stage from the low-income stage. The development issue it now faces is no longer getting rid of poverty, but rather going beyond the "middle-income trap" and marching toward modernization by realizing an overall prosperous society in moderate terms. In addition, China's economy has entered a phase that we might call the "new normal". It needs to adapt to these conditions and guide the way, requiring new ideas about development that center around innovation, coordination, greenness, openness, and sharing. These are both a theoretical summary of the practices of promoting economic development and a significant breakthrough in the theory of socialist economic development with Chinese characteristics. Relatedly, the theory of economic development makes new breakthroughs in the following four ways.

The first part relates to the ways in which China is entering a "new normal". This phrase refers to conditions including the change of speed (meaning that economic growth needs to change from high speed to medium-high speed while the development mode needs to change from focusing on scope and speed to quality and efficiency); structural optimization (meaning that the principal adjustment of economic structure needs to change from increment and capacity expansion to stock adjustment and the simultaneous development of quality and incrementalism); and motivation conversion (meaning that the developmental drive needs to rely more on innovation rather than on factors such as resources and low-cost labor).

The second part is the theory of innovation-driven economic development. First, innovation should be considered as the driving force of a new development mode. While resources, environment, and low-cost labor are in short supply, it should be proposed that the economic development can be driven by innovation instead of investment. In this scenario, technological innovation should play a leading role. Second, the innovation of technology highlights independent innovation. Over a long period of time, China's technological innovation had mainly depended on the introduction and imitation of innovations. Following and imitating other developed countries, China could not achieve modernization. An innovation-driven economy needs to highlight independent innovation and stand on the same starting line as the developed countries, running neck and neck with them and eventually taking the lead in technology and industry. Third, the innovation of technology needs to connect with the innovation of industry, promoting industries toward the medium-high end. For one, it needs innovation in green technology and in strategic emerging industries. Additionally, it needs to make stock adjustments, resolve excess capacities, and eliminate those that are polluting and outdated. Adjustments could bring temporary hardships, but they will eventually lead to an ideal scenario that will result in a faster growth in the service and high-tech industries. Fourth, it needs to promote the cooperation among the fields of production, academics, and research in order to develop new technology.

The third part concerns the demand-pull theory including the following components. First, the development engine is shifted to domestic market. Chinese economic aggregates rank the second in the world and the size of the domestic market also takes the lead within the world economy. Thus, gross demand is needed to realize a sustainable growth of the economy. Given the changes in the global economic environment, the strategy of promoting economic development mainly through export and foreign direct investment would become less important. Also, in this case the domestic economy has become the engine of growth. Second, the important aspect of the transformation of the modes of development is that economic growth will no longer be simply driven by investment and export. Instead, it will be propelled by a coordination between consumption, investment, and export. To be more specific, when it comes to growth, consumption plays a fundamental role, investment a key role, and export a promoting role. Third, expanding consumer demand becomes the new driver for economic growth, but it still needs cultivation. The approaches to do so may include the cultivation of spending power and the development of consumption economy along with new industries and services that meet consumer demands.

The fourth part is the theory of supply-side structural reform. Experience has proven that in developing countries, relying on demand only could not effectively promote economic growth even though they adopt market economies. On the basis of achievement in demand-side reform, we need to promote economic development on the supply side in order to achieve development with quality and efficiency. The following principles apply. First, in order to promote effective supply, we must avoid structural supply shortage or ineffective and low-end supply of excess. The aim of supply-side reform is to enhance the supply structure's adaptability and flexibility to the changes of demand and to improve the quality and efficiency of the supply system. Second, we must provide the driving force for growth on the supply side. Growth is driven by both demand and supply. Supply factors include technology, structure, efficiency, and systems apart from the input of material factors. The promotion of total factor productivity could largely make up for a deficiency in the input factors. The drive from innovation, the structural adjustment, and the increase of efficiency can all become new driving forces for supply. The implementation path is structural reform, which involves the system of scientific and technological innovation, the system of refined management, and the incentive system. Third, we must stimulate initiative in all walks of life. If the demand side emphasizes the choices of the market and provides the pressure for development, then the supply side emphasizes economic incentives and provides the driving force for development. For instance, in the face of ineffective and low-end supply, in order to achieve the goal of reducing overcapacity, destocking, deleveraging and reducing cost, the demand side counts on the competitive market system, while the supply side adopts the way of recombination and optimization. As another example, when confronted with the pressure of an economic slowdown, the demand side adopts an expansionary monetary policy, while the supply side cuts tax and interest rate for the entity enterprises to arouse their initiative and release their vitality.

In summary, socialist political economy with Chinese characteristics is the great achievement of Chinese Marxism. Just as General Secretary Xi Jinping says, our party combines the basic principles of Marxist political economy with China's new practices of reform and opening up, continues enriching and developing Marxist political economy, and makes many important theoretical achievements in contemporary Chinese Marxist political economy. These theoretical achievements adapt to the national conditions and the features of contemporary China. They not only provide guidance for our country's economic development practices, but also open up new horizons for Marxist political economy. Socialist political economy with Chinese characteristics is the theoretical generalization of socialist economic system with Chinese characteristics and of the road of economic development. In other words, it is telling the story of China and guiding its practices with China's own theories. Under its guidance, China's economic system realizes its transformation toward the socialist market economy, the national economy steps onto the track of scientific development that is stable and fast, and Chinese people enter a moderately prosperous society in a holistic way from a moderately prosperous society in a general way. All these transformations play an important role in liberating and developing productive forces. By guiding China's economic construction with Marxist political economy with Chinese characteristics, we will certainly deliver even more splendid achievements.

Bibliography

卫兴华:《中国特色社会主义经济理论体系研究》, 中国财政经济出版社 2015 年版. Wei Xinghua. *Study on the Theoretical System of Socialist Economy with Chinese Characteristics* (Beijing: China Financial & Economic Publishing House, 2015).

洪银兴主编:《马克思主义经济学经典选读·当代价值》, 高等教育出版社 2012 年版. Hong Yinxing (ed.). *Close Reading on the Classics of Marxist Economy · Contemporary Values* (Beijing: Higher Education Press, 2012).

Chapter 2

Innovating the Theoretical System of Socialist Political Economy with Chinese Characteristics

The cause of socialism with Chinese characteristics is under construction, and the theoretical system of socialist political economy with Chinese characteristics is under construction as well. To construct a socialist political economy with Chinese characteristics, we should base ourselves on China's national conditions and development practices, reveal new characteristics and principles, refine and summarize the regular results of Chinese economic development practices, as well as elevate practical experiences to systematic economic theory. The practice of reform and opening up is interactive with the innovations of political economy theory. This requires the systematization of successful practices and theoretical innovations to build up the theoretical system of socialist political economy with Chinese characteristics.

2.1 Socialist Political Economy with Chinese Characteristics is Marxist Political Economy of Contemporary China

Socialist political economy with Chinese characteristics is the result of the localization and modernization of Marxist political economy. It is a systematic economic theory based on the refined and summarized practices of socialist economic construction with Chinese characteristics.

The construction of a disciplinary system for socialist political economy with Chinese characteristics should initially clarify its subject orientation.

Subject Orientation 1: Socialist political economy with Chinese characteristics belongs to Marxist political economy, and it is manifested in the paradigm of inheriting Marxist political economy. The so-called theoretical paradigm involves the basic structure, functions, categories, and methods of the theoretical system. The economic paradigm of today's world generally includes two major systems: The paradigm of Marxist economics and Western economics. The paradigm of Marxist political economy, represented by Marx's *Capital,* generally includes the following five aspects: First, the basic position represents the fundamental interests of the proletariat. Second, the research object is the relationship based on a certain level of productive forces. Third, the basic task is to illustrate economic laws, especially the inevitability of socialism to replace capitalism. Fourth, the research methods are materialist dialectics and historical materialism. Fifth, the discourse system is based on the basic principles and categories of *Capital.* The reason why socialist political economy with Chinese characteristics belongs to Marxist political economy is rooted in its inheritance from the latter. The paradigm of Marxist political economy runs through the construction of socialist political economy with Chinese characteristics.

However, socialist political economy with Chinese characteristics is not simply a copy of Marxist political economic theories. Based on practices from socialist economic construction with Chinese characteristics as well as reform and opening up, it makes innovations and develops from its inheritance of Marxist paradigms: First of all, as for its basic position, since the interests of the proletariat represent the fundamental interests of all people after the seizure of power by the proletariat, socialist political economy with Chinese characteristics puts people first and serves the well-being and common prosperity of people. Second, as far the research objects, it studies the relations of production based on certain levels of productive forces, emphasizing the relations of production in the primary stage of socialism. Third, as for its basic tasks, the economic laws are still being elaborated, but emphasizes economic laws in the primary stage of socialism. Fourth, as for the foundation of methodology, it insists on materialist, dialectics, and historical materialism, especially highlighting the two-point theory and focal-point theory. However, the application of current methods (mathematics and model analysis for instance) is not excluded. Fifth, the discourse system of economics is based on Marxist political economy discourse, but first, it is open to practices of reform and development as it generalizes new practices with new discourse. It also opens to positive theoretical achievements of human development in the contemporary world, which includes absorbing useful elements of Western economics. After China's transition to a market economy, the modern market economy theories are generalized by the countries that first took the initiative to develop market economy. If contemporary Chinese Marxist political economy critically absorbs the above theories, it will be more scientifically advanced.

Subject Orientation 2: Socialist political economy with Chinese characteristics is the Sinicization of Marxist economics. The economics established by Marx interprets the problem of the economic system and economic development in the future society, while the practices of developing socialism with Chinese characteristics are solving this problem. To construct and develop a socialist economy, socialist political economy with Chinese characteristics needs to research new problems as required by the times, discover new laws, generalize new theories, and continue to make theoretical innovations. This process engages the Sinicization and modernization of Marxist economics, which is highlighted in the following three aspects.

(1) Regarding the conception of time and space, Marx researched capitalism in capitalist societies when socialist countries did not exist yet. The socialist economy as he foresaw follows capitalist economy continually through time. In the present era, socialism and capitalism coexist in the same space. Internationally, socialist countries coexist with capitalist countries, while the dominant socialist economy coexists with multi-ownership economy in China. Thus, the subject of Sinicization of Marxist economics faces the following problem: on the one hand, two different kinds of economies with common background for economic organizations, methods, rules, and orders are similar in forms; on the other hand, there are contradictions and competitions among the coexisting different kinds of economies with different natures. In this context, the task of socialist political economy with Chinese characteristics is not only to elaborate the superiority of socialist economic system, but also to find out ways to enhance the competitiveness and influence of socialist economy, and mutual learning is necessary.

(2) Regarding the material foundation, Marx believed that developed capitalism leads to socialism, which is related to high productive development. Before the founding of the People's Republic of China is born out

of semi-colonial and semi-feudal society. Although the country's industrialization has been built, the level of productivity still lags behind developed capitalist countries. The material foundation of socialism has not been fully established and the development of socialism should go through a primary stage of socialism. At this stage, China should accomplish the tasks of socialization, marketization, and modernization of production, which other countries have already accomplished under capitalist circumstances. The fundamental task of developing socialism at this stage is to develop productive forces. Correspondingly, socialism in the primary stage of socialism is not the complete elimination of private ownership, but rather, to take advantage of the variety of private ownership to develop productive forces of the economy.

(3) Regarding the analysis of successful practices of socialism with Chinese characteristics, the 70 years since the founding of the People's Republic of China in 1949, especially in the 40 years since the reform and opening up, show a history of exploring and constructing socialism with Chinese characteristics. China has leaped from a poor and backward agricultural country to the world's second largest economy. The Chinese model of economic reform and the Chinese road to economic development have been tested in practice. Great practice promotes theoretical innovation. The socialist political economy with Chinese characteristics generalizes theories from successful practices of socialist economic construction with Chinese characteristics, and it tells China's story with Chinese theories.

Subject orientation 3: Socialist political economy with Chinese characteristics is the economics of innovation in the new historical era. The new practice of the development of socialism with Chinese characteristics will promote the refinement and summary of regular results of economic development practices, as well as elevate practical experiences to draw from systematic economic theories. Currently, China's economy is the second largest in the world. Per capital GDP has entered the ranks of middle-income countries, and urbanization rate has entered the middle stage of urbanization. At this historical starting point, the development problems to be solved are not merely the problems of growing GDP in the low-income stage, but the pursuit of full development of economy and society. Its tasks involve going beyond the "middle-income trap", supporting the "new normal" phase of economic development, and achieving the "Two Centenary Goals". To accomplish these new tasks in the new era, we must avoid fatal mistakes and use scientific theoretical guidance.

This requires that the socialist political economy with Chinese characteristics be problem-oriented. Not only should it adhere to the basic tenets of Marxism and methodology, but it should also consider the reality of Chinese economic development to form and recognize new theoretical achievements.

Therefore, the subject orientation of socialist political economy with Chinese characteristics at the current stage is political economy for the primary stage of socialism in terms of productive relations, as well as the political economy for the middle-income development phrase in terms of productive forces. Thus, it maintains its mainstream status in economics and the theoretical position of guiding ideology of China's reform and development.

The above-mentioned disciplinary orientation determines the level of the research. Generally speaking, the analytical level of Marxist economics is limited to the essential level of economic relations, in other words, the analysis of production relation. The theory is that the development of productive forces relies on adjusting and changing productive relations. The problem of developing productive forces in the current stage of socialism not only involves the level of productive relation improvement and development, but it also involves levels of economic operation and economic development. These two levels are both related to the productive relations. Socialist political economy with Chinese characteristics expands the horizon of the political economics.

2.2 Building a Systematic Economic Theory Concerning the Liberation, Development, and Preservation of Productive Forces

Like many other disciplines, socialist political economy with Chinese characteristics has specific research objects and tasks, which are related to Marxist political economics and other new developments. The main manifestation is reflected in the fact that it researches not only the relations of production, but also productive forces.

According to Marx's definition, Marxist political economy starts from researching production. The production it studies here is not a common type of production but social production. It involves not only relations of production, but also the productive forces which are interactive with each other. Its basic tenets as stated by Marx is: "No matter which social form, before all the productive forces it can hold, it will never die; and new and higher production relations. It will never appear until its material existence conditions mature in the birthplace of the old society".[1] This explains that the existence and change of certain productive relations rely on productive forces. Marxist political economy is linked to productive relations. The reason is that certain production relations are always associated with a certain level of social productivity. The historical development of productive technology and organization form plays a decisive role in the choice of the productive relations dominated by society. Research on the development level of productive forces provides the evaluation criterions for the relations of production at a certain stage.

The basic methodology of Marxist political economy is the contradictory analysis of productive forces and the relations of production. The subjects of the research and the tasks differ. In capitalist economy, the contradiction between productive forces and productive relations is manifested in that the development of productive forces is hindered by the relations of production, so the task of Marxist political economy is to reveal the objective law of socialism replacing capitalism. Yet after the seizure of power by the proletariat, the task changes. It changes to "increase the total amount of productivity as rapidly as possible", and to produce for the prosperity of all. The basis is that socialism finally substitutes capitalism on the material condition that its level of productive forces reaches and exceeds that of capitalism. Socialism does not mean poverty. Especially after countries that are economically backward enter the socialist society, the contradiction between productive forces and productive relations manifests in the relative backwardness of productive forces. The biggest obstacle during socialism's victory over capitalism is not the backwardness of productive relations, rather it is the backwardness of productive forces. Based on the reality that when China enters the socialist society, its level of productive forces has not yet reached that of the capitalist countries. One of the major breakthroughs for socialist political economy with Chinese characteristics is to clarify that China is still at the primary stage of socialism and the nature of socialism at this stage is to liberate and develop productive forces, eradicate exploitation, eliminate polarization, and gradually achieve common prosperity. It is mentioned here that developing productive forces is the essential demand

[1] Karl Marx and Frederick Engels. *Marx & Engels Collected Works*. Vol. 29, Trans. Ben Fowkes and Emile Burns (London: Lawrence & Wilshart, 2010), p. 263.

and the fundamental task of socialism. Thus, it is decided that the fundamental task of socialism at the primary stage is to develop productive forces to meet people's material and cultural needs, as well as to construct the material foundation of socialism. In this way, socialist political economy with Chinese characteristics emphasizes the vital position of researching productive forces, promoting national wealth as its goal and end result. It can be conferred that socialist political economy with Chinese characteristics is based on the theoretical breakthrough of this research object and task.

What is the study of productive forces? According to the essential demands of socialism in the primary stage, Deng Xiaoping stresses that a mere talk of developing productive forces is not enough. To liberate productive forces and develop productive forces are aspects that should be separately taken into consideration. On May 24, 2013, when General Secretary Xi Jinping moderated the sixth group study for the Political Bureau of the Communist Party of China (CPC) Central Committee, he emphasized on firmly establishing the idea that "protecting the environment equates to protecting productivity and that improving the environment also equates to developing productivity".[2] Thus, socialist political economy with Chinese characteristics includes three levels for productive forces: to liberate productive forces, to develop productive forces, and to protect productive forces. The construction of the theoretical system of socialist political economy with Chinese characteristics is the systematic construction of an economy that liberates, develops, and protects the productive forces.

The first level is to liberate productive forces. The so-called liberation of productive forces is to promote the reform and opening up according to the characteristics of the stage of Chinese socialism and to fundamentally change the economic system that restricts the development of productive forces. Here, the liberation of productive forces is the driving force, while the development of productive forces is the end goal. The adjustments of the productive relations involved in liberating the productive forces are concerned with the self-reform and self-improvement of the socialist economic system with Chinese characteristics, including the reform and improvement of the basic economic system, resource allocation, state-owned enterprises, basic distribution system, and the macro control

---

[2]Xi Jinping. *The Governance of China*. Vol. 1 (Beijing: Foreign Languages Press, 2014), p. 231.

system. All these mentioned above will be elaborated in later paragraphs.

The second level is the development of productive forces for economic development. Though liberating productive forces provides motive for developing productive forces, it cannot replace the study of the development of productive forces and economic development. The reason is that the development of productive forces has its own laws and its own theoretical system. According to the generalization of Marx, the development of social productive forces derives from the three aspects: "This development in productivity can always be reduced in the last analysis to the social character of the labor that is set to work, to the division of labor in society, and to the development of intellectual labor, in particular of the natural sciences".[3] These three aspects are the theoretical basis for the research and development of productive forces.

The third level is to protect productive forces. This involves the relationship between economic development and ecological environment protection. As Marx said, "Even if we leave aside the question of the level of development attained by social production, the productivity of labor remains fettered by natural conditions".[4] The richer the soil is and the better the climate is, the higher the rate of labor productivity is. This productive effect resulted in the protection of productive forces. In this sense, environment and ecology are wealth, and lucid waters are lush mountains are invaluable assets. The concept of protecting productive forces is consistent with the concept of green development. The style of green development and green life is the essential condition for sustainable development and the important embodiment of people's pursuit for a better life. It is only when the resources, environment, and ecology are effectively protected that the harmonious coexistence between humans and nature can be achieved, as well as sustainable development.

The research on the development and protection of productive forces can be categorized as theoretical research on economic development. Over the past 40 years, socialist political economy with Chinese characteristics has made great theoretical contributions to economic development, including the theory of socialist modernization with Chinese

---

[3]Karl Marx. *Capital: A Critique of Political Economy*. Vol. 3, Trans. David Fernbach (New York: Penguin Books, 1981), p. 175.

[4]Karl Marx. *Capital: A Critique of Political Economy*. Vol. 1, Trans. Ben Fowkes (New York: Penguin Books, 1976), p. 647.

characteristics, the theory of science and technology as the primary force of productivity, the theory of new industrialization and urbanization, and the theory that emphasizes making good use of international and domestic markets and resources, etc.

China's economic development entered a new phase after the 18th National Congress of the CPC. On the one hand, China's economic development entered the middle-income stage from the low-income stage, where the development problem it faces is not to rid poverty, but rather to go beyond the "middle-income trap", and to realize an overall moderately prosperous society, moving forward toward modernization. On the other hand, the economic development enters the "new normal" phase. It is reflected as General Secretary Xi Jinping concludes in the explanation of "Central Committee of the Communist Party of China Recommendations for the 13th Five-Year Plan for Economic and Social Development". The first is the change of speed, as the economic growth needs to transition from high speed to medium-high speed and the development mode needs to turn from the type of scope and speed, to the type of quality and efficiency. The second is structural optimization as the principal adjustment of economic structure that shifts from increment and capacity expansion to stock adjustment and simultaneous development of quality and increment. The third is power transformation as the drive of development relies more on innovation rather than on factors such as resources and low-cost labor. The adaptation of the "new normal" leads to the new development concept, which is the concept of innovative, coordinated, green, open, and shared development. This is the theoretical conclusion on the practices of promoting economic development in the economic "new normal" phase that will become the cutting-edge theory for socialist political economy with Chinese characteristics.

In the economic "new normal" phase, it is necessary to look out for new drives of developing productive forces. Socialist political economy with Chinese characteristics indicates the following two new drives.

The first driving force is innovation. It was Marx who first talked about the notion of innovation.[5] Schumpeter first raised the concept of innovation. Yet even in Western economics, as Stiglitz states, standard

[5] C. Freeman. "Marx and Engels (1848) probably more than any other economist assigned to technical innovation the driving force in economic development and competition". *The New Palgrave Dictionary of Economics*. Third Edition (London: Palgrave Macmillan, 2018), p. 6562.

market economy model ignores the role of innovation. The 18th National Congress of the CPC proposed innovation-driven economic development, and the Fifth Plenary Session of the 18th Central Committee of the CPC clearly put forward the concept of "innovative development", and regarded it as the first driving force and basic point of development. Its theoretical contribution lies in the so-called transformation of development mode. What kind of development mode is the goal? This requires not only intensive growth but also innovative development approaches. This content includes the following:

1. Innovative development as a new approach of development. Of these developments, scientific and technological innovation takes the lead.
2. The innovation of technology highlights independent innovation. The innovation of science and technology has changed from following and imitating other developed countries to keeping pace with them, and eventually taking the lead in technology and industry.
3. The innovation of technology needs to connect with the innovation of industry and promote the industry shift toward the medium-high end.
4. The collaborative research calls for promoting cooperation among enterprises, universities, and research institutes to develop new technology. This innovation and entrepreneurship call for the participation from the masses.

It is obvious that innovation, as a new approach of development is the innovation of Chinese development theories as well as the theoretical creation of socialist political economy with Chinese characteristics.

The second is the driving force of consumption. Political economy should not only research production but also consumption. It should not only research productive forces but also consumption capacity. The improvement of productive forces cannot be achieved without the increase of the consumption capacity. The consumption capacity is an important concept raised in Marx's *Capital*. The 18th National Congress of the CPC clearly proposed the strategy of boosting domestic demand and put consumption capacity as the vital element among the troika of investment, export, and consumption to promote economic growth. In the suggestions for the 13th Five-Year Plan, the CPC clarified that it is essential to speed up the establishment of a long-term mechanism to expand consumer demand and to release the potential of individual consumption. Socialist political economy with Chinese characteristics researches on the consumption and the consumption capacity for the following three reasons: First, the transformation of economic development pattern should emphasize on the fundamental role that consumption plays on growth. Economic growth should no longer be promoted through mere investment and export but through the combined forces of consumption, investment, and export. And the consumer demand, with its topmost significance, is the reliable and sustainable force. Second, the balanced relationship in macroeconomy actually relies on the balanced relationship between productive forces and consumption capacity. Third, the people-oriented economics should promote the level of people's consumption, the factors that influence consumption capacity, and the level of income, employment, and social welfare, and it should also indicate the nature of the distribution relationship and system. The percentage of accumulation and consumption is the comprehensive reflection of the development mode. Thus, the consumption capacity should always be included in the research on socialist political economy with Chinese characteristics.

Based on the essential demands of socialism in its primary stage, socialist political economy with Chinese characteristics makes its pioneering research combining the three levels of liberation, development, and protection of productive forces in its research to form its systematic economic theories. It presents great theoretical and practical significance. It indicates that Marxist political economy does not merely talk about socialism and capitalism, or just productive relations, but it also includes substantial materials regarding the liberation, development, and protection of productive forces. On this basis, the new concept of economic development is based on a theoretical conclusion of promoting economic development. To lead and promote Chinese economic development with these new concepts and to solve the difficult problems in economic development leads to a new economic landscape. In this way, political economy can not only function in educational terms, but also guides the national and entrepreneurial economic decision-making and economic policymaking.

2.3 The Theoretical Innovation on Economic System Analysis

The basic economic system and the basic revenue system are the two aspects of the social economic system. The systematic economic theory of theoretical innovation constitutes the core of socialist political economy with Chinese characteristics.

The theory of ownership is the fundamental theory of Marxist political economy. The basic socialist economic system is defined as socialist public ownership. In order to develop productive forces at the primary stage of socialism, it is required that we should start from reality and seek new drives and factors to promote productive force, thus promoting socialist development in the primary stage of socialism to make full use of all the resources for the creation of social prosperity. Therefore, the basic economic system allows for public ownership to play the dominant role and diverse forms of ownership to develop together as the primary stage of socialism.

After the reforms and opening up, a series of significant theories have been developed in the reform and improvement process of the basic economic system, which show in the following three aspects: (1) A variety of non-public sectors of the economy such as the individual economy, private economy, and foreign investment economy, which have been "outside the system" for a long time, now "enter the system" and become an integral part of the basic economic system. The relationship between them and the public economy is not one who wins but one of equal competition. (2) The public ownership makes a breakthrough in materializing forms. In the past, the theory emphasized that public assets can only be managed by public enterprises. It is now clear that public ownership is a concept of assets and capital, and it does not merely refer to public enterprises (including state-owned enterprises and collective enterprises) but refers to public assets (which include state-owned assets and collective assets). This means that public assets can be managed in various types of enterprises, and public ownership can be materialized through various forms, including mixed economy like the shareholding system. (3) The breakthrough of public ownership that play a dominant role. Past theories define public ownership as having a dominant role in public enterprise that occupies the majority. Now the public ownership that plays the dominant role acquires a new meaning, that is, the public assets play a dominant role in the total assets of society; the state sector controls the national lifeblood of the economy and plays the leading role in economic development. According to this theory, the state sector makes the strategic adjustment of advancing and retreating, and it maintains control over the national economy.

According to the Third Plenary Session of the 18th Central Committee of the CPC, the reform and improvement of the basic economic system should not only adhere to "two unswervinglys" but also "two inviolabilities":

to unswervingly consolidate and develop the public sector of the economy as well as ensure its dominant position, support and guide non-public economic development; the property rights of the public economy are inviolable, as well as the property rights of the non-public economy. It is on this basis that four aspects of reform with significant theoretical breakthroughs should be promoted:

(1) Implement unified market access for all forms of ownership on the basis of a negative list, abolish all forms of unreasonable regulations on the non-public economy, eliminate hidden barriers, and fix specific measures to establish specific measures for non-public enterprises to enter franchising fields. Therefore, the non-public economy and the public economy has equal access to the market.

(2) A mixed economy of government capital, collective capital, and non-public capital is an important way to materialize the basic economic system. Allow more state-owned and other ownership enterprises to develop into a mixed-ownership economy. Allow non-state shares to enter state capital investment projects and encourage the development of non-public capital holdings of mixed-ownership enterprises. The public ownership system plays a dominant role, and diverse forms of ownership developing side by side shift from the development outside of the enterprises to the development within the same enterprise.

(3) Rural collective separates the land-owning, land-contracting, and land-operating rights. The operation rights of the contracted collective-owned land can be switched around. Thus, farmers can obtain income from the land property rights. This is a major breakthrough in China's rural land system theories.

(4) In the mixed-ownership, public ownership manifests a new dominant role. The state-owned enterprises are divided into the public service type and the commercial type. The commercial type of public enterprises is in the field of competition and focuses more on the running benefits of public capital. Therefore, they will not seek enterprise shareholding, instead they pursue the proliferative ability of the enterprises. Thus, in enterprises with strong proliferative ability, the total quantity of public capital is large enough to occupy the majority even without shareholding. Enterprises of the public service type will not dominate the market, in this way, non-state shares will be allowed in state capital investment projects and enterprises. The dominant role of the public ownership is presented in shareholding and mixed-ownership. The public ownership not only controls its own capital, but also controls the participated non-state capital.

Its control power lies not only in its shareholding, but also in its attraction generated by its equal treatment of other ownership economies and the associated shared benefits.

In general, the reform and improvement of the basic economic system is the great achievement of socialist political economy with Chinese characteristics, because it solves the theoretical and practical problems that comes along with activating various non-public economies and keeping the dominant role of public economy.

The relation of distribution is the other side of the relation of production. With the gradual establishment of the basic economic system in which public ownership plays the dominant role and diverse forms of ownership develop together, the basic distribution system whereby distribution according to work is dominant and multiple forms of distribution coexist is established accordingly.

Two rules exist in the Marxist political economy for the basic distribution system of socialism: (1) The elimination of exploitation and the pursuit of common prosperity are the basic requirements of socialism. (2) The distribution according to work is the distribution law of socialism because the means of production are public while only labor is private. In the real primary stage of socialism, theoretical breakthroughs are made on the following two conditions.

First, the existence of diverse forms of ownership is recognized. It means that the private ownership of factors other than labor, such as capital, technology and entrepreneurs are recognized as private. Accordingly, the income distribution system that follows should not only stimulate labor efficiency, but also stimulate the element owner to invest various elements like capital, technology, and management. Not only should labor be respected, but elements of creation and entrepreneurship, knowledge and talents should also be respected. It is in this way that all elements of wealth creation like labor, capital, technology, and management can be activated.

Second, how to achieve common prosperity in the primary stage of socialism with relatively lacking material wealth? Throughout a long period of history, the common prosperity is taken as egalitarianism, which results in common poverty. Deng Xiaoping clarifies that common poverty is not socialism, as promoting that policy allows some people to get rich first. Common prosperity is understood as the existence of prior prosperity and later prosperity, whereas prior prosperity should help the later prosperity. The participation of various non-labor factors in the income distribution according to the market laws provides a mechanism for some people to get rich first. The formation of this kind of distribution system indicates the efficiency principle of income distribution.

The theory of various production factors participating the income distribution develops with the development of reform. The major theoretical results include the following.

(1) The principle with which various production factors can participate in the distribution. From the 14th to 16th National Congress of the CPC, the principle was settled that the production factors such as labor, capital, technology, and management should participate in distribution according to their contributions. Both the 17th and 18th National Congress of the CPC proposed to refine the system in which production factors like labor, capital, technology, and management should participate in distribution according to their contributions. Based on that, the Third Plenary Session of the 18th Central Committee of the CPC proposed that the reward of the production factors should be determined by the respective markets of the factors. Such statements indicate that the portion of income distribution depends not only on the input of each production factor but also its respective contribution and the market's supply and demand. This being said, distribution is made according to market principles and is the practical presentation of market economy system. The participation of all factors in distribution, according to contribution and market principles can fully stimulate the vitality of all factors. Generally speaking, it can meet socialism's basic requirement of productive force development. Multiple production factors are brought into full play to increase social wealth, along with it comes the significant increase in the workers' absolute income, which coincides with their interests.

(2) How to reflect the dominance of distribution according to work with various non-labor factors' participation in income distribution. Different people may have different factors, and it may lead to different levels of income. People with bigger saving capacity, higher technological level, and stronger management ability tend to become wealthier. As the ownership of the production means can be mixed, so can the ownership of the production factors. This being said, labor investment not only involves the laborer's labor in the direct process of production but also involves the labor of the technicians and administrators, absent from the production site but still work for the production. It involves the management of the enterprise managers as well. According to Marxist theory, these parts of

labor also belong to productive labor. Even those direct laborers may also have technological factors as human capital and complex labor, aside from their simple labor output. It is obvious that if the labor reward of technicians and managers is included in the entire labor reward, then the dominance of distribution according to work can be highlighted. As its premise, three principles should be adhered to: the first is to ensure higher reward for complex labor so that technological and management labor can be highlighted; the second is to ensure that labor reward grows in step with the improvement of labor productivity; the third is not to ignore the contribution of the laborers in the growth of enterprise efficiency whose labor may not be complex. If these three principles are pursued, the dominance of distribution according to work can then be highlighted in the total income distribution.

(3) How to bridge the income gap when the share of the front-line workers' reward in the distribution of income has dramatically declined. There is the tendency that the share of the direct labor providers' reward in the distribution of income is declining, even if technology and management factors are not taken into consideration. The Third Plenary Session of the 18th Central Committee of the CPC identifies the demand of fairness and justice, as well as the gradual achievement of common prosperity. Shared development is the essential demand of socialism with Chinese characteristics that prioritizes the people. According to this requirement, it is necessary to improve the basic revenue system so that people can enjoy the fruit of the shared reform and development in the improvement of living standards. People can gain benefits and achieve more of a "sense of gain". This involves the following aspects: the first is to highlight the fairness of rights, which includes eradicating the loophole of the abuse of power for personal gain with and by the system; anti-monopoly and obtaining income in a market of fair competition; as well as the creation of opportunity for more people to gain income from property. People should have equal access to basic public services. The equality should be well-rounded so that low-income groups can have equal access to basic public services. The second is to improve primary distribution and redistribution, to elevate the share of the citizen's income in the distribution of national income, to change the long-held opinion that primary distribution should emphasize efficiency while redistribution should emphasize fairness, to clarify that primary distribution and redistribution should both deal with the relationship between fairness and efficiency, while redistribution should lay more emphasis on fairness. The third is that according

to Marxist economic principles, the reason why distribution should be according to work is that labor is still the means to earn a living. Thus, the growth of labor reward is not limited to labor's contribution but should include other requirements for making a living. The range of making a living is the range of necessary labor. The range of necessary labor involves historical and moral factors. The necessary range of labor develops along with the development of the society and culture, and the labor reward grows accordingly. The fourth is that in terms of socialist sense of fairness, the gap of labor income is caused by the differences of respectively owned factors, such as technology. With equal access to education, the gap between factors owned by each distribution subject may diminish and common laborers can also gain complex labor income, so the gap between distribution results may further diminish.

Therefore, the task of economic system analysis for socialist political economy with Chinese characteristics is to analyze and define the nature of various ownerships. Though its focus is not the battle among different forms of ownership but on the mission of constructing a new society, on seeking effective ways for diverse forms of ownership to compete on a fair basis, cooperating and developing, and seeking ways for owners of various factors such as labor, knowledge, technology, management and capital to make full use of their ability, to play their respective roles, and to live in harmony. It aims to give full play to all sources that can create social wealth and benefit the people.

2.4 Innovative Theories on Economic Operation Analysis

Economic operation involves the analysis of the means of resource allocation as well as the relationship between supply and demand. It aims at achieving two goals: (i) efficiency and (ii) coordinated development. It is inherently demanded by the sustainable and sound development of the economy. For a certain period of time, Western economics concerned itself with discourse power over economic operation analysis. The market-based reform in China promotes the study of political economy into the field of economic operation analysis. The establishment of socialist market economy theories seized back the power over economic operation analysis. These are significant contributions of socialist political economy with Chinese characteristics.

The primary theoretical development is the identification that in the socialist market economy, market acts fundamentally in resource allocation under state macro control. It solves the problem of the combination of socialist public ownership and market economy, both in theoretical and practical terms. A series of reforms, such as the reform on the system of property rights of state-owned enterprises, the development of diverse forms of ownership, the cancelation of mandatory plans, the deregulation of control over market prices, and the entrance of foreign capital promote the development of socialist market economy, having obviously vitalized economy and improved the efficiency of resource allocation.

The further theoretical development is that, with the establishment of the Chinese socialist market economy system and the improved knowledge and control over market laws, the Third Plenary Session of the 18th Central Committee of the CPC identified the market's determination on resource allocation and it demanded better role of the government. It is a breakthrough of the socialist market economy theories. To clarify the determination of the market on resource allocation is actually a return to the nature of a market economy. The market's autonomy is emphasized when the market determines resource allocation. Its autonomy is presented in the fact that the market independently determines the direction of resource allocation and at the same time, the government will not improperly interfere in the independent determination of market prices, regarded as market regulation signals. It has greatly promoted the reform on the cancelation and decentralization of administrative examination and approval right for governments at all levels.

Then how does one show that socialism demands the new project raised by the new resource allocation pattern for political economy? How should the government play a better role? New liberalism theories put the government and the market in opposition, indicating that the government cannot function in the market economy, and a strong government will prevent a strong market. The practice of socialist market economy operation answers these questions in a scientific way. To term market economy as a socialist market economy is uniquely Chinese. It is with solid meaning rather than a mere label, which shows in the active role of the government. A strong government does not indicate a weak market. The coordination of a strong government and a strong market is the characteristic of socialist market economy operation. The better role of the government is shown in the following two aspects.

(1) The government and the market have their clarified function boundaries. As for the fields where the government functions, different economists have different voices. Some advocate that the government should function in the fields where the market malfunctions, such as in the external problems of overcoming the polarization of wealth and environmental pollution. Some state that as the significant basis of system change, the government (the state) should function primarily to protect the property right structure that will benefit efficiency. Others emphasize that the government should interfere with the macroeconomy to prevent the loss of macroeconomic control such as high unemployment and high inflation. There is no doubt that the socialist market needs the government to function in these ways. Apart from these, the government should also function in the following ways according to the practical situation of China: First, to lead the construction and improvement of a market system and market mechanism. The Chinese market economy is transformed from a planned economy that has led to serious chaos in the market system and market mechanism, and it is difficult to have effective market resource allocation. The effectiveness of market resource allocation is based on the perfection of market mechanism. A perfect market economy will not be born or grow on its own. The government should shoulder the responsibility of constructing and improving the market, which includes the construction of a perfect market system, the establishment of a unified and open competition order, the clarification of the fair market regulations, and the supervision of market orders. Second, to allocate the public resources. The decisive role of the market on resource allocation should not be enlarged to the market's determination on public resources. The allocation of public resources is to meet the demands of the public. Based on the principle of fairness, it can only be decided by the government. In projects involving national security, ecological safety, environmental protection, important nation-wide arrangements for manufacturing capacity, development of strategic resources and crucial public interests, as well as fundamental public service allocation, the government should not only interfere but take a strong hand and play its full role. Third, to promote development. For a developing country at the primary stage of socialism, only development counts. The promotion of development is the important function of the government. The government should plan and guide in the fields, such as promoting integration of urban and rural development, urbanization, developing the innovation-driven economy, adjusting

economic structure, constructing ecology and environment, as well as developing an open economy.

(2) The government function mechanism should effectively connect with the market mechanism. The function of the government should not conflict with the decisive role of the market, instead it should act in cooperation with the market. On the one hand, the public services provided by the government should conform to the laws of the market and make use of the market mechanism. On the other hand, the public services provided by the government do not have to be produced and operated by governmental departments. Sometimes, production and operation by private departments will be more effective; services brought from private department by the government will enable public services to be of higher efficiency and quality; and market approaches such as emission charges and emission rights, trading system can be applied to environmental protection. In addition, the government allocation of public resources can be mainly recognized by policymaking, which includes using income allocation policies to promote social equality and justice, using industrial policies and the negative list to lead the transformation, upgrading the industrial structure, and using financial and monetary policies to adjust the macroeconomic operation. The government's adjustment of macroeconomy is not a direct adjustment of the market, but rather a supervision of the overall price and employment level, which shows the effectiveness of the market adjustment. Within the reasonable range of the macroeconomy, the state will not freely control and regulate so that it will give more independence for the market.

It is obvious that the market's determination on resource allocation is combined with a more effective government as an organic whole. This is a successful creation for the method of the socialist market economy operation, which not only gives the economic operation vitality and efficiency, but also recognizes the socialist development goal. To elevate this economic operation method to systematic economic theory is a landmark achievement of the socialist political economy with Chinese characteristics.

The analysis of the relationship between supply and demand is also an important aspect of economic operation. Existing economics analyzes the relationship between supply and demand in the following ways: political economy focuses on the analysis of the effect and mechanism of the law of value; Western economics focus on the analysis of balance and imbalance among supply, demand, and price. China, at present, places more emphasis on the system of demand side and supply side, and their related reform, which opens a new prospect for the political economy analysis of the economic operation.

For 40 years, the transformation into the system of market economy has actually been the reform on the demand side. It involved improving the market competition mechanism, to highlight market demand orientation and abolish mandatory plans in the micro system; clarifying the transformation of macro system to a system in which the troika of investment, export, and consumption are in tune with economic growth, and the transformation of macro control to an overall demand and supply control of the financial and monetary policies. On this basis, the focus of the demand side is to improve the management of the demand and supply, especially the drive of consumption. The new problem appearing in the practices is that in the transformation to the market economy, mere demand cannot effectively drive the growth of economy. It is indicated that economic growth requires the drive from the supply side. Unlike developed countries, developing countries need to solve problems of the supply side to achieve economic growth in the transformation to the market economy.

The first is to promote effective supply. The coexistence of structural supply shortage and ineffective and low-end supply of excess is typical in the developing countries. Structural supply shortage is reflected in problems related to product quality, technological level, efficiency, service, and food hygiene. At the same time, ineffective and low-end supply of excess exists. These problems on the supply side will not automatically disappear in the transformation to the market economy, and demand will not drive effective supply. Therefore, the target of reform on the supply side is to improve the adaptability and flexibility of structural supply for the change of demand, to improve the quality and efficiency of the supply system. The reduction of overcapacity and destocking is to make way for the resources occupied by the ineffective and low-end supply, and to also increase effective supply.

The second is to provide the drive for growth from the supply side. People used to take the transformation from the drive of supply to the drive of demand as the drive for economic growth in the transformation to the market economy, so that the drive on the supply side will usually be ignored. The actual drive for growth not only involves the drive of demand, but also involves the drive of supply. If there is a lack of sufficient drive on the demand side, it is more necessary for the supply side to have the drive for economic growth. Apart from all the material factors, the technological, structural, and efficient system factors are also included in the supply factors. When the supply drive from material resources and low-cost labor recedes, there are still other drives provided by the supply side. The improvement of total factor productivity to a large extent makes up for the insufficiency of factors. The innovation drive, the adjustment of the structure, and the improvement of efficiency will prove to be new supply drives. Structural reform is the very approach to these drives, which involves the system of scientific and technological innovation, the system of refined management and the incentive system.

The third is to stimulate the vitality of the market. The key questions of economics can be summarized as "choice" and "stimulation". Generally speaking, economics on the demand side focuses on the question of choice: when the market determines the allocation of resources, the market will choose the resource flow — in which region, field, and enterprise. A market with fierce competition will choose the survival of the fittest and this choice exerts external pressure to the enterprises. Economics on the demand side focuses on the question of stimulation. One major principle of political economy with Chinese characteristics is to insist on boosting enthusiasm from all aspects, which should be taken as a major principle for the structural reform on the supply side. Analyzed from the perspective of economic development, stimulation involves the following three aspects: (1) The stimulation of innovation. Innovation is different from other economic activities. First, the innovated knowledge and technology can be extended and shared, and the society will benefit from the new knowledge and technology. Second, the innovated technology can be copied. The cost of copying is so low that the cost of innovation then will not be compensated. Third, compared with the material product market, there is more informational asymmetry in the knowledge product market, so that the true value of knowledge will usually be seriously undervalued. Therefore, innovation should not merely rely on market pressure, but rather on the internal drive provided by stimulation, which includes the acquirement of innovation profit under strict intellectual property protection and the stimulating policies and guided investment incentives provided by the government. (2) The stimulation for overcoming opportunistic behaviors. Establish the stimulation system with information insufficiency, rid opportunistic behaviors with moral dangers that do harm to supply quality and efficiency, and overcome the Gresham's Law from the perspective of the system. (3) The stimulation of enterprise vitality.

For the subjects of micro economy, relieve the burden of enterprises, reduce administrative intervention on enterprises, so as to stimulate the enterprise vitality. The stimulation of enterprise vitality is especially demanded, for enterprises are the essential factors in economic operation. It is necessary to deal well with the relations among the state, the enterprise, and the employees in terms of their interests in the national income allocation. On the one hand, the interest of the enterprise should be emphasized in the relationship between the enterprise and its employees. Employees should share the achievement as well as the risks from enterprise development. If the enterprise goes bankrupt or lays off its employees with the overburden of unqualified employees, the employees are still the victims. On the other hand, the interest of the enterprise should be emphasized in the relationship between the enterprise and the government. The government should make profit for the enterprises. Greatly reduce taxes, interests, fees (the five major social insurance programs and housing provident fund), and debts from the perspective of the system. Let more enterprises get rid of their burden.

It is a great development for political economy with Chinese characteristics to research respectively from the perspective of system and reform on the operation efficiency of the demand side and the supply side, to reflect the development of China's research on economic operation theories, and to elevate its achievement to systematic economic theories.

2.5 Innovative Theories on Economic Development Analysis

To tell China's story with Chinese development theories can present Chinese wisdom. The Chinese road to economic development requires the conclusion and summary of Chinese theories. It is impossible to be explained by Western economics. Chinese industrialization and urbanization are examples. Chinese industrialization and urbanization are promoted when the urban–rural dual structure has not been completely reformed and agriculture is still greatly underdeveloped. At that time, the urban areas are as underdeveloped as the rural areas, so it is impossible for the cities to take the hundreds of millions of rural surplus labors removed from their land. Under these circumstances, industrialization and urbanization cannot repeat the path paved by the Western countries. Chinese farmers created their own paths for rural industrialization and urbanization, and it has proven to be successful. The economic theory that summarizes these great creations and practices will not only highlight the Chinese characteristics of the socialist political economy with Chinese characteristics but also contribute to the whole world.

The existing development theory is primarily based on the low-income stage. The development problem that China faces when it enters the middle-income stage is to get rid of poverty and to enter into a condition of moderate prosperity. An important path for development is to promote industrialization and urbanization. Related development theories involve the pursuit of GDP growth, high accumulation and low consumption, high input for high speed, extensive development mode, and rural surplus labor transfer, and so on. It can be said that these development theories are of theoretical guidance for China to get rid of poverty and enter the middle-income stage. The problem is that when China has already entered the middle-income stage, a continued guidance of these theories without the innovation of development theories will not help the development at a new stage. It is even possible that China will suffer from the "middle-income trap".

At present, the Chinese economy is characterized by obvious middle-income traits. At this new historical starting point, with the full establishment of the moderately prosperous society, the development task is to step from a middle-income country to a high-income country. Compared with the past low-income stage, the economy in the middle-income stage has already been or is under great transformation, and new development tasks are on the way. Developing countries will generally encounter the "middle-income trap" when they enter the middle-income stage. The "middle-income trap" is concerned with the problem of development mode. If a country in the middle-income stage cannot rid the development mode of the low-income stage, the result is that it cannot compete with the low-income countries in terms of income and it cannot compete with the wealthy countries in terms of advanced technology and research. This development mode poses three types of threats: (1) The income gap reaches the peak point of the Kuznets curve and it becomes difficult for it to go downward; (2) The frequency of corruption reaches the peak point of the Kuznets curve; (3) The environmental pollution also reaches the peak point of the Kuznets curve and it is difficult for it to go downward. With the development of civilization in the middle-income stage, citizens will not tolerate the widening income gap caused by the injustice of rights and they will pay more attention to health and education, and relative awareness of rights protection will also be greatly raised. Practices prove that not all countries fall into this trap. Countries like Singapore and South Korea overcame the middle-income trap with the process of modernization. China is threatened by this trap, yet it is not to say that it will surely enter the trap. When China realizes the possibility of the trap, it is required that with the guidance of the correct development theories, China can avoid the trap.

The series of new and important development problems mentioned above, which China faces when it enters the middle-income stage, are the starting point and source of motivation for the innovation of development theories. In responding to the great development problems in the middle-income stage, it is required that new economic development goals should be identified. The development problem in the low-income stage is actually the problem of growth, and its target is singular. Yet when China has entered the middle-income stage, the development problem will not merely restrict itself to the problem of growth. Growth is not equal to development. Economic development has more extensive meanings than economic growth, and it involves various levels of an economic society. Not only does it include the elimination of poverty, but a fair allocation and the increase of social welfare should also be counted as development targets. Economic growth not only involves benefits, but it also considers its costs, such as resource input and environmental pollution etc. Only growth with an effective use of resources, an effective control over environmental pollution, and an increase of social welfare will be valuable. It will be meaningless if the economy grows with ruined environment, harmful health of citizens, and the polarization between the rich and the poor. Economic development is concerned with a sustainable growth of the production. It involves the growth of the output capacity and it includes not only the growth of quantity and scale, but also the advance of technology, the improvement of system, and innovation culture on which sustainable economic growth relies.

The significant development problems and targets have promoted a series of great innovations for economic development theories.

2.5.1. *The "new normal" phase theory*

In 40 years after the adoption of reform and opening up policies, Chinese economic growth has primarily been at its high-speed stage. When China entered the middle-income stage, its economy went into the new normal phase. It is reflected in the change of speed, as the speed of growth shifts from a high speed to a middle-high speed. The main reasons are the following: (1) The supply of material and environmental resources has reached its limits. (2) With the slowdown of rural labor transfer, the supply of the low-cost labor has reached its limit. (3) The supply and demand structure is seriously imbalanced. When China has entered the middle-income stage, consumption needs of its citizens started to change after they have fulfilled their basic living needs. They started to pay more attention to the needs concerning health, safety, hygiene, and class. Yet production and service still lagged behind in the supply of the low-income stage, which emphasizes on quantity instead of quality. The production for production's sake will lead to stocking and surplus caused by the insufficiency of effective supply, ineffective and low-end supply. It is obviously inevitable that Chinese growth will turn medium-high speed, yet efforts are still necessary to sustain the medium-high speed. When traditional mode of development has not lifted the pressure that leads the economy downhill, the development mode needs to turn from the type of scope and speed to the type of quality and efficiency, the structural reform from the supply side needs to be promoted, and new drive of development needs to be sought.

2.5.2. *The new development concept*

General Secretary Xi Jinping states that development should be scientific development guided by economic laws, and it should be sustainable development guided by laws of nature. He raises five new development concepts of innovative, coordinated, green, open, and shared development. New concepts for economic development are the theoretical summary of our practice of promoting economic development as well as the systematic guidance for Chinese economy when it enters the middle-income stage.

Innovative development concepts can promote the innovation of development drive theory. In the low-income stage, the drives of development are the drives supplied by the relative sufficiency of resources and low-cost labors. Now that the drives provided by factors such as resources and the low-cost labor are dying out, the drive of development should turn to the drive for innovation. Innovation is the primary driving force for development. It determines the speed, efficiency, and sustainability of development. The core of innovation-driven development is the innovation of science and technology. To adopt the strategy of innovation-driven development is to depend on the innovation of science and technology, which will drive to change the mode of development, to turn industrial structure to middle-high end, and to promote green production and consumption. The innovation of science and technology highlights independent innovation. The innovation of science and technology needs to turn from following and imitating other developed countries to keeping pace with them, and eventually taking the lead in technology and industry. If scientific and technological innovation is to become the drive of industrial innovation, it needs to connect with the innovation of industry to emphasize the conversion of scientific and technological achievements into actual productive forces. It needs collaborative innovation through the joint efforts of enterprises, universities, and research institutes to promote their cooperation to develop new technology, in order to create an environment where innovation and entrepreneurship call for the participation from the masses. It is clear that regarding innovation as a new mode of development is an innovation of Chinese development theory, and a theoretical creation of the socialist political economy with Chinese characteristics.

Coordinated development concepts can promote the innovation of development structure theory. The development of national economy is holistic. With multiple aspects of weakness, coordinated development is required to achieve balanced development and the holistic improvement and elevation of economic structure. Marxist social reproduction theory can be deduced from coordinated development theory. These two types of balance theory are to call for development in proportion among all departments on the basis of comprehensive coordination. In the phase of entering from the low-income stage to the middle-income stage, allowing some areas and people to get rich first is to adopt a strategy of imbalanced development. After entering the middle-income stage, we should turn our development concepts to coordinated development, or in other words, to balanced development. For the existing imbalanced economic development, we should make efforts to correct the weaknesses, which include correcting the weakness in agricultural modernization to promote the synchronous development of new industrialization, information technology, urbanization and agricultural modernization; correcting the weakness in poor areas to promote coordinated urban and rural development; correcting the weakness in social development to promote coordinated economic societal development; and a continuous holistic development.

Chinese economic development has opened up in a modernized way with Chinese characteristics for the synchronous development of new industrialization, information technology, urbanization, and agricultural modernization. The moderately prosperous society in all respects is to be shared by all, and it involves the coordinated development of economy, society, culture, politics, and ecology. In the low-income stage, in order to speedily get rid of poverty and gain a rapid growth in GDP, allowing some areas and people to get rich first is actually to adopt a strategy of imbalanced development. After entering the middle-income stage, the problems of imbalance and the weaknesses are very obvious. To build the moderately prosperous society in all respects and to promote modernization requires the correction of weakness according to the demands of shared and coordinated development. It includes: (1) the correction of weakness in agricultural modernization; (2) the correction of weakness in rural development to overcome the binary rural and urban structure; (3) the correction of weakness in the poor areas and population; (4) the correction of weakness in ecological civilization; and (5) the correction of weakness in human development. If these weaknesses cannot be corrected, it is very difficult to build the moderately prosperous society in all respects, and even more difficult to enter the high-income stage.

Green development concepts can promote the innovation of wealth theory. The traditional view of wealth includes only the material wealth. Green development concepts emphasize the harmonious coordination between nature and human beings. It is clear that ecology and environment are also considered wealth. Clean water, fresh air, and green environment are precious. Lucid waters and lush mountains are invaluable assets. In the low-income stage, promoted industrialization, urbanization, and heavy industrialization inevitably lead to the exhaustion of resources and unsustainable supply, which is ultimately the price of development. General Secretary Xi Jinping states that the human society lasts for thousands of years, for in the stages where productive forces lagged behind and physical poverty prevailed, not very much ruin was done to the ecological system. Yet in a mere 300 years from the start of industrial civilization to the present, great productive force of the human society leads to the Western modernization of a few developed countries, which have already threatened the life of human beings and sustainability of the creatures on the earth. If it goes on like this, the human civilization will crash down. Ecology and environment refer to the space where human beings live and work. The capacity of the environment taking in pollution is limited. The remaining pollution will do harm to human health and production. It means that unlike the past approaches of those Western countries, Chinese modernization not only requires more material wealth, but also more spiritual and ecological wealth so as to promote the approaches of green development and green life. If ways of human life and production are the most suitable and civilized way to influence and interfere with nature, then nature will respond in its best way to the productive force. And it is in this concept that the improvement of ecological environment is the development of the productive force.

Open development concepts can promote the innovation of international division theory. To make full use of national and international resources and to open up national and international markets is the only way for national prosperity. In the past, like many other developing countries, China entered the international division and global value chain with relatively high resource endowment. Now as the world's second largest economy and the world economic power, China wants to further enhance its own international competitiveness and improve the quality and standard of an open economy. Aiming to switch the comparative advantages to the competitive advantage in the international division, to reach the medium-high level of global value chain, and to actively participate and dominate in the global economic governance. The Belt and Road, Asian Infrastructure Investment Bank, and free trade areas are among the ways to participate in the global economic governance so that China's institutional discourse power can be elevated.

Shared development concepts can promote the innovation of development goal theory. Shared development reflects the demand of common prosperity and the development idea that puts people first, which is the basic demand of socialism with Chinese characteristics. In the early phase where economy starts to grow, it is allowed that some people can get rich first. But at present, it is required that the majority of people should get rich. On the one hand, development ideas such as "production for production's sake" and a unilateral pursuit of high accumulation should be avoided; on the other hand, fairness and justice should be embodied in income allocation and polarization should be avoided. The fruits of reform and development should be shared by all people, by all fields, in joint efforts and in gradual processes. The people share the fruits of reform and development in the improvement of livelihood, obtaining solid interests, and a "sense of gain". This is the source of motivation for reform and development. On the way of building a moderately prosperous society in all respects, promoting modernization puts more emphasis on the modernization of human beings, and this is what Marx states as the all-round development of an individual. It involves the all-round development of one's knowledge, the all-round development of one's ability, and the all-round uses of one's talent. With the present income differences, because of the differences of people's development capacity, to a great extent they cannot share the fruits of the development. Therefore, to develop education and elevate the cultural level of the whole nation is not only the necessary process of promoting the modernization of human beings, but also the significant approach to achieve shared development.

2.5.3. *To seek development drives on both the supply side and the demand side*

The major function of political economy research is to seek economic drives. Economic drives relate to economic interests. To seek development drives from the level of productive force involves both the supply side and the demand side. In the low-income stage, or in the past 40 years, the drives for Chinese economic development are mainly drives from the supply side, which are the supplies of abundant material resources and the low-cost labor in the early stage of development. The reform and opening up has fully activated these drives and supported rapid growth in the past. At present, the supply capacity of those factors used to drive the rapid growth of economy obviously starts to diminish. Therefore, the drives for economic growth need to change and new drives from both the supply side and the demand side should be sought.

The pulling power from the demand side is produced on the basis of market economy developed by reforms. The pressure from competition is regarded as the pulling power from the demand side. It is now identified macroscopically from the aggregate demand decision, that the pulling power from the demand refers to the coordinated pull of economic growth by the troika of investment, export, and consumption. At the same time, macro control of the state also emphasizes on the control of aggregate demand by financial and monetary policies. "The troika" from the demand side each have their own merits, yet the consumption demand is the basic. The Central Committee of the Communist Party of China Recommendations for the 13th Five-year Plan for Economic and Social Development clearly put forward the idea of speeding up the establishment of a long-term mechanism for increasing consumer demand and unleashing the potential of individual consumption. In *Capital*, Marx clearly puts forward the concept of social consumption capacity. In social reproduction, consumption force is equally important as a productive force. The present emphasis on the pulling power of consumer demand is not merely for the reason that consumption is not emphasized in the past, but more for the reason that consumption is irreplaceable in the pulling of economic growth. (1) The transformation of economic development methods needs to emphasize the basic function of consumption on growth. Consumption is the ultimate demand. Consumption is the reliable and sustainable drive for economic growth. As Marx says that in reproduction, consumption is the destination as well as the starting point. Production stops where consumption stops. (2) The economics that put people first require consumer demand's pull of economic development. People's consumption level that determines the consumer demand also determines the nature of the distribution relationship and the distribution system. (3) The balanced relationship of macroeconomy is actually the balanced relationship of the productive force and the consumption force. The ratio of accumulation and consumption is the comprehensive reflection of development method. Therefore, the socialist political economy with Chinese characteristics should not research on the development of productive force without the research on consumption capacity. Political economy should research not only production, but also consumption. It should research not only productive force, but also consumption capacity. Without the improvement of consumption capacity, there will be no improvement of productive force. From the perspective of productive force development, it is essential to cultivate the consumption capacity so as to improve consumer demand's pull of economic development, which involves increasing people's income, expanding employment, and improving the social security system.

Factors that affect the increase of economy includes both demand factors and supply factors. When consumers' demand pull cannot fully stop the downward mobility of economy, we should seek out the drive for economic increase from the supply side. The supply factors for potential economic growth that influence increase in its rate include not only the input of material and labor factors, but also the factors of technology, structure, and efficiency. The present subsiding drives from the supply side involve only material resources and low-cost labor. Yet on the supply side, there are other drives to be sought. The innovation drive, the adjustment of structure and the improvement of efficiency are all regarded as the drives provided by the supply side to promote economic growth. Compared with drives from the demand side, drives from the supply side sustains in the long term. Thus, the structural reform from the supply side becomes the major drive for economic development.

The major development problem for developing countries is the structural problems, among which the biggest one to overcome is the urban–rural dual structure. In the low-income stage, the urbanization based on moving farmers to cities is the great drive for development. After entering the middle-income stage, more should be included in overcoming the urban–rural dual structure. The two sides of the coin are the urban modernization and the integration of urban and rural development. Both sides contain great demands and great space for supply increase: the factors for the development of cities expand toward the rural areas, and there is an increase in the supply of urban factors and facilities in the rural and especially various types of towns so as to increase and promote industrial development, public service, employment attraction, and population aggregation functions in towns located in the vast rural areas. To push the urbanization of people not only grants citizenship to rural population which have been transferred to the cities so that new demands for city housing and welfare appear, but also enables farmers to have citizenship in rural towns, as well as enjoy rights of urban citizens, so that new demands for town housing and welfare appear. It is obvious that the integration of urban and rural development will become the great drive for economic development in the middle-income stage. Apart from changing the urban–rural dual structure, the drives for structural adjustment also include the transformation and upgrading of industrial structure, the coordination of regional structures, and so on. The structural adjustment in these aspects will become great drives for economic development.

2.5.4. *To improve total factor productivity*

The concept of factor productivity is mentioned in Marxist economics, which refers to labor productivity, capital productivity, and land productivity. Robert M. Solow, winner of the Nobel Memorial Prize in Economic Sciences in 1987, introduces the concept of total factor productivity. When total productivity outgrows the productivity generated by respective input of each factor, the extra portion is referred to as total factor productivity, the improvement of which involves the improvement of the input factor's quality, the improvement of the resource allocation efficiency, the advance of technology, and the economics of scale. The key to total factor productivity improvement lies in the "gathering" of all factors. When capital is taken as "the gathering factor", the focus of total factor productivity improvement is to improve the efficiency of capital factor allocation. The proportion of investment on factors as material capital, labor capital, land and technology form the structure of factor allocation. The structural mistakes in factor allocation, like more investment on real estate and virtual economy rather than material capital and technology factors related to new industries, like more emphasis on material capital investment rather than labor capital investment, is where the problem lies in low total factor productivity. Therefore, an emphasis on high-tech industry investment and labor capital will lead to the improvement of total factor productivity. At present, special attention should be paid to "the gathering factor" of entrepreneurs. The innovation provided by entrepreneurs in promoting new combinations of factors decides the improvement of total factor productivity. The structural reform on the supply side encourages operators to become entrepreneurs and let them gather factors while the market decides the resource allocation. The entrepreneurs lead and improve the quality and efficiency of the supply system so as to improve the total factor productivity.

Based on the essential demands of socialism in the primary stage of socialism and development goals in the middle-income stage, to combine the development and protection of productive forces and form the systematic economic development theory is the pioneering research of socialist political economy with Chinese characteristics, which is of great theoretical and practical significance. The economic development theory thus constructed is loaded with Chinese characteristics, Chinese style, and Chinese manner.

Chapter 3

Capital and the Discourse System of Socialist Economy with Chinese Characteristics

The construction of socialist political economy with Chinese characteristics plays an important role in building a philosophy and social science system and an academic discourse system that also has Chinese characteristics. It is necessary to adhere to the theoretical guidance of Marxism, interpreting Chinese practice with Chinese theories, and also sublimating Chinese theories based on Chinese practices. The socialist political economy with Chinese characteristics is the theoretical accomplishment of Chinese Marxist economics. It is a theory of innovation, but it is not created out of thin air. The economic discourse system is part of the Marxist economy theory provided by Marx's *Capital: A Critique of Political Economy*.

3.1 *Capital: A Critique of Political Economy* Provides a Theory for the Discourse System of Socialist Economy with Chinese Characteristics

Every discipline has its own discourse system. Generally speaking, the discourse system of theoretical economics includes both economic theories and terms. Economic theories involve basic standpoints, basic principles, and basic methods.

There are two main contemporary economic theories: Western economy theory and Marxist economy theory. Although both fields study economic problems, their research objects, levels, and tasks are not the same. The difference between Marxist political economy and Western economy is that the latter emphasizes the description of economic phenomena and the relationship between various economic variables in the operation of micro- and macroeconomies; the former emphasizes the analysis of the nature of economic relations, studying social relations among people and reflecting certain relations of social production. Western economics focus on the analysis of economic operations and regards the system as its prerequisite. In addition, it involves the analysis of economic systems. Marxist economics focuses on the analysis of economic systems (including economic institutions) and involves economic operations, but the analysis of economic operation emphasizes on the allocation and adjustment of various relations of production. These two theoretical systems have different degrees of theoretical and practical significance for the analysis of economic process. They cannot be replaced nor be simply excluded, and they can even learn from each other. However, the appropriate discourse system can only be determined by specific research objects and tasks appropriate to certain economic theories.

Socialist political economy with Chinese characteristics is first of all a political economy. Its object of study is the relations of production at the primary stage of socialism that are determined by the level of development of productive forces. The research task is to develop the basic economic system in which public ownership plays the dominant role and diverse forms of ownership develop side by side. It involves the analysis of both the essential and systemic levels of the economy. Therefore, the discourse system should be based on Marxist economy theory. *Capital* contributes to the construction of the discourse system of socialist political economy with Chinese characteristics in the following three ways.

The first way it affects the discourse concerns the systematic economic terms established in *Capital*. These terms have been widely used in political economics textbooks, even in modern textbooks that are popular in the West. In particular, the discourse system about the relations of production in *Capital* deals with the stipulations of socialist and capitalist economies, including various forms of ownership and characteristics under public and private forms of ownership. It also deals with various economic laws, wages, rent, interest, etc. These economic terms involve the basic provisions of Marxist economics; they are the core categories of socialist economic theory system with Chinese characteristics.

Some capitalist crimes criticized by Marx in *Capital* are not necessarily negated during the primary stage of socialism. For example, competition and accumulation may cause polarization, but the effect of improving the efficiency of resource allocation needs to be fully affirmed under the conditions of the market economy. Another example concerns private capital and surplus value. In the analysis of capitalism, while the historical role of private and surplus value is affirmed, they are both also seen as negative because of the exploitation of labor. In the economic analysis of the primary stage of socialism, personal possessions cannot become the mark of political standards of progress or backwardness. Therefore, private capital and its surplus value are affirmed as a part of a variety of forms of ownership in the economy.

The second way it affects the discourse concerns the basic principles of economics elaborated in *Capital*. To a certain extent, *Capital* is the theory of the market economy. Many economic phenomena are similar to those analyzed in *Capital* after China's economic system has turned to a socialist market economy. Theories in *Capital,* such as the theories concerning commodity currency, competition, capital accumulation, capital organic composition, capital cycle and turnover, the conditions for the realization of total social products, the law of average profit margin, circulation cost, land rent, credit economics, and business cycles can all be the basis of the discourse system of socialist economy with Chinese characteristics.

Some of the principles used for analyzing capitalism in *Capital* can also be used to analyze the current socialist economy. One such example is the principle of capital. The term capital was not used for quite a long time, and there were attempts to replace it with the concepts of assets, fund, and even social capital such as state-owned assets and funds. These alternative concepts have proven to be unscientific. According to Marx's principles, capital has three definitions. First of all, capital is a kind of relations of production, which means that capital employs labor. Second, the nature of capital is to achieve value proliferation. Third, capital is the movement of life, in which capital achieves the appreciation of capital in the movement. At the present stage, these three definitions of private capital are complete. While public capital does not include its first definition, the latter two are indispensable. If capital value neither proliferates nor adds value in its movement, capital cannot be defined. Moreover, if public ownership is not capital, it is hardly possible to establish a form of mixed-ownership with private capital. This is particularly true when it comes to the reform of state-owned enterprises. The state has changed the status of state-owned enterprises from managing assets to managing capital, and the analysis of capital principles in *Capital* has become an important discourse of socialist political economy with Chinese characteristics. Furthermore, once the role of capital is confirmed in the socialist economic analysis, fixed, circulating, and virtual capital will naturally enter its discourse system. This illustrates that even the analysis of capitalism can be the analysis of socialism with Chinese characteristics after capitalism has been withdrawn.

The third way it affects the discourse concerns the foresight and regulation for the future society in *Capital*. Being in a capitalist society, Marx made logical predictions about a future society after it has replaced capitalism. These include the provisions of socialist economic systems such as public ownership, distribution according to work, planned distribution of social labor according to proportion, etc. All these factors should be part of the discourse of socialist political economy with Chinese characteristics. It must be noted that some provisions no longer exist in the future society in *Capital*, but still function in the practices of the primary stage of socialism, and they still need to enter its discourse system. For example, Marx imagined that the future society could directly distribute social labor, without a need for "value". In reality, commodity money still exists, and the distribution of social labor needs to be regulated by the market and law of value. Another example is that Marx envisioned that the distribution of personal income in a future society will only exist according to work. The reason is that all other productive factors are public. In reality, it is not just the private ownership of labor. The capital, technology, management, etc., all belong to different owners. When it comes to distribution, it is necessary to insist on a form that is determined according to work and confirms the participation of various productive factors in the distribution of income. Therefore, there is a need for the discourse system of factor ownership that is involved in income distribution that is described in *Capital*. This means that the discourse system of socialist economy with Chinese characteristics not only includes Marx's expectations about the future society, but also the basic principles of economics from the future society described in *Capital*. This belongs to the Chinese modernization of Marxist economics.

There is one phenomenon in the realistic discourse system of economics that needs to be noted: problems which can be explained by Marxist economic discourse seem only to be interpreted by Western economics. This is unfair. Without prejudice, some concepts and principles of Western economics are not only found in *Capital*, but also in the interpretation of reality in its discourse. For instance, Western economics essentially uses Pareto improvement to explain the allocation of resources while Marx's *Capital* uses the law of value to explain the distribution of social labor time by market mechanisms. It is clearly pointed out that "the law of the value of commodities ultimately determines how much of its disposable labor-time society can expend on each kind of commodity".[1] The second example of this trend concerns the theory of property rights. Coase theory is most often mentioned in discussions of property rights. In fact, the issue of ownership in many aspects of *Capital* is related to property rights. Chapter 2 in Volume I points out that an exchange of relations is actually the transfer of ownership, and the mutual recognition of two people's private ownership is a contractual form of "the content of this juridical relation (or relation of two wills) is itself determined by the economic relation".[2] The concentration of capital and the form of mergers and acquisitions analyzed in Chapter 23 of *Capital* is actually the theory of enterprises that will replace or adjust market and property rights. The third example is corporate governance. Western economics applies team production theory and principal–agent theory. In the analysis of supervising and managing cooperation, *Capital* makes a comprehensive analysis of the characteristics and the necessity of supervision in the present theory of "team production". "The work of directing, superintending and adjusting becomes one of the functions of capital, from the moment that the labor under capital's control becomes cooperative". "An industrial army of workers under the command of a capitalist requires, like a real army, officers (managers) and N.C.O.s (foremen, overseers), who command during the labor process in the name of capital. The work of supervision becomes their established and exclusive function".[3]

Of course, as economic practices develop, the discourse system is becoming increasingly rich. When Marx wrote *Capital* more than

---

[1]Karl Marx. *Capital: A Critique of Political Economy*. Vol. 1, Trans. Ben Fowkes (London: Penguin Books, 1976), p. 476.

[2]*Ibid.*, p. 178.

[3]*Ibid.*, pp. 449–450.

100 years ago, the socialist economy and its related discourse system were only products of his logical deduction. When socialism is put into practice, it needs to study new issues, discover new laws, and generalize new theories for the new era. Chinese practices need to be explained by Chinese theory, and Chinese theories needs to be sublimated based on Chinese practice. It is necessary to scientifically explain what kind of socialism should be developed in a country with a developing economy and culture. In addition, it is important to have the need for a discourse system that emerges from Chinese practices and reflects the innovations of economic theory. Based on the practice of China's reform and development, a series of economic discourses have been created. These include the primary stage of socialism, the socialist market economy, state-owned capital, and new development concepts. These discourses can be found in works like *Capital* that subscribe to Marxist economy theory and its innovation in the discourse system, embodying the Sinicization of Marxist economics.

3.2 Explaining the Primary Stage of Socialism and Its Basic Economic System in the Discourse System of the Productive Forces and the Relations of Production

The basic terms of Marxist economics include the productive forces, the relations of production, and the unity of the two. An analysis of the contradiction between the productive forces and the relations of production is the basic methodology of Marxist economics. In every society, the productive forces and the relations of production are a unified whole. The relations of production are both the core qualities of certain social economic systems and an essential attribute of society's economic system. Political economics is a field that explains the basic economic system of society and its changing law of economic development.

The primary stage of Chinese socialist development is determined by the level of productive forces. At this stage, it is necessary to accomplish tasks that have been completed by other countries under capitalist conditions such as socialization, marketization, and the modernization of production. The primary stage of socialism is a new discourse of Chinese economics and can be found in the discourse system of Marx economics, so it is not being produced out of a void. The proposition of the discourse at the primary stage of socialism is the theoretical accomplishment of Chinese Marxist economics.

According to *Capital*, the development of capitalism is the entry point to a socialist society. The highest level of the productive forces in a capitalist society is as follows: "other developments take place on an ever-increasing scale, such as the growth of the cooperative form of the labor process, the conscious technical application of science, the planned exploitation of the soil, the transformation of the means of labor into forms in which they can only be used in common, the economizing of all means of production by their use as the means of production of combined, socialized labor, the entanglement of all peoples in the net of the world market, and, with this, the growth of the international character of the capitalist regime".[4] These may be regarded as the material conditions for socialism to eventually replace capitalism. New China was born out of a semi-colonial and semi-feudal society. After decades of development, China's productive forces have not yet reached the level of developed capitalist countries, meaning that the socialist material foundation has not been fully established. For establishing the material basis of socialism, "this requires a certain social material basis or a series of conditions of existence, which are the natural products of long-term, painful historical development".[5]

Capital contains a discussion about the mode of production in Chinese society: the internal solidarity and structure of the previous capitalist and national production methods can be clearly seen in relations between the United Kingdom and India and China. In China, "the broad basis of the mode of production is formed by the union between small-scale agriculture and domestic industry".[6] The reason is for this is the fact that the direct combination of agriculture and handicrafts has resulted in substantial savings and increased efficiency in time, prompting a stubborn resistance in industries. This means that the underdeveloped market economy and the strength of the small-scale peasant economy have firmly preserved the old production methods. This can also be regarded as the historical reason for the existence of natural economic production methods in the primary stage of socialism.

---

[4] *Ibid.*, p. 929.

[5] *Ibid.*, p. 50.

[6] Karl Marx. *Capital: A Critique of Political Economy*. Vol. 3, Trans. David Fernbach (London: Penguin Books, 1981), p. 451.

China is still at the primary stage of socialism, a status which is determined by the level of development of the productive forces. The main task at this stage is to develop the productive forces. The corresponding essence of socialism at the primary stage is to liberate and develop the productive forces, eliminate exploitation, eliminate polarization, and gradually achieve common prosperity. This judgment directly affects the choice and establishment of the basic economic system.

In Marxist economy theory, the structures of ownership constitute a society's basic economic system. Socialism means eliminating private ownership: the goal of socialist development. After the primary stage of socialism is confirmed, an important task of theoretical innovation is to make it clear that the fundamental task of socialism at the primary stage is not to completely eliminate private ownership, but rather to develop productive forces. The corresponding ownership structure should include not only public ownership, but also various other types, forming a basic economic system in which public ownership is the main body and multiple ownership economies develop alongside each other. Among them, public ownership is the main feature of socialism, and the common development of multiple ownership economies has uniquely Chinese characteristics.

The development of multiple ownership economies can also be found in Marx's *Capital*. At the time of its composition, Marx discovered that when the Western European continent was compared with the more capitalist and developed Britain: "here the capitalist regime has either directly subordinated to itself the whole of the nation's production, or, where economic relations are less developed, it has at least indirect control of those social layers which, although they belong to the antiquated mode of production, still continue to exist side by side with it in a state of decay".[7] Although this refers to the primary stage of capitalist society, these words show that in the primary stage of socialism it is inevitable to retain the varying modes of production that previously existed. Marx described this theory in the following way: "No matter which state of society it can accommodate, it will never perish until all the productive forces are brought into play; a new higher relation of production will never appear until its material conditions of existence mature in the old society".[8]

[7] Karl Marx. *Capital: A Critique of Political Economy,* Vol. 1, Trans. Ben Fowkes (London: Penguin Books, 1976), p. 931.

[8] Karl Marx and Friedrich Engels. *Marx & Engels Collected Works.* Vol. 31, Trans. Ben Fowkes and Emile Burns (London: Lawrence & Wilshart, 2010), p. 413.

Socialism with Chinese characteristics not only adheres to the basic tenets of Marxism in terms of the basic economic system, but also carries out theoretical and institutional innovation in light of Chinese practices. That is to say, a variety of non-public economies, such as those that are individual, private, or due to foreign investments flowing from "outside the system" into "inside the system", have become an important part of the basic economic system of the primary stage of socialism. With public ownership playing the dominate role, it is necessary to focus on the mission of building a new society, seeking an effective method for the harmonious and cooperative development of different ownership economies, and creating a market environment of equal competition instead of focusing on the struggle between public and nonpublic ownership. This includes the implementation of a unified market access system based on a negative list, the abolition of various forms of unreasonable regulations on the non-public economy, the elimination of various hidden barriers, the permission for private capital to enter not only competitive fields but also those that were previously thought to be monopolized by the state-owned economy. The Third Plenary Session of the 18th Central Committee of the Communist Party of China (CPC) further clarified that a mixed economy with cross-shareholding and blending of state-owned, collective, and non-public capital is an important way to materialize China's basic economic system.

In *Capital*, Marx did not propose the term "mixed-ownership". Instead, he proposed the concept and the role of joint-stock company. The main contents are as follows. First, the stock company is a way to socialize private capital; therefore, it is the entrance to socialism. "Capitalist joint-stock companies as much as cooperative factories should be viewed as transition forms from the capitalist mode of production to the associated one".[9] Second, in a joint stock company, "the function is separated from capital ownership, so labor is also completely separated from ownership of the means of production and of surplus labor. This result of capitalist production in its highest development is a necessary point of transition towards the transformation of capital back into the property of the producers, though no longer as the private property of individual producers, but rather as their property as associated producers, as directly social property. It is furthermore a point of transition towards the transformation of all

[9]Karl Marx. *Capital: A Critique of Political Economy.* Vol. 3, Teans. David Fernbach (New York: Penguin Books, 1981), p. 572.

functions formerly bound up with capital ownership in the reproduction process into simple functions of the associated producers, into social functions".[10] Third, the stock company provides a more effective mechanism for governance. Marx proposed that the share-holding system can be a transition to socialism. "This is because a great part of the social capital is applied by those who are not its owners, and who therefore proceed quite unlike owners who, when they function themselves, anxiously weigh the limits of their private capital".[11] The mixed-ownership system established at the present stage in China essentially adopts the form of a shareholding system that can also become a realized form of public ownership. Marx's discourse about the shareholding system can be used to illustrate the property rights, functions, and operations of the current shareholding economy.

3.3 Explaining the Socialist Market Economy in the Discourse System of Commodity Economy and the Law of Value

The theory of the socialist market economy is an important part of the socialist economy with Chinese characteristics as well as a major innovation in the theory of socialist economics. General Secretary Xi Jinping pointed out: "Both theory and practice have proved that the allocation of resources by the market is the most effective means to this end. It is a general rule of the market economy that the market decides the allocation of resources, and a market economy in essence is one in which the market determines resource allocation".[12] A discourse is then necessary to explain the socialist market economy and its operation.

Some people think that market economic theory can only be explained by the discourse system of Western economics. This is because there is no concept of a market economy in Marx's *Capital* and Marxist economics explains the essence of economic relations instead of economic operation. Contrary to that expectation "commodity production", "commodity exchange", "circulation process", and "market" are the most

---

[10] *Ibid.*, p. 568.

[11] *Ibid.*, p. 572.

[12] Xi Jinping. *The Governance of China*. Vol. 1 (Beijing: Foreign Languages Press, 2014), p. 84.

frequently used concepts by Marx in *Capital*. In fact, *Capital* provides a relatively complete theory of the market economy. Most of the contemporary discourses concerning the market economy actually originate in *Capital*, including that which concerns the market economic system and the market economic operations. This has a direct impact on the discourse system of the socialist market economy.

First, one must discuss the discourse about the characteristics of the market economy system. According to Marx, commodity economies existed in late primitive societies. The idea of a market economy as one that allocates resources throughout the society only emerged after entering the capitalist era. Its institutional characteristics are pointed out in *Capital*'s discussions of the labor market: "the sphere of circulation or commodity exchange, within whose boundaries the sale and purchase of labor-power goes on, is in fact a very Eden of the innate rights of man. It is the exclusive realm of Freedom, Equality, Property and Bentham". More specifically, the first characteristics refers to a free contract economy. "They contract as free persons, who are equal before the law. Their contract is the final result in which their joint will finds a common legal expression". The second is equality. "they exchange equivalent for equivalent". The third is ownership. "The guardians must therefore recognize each other as owners of private property. This juridical relation, whose form is the contract, whether as part of a developed legal system or not, is a relation between two wills which mirrors the economic relation".[13] These three characteristics should be common in a market economy whether it is capitalist or socialist.

Second, one must discuss the discourse about the market's role in resource allocation. The original meaning of the market economy concerns its allocation of resources. Marx's discourse system in *Capital* explains how the market allocates resources. The allocation of resources means that all of the labor time under the control of a society must adjust to production in one way or another. The standard for the effective allocation of resources is the amount of time for labor that is socially necessary. Its two meanings are as follows. First, the labor time consumed by the production of each commodity is socially necessary labor time; second, the labor-time consumed by the total amount of commodities produced by each department is socially necessary labor time. "In the midst of the

[13]Karl Marx. *Capital: A Critique of Political Economy.* Vol. 1, Trans. Ben Fowkes (London: Penguin Books, 1976), p. 178.

accidental and ever-fluctuating exchange relations between the products, the labor-time socially necessary to produce them asserts itself as a regulative law of nature. In the same way, the law of gravity asserts itself when a person's house collapses on top of him".[14] This rule is the law of value. "If a commodity is to be sold at its market value, i.e., in proportion to the socially necessary labor contained in it, the total quantity of social labor which is applied to produce the overall amount of this kind of commodity must correspond to the quantity of the social need for it, i.e., to the social need with money to back it up".[15]

Third, one must discuss the discourse about the market mechanism. According to Marx's theory, the market mechanism is the functionary mechanism of the law of value. Unlike planned regulation, the market regulation of resource allocation "only plays a role as an inherent, silent natural necessity after the event, which can be detected by the barometer of market and it must overcome the random actions of commodity producers". "The division of labor within society brings into contact independent producers of commodities, who acknowledge no authority other than that of competition, of the coercion exerted by the pressure of their reciprocal interests".[16] The market mechanism includes using the market as a barometer as well as the influences of competition and authority on independent commodity producers. The full competition is determined by the basic conditions and premises of resource allocation in the market, which then manifests in two ways. First, "the more mobile capital is, i.e., the more easily it can be transferred from one sphere and one place to others". The premise is that there has been complete trade freedom within the society and it has eliminated all monopolies other than those that are natural; small-scale farming agriculture has been transformed. Second, "the more rapidly labor-power can be moved from one sphere to another and from one local point of production to another".[17] The premise is to abolish laws that impede labor mobility. Workers have abandoned all occupational prejudice and are not concerned about the content of their own labor.

---

[14] *Ibid.*, p. 168.

[15] Karl Marx. *Capital: A Critique of Political Economy*. Vol. 3, Trans. David Fernbach (New York: Penguin Books, 1981), p. 294.

[16] Karl Marx. *Capital: A Critique of Political Economy*. Vol. 1, Trans. Ben Fowkes (London: Penguin Books, 1976), p. 477.

[17] Karl Marx. *Capital: A Critique of Political Economy*. Vol. 3, Trans. David Fernbach (New York: Penguin Books, 1981), p. 298.

Fourth, one must discuss the discourse about credit and financial activities. Finance is the core of the modern economy. When Marx was writing, the financial system was far from developed. However, the discussion of credit and finance in *Capital* has laid a foundation for understanding today's developed financial system. *Capital*'s discourse system concerning finance mainly involves two aspects. The first way in which *Capital* covers finance involves four categories explaining credit and finance. First, it explains the financial function of money, particularly the means of payment and storage. Second, it explains the leverage effect of credit on capital concentration from the perspective of capital accumulation. The development of the credit system has concentrated a large amount of dispersed capital, so that capital may flow freely between departments. Third, it explains credit's expansive effects on social reproduction from the perspective of both commercial and bank credit. Because of the intermediary effect of credit, the credit system can make the circulation of social reproduction and government break through the limitations of both time and space; thus, the process of expanding reproduction can be strengthened to its maximum capacity. Fourth, it illustrates the role of financial expansion from the perspective of virtual capital in the form of credit. Commercial credit and bank credit enable the same monetary capital to be reused. This same currency can be used as a tool to deposit many times; also, it can perform the function of a loan many times. It also comes in the form of securities, such as bonds and stocks, which generate virtual capital in the form of capitalization of income. As Marx said, "The formation of fictitious capital is known as capitalization. Any regular periodic income can be capitalized by reckoning it up, on the basis of the average rate of interest, as the sum that a capital lent out at this interest rate would yield".[18] The second way in which *Capital* concerns finance involves the explanation of the market and macro problems that arise from credit and finance. A system of credit has the function of promoting speculative trading. Credit will become the main lever of overproduction and excessive speculation. In macroeconomy, credit-based production system in which all the links in the reproduction process are based, credit is closely related to cyclical fluctuations in the economy. "In a system of production where the entire interconnection of the reproduction process rests on credit, a crisis must evidently break out if credit is suddenly withdrawn and only cash payment is accepted, in the form of a violent scramble for

[18] *Ibid.*, p. 597.

means of payment".[19] Moreover, the important manifestation of the economic crisis is a crisis in currency. "When credit contracts or dries up altogether, money suddenly confronts commodities absolutely as the only means of payment and the true existence of value".[20] Currency crises are inevitable.

Fifth, one must discuss the discourse about the virtual and real economies. The analysis of modern market economy is inseparable from the analysis of correlation between the virtual economy and the real one. In recent years, financial crises are mostly caused by the excessive expansion of the virtual economy; therefore, the correct handling of the relations between these two economies, the virtual and the real, is an indispensable part of the socialist economy with Chinese characteristics. The analysis of virtual and real capital in Marx's *Capital* provides a discourse for this analysis. Firstly, virtual capital operations should be separated from those that are real. There are two types of separation. When the minimum capital limit is raised, the capital that cannot reach the minimum limits of the real economy often enters the market or other channels of credit. One case is to "hand over to the commanders of large industrial departments in the form of credit". In another case, "The mass of small fragmented capitals are thereby forced onto adventurous paths: speculation, credit swindles, share swindles, crises".[21] The second type of separation is that the capital raised by securities enters the operation of enterprises and forms the operation of real capital. As a certificate of ownership, securities represent the right to claim that future earnings can actually enter the market's circulation. "On the one hand their market values fluctuate with the level and security of the receipts to which they give a legal title". On the other hand, "the market value of these securities is partly speculative, since it is determined not just by the actual revenue but rather by the anticipated revenue as reckoned in advance".[22] Interest rate, the number of securities entering the market, speculative psychology, false information, manipulation of the market, and other factors will separate the market value from the value of its real capital. Second, the securities market is actually a speculative market. Because property exists in the form of stocks, the movement and transfer of the joint-stock system

[19] *Ibid.*, p. 621.

[20] *Ibid.*, p. 648.

[21] *Ibid.*, p. 359.

[22] *Ibid.*, p. 598.

becomes the result of exchange gambling. "An entire system of swindling and cheating with respect to the promotion of companies, issue of shares and share dealings".[23] "It lays open, in the form of speculation and the credit system, a thousand sources of sudden enrichment".[24] Third, excessive virtual capital speculation leads to financial crisis. *Capital* points out that securities trading far exceeds the limits of social needs and is the basis of both credit and monetary crises. In the inflated virtual capital, "a tremendous number of these bills represent purely fraudulent deals, which now come to light and explode; as well as unsuccessful speculations conducted with borrowed capital, and finally commodity capitals that are either devalued or unsaleable, or returns that are never going to come in".[25] Marx revealed these problems more than 100 years ago, but they are common in the modern virtual economy; therefore, it is necessary to strengthen financial supervision and regulation, especially the supervision of virtual capital markets.

The decision to comprehensively continue the reform, which comes from the Third Plenary Session of the 18th Central Committee of the CPC, can be scientifically confirmed from the above analysis of *Capital* concerning the market economy; it mainly involves the market playing a decisive role in the allocation of resources. This decision also indicates the necessity of constructing a unified and open market system with orderly competition, fair and transparent market rules, and a unified market supervision system.

3.4 Explaining the Distribution System at the Primary Stage of Socialism with the Relations of Production and the Relations of Distribution

In Marx's discourse system about the future society, a socialist society's personal consumer goods should only be distributed according to work. China's reform practices have clarified that the distribution system at the primary stage of socialism is one in which the distribution according to work is dominant and multiple forms of distribution exist side by side. The 14th National Congress of the CPC proposed that productive factors

[23] *Ibid.*, p. 569.

[24] Karl Marx. *Capital: A Critique of Political Economy*. Vol. 1, p. 741.

[25] Karl Marx. *Capital: A Critique of Political Economy*. Vol. 3, p. 621.

such as individual capital should be allowed to participate in the distribution of income. The 16th National Congress of the CPC then proposed establishing the principle that labor, capital, technology, management, and other productive factors should participate in distribution according to their contributions. Based on those precedents, the Third Plenary Session of the 18th Central Committee of the CPC proposed that the rewards from productive factors should be determined by their respective markets. In this regard, some scholars believe that a discourse that sees factors of production as being rewarded by their contributions is derived from the Western economic theory of marginal productivity formulated by John Bates Clark. Even though Marx only envisioned a future society in which a form of distribution according to work operated without other methods, it is undeniable that the various distribution methods at this stage still belong to the discourse system of *Capital*.

First, there is a discourse about the relationship between production and distribution. *Capital* uses a special chapter to examine the relations of production and distribution, pinpointing that "the specific relation of distribution thus simply expresses the historically determined relation of production". The historical nature of the relations of distribution is also the historical nature of relations of production; "they simply express one side of these".[26] Since the confirmation of the basic economic system at the primary stage of socialism in which public ownership is the main body and multiple ownership economies develop alongside each other, it has been natural to have a distribution system whereby the distribution according to work is dominant and multiple forms of distribution exist side by side.

Second, there is a discourse about the distribution according to factors and the realization of ownership. All production requires laborers to combine with various productive factors. Marx's labor theory of value holds that labor is the only source of value creation. However, "labor is therefore not the only source of material wealth, i.e., of the use-values it produces. As William Petty says, labor is the father of material wealth, the earth is its mother".[27] The necessity of various factors participating in production and distribution is determined by the ownership of productive factors. The involvement of various productive factors in distribution is actually the economic realization of factor ownership, that is,

[26] *Ibid.*, pp. 1022–1023.

[27] Karl Marx. *Capital: A Critique of Political Economy*. Vol. 1, p. 134.

the distribution of newly created value among different factor owners. "One part of this value as belonging or accruing to the owner of labor-power, one part to the owner of capital and a third part to the owner of landed property. These are thus relations or forms of distribution, for they express the relationships in which the total value newly produced is distributed among the owners of the various agents of production".[28] Obviously, wage, interest, and the rental of land are the economic realizations of labor, capital, and the ownership of land, respectively. This is different from Clark's theory of marginal productivity. Marx believed that the public ownership of production should mean that only laborers own the labor force; other factors such as capital, labor, technology, and management are public. Correspondingly, there is only distribution according to work. In reality, at the primary stage of socialism, it is not just the labor force that belongs to private ownership. Capital, technology, management, and other elements also belong to different owners (including private owners). Income distribution is the realization of ownership of various factors. In order to sufficiently mobilize various factors into the process of economic development and engage the vitality of wealth creation, it is necessary to recognize factor rewards in the system of income distribution. It is not only necessary to stimulate the efficiency of labor but also to stimulate the input of capital, technology, management, and other factors from the owners of various productive factors. The method to do so is to obtain the corresponding reward according to the input and contribution of capital, labor, resources, technology, and management in the production process. As for the method by which labor and other various factors of production will participate in distribution according to their contributions, *Capital* provides the following demonstration: the new creation value ($v + m$) and the labor element remuneration v. These include not only the rewards of the workers on the production site but also the rewards of the managers and technicians belonging to the "collective laborer". Non-labor productive factors participate in the distribution of m and their contribution is mainly in increasing surplus products. The origin for the decision to reward production factors at the Third Plenary Session of the 18th Central Committee of the CPC is also in *Capital*. "Capital further appears as a commodity in so far as the division of profit into interest and profit proper is governed by supply and demand,

[28]Karl Marx. *Capital: A Critique of Political Economy*. Vol. 3, p. 1017.

i.e., by competition, just like the market prices of commodities".[29] The manager's salary is "regulated in the labor market like that of any other labor".[30]

Third, there is a discourse about the distribution of resources according to work and labor compensation. The form of distribution according to work at the primary stage of socialism is consistent with Marx's vision because labor is still a means of earning a living. This is based on the principle of "more pay for more work, less pay for less work". However, the actual mode and the environment of distribution according to work are indeed at a certain distance from Marx's original assumptions. Most notably, under the conditions of a market economy, the distribution must be in the form of currency instead of labor vouchers, and there are also many non-labor productive factors participating in income distribution. This situation is very close to the analysis of *Capital* in many respects. The corresponding discourse on income distribution in *Capital* can be applied to the analysis of realistic distribution according to work. First of all, there are two forms of monetary wages adopted for distribution according to work. One is hourly wages and the other is piece-rate wages. When they are compared, piece-rate wages can provide a certain measure of labor intensity. Therefore, Marx pointed out, "since the quality and intensity of the work are here controlled by the very form of the wage, superintendence of labor becomes to a great extent superfluous".[31] The contracting system in China is the embodiment of this thought. The second is the determinant of wage levels. Under the condition that a variety of non-labor productive factors participate in income distribution, it is important to ensure that the form of distribution according to work is the main body and labor compensation grows as it is necessary. Although Marx's analysis of the value of labor force is concerned with the distribution of capitalism, the necessary labor (essential product) and the withdrawal of its relations of production have important guiding significance for the income distribution at the primary stage of socialism. The necessary labor factors that Marx pointed out when comparing national wages in the determinants of level of wages include the following: "the price and the extent of the prime necessities of life in their natural and historical development, the cost of training the workers, the part played by the labor of

[29] *Ibid.*, p. 477.

[30] *Ibid.*, p. 567.

[31] Karl Marx. *Capital: A Critique of Political Economy*. Vol. 1, p. 695.

women and children, the productivity of labor, and its extensive and intensive magnitude".[32] Obviously, labor rewards grow in step with the progress of society. Third, complex labor creates more values than simple labor, so the amount of remuneration is higher than that of simple labor. Marx not only acknowledged this difference, but also demanded to adapt to the technological basis of large industries and to strengthen the education of workers and their children to become "the totally developed individual".[33] This is also an important method for China to solve the inequitable distribution caused by the disparities in the levels of technology and education among laborers.

3.5 Explaining the Economic Development of the New Stage in the Discourse System of Developing Productive Forces and Expanding Reproduction

Economic development is the development of productive forces. It is generally acknowledged that Marxist economics studies the relations of production. Even if these productive forces are studied, such research mainly refers to the relations of production in accordance with the development of productive forces, coordinating and promoting the productive forces by adjusting the relations of production. Therefore, the discourse system concerning the economic development at the primary stage of socialism can only come from Western economic theories of development. In fact, Marx's analysis of productive forces and relations of production in *Capital* includes both the relations of production and productive forces, especially the development of social productive forces contained in the contradiction between capitalist relations of production and productive forces. The discourse system revealed in *Capital* can be the foundation for economic theory at the primary stage of socialism.

First, there is a discourse about social productive forces. Western economics uses a model of economic growth to illustrate that the factors of productive forces indicated by Marx are more comprehensive. In *Capital*, Marx pointed out the following factors that determine labor productivity: "it is determined amongst other things by the workers' average degree

[32] *Ibid.*, p. 701.

[33] *Ibid.*, p. 618.

of skill, the level of development of science and its technological application, the social organization of the process of production, the extent and effectiveness of the means of production, and the conditions found in the natural environment".[34] Based on this, Marx traces the resources of social productive forces to the following three aspects: "to the social character of the labor that is set to work, to the division of labor in society, and to the development of intellectual labor, in particular of the natural sciences".[35] In *Capital*, Marx carefully analyzed each of the production methods in terms of both the technical specifications and the social division of labor, from simple cooperation to handicraft industry and machinery industry. All discourses about productivity factors and resources of productive forces can be the basis of today's economic development discourse. The major progress in economic development theory in recent years is that science and technology have become the primary productive forces and human resources are in turn the primary resources. These theories are based on the discourse of Marxist economics.

Second, there is a discourse about the way in which the economy develops. The two methods of expanded reproduction Marx that explicitly distinguished in *Capital* are, in fact, the earliest distinctions made to differentiate economic development methods. One distinction divides the extended reproduction from the expanded reproduction. "Extensively, if the field of production is extended; intensively, if the means of production are made more effective".[36] The other distinction divides farming methods from agriculture into extensive management and intensive farming. "A family tills, say, 100 acres superficially, and even though the product per acre is not large, the product of 100 acres provides a sizable surplus for sale". Intensive farming, on the other hand, means "the concentration of capital on the same piece of land instead of its distribution over adjacent tracts".[37] The connotation of the present mode of economic development may be richer than in Marx's time, but the study of the present modes of economic development still has obvious continuity with *Capital*.

Third, there is a discourse about innovation and development. In the current new normal economic situation, economic development needs to

[34]*Ibid.*, p. 130.

[35]Karl Marx. *Capital: A Critique of Political Economy*. Vol. 3, p. 175.

[36]Karl Marx. *Capital: A Critique of Political Economy*. Vol. 2, Trans. David Fernbach (London: Penguin Books, 1978), p. 251.

[37]Karl Marx. *Capital: A Critique of Political Economy*. Vol. 3, p. 813.

turn to innovation, and scientific and technological innovation should play a leading role. Schumpeter is generally credited with the discourse of innovation; however, the earliest idea of innovation can actually be traced back to Marx's *Capital*.[38] The first discourse about innovation relates to managerial and institutional innovation. This includes the productive forces produced by cooperation and corresponding management, the productive forces produced by the division of manufacturing labor, and the division of labor in society. The second discourse about innovation relates to scientific and technological innovation. "Intellectual labor, especially the development of natural sciences" is an important source of the development of productive forces. It mainly involves the decisive role of science and technology in the productive forces. The determinants of the labor productive forces include the state of science and the degree of its practical application. The foundation of the large-scale mechanized industry is revolution, and it is manifested as "the conscious technical application of science".[39] In mechanized production, each division of labor is "solved by the application of technology like mechanics, chemistry, etc.". The third discourse about innovation relates to the sufficient input into technological innovation and its applications. Institutional innovation, "as the productive forces generated by collaboration and division of labor, does not cost capital. It is the natural force of social labor". However, technological innovation is necessary "as a man requires lungs to breathe with, so he requires something that is the work of human hands in order to consume the forces of nature productively. A water-wheel is necessary to exploit the force of water, and a steam-engine to exploit the elasticity of steam. Once discovered, the law of the deflection of a magnetic needle in the field of an electric current, or the law of the magnetization of iron by electricity, cost absolutely nothing. But the exploitation of these laws for the purposes of telegraphy, etc., necessitates costly and extensive apparatus".[40]

Fourth, there is a discourse about coordinated development. Coordinated development is a new economic development concept under

---

[38] C. Freeman. "Marx and Engles (1848) probably more than any other economist assigned to technical innovation the driving force in economic development and competition". *The New Palgrave Dictionary of Economics*. Third Edition (London: Palgrave Macmillan, 2018), p. 6562.

[39] Karl Marx. *Capital: A Critique of Political Economy*. Vol. 1, p. 929.

[40] *Ibid.*, Vol. 1, p. 508.

this new normal and one of its important aspects is structural coordination. Marx's theory of social reproduction can be attributed to the theory of coordinated development. The central issue of social reproduction is the realization of the market as an aggregate product of society, involving the proportionality of various sectors. The theory of balancing these two major departments requires them to develop proportionately on the basis of overall coordination. Because periodic economic crises are inevitable in that they are caused by the imbalance of the proportion of social reproduction under capitalist conditions, Marx developed the discourse of collective rationality and joint control. That is, "within capitalist production, the proportionality of the particular branches of production presents itself as a process of passing constantly out of and into disproportionality, since the interconnection of production as a whole here forces itself on the agents of production as a blind law, and not as a law which, being grasped and therefore mastered by their combined reason, brings the productive process under their common control".[41] In other words, in order to consciously realize a balance between various production sectors, it is necessary to subordinate the laws of collective rationality in production process to common control. Therefore, in the future, "the matter would be simply reduced to the fact that the society must reckon in advance how much labor, means of production and means of subsistence it can spend, without dislocation, on branches of industry which, like the building of railways, for instance, supply neither means of production nor means of subsistence, nor any kind of useful effect, for a long period, a year or more, though they certainly do withdraw labor, means of production and means of subsistence from the total annual product".[42] The socialist society that was later established tried to generally achieve this requirement through a planned economy and paid the price of inefficiency. The current shift from a planned to a market economy does not mean abandoning the requirements for proportional development of various sectors. Instead, it needs to work out a new method of realizing well-rounded and coordinated development in the context of a market economy. This is an important topic for Chinese Marxist economics.

Fifth, there is a discourse about green development. Green development requires establishing a society that is environmentally friendly and conserves resources, involving a harmony between man and nature.

---

[41] Karl Marx. *Capital: A Critique of Political Economy*. Vol. 3, p. 365.

[42] Karl Marx. *Capital: A Critique of Political Economy*. Vol. 2, p. 390.

Marx divides external natural conditions into two categories from an economic perspective: first, there are natural resources that consist of living materials such as soil fertility, fish-rich water, etc.; second, there are natural resources that consist of the means of labor such as a torrential waterfall, a navigable river, forests, metals, coal, etc. These two types of natural resources play different, yet decisive, roles in different stages of development. "At the dawn of civilization, it is the first class that turns the scale; at a higher stage of development, it is the second".[43] This can also explain the natural conditions of regional differences at different stages of development. Under the same conditions, "the quantity of surplus labor will vary according to the natural conditions within which labor is carried on, in particular the fertility of the soil".[44] However, "the productivity of labor is also tied up with natural conditions, which are often less favorable as productivity rises — as far as that depends on social conditions. We thus have a contrary movement in these different spheres: progress here, regression there. We need only consider the influence of the seasons, for example, on which the greater part of raw materials depends for their quantity, as well as the exhaustion of forests, coal and iron mines, and so on".[45] "Moreover, all progress in capitalist agriculture is a progress in the art, not only of robbing the worker, but of robbing the soil; all progress in increasing the fertility of the soil for a given time is a progress towards ruining the more long-lasting sources of that fertility".[46] Marx uses the concept of human domination of nature in the relations between man and nature. The connotations of this idea can be divided into three categories. First, one might adapt to nature. The natural basis for social division of labor proceeds from differences between natural conditions and the diversity of its natural products. Through the changes in the natural environments in which people live, they tend to diversify their own needs, abilities, means of labor, and ways of labor. Second, one might control nature. "It is the necessity of bringing a natural force under the control of society, of economizing on its energy, of appropriating or subduing it on a large scale by the work of the human hand, that plays the most decisive role in the history of industry".[47] Third, one might rely on science to

---

[43]Karl Marx. *Capital: A Critique of Political Economy*. Vol. 1, p. 648.

[44]*Ibid.*, Vol. 1, p. 648.

[45]Karl Marx. *Capital: A Critique of Political Economy*. Vol. 3, p. 369.

[46]Karl Marx. *Capital: A Critique of Political Economy*. Vol. 1, p. 638.

[47]*Ibid.*, p. 649.

achieve a circular economy. "Every advance in chemistry not only multiplies the number of useful materials, and the useful applications of those already known, thus extending capital's sphere of investment along with its growth; it also teaches capital how to throw back the waste from the processes of production and consumption into the cycle of the process of reproduction, and thus, without any previous outlay of capital, it creates fresh materials for it".[48] Although the role of human beings is more prominent in Marx's analysis of the relations between man and nature, this economic perspective is of great value in studying sustainable development.

Sixth, there is a discourse about shared development. The thought and discourse involving development's reason and driving force can be traced back to *Capital*'s criticism of the capitalist mode of production. The direct reason for economic crises in capitalism is the contradiction between production and consumption, and the fundamental reason is that the purpose of production is not for the people. "Since capital's purpose is not the satisfaction of needs but the production of profit, and since it attains this purpose only by methods that determine the mass of production by reference exclusively to the yardstick of production, and not the reverse, there must be a constant tension between the restricted dimensions of consumption on the capitalist basis, and a production that is constantly striving to overcome these immanent barriers".[49] Not only does this line of thinking point out the purpose of production, but it also proposes the concept of the power of consumption. Under capitalist conditions, social consumption "is determined neither by the absolute power of production nor by the absolute power of consumption but rather by the power of consumption within a given framework of antagonistic conditions of distribution, which reduce the consumption of the vast majority of society to a minimum level, only capable of varying within more or less narrow limits. It is further restricted by the drive for accumulation, the drive to expand capital and produce surplus-value on a larger scale". Therefore, "but the more productivity develops, the more it comes into conflict with the narrow basis on which the relations of consumption rest".[50] The result is a crisis of overproduction. These arguments of *Capital* in turn require that the purpose of economic development under socialist conditions is to meet the increasing material and cultural demands of the people. It is essential

---

[48] *Ibid.*, p. 754.

[49] Karl Marx. *Capital: A Critique of Political Economy*. Vol. 3, p. 365.

[50] *Ibid.*, p. 353.

to fundamentally change the antagonistic distribution system, overcoming the idea of "production for production's sake" and the one-sided pursuit of high accumulation of development. It also shows that consumption drives economic growth and its power is as important as the concept of productive forces. Sharing development and improving the consumption power of the masses is the power source of economic development in itself.

Of course, the practice of socialist economics with Chinese characteristics is richer than that of Marx when he wrote *Capital*. Socialist economy with Chinese characteristics, as its theoretical discourse system, is bound to have many innovations and creations. These innovative theories and discourses are not fabricated out of thin air; instead, they are based on the basic principles and analytical tools of Marxist economics, in combination with the scientific knowledge that is formed by contemporary Chinese practices of socialist economic development. Furthermore, they are supported by the basic theories of Marxist economics and accurately reflect the objective reality. In addition, they are consistent with the development direction pointed out by Marxist economics. It is precisely for this reason that Marxist economics has maintained its theoretical basis and the guiding principle in the field of economic reform and economic construction in China.

Bibliography

习近平: 关于《中共中央关于制定国民经济和社会发展第十三个五年规划的建议》的说明, 2015 年 11 月 13日. Xi Jinping. Explanations on recommendations for the 13th five-year plan for economic and social development. *Xinhuanet.com*. Nov 13, 2015. http://www.xinhuanet.com//politics/2015-11/03/c_1117029621.htm.

洪银兴: 《资本论的现代解析》(修订版), 经济科学出版社 2011 年版. Hong Yinxing. *Modern Analysis of Capital*. Beijing: Economic Science Press, 2011.

Chapter 4

A Scientific Foresight of the Characteristics of Socialist Economy in Capital

The idea of *Capital* is based on class struggle, and its goal is to overthrow the old system. In the primary stage of socialism, our goal is to build a new society. Though it is required to strengthen the belief in the replacement of capitalism by socialism, studying *Capital* cannot be limited to this requirement. To adapt to our central tasks and the characteristics of the economic background which we face, our way of studying *Capital* should also be changed accordingly. The basic requirement is to turn our attention from class struggle to economic construction. In the face of capitalist society, *Capital* is a weapon for class struggle, and it is the theoretical guidance of economic construction in today's socialist society. To study *Capital*, we must turn our focus from critique to construction, from how to overthrow capitalist society to how to build a socialist society, and how to adjust the relations of production, improve social productivity, increase social wealth, and promote social welfare.

4.1 The Inevitability of the Replacement of Capitalism by Socialism

Capitalism is an inevitable stage in the development and progress of human history, but capitalism is temporary. It must develop into a new, more advanced state of society. Based on the overall logical relationship of mankind's development, Marx demonstrates the historical destiny of the emergence and development of capitalist private ownership and its replacement by socialist public ownership. In a certain sense, *Capital* is not only a profound revelation of the nature and operation of capitalist private ownership, but it is also a logical argument for the historical inevitability of socialist public ownership.

4.1.1. *The expropriation of exploiters is the inevitable result of history*

Studying the primary accumulation of capital, Marx examines the emergence and development of the capitalist mode of production and the historical trend toward the replacement of capitalism by socialism. The capitalist mode of production is a special mode of production uniquely regulated by history. Like any other mode of production, the capitalist mode of production exists in a particular stage of the development of social productive forces. The capitalist mode of production is the historical conditions and foundations of their existence.

Capitalist private ownership is generated from small private ownership. On the one hand, capitalist private ownership originated from the differentiation of small commodity producers. On the other hand, it is derived from usury and capitalization of the commercial monetary system. With the formation of commodity markets and increasingly fierce market competition, the gap between the rich and the poor has widened, and wealth has gradually gathered in the hands of a few. The small commodity producers, who have developed in the competition, gradually begin to hire workers, and then developed into capitalists, yet the small producers, who have lost in the competition, gradually decline and turn into the employed workers. Capitalist private ownership's negation of small-capital private ownership is accomplished utilizing primary accumulation. The primary accumulation of capital is the exploitation of small farmers by capitalists. The primary accumulation concentrates on the scattered production materials of the individual and turns them into socialized production material for the capitalist. It deprives the laborers of their land, production tools, and means of subsistence and defies the private ownership in which one uses his labor to obtain private property. Personal ownership is replaced by the private ownership of the bourgeoisie based on wage labor.

After capitalists have concentrated their means of production by expropriating small producers and plundering colonies, the new production conditions that they have acquired are incomparable to small producers. "A consistent foundation for capitalist agriculture could only be provided by large-scale industry, in the form of machinery; it is a large-scale industry which radically expropriates the vast majority of the agricultural population and completes the divorce between agriculture and rural domestic industry, tearing up the latter's roots, which are spinning and weaving. It therefore also conquers the entire home market for industrial capital for the first time".[1] Therefore, the socialized mass production and market economy of capitalism have negated the small production mode of the natural economy.

The socialization of production is a double-edged sword. It has defeated many small individual producers, concentrated the means of production that can be concentrated, promoted the development and function of the machine, and created labor productivity that could not be achieved in the past. "Only capitalist commodity production is an epoch-making mode of exploitation, which in the course of its historical development revolutionizes the entire economic structure of society by its organization of the labor process and its gigantic extension of technique, and towers incomparably above all earlier epochs".[2] The capitalist private system extracts the methods and conditions of surplus labor, so that "it extorts this surplus labor in a manner and in conditions that are more advantageous to social relations and to the creation of elements for a new and higher formation than was the case under the earlier forms of slavery, serfdom, etc.".[3]

"As soon as the capitalist mode of production stands on its own feet, the further socialization of labor and the further transformation of the soil and other means of production into socially exploited and therefore communal means of production takes on a new form. What is now to be expropriated is not the self-employed worker, but the capitalist who

---

[1]Karl Marx. *Capital: A Critique of Political Economy*. Vol. 1, Trans. Ben Fowkes (London: Penguin Books, 1976), pp. 912–913.

[2]Karl Marx. *Capital: A Critique of Political Economy*. Vol. 2, Trans. David Fernbach (London: Penguin Books, 1978), p. 120.

[3]Karl Marx. *Capital: A Critique of Political Economy*. Vol. 3, Trans. David Fernbach (London: Penguin Books, 1981), p. 958.

exploits a large number of workers".[4] Through capital concentration, large capital deprives small capital and the capitalist strikes down many others. Related to this, "the growth of the cooperative of the labor process, the conscious technical application of science, the planned exploitation of the soil, the transformation of the means of labor into forms in which they can only be used in common, the economizing of all means of production by their use as the means of production of combined, socialized labor, the entanglement of all peoples in the net of the world market, and, with this, the growth of the international character of the capitalist regime".[5] A monopoly of capital has become shackles for socialized production methods. "The centralization of the means of production and the socialization of labor reach a point at which they become incompatible with their capitalist integument".[6]

The accumulation of capital in capitalist production not only means the increase of production scale, but also the adoption of new technologies, the development of new products, and the development of new markets. It not only enhances the expansion of productivity but also improves productivity. Capital accumulation and productivity development are mutually reinforcing. In this kind of interaction, social productivity advances at an unprecedented rate. Therefore, the historical responsibility of the capitalist relations of production lies in that "he [the capitalist] is fanatically intent on the valorization of value; consequently, he ruthlessly forces the human race to produce for production's sake. In this way, he spurs on the development of society's productive forces, and the creation of those material conditions of production which alone can form the real basis of a higher form of society, a society in which the full and free development of every individual forms the ruling principle".[7] The unrestricted development of capitalism is bound to fall into new contradictions. Its historical mission is to promote the development of human labor productivity by geometric progression without scruple. If the people's purchasing power and scope are restricted by the system, which hinders the development of productivity, this mission is betrayed. "It thereby simply

---

[4]Karl Marx. *Capital: A Critique of Political Economy*. Vol. 1, pp. 928–929.

[5]*Ibid.*, p. 929.

[6]*Ibid.*, p. 929.

[7]*Ibid.*, p. 739.

shows once more that it is becoming senile and has further and further outlived its epoch".[8]

It can be seen that the socialization of production is the internal motivation for the capitalist private ownership to negate itself. This reveals that capitalist ownership cannot continue to harness this productivity. Moreover, with increasing power, this productivity requires to eliminate this contradiction, demanding that it be removed from its attributes as capital and that it is recognized as the nature of social productivity. In this case, capitalist ownership needs to be adjusted within itself. "Once these have reached the point where they have to be sloughed off, then the material source, the economically and historically justified source of the title that arises from the process of life's social production, disappears, and with it all transactions based on it".[9]

In addition to the basic contradictions of the capitalist society mentioned above, the capitalist economy has a series of social contradictions that it cannot overcome.

First, the strict management within the capitalist production enterprises has sharp contradictions with the anarchy of social production. Marx found that "Although on the basis of capitalist production the social character of their production confronts the mass of immediate producers in the form of a strict governing authority, and the social mechanism of the labor process has received here a completely hierarchical articulation, [...] the most complete anarchy reigns among the bearers of this authority, the capitalists themselves, who confront one another simply as owners of commodities, and within this anarchy the social interconnection of production prevails over individual caprice only as an overwhelming natural law".[10] The economic crisis in the social sphere is inevitable.

Second, under the condition of separation of capital ownership and management, capitalists become redundant, which provides conditions for the elimination of the capitalist system and also provides an entry point for the establishment of a socialist economic form. Marx discovered the separation of managerial work and capital ownership from the phenomenon that in the enterprise supervision and command of labor are handed to particular persons. "Joint-stock companies in general (developed with the credit system) have the tendency to separate this function of

[8]Karl Marx. *Capital: A Critique of Political Economy*. Vol. 3, p. 371.

[9]*Ibid.*, Vol. 3, p. 911.

[10]*Ibid.*, p. 1021.

managerial work more and more from the possession of capital".[11] Thus, "it has [...] become superfluous for this work of supervision to be performed by the capitalist. A musical conductor needs in no way be the owner of the instruments in his Orchestra. [...] The capitalist has become just as superfluous as a functionary in production as he himself".[12]

Third, with the development of credit, not only is production socialized, but also capital has a social nature. The monetary capital lent by the bank is no longer lent by its direct owner. With the socialization of production and the development of economic linkages between enterprises, the credit system has been greatly improved, and the role of financial organizations has become increasingly prominent. When Marx studies the role of credit in the capitalist economy, he proposes the notion of social capital in opposition to private capital in his analysis of the stock company. In the share-based economy, "Capital, which is inherently based on a social mode of production and presupposes a social concentration of means of production and labor-power, now receives the form of social capital (capital of directly associated individuals) in contrast to private capital, and its enterprises appear as social enterprises as opposed to private ones. This is the abolition of capital as private property within the confines of the capitalist mode of production itself".[13]

To sum up the above analysis, on the one hand, capital has a social nature; on the other hand, some functions that should be performed by functional capitalists are carried out by managers. Only managers are left. Capitalists disappear in the production process as redundant people. Thus, Marx concludes, "so far therefore as it arises from the form of labor as social labor, from the combination and cooperation of many to a common result, it is just as independent of capital as is this form itself, once it has burst its capitalist shell".[14]

According to the development of monopoly at that time, Engels adds to Marx's analysis of the role of credit in the capitalist economy that the socialization of production is further improved, and free competition is on the way. "A further reason is that in each country the big industrialists in a particular branch of the industry come together to form a cartel to regulate production. A committee fixes the quantity each establishment is to

[11] *Ibid.*, p. 512.
[12] *Ibid.*, p. 511.
[13] *Ibid.*, p. 567.
[14] *Ibid.*, p. 511.

produce and has the last word in dividing up the incoming orders".[15] He here finds a trend: "Competition has been replaced in England by monopoly, thus preparing in the most pleasing fashion its future expropriation by society as a whole, by the nation".[16]

Of course, the shareholding system and the form of credit pointed out by Marx that leads to the above contradictions belong to the sublation within the scope permitted by capitalist production relations. "[T]he transformation into the form of shares still remains trapped within the capitalist barriers; instead of overcoming the opposition between the character of wealth as something social, and private wealth, this transformation only develops this opposition in a new form".[17] The fundamental way of overcoming this opposition is to eliminate capitalist private ownership.

In summary, the development of the capitalist economy has created the necessary conditions for the establishment of a socialist economic system: First, the highly developed science and technology, productivity, and social wealth under the conditions of capitalism are important material foundations for the establishment of a socialist economic system. Second, the credit system developed under the capitalist system, which improved day by day, is a transitional form for the transfer to a new mode of production. Third, the sharing economy developed under the capitalist system and the monopoly formed are the important entry point to socialism.

Thus, Marx concludes at the end of the book *Capital*: "Once a certain level of maturity is attained, the particular historical form [of Capitalism] is shed and makes way for a higher form".[18] This higher form is nothing but socialism.

4.1.2. *The material basis of the new society's establishment*

The inevitability of socialism to replace capitalism can be explained by the contradiction between productivity and production relations. Similarly, the improvement and development of a socialist society should also be explained by the development of social productivity. This raises

---

[15] *Ibid.*, p. 570.

[16] *Ibid.*, p. 570.

[17] *Ibid.*, p. 571.

[18] *Ibid.*, p. 1024.

the question about the material basis of the new society that Marx envisioned in the past. This is Marx's famous argument of the "two nevers": "No matter which social form, before all the productive forces it can hold, it will never die; and new and higher production relations. It will never appear until its material existence conditions mature in the birthplace of the old society".[19]

After Marx demonstrates his visions on the basic characteristics of the future society in *Capital*, he points out that these prescriptive realizations "requires that society possess a material foundation, or a series of material conditions of existence, which in their turn are the natural and spontaneous product of a long and tormented historical development".[20] He points out that not only the new society needs a certain material foundation but also the formation of these material foundations requires long-term historical development.

According to Marx's thinking, the material basis of the so-called new society must be higher than the level of productivity that has been achieved under capitalist conditions. The reason is that the future society is a positive sublation of the capitalist society. It should be based on the material foundation that the capitalist system cannot accommodate its productivity, so that "it is the historical task of the capitalist mode of production to bring to a certain level of development, as material foundations for the new form of production".[21]

The socialist economic system is successive to the capitalist economic system. The capitalist mode of production is the institutional basis on which public ownership is derived. In the full development of capitalism, the components of public ownership have been bred. Otherwise, public ownership cannot appear in human society as a system and a complete worldwide system. This is what Marx says: "at a certain stage of development of the material forces of production, and of the social forms of production corresponding to them, a new mode of production develops and is formed naturally out of the old".[22] However, "Even when a society has begun to track down the natural laws of its movement", "it can neither

[19]Karl Marx and Frederick Engels. *Marx & Engels Collected Works*. Vol. 29, Trans. by Ben Fowkes and Emile Burns (London: Lawrence & Wilshart, 2010), p. 263.

[20]Karl Marx. *Capital: A Critique of Political Economy*. Vol. 1, p. 173.

[21]Karl Marx. *Capital: A Critique of Political Economy*. Vol. 3, p. 572.

[22]*Ibid*., p. 357.

leap over the natural phases of its development nor remove them by decree. [...] But it can shorten and lessen the birth-pangs".[23]

In *Capital*, Marx criticized the capitalist system but fully affirmed the social productivity and its historical role in the capitalist society. Marx writes, "The development of the productive forces of social labor is capital's historic mission and justification. For that very reason, it unwittingly creates the material conditions for a higher form of production".[24] Capital is not only the concentrated expression of the contradiction in capitalist society, it is also a booster for the accumulation of material wealth in a capitalist society. To strive to increase productivity indefinitely is the logical result of the unrestrained pursuit of wealth. Capital is achieved by the pursuit of profit by controlling production. The growth of capital and the increase of domestic wealth are mutually conditional. Without the increase of domestic wealth, it is impossible to generate more capital. Without growth and a large amount of capital, it is difficult for national wealth to achieve sustainable and substantial growth. Marx's affirmation of capital lies in that "[i]t is one of the civilizing aspects of capital that it extorts this surplus labor in a manner and in conditions that are more advantageous to social relations and to the creation of elements for a new and higher formation than was the case under the earlier forms of slavery, serfdom, etc.".[25]

More importantly, the material foundation of a socialist society is reflected in the satisfaction of the material needs of people. "On the one hand, necessary labor-time will be measured by the needs of the social individual; and, on the other, society's productive power will develop so rapidly that, although production will now be calculated to provide wealth for all, the DISPOSABLE TIME of all will increase. For real wealth is the developed productive power of all individuals".[26] The economic activities of the Community of Freemen are aimed at the comprehensive and free development of everyone. Therefore, we should not only consider the interests of certain people or certain groups but must pay attention to everyone to respect the interests of all members of society. Otherwise, it will violate the "fundamental principles" of the Community of Freemen. To meet the multifaceted and growing needs of the people, the material

---

[23] Karl Marx. *Capital: A Critique of Political Economy*. Vol. 1, p. 92.

[24] Karl Marx. *Capital: A Critique of Political Economy*. Vol. 3, p. 368.

[25] *Ibid.*, p. 958.

[26] Karl Marx and Frederick Engels. *Marx & Engels Collected Works*. Vol. 29, p. 94.

wealth created by the full development of productive forces needs to be abundant. "ABUNDANCY [...] includes both mass and variety of use-values, and which in turn implies a profuse development of man as a producer, an all-round development of his productive capacities".[27]

4.2 The Basic Characteristics of Socialist Society

It is according to the conditions of the capitalist society in which he lived that Marx envisioned the future socialist society. Many socialist regulations were carried out under rational deductions while he was criticizing capitalist contradictions. Marx scientifically foresaw and underpinned the fundamental characteristics of the relations of production of the future society in *Capital*.

4.2.1. *The public ownership of the means of production*

Marx takes developed and comparatively developed countries as the background, considering the paradox between the socialization of production and the private ownership in the capitalist society. According to the law that relations of production must fit the feature of productive forces, Marx comes to the conclusion of expropriating the exploiters and building an ownership of productive means that is shared by the entire society. As Marx writes, primitive accumulation is accomplished by expropriating small producers, the concentration of capital by expropriating small and medium capitalists; "and even in the last instance to expropriate all individuals from the means of production — which, with the development of social production, cease to be means and products of private production, and can only remain means of production in the hands of associated producers, as their social property, just as they are their social product".[28] Therefore, a socialist society should transfer all the productive means of the bourgeois to "their property as associated producers, as directly social property".[29] Direct public ownership of socialism is the direct combination of labor and productive means. It is "the result of the way [...] in

[27]Karl Marx and Frederick Engels. *Marx & Engels Collected Works*. Vol. 32, Trans. Victor Schnittke and Yuri Sdobnikov (London: Lawrence & Wilshart, 2010), p. 247.
[28]Karl Marx. *Capital: A Critique of Political Economy*. Vol. 3, p. 571.
[29]*Ibid.*, p. 568.

which they serve as conditions of directly social, socialized labor, of direct cooperation within the production process".[30]

Regarding the pattern of future socialist ownership, Marx originally stipulates it as a "social property",[31] in which productive means belongs to society. In *Anti-Dühring*, Engels explains it like that "[f]rom the moment when society enters into possession of the means of production and uses them in direct association for production".[32] In *Capital*, Marx envisages the future society as "an association of freemen, working with the means of production held in common, and expending their many different forms of labor-power in full self-awareness as one single social labor force. [...] The total product of our imagined association is a social product. One part of this product serves as a fresh means of production and remains social. But another part is consumed by the members of the association as a means of subsistence".[33] According to Marx, the public ownership of productive means is the shared ownership of land and the productive means that are produced by labor.

According to Marx's analysis of the conditions of the appearance of commodity and currency, if the entire society possesses the productive means, the relationship between commodity and currency would not have existed. If the personal labor of the worker does not need to be indirectly expressed as social labor through the form of value, and if that personal labor is economically presumed as social labor becomes the common premise in production, the application of currency in the economy would be unnecessary. "With collective production, money capital is completely dispensed with. The society distributes labor-power and means of production between the various branches of industry. There is no reason why the producers should not receive paper tokens permitting them to withdraw an amount corresponding to their labor-time from the social consumption stocks. But these tokens are not money; they do not circulate".[34] Because a planned distribution of labor-time is capable of adjusting the proportion of various labor functions and demands to the appropriate

[30] *Ibid.*, p. 198.

[31] Karl Marx and Frederick Engels. *Marx & Engels Collected Works*. Vol. 24 (London: Lawrence & Wishart, 2010), p. 200.

[32] Karl Marx and Frederick Engels. *Marx & Engels Collected Works*. Vol. 25 Trans. Emile Burns and Clemens Dutt (London: Lawrence & Wishart, 2010), p. 294.

[33] Karl Marx. *Capital: A Critique of Political Economy*. Vol. 1, pp. 71–72.

[34] Karl Marx. *Capital: A Critique of Political Economy*. Vol. 2, p. 434.

level, the personal labor of a laborer is expressed as social labor from the very beginning of production. "[M]oney capital would immediately be done with, and so too the disguises that transactions acquire through it".[35]

Marx demonstrates the ownership and relationship of possession of the productive means in the future society with land ownership as an example. In the future society, "the private property of particular individuals in the earth will appear just as absurd as the private property of one man in other men. Even an entire society, a nation, or all simultaneously existing societies taken together, are not the owners of the earth. They are simply its possessors, its beneficiaries, and have to bequeath it in an improved state to succeeding generations, as *boni patres familias*".[36]

"To re-establish the private property" is another assumption Marx has toward public ownership. Marx states that "[t]he capitalist mode of appropriation, which springs from the capitalist mode of production, produces a capitalist private property. This is the first negation of individual private property, as founded on the labor of its proprietor. But capitalist production begets, with the inexorability of a natural process, its own negation. This is the negation of the negation. It does not re-establish private property, but it does indeed establish individual property on the basis of the achievements of the capitalist era: namely cooperation and the possession in common of the land and the means of production produced by labor itself".[37] Scholars disagree on the definition of Marx's individual ownership. Some believe that individual ownership refers to the private ownership of consumption materials, while others define it as the ownership of productive means. According to a series of classical discussions by Marx, the situation can be understood as follows. First, to replace the capitalist private ownership is not to re-establish private ownership that bases on personal labor, but to eliminate the private ownership of productive means and build up a public ownership of productive means. Hence the illegitimacy of understanding it as re-establishing an individual property of productive means. Second, the individual here does not refer to separate ones with conflicting interests, but the united individuals with the same fundamental interest. This is what Marx defines in another statement as "the property of the non-individual in its independent singularity, hence of

---

[35] *Ibid.*, p. 390.

[36] Karl Marx. *Capital: A Critique of Political Economy.* Vol. 1, p. 911.

[37] *Ibid.*, p. 929.

the associated, social individual".[38] Third, whenever ownership is mentioned, it usually refers to that of the productive means. Therefore, despite that, it is certain that consumption materials in the future society will belong to the individual, but here it does not imply the re-establishment of the individual ownership of consumption materials. This individual ownership is a synonym of socialist public ownership. So, "to re-establish the private property" contrary to the capitalist private ownership is another expression of Marx on public ownership. Under such circumstances, the entire society possesses all the productive means, and everyone is the owner of the means. Therefore, society is a "united community of freemen".

The above pattern of public ownership in the future society as is defined by Marx can be addressed as complete, mature, as well as directional. Marx does not only logically deduce the complete pattern of public ownership in *Capital*, but he also carries out the transitional pattern of public ownership according to the social reality of his time. In *Capital*, Marx has discussed cooperative factories, consumer cooperatives, etc., and he thinks that these movements are the proactive sublation that capitalist possession conducts. He says that the result of the extreme development of capitalist production is the possession of the united producers transferred from capital, i.e., "a necessary point of transition" to direct social possession, and at the same time "a point of transition toward the transformation of all functions formerly bound up with capital ownership in the reproduction process into simple functions of the associated producers, into social functions".[39]

Marx's presumption toward public ownership is reasonable and scientific both theoretically and logically. Consequently, these presumptions are undoubtedly inspirational for us to understand and grasp the fundamental definition of public ownership. Regarding "[t]he thing to be done at any definite given moment of the future, the thing immediately to be done, [it] depends, of course, wholly and entirely on the actual historical circumstances in which action is to be taken".[40]

---

[38] Karl Marx and Frederick Engels. *Marx & Engels Collected Works*. Vol. 34, Trans. Ben Fowkes (London: Lawrence & Wishart, 2010), p. 109.

[39] Karl Marx. *Capital: A Critique of Political Economy*. Vol. 3, p. 568.

[40] Karl Marx and Frederick Engels. *Marx & Engels Collected Works*. Vol. 46, Trans. Rodney Livingstone, Stanley Mitchell, Peter and Betty Ross, and Stephen Smith (London: Lawrence & Wilshart, 2010), p. 166.

4.2.2. *Distribution according to work*

Marx believes that "[t]he so-called relations of distribution, therefore, correspond to and arise from historically particular and specific social forms of the production process and of the relationships which men enter into among themselves in the process of reproducing their human life. The historical character of these relations of distribution is the historical character of the relations of production, and they simply express one side of these".[41] Following his presumptions about public ownership, Marx naturally deduces that distribution according to work is the distribution pattern of individual consumer goods in the socialist society. Under the circumstances of public ownership, laborers possess the productive means of the society as a whole, which means that the laborers are equal in front of the productive means, i.e., no other entity could provide anything except the laborer's labor itself. It makes it impossible for the laborers to attain individual consumer goods if it is not through personal labor, and eliminates the possibility of exploitation as well.

Marx entitles the future society as the united community of freemen. Within such a social form, the entire products of society are partly consumed by production and partly by individuals, with the distribution according to work as its principle regarding the individual consumer goods. Marx believes that, among the members of the united community of the means of consumption, "[t]he way this division is made will vary with the particular kind of social organization of production and the corresponding level of social development attained by the producers. We shall assume, but only for the sake of a parallel with the production of commodities, that the share of each individual producer in the means of subsistence is determined by his labor-time". Therefore, "labor-time would [...] play a double part. Its apportionment in accordance with a definite social plan maintains the correct proportion between the different functions of labor and the various needs of the associations. On the other hand, labor-time also serves as a measure of the part taken by each individual in the common labor, and of his share in the part of the total product destined for individual consumptions".[42] It is the notion of distribution according to work that functions in here.

---

[41] Karl Marx. *Capital: A Critique of Political Economy*. Vol. 3, p. 1023.

[42] Karl Marx. *Capital: A Critique of Political Economy*. Vol. 1, p. 172.

Theories on the income distribution of the future social system are completed in *Critique of the Gotha Programme*. On the one hand, Marx differentiates the two stages of communism, i.e., the primary and the higher stages of communism; he also reveals the fundamental characteristics of the two stages. On the other hand, based on his criticism of Ferdinand Lassalle's "no-deduction" theory, Marx brings forward the different distributive patterns of the two stages and the corresponding reasons. Marx believes that the primary stage of the future society, i.e., the socialist society, owing to the fact that it has just been born from the capitalist society, and that the newly born society brings with it traces of its predecessor either economically, ethically, or spiritually, has to practice the principle of distribution according to work. The society can only distribute according to needs when it reaches the higher stage of communism where people do not have to obey the division of labor like slaves, leading to the disappearance of the contradiction between mental labor and manual labor; where labor itself has become the first need in life instead of a mere means for personal survival; where the productive forces grow along with the comprehensive development of the individuals, and every branch source of the commonwealth is abundant.

In *Critique of the Gotha Programme*, Marx gives scientific analyzes on such issues as the origin of the socialist society's practice of distribution according to work, in what form the principle is achieved, and so forth.

First of all, public ownership is the economic premise for distribution according to work. Marx said that only "[w]ithin the cooperative society based on common ownership of the means of production [can] a given amount of labor in one form is exchanged for an equal amount of labor in another form".[43] In other words, within the social forms other than public ownership, distribution according to work can by no means exist. This economic condition distinguishes the socialist distribution principle from capitalism.

Second, the old social division of labor is the direct economic condition for distribution according to work. The socialist society still carries with it traces from the society that it derives from either in the economy, ethics, or spirit. In particular, laborers are still in a certain social division

[43] Karl Marx and Frederick Engels. *Marx & Engels Collected Works*. Vol. 24, Trans. David Forgacs, Rodney and Krystyna Livingstone, Peter and Betty Ross, Barrie Selman, Joan and Trevor Walmsley (London: Lawrence & Wilshart, 2010), pp. 85–86.

of labor. The labor here differs hugely in itself; it is often compulsory and is merely a means of surviving. Such economic condition makes distribution according to work inevitable. The existence of such economic conditions differentiates the distribution principle of the primary stage of communist society from its higher stage.

Finally, means of materializing distribution according to work are decided by a series of economic conditions. In the future, society directly possesses all productive means, i.e., with a single ownership structure; currency as a commodity no longer functions and the national economy is under a unified planned arrangement; laborers directly combine with productive means throughout the society. Therefore, distribution according to work adopts a direct means of achievement — "individual labor no longer exists in an indirect fashion but directly as a part of total labor";[44] the society distributes according to the amount of personal labor straightforwardly *sans* any other intermediary procedures; the labor token or certificate serves as the distributive medium, which can most directly reflect the feature of the socialist distribution.

The notion that distribution according to work actually comes after the distribution within the social range is what Marx reveals as the "social products deduction theory". It means that the total products of society, before going into the distribution procedure of personal consumer goods, have to undergo a series of deduction that involve two major categories and six aspects altogether. On the one hand, before it is to be distributed as personal consumption means, what has been consumed as remuneration for productive means should be deducted; on the other hand, the additional part that is for enlarging production shall be deducted as well; moreover, back up fund or insurances to meet the contingencies of accidents or natural disasters shall also be counted out. The left total product of society after the first deduction can be seen as the national income; the second and third steps of deduction are accumulation funds; the rest of the total product of society after all the above three steps of the deduction is consumer fund. This consumer fund, before being distributed among individuals, has to go through another three steps of the deduction: the first step is to deduct the general costs of administration not belonging to production — this part diminishes in proportion as the new society develops; the second is to deduct what is intended for the satisfaction of common needs, such as schools, health services, etc., which grow in proportion as the new

[44]Karl Marx and Frederick Engels. *Marx & Engels Collected Works*. Vol. 24, pp. 85–86.

society develops; the third is to deduct funds for those unable to work, etc., in short, for what is included under so-called official poor relief.

Regarding the definition of the labor that serves as a measure to distribution according to work, Marx has provided with a general explanation in *Critique of the Gotha Program*, in which he notes that "the individual producer receives back from society — after the deductions have been made — exactly what he gives to it. What he has given to it is his individual quantum of labor. For example, the social working day consists of the sum of the individual hours of work; the individual labor-time of the individual producer is the part of the social working day contributed by him, his share in it".[45] However, scholars have disagreed on the definitions of the "individual amount of labor" and "individual labor-time", which are said to serve as the measure to distribution according to work. In the light of Marx's analytical framework, the "work" as in distribution according to work is a converted labor-time that has with it the social average nature, i.e., "the social average labor-time", which is the labor-time that is calculated based on social average labor intensity, and the levels of proficiency and complexity after eliminating influences from advantages or disadvantages of the productive means. Every producer's labor-time has to be converted by the unified measurement — social average labor-time before it measures the distribution of his consumer goods. One shall not seek his benefits through the possession of better productive means; before the distribution of personal consumer goods, such objective influences must be removed.

Distribution according to work, in fact, belongs to the distribution of personal consumer goods; it is to exchange for personal consumer goods with the same amount of labor. After the laborer has provided a certain amount of labor, he will be granted a piece of labor certificate from the society; "He receives a certificate from society that he has furnished such-and-such an amount of labor (after deducting his labor for the common funds); and with this certificate, he draws from the social stock of means of consumption as much as the same amount of labor cost. The same amount of labor which he has given to society in one form, he receives back in another".[46] What does Marx mean by "equivalent" and "all gained back" then? Does it mean that when a laborer gives out X hours of social labor he would take back in X hours of materialized consumer goods?

---

[45] *Ibid.*, p. 86.

[46] *Ibid.*

According to Marx, within the total product of society, what is for distribution according to work is the part of the individual consumption means, i.e., the rest part after various social deduction. In the total product of society, except for the materialized labor that takes part in the labor process, the actual functioning labor is the total of surplus labor and necessary labor. Although regarding the physical forms it is necessary to labor that forms individual consumer goods, it is the functioning labor, which is the result of total labor of society minus materialized labor that serves as the distribution basis for individual consumer goods. As for each producer, there is no such equivalence where X hours of labor exchanges for materialized X hours of individual consumer goods. The "equal" as in the exchange of equal labor, or "equivalent" as is mentioned by Marx, refers *de facto* to a certain equivalence in proportion. In other words, the proportion of the individual consumer goods each laborer deserves in the total individual consumer goods of society ought to be equivalent to the proportion of the laborer's amount of labor he offers to the society with total average labor of society, or, that different laborers' equal amount of labor is granted equal rewards is the essence of distribution according to work.

Marx's theory of distribution according to work can be briefly summarized as the following: distribution according to work is the distribution principle of individual consumer goods in the socialist society; labor — instead of individual labor, it is the socially necessary labor that is acknowledged by the society — is the only measure of distributing laborers' consumer goods; the object of distribution according to work is not the entire total product of society but the part that has removed the consumed productive means, means reserves, and social consumption; equal labor exchange is a relationship that has equal proportions — the reward granted to the laborers is equal in proportion in terms of their labor and the total average labor of society.

Lastly, we need to pay attention to the tendency which Marx has revealed: as the social productivity is developing faster and faster, the amount of labor has less influence and effect toward distribution, while the decisive influence of the laborers' need on distribution is growing stronger.

4.2.3. *The comprehensive development of people's freedom*

Marx has explicitly pointed out that a significant characteristic of the future society is that people's freedom shall develop comprehensively.

He depicts such comprehensive development of the people from the united community of freemen as follows: "[j]ust as the savage must wrestle with nature to satisfy his needs, to maintain and reproduce his life, so must civilized man, and he must do so in all forms of society and under all possible modes of production. This realm of natural necessity expands with his development, because his needs do too, but the productive forces to satisfy these expand at the same time. Freedom, in this sphere, can consist only in this, that socialized man, the associated producers, govern the human metabolism with nature in a rational way, bringing it under their collective control instead of being dominated by it as a blind power; accomplishing it with the least expenditure of energy and in conditions most worthy and appropriate for their human nature".[47]

Freedom of the employed laborers under capitalism, compared with laborers of the past eras, can be concluded into three aspects: the lawful freedom, which means that workers are freemen protected by law; freedom in choosing employers, labor locations, labor conditions, careers, and level of salary; freedom in choosing one's own skill development. Freedom is one step further than past society. It has positively influenced the general changes in social materials and the overall development of human demand and capabilities. The reproduction of labor, because productive means are still held by the minorities, affiliates to capital, so this freedom has only formal meanings. "The form becomes *freer* because the subordination is now only of an *objective* nature; it is formally speaking voluntary, *purely economic*".[48]

It is in the socialist society when the capitalist society is destroyed can the laborers truly attain freedom. In the new social form, the feature of freedom is materialized not only formally but also essentially. The fundamental reason is that social wealth has become the material condition that people share and develop together. The comprehensive development of humankind is the historical product through the process of human beings' knowing, transforming, and conquering nature when men liberate and develop themselves.

In terms of the definition of freemen of the future society, Marx thinks that freemen are "freely associated men, and stand under their conscious

---

[47]Karl Marx. *Capital: A Critique of Political Economy*. Vol. 3, p. 959.

[48]Karl Marx and Frederick Engels. *Marx & Engels Collected Works*. Vol. 34, Trans. Ben Fowkes (London: Lawrence & Wilshart, 2010), pp. 432–433.

and planned control".[49] Freemen are not separate individuals who have no connections with each other but individuals who have achieved socialization. It means that everyone's freedom only exists when there is a social connection within a social connection, each individual's talent and wisdom can get comprehensive development; the economic and social status of a person is equal with the others, and all hierarchies disappear. This is what Marx says, "Only within the community has each individual the means of cultivating his gifts in all directions; hence personal freedom becomes possible only within the community".[50]

Regarding the conditions of the formation of freemen, Marx brings about four aspects: First of all, social productive forces highly develop, and the labor provided by the people has enough surplus, so that shortening working days is possible, and the free time that every individual can have in the society increases. "[T]he creation of disposable time is then also the creation of time for the production of science, art, etc.".[51] It guarantees that people have time to make free choices and develop. If men have to spend their major energy and time in dealing with the issue of survival, and heavily depend on natural products, freedom can only be a meaningless word. Second, productive means are possessed by society, therefore nobody would gain consumption means with methods other than laboring. Third, theoretical education organically combines with applied skill education. Consequently, "this education will, in the case of every child over a given age, combine productive labor with instruction and gymnastics, not only as one of the methods of adding to the efficiency of production, but as the only method of producing fully developed human beings".[52] Fourth, the universality of labor. "The intensity and productivity of labor being given, the part of the social working day necessarily taken up with material production is shorter and, as a consequence, the time at society's disposal for the free intellectual and social activity of the individual is greater, in proportion as work is more and more evenly divided among all the able-bodied members of society, and a particular social stratum is more and more deprived of the ability to shift the burden

[49] Karl Marx. *Capital: A Critique of Political Economy*. Vol. 1, p. 173.

[50] Karl Marx and Frederick Engels. *Marx & Engels Collected Works*. Vol. 5, Trans. Clemens Dutt, W. Lough, and C. P. Magill (London: Lawrence & Wilshart, 2010), p. 78.

[51] Karl Marx. *Grundrisse: Foundations of the Critique of Political Economy*. Trans. Martin Nicolaus (London: Penguin Books, 1973).

[52] Karl Marx. *Capital: A Critique of Political Economy*. Vol. 1, p. 614.

of labor (which is a necessity imposed by nature) from its own shoulders to those of another social stratum".[53]

In the economic activities of the united community of freemen, regulations on time are still vitally significant. The economic activities of freemen also demand efficiency and will need analysis and accounting on the input–output relationship as well. Because "the multiplicity of [an individual's] development, its enjoyment and its activity depends on economization of time".[54] While the time it needs in producing wheat, cattle, and so on becomes less, the time that the society gains in conducting other productions, either materially or spiritually, will be more. The level of how much time saved directly determines the level of the comprehensive development of freemen.

The fundamental influence of free time on a person's comprehensive development can be summarized as follows.

First, free time guarantees that everyone can share such cultural fruits as science, arts, and social patterns, inherited from history, i.e., to freely develop individualities. "The free development of individualities, and hence not the reduction of necessary labor-time so as to posit surplus labor, but rather the general reduction of the necessary labor of society to a minimum, which then corresponds to the artistic, scientific, etc.".[55]

Second, free time is an important ruler that measures the wealth of the future society. According to Marx, labor-time as the measure of wealth implies that wealth is based on poverty. When the free time becomes the decisive element in the growth of wealth, it is the possession of men's general productive forces that serves as the grand foundation of production and wealth instead of the direct labor that men complete, or the labor-time that people spend. Then, the value measure of wealth would shift from labor-time to free time, and increasing free time means increasing the "time for the full development of individuals, which in turn reacts back upon the productive power of labor as itself the greatest productive power".[56]

Third, the increase of free time is the fundamental condition to found a realm of freedom. Marx points out that the material field is always a realm of necessity. "The realm of freedom really begins only where labor

[53]Karl Marx. *Capital: A Critique of Political Economy*. Vol. 3, p. 667.

[54]Karl Marx. *Grundrisse*. pp. 172–173.

[55]*Ibid.*, p. 706.

[56]*Ibid.*, p. 711.

determined by necessity and external expediency ends; it lies by its very nature beyond the sphere of material production proper. [...] The true realm of freedom, the development of human powers as an end in itself, begins beyond it, though it can only flourish with this realm of necessity as its basis. The reduction of the working day is the basic prerequisite".[57] Here, the contradiction between "this side" and "the other side" of material production is the contradiction between labor-time and free time.

Lastly, more free time means that the comprehensive and free development of individuals is the basic characteristic and content of the ideal future society. "The whole of human development, so far as it extends beyond the development directly necessary for the natural existence of human beings, consists merely in the employment of this free time and presupposes it as its necessary basis".[58]

4.2.4. *Planned economy*

On the anarchical circumstance of social production under capitalist conditions, Marx logically deduced that the future society ought to establish a planned economy in the whole society. A significant feature of the economy of the united community of freemen is that "the social life-process, i.e., the process of material production [...] becomes production by freely associated men, and stand under their conscious and planned control".[59] The alleged planned control is that "[i]ts apportionment in accordance with a definite social plan maintains the correct proportion between the different functions of labor and the various needs of the associations".[60]

A planned economy is the automatic adjustment and control of economic activities. Under the condition of public ownership, the whole society keeps high collective rationality; it can automatically control economic activities with its power. "Society likewise has to distribute its time in a purposeful way, in order to achieve a production adequate to its overall needs; just as the individual has to distribute his time correctly in order to achieve knowledge in proper proportions or in order to satisfy the

---

[57] Karl Marx. *Capital: A Critique of Political Economy*. Vol. 3, pp. 958–959.

[58] Karl Marx and Frederick Engels. *Marx & Engels Collected Works*. Vol. 30, Trans. Ben Fowkes and Emile Burns (London: Lawrence & Wilshart, 2010), pp. 191–192.

[59] Karl Marx. *Capital: A Critique of Political Economy*. Vol. 1, p. 173.

[60] *Ibid.*, p. 172.

various demands on his activity. Thus, the economy of time, along with the planned distribution of labor-time among the various branches of production, remains the first economic law on the basis of communal production. It becomes law, there, to an even higher degree".[61] It means that, through a planned distribution of labor-time, the entire society's labor functions and the supply of their products fit the demand of the society for various social functions and products. The logical premise of Marx's analysis here is based upon an adequate supply of material sources, so there would not be any problem with the planned function regarding the planning deployment of material data. As a result, the focus of planned distribution shifts onto the aspect that concerns people. In the light that labor functions are personified expression of labor-time, the adjustment to labor functions would concert to that to labor-time.

According to Marx, the rationality of the capitalist society always functions after a problem breaks out, while that of the socialist society functions beforehand. "[T]he society must reckon in advance how much labor, means of production and means of subsistence it can spend, without dislocation".[62] Only through proactive control of the production process can the society achieve direct planned production. This shows that planned production includes society's personal development and social material productive force, two mutually dependent conditions.

4.3 Scientific Understanding of Socialism in Practice

The task of political economy to analyze socialism has but does not limit to the requirement of strengthening the belief in socialism replacing capitalism. To adapt to the demand of China's reform and opening up policy and modernization, the political economy should aim at reforming and perfecting the socialist economic system, stimulating the development of advanced social productivity, and increase national wealth. Correspondingly, research on and educational ideas about the political economy calls for changes in two aspects. On the one hand, the attention should be turned from class struggle to economic construction. Political economics has been the weapon in the class struggle in a capitalist society,

---

[61] Karl Marx. *Grundrisse*. p. 173.

[62] Karl Marx. *Capital: A Critique of Political Economy*. Vol. 2, p. 390.

while in today's socialist society, it is the theoretical guidance to economic construction. On the other hand, the past dogmatization of political-economic theories should be turned into an action guide. Over a hundred years ago when he was criticizing capitalism, Marx logically deduced certain characteristics of the socialist society, which ought to be taken as the action guide instead of dogmas in building a socialist society today. We must not stiffly receive particular theories proposed by Marx at his time, but rather expand Marx's socialism along with the developmental practices of the socialist society.

When he analyzed the economic paradoxes within capitalism, Marx logically deduced certain economic characteristics of the future socialist society. Examples are the envisioned characteristics of the economy of the united community of freemen in the part of commodity fetishism, the characteristics of the newly founded social ownership after exploiting the exploiters when he looks into the historical trend of capital accumulation, the system of plan adjusting the distribution of social labor as is covered in Volume II of *Capital*, and discussions on socialist economy that can be found in some other parts.

It should be mentioned that the stipulations deduced by Marx in *Capital* on the future society after capitalism are logical as well as scientific. According to Marx, these stipulations are mature economic characteristics of the socialist society that have been founded based on the mature capitalist society. However, China turned itself into a socialist society based on a relatively economically backward semi-colonial and semi-feudal society. When he analyzed the productive relations of the countries other than England, Marx pointed out that these countries "suffer not only from the development of capitalist production but also from the incompleteness of that development. Alongside the modern evils, [they] are oppressed by a whole series of inherited evils, arising from the passive survival of archaic and outmoded modes of production, with their accompanying train of anachronistic social and political relations".[63] When he was analyzing the historic function of merchant capital, Marx had a discussion that concerns China: Before capitalism, the ethnic mode of production has an internal solid structure. In the case of how much hindrance this fact has influenced the deconstruction effect of commerce toward the feudal productive mode, we can see clearly from the communion between the Englishmen and the Indians and the Chinese. In China,

[63] Karl Marx. *Capital: A Critique of Political Economy*. Vol. 1, p. 91.

"the broad basis of the mode of production is formed by the union between small-scale agriculture and domestic industry".[64] The process of commerce deconstructing this productive mode has been extremely slow. Except for the fact that there is no direct political power involved, the reason is also that the direct combination of agriculture and handicraft industry greatly saves resources and time so that it forms a tenacious resistance against large industrial products. "[P]rices [of the products of the large-scale industry] include the *faux frais* [overhead expenses] of the circulation process with which they are everywhere perforated".[65] The analysis reveals that the underdevelopment of the market economy and the dominance of the small peasant economy contribute to the fact that the old productive mode is steadily maintained until the primary stage of socialism.

Therefore, China had also witnessed the same productive relations when it first turned into a socialist society, i.e., the existence of both capitalist productive relations and several pre-capitalist relations. Even though the society has undergone socialist transformation, the traces and influences of many pre-capitalist productive modes still exist. All these elements prove that Chinese socialism is still in its primary stage.

After confirming China being in the primary stage of socialism, we then need to check such issues as the persistence and development of the socialist theories in *Capital*. To persist on is to confirm; stipulations on socialism as is written in Marx's *Capital* can still be the aim of building socialism. To develop is to closely research the demanded economic conditions of the stipulations in *Capital*, based on which such a conclusion shall be achieved that the primary stage of socialism would not fully accomplish the stipulations given the logic of *Capital*. By Marx's thought method, the fundamental way of achieving the socialist goals is to create and realize the economic condition of definition, especially creating and realizing the material basis of definition depending on the development of productive forces.

Marxist political economy, with the *Capital* system as the representative, takes capitalism as its subject. Its foresight and stipulations about socialist economic relations are involved in the framework of the analysis of capitalism. Therefore, we need theoretical innovation while taking the

---

[64] Karl Marx. *Capital: A Critique of Political Economy*. Vol. 3, p. 451.

[65] *Ibid.*, p. 452.

Marxist political economy as the theoretical foundation of the guiding ideology and analyzing socialist economic relations.

The guiding ideology that *Capital* provides to the development of the socialist economy in practice is not only its discussion on its characteristics but more importantly is general economic theories. And the market economic theory is the most important among general economic theories. Although *Capital* explains economic theories in the economic form of capitalism, after peeling off the definition of a capitalist economic relation, many theories play an obvious guiding role in the contemporary socialist economy. China's reformative and opening practices confront with many aspects of adjusting economic relations, such as the adjustment of the structure of ownership, the construction of enterprise system, the adjustment of distribution structure and distribution system, the construction of market economy, the adjustment of the relationship between the state and its enterprises, etc. Principles and methods in *Capital* play a guiding role in research on and analyzes of these aspects.

According to Marx, the solid material conditions and spiritual conditions created by the adequate development of productive forces are the premises of a functioning public society. "If we did not find concealed in society as it is the material conditions of production and the corresponding relations of exchange prerequisite for a classless society, then all attempts to explode it would be quixotic".[66] When human society is not fully equipped with such conditions or public ownership is not economically free, the application and exertion of its various social functions must be incomplete. As a result, the efficiency of public ownership can by no means be demonstrated.

Marx gives an extensive analysis of productive forces in *Capital.* For example, from simple cooperation to the division of labor of manufacture to large-scale mechanic industry, Marx analyzes each production mode in detail including the technical aspects. Similarly, analysis of the socialist economic relations should also abide by such a scientific method. Developing the socialist economic relations, in the end, depends upon the development of productive forces. Although China's being in the primary stage of socialism is decided by the disadvantaged productive forces, it does not mean that the currently developing productive forces are inferior. Instead, the development should follow the standards of advanced productive forces.

[66] Karl Marx. *Grundrisse: Foundations of the Critique of Political Economy*. p. 159.

While explaining the issue of the united community of freemen achieving conscious and planned control of material production, Marx specially adds that "[t]his, however, requires that society possess a material foundation, or a series of material conditions of existence, which in their turn are the natural and spontaneous product of a long and tormented historical development".[67] What we are supposed to do is not to abduct the fundamental definition of socialism but to create the material basis for the realization of the socialist definition. To make it clearer, the focus of developing the socialist economy at the moment is not to pursue the advantage of the system, but the advantage of social productive forces push forward the development of the system on this account.

Economics always represents a certain interest group. *Capital* has been called the "Bible"for the proletariat. For a long time, people learn about *Capital* and political economy from the perspective of analyzing class and class struggle, which is understandable in the era of class struggle. While in the era of constructing a new society, the political economy ought to provide a theoretical contribution to the forming of the adaptability of thinking, ideas, and entrepreneurship mechanism to the basic economic system at the primary stage of socialism. The analysis of the political economy on the socialist economy is not to offer theories on class struggle but on constructing a harmonious society. The political economy facing capitalism is to seek the gravedigger of capitalism. But the political economy facing socialism is to seek the builders of the society to completely solve the problem of the fundamental power that constructs the new society and develops advanced social productive forces.

The key to constructing the new society is pushing the development of productive forces, especially that of advanced productive forces. According to Marx, productive means, a tool of production, in particular, is the sign that differentiates economic eras. This is what he says, "[i]t is not what is made but how, and by what instruments of labor, that distinguishes different economic epochs".[68] Marx's historical analysis reveals that the social productive forces catering the capitalist economic relations started with simple cooperation, went through the division of labor of manufacture, and it is not until during the large-scale mechanic industry that the material-technical base had been founded. The characteristic of large industry is machines producing machines. "Large-scale industry,

---

[67] Karl Marx. *Capital: A Critique of Political Economy*. Vol. 1, p. 173.

[68] *Ibid.*, p. 286.

therefore, had to take over the machine itself, its characteristic instrument of production, and to produce machines using machines. It was not till it did this that it could create for itself an adequate technical foundation, and stand on its own feet".[69] The functions of the productive forces produced by machines, according to Marx, have two aspects: "[a]s machinery, the instrument of labor assumes a material mode of existence which necessitates the replacement of human force by natural forces, and the replacement of the rule of thumb by the conscious application of natural science".[70] The two aspects of the requirement of the large-scale mechanic industry pose as the frame of reference to the development of advanced social productive forces of contemporary China. In general, advanced social productive forces are based on modern science technologies. Advanced social productive force is a fluid concept. Just as Marx has said, the technical foundation of the large industry is revolutionary. The level of productive forces that China is at today may have greatly exceeded that of the capitalist country where Marx lived, but we still cannot say that the socialist material foundation of China is established. The reason is that developed capitalist countries continuously innovate technologies and industries depending on their basis of the large-scale mechanic industry, and their productive forces thus reach to a higher level. Under such conditions, what we have mentioned representing the advanced social productive forces shall not be limited to level of the large-scale mechanic industry as is depicted in *Capital*, but we should set the level of the productive forces that have been reached by contemporary developed countries as the frame of reference to the advanced social productive forces. The advanced social productive force a hundred years ago is the large-scale mechanic industry, but today it is the new high-tech industry, with the information industry as its representative.

At present, the stage which capitalism is at and the level of development of productive forces or enterprise systems are all different from those when Marx wrote *Capital* more than a hundred years ago. The developmental practices of the socialist society and the situations that Marx envisioned are not the same either. All these demand that principles of political economy develop along with the development of practices. An example is the labor theory of value. When Marx lived, labor had a decisive influence on economic growth, and the labor then was mainly the

[69] *Ibid.*, p. 506.

[70] *Ibid.*, p. 508.

labor of workers. Regarding the development of the economy in the modern period, functions of knowledge and technologies toward economic growth greatly exceed that of labor. The content and range of labor are also broadened. Except for workers, technical staff, managers, service personnel, etc. all provide labor, even private entrepreneurs provide labor while managing their firms. Consequently, while analyzing the modern economy with the labor theory of value one needs to make new explanations by the changed situations. Another example is that in the capitalist analysis, personal properties and private capital are seen as the tool for expropriation because they fall within the category of the private economy, and proletarians who possess nothing are applauded as the society's gravediggers. However, the same theories shall not be blindly adopted in the analysis of the socialist economy. In the socialist society, working class as the hosts and builders should also be able to become possessors; whether one has property or not and how much property one owns shall not be the standard that measures the extent of one's political advancement. The political economy should carry out and research on conceptions about the constructors who are actively involved in building socialism with Chinese characteristics as well as the system of protecting private properties. It also needs to follow that various elements including the capital, labor, and management participate in distribution according to contribution as well as the set proportion by the enterprises. It needs to find an efficient way of labor–management cooperation as well. The political economy should make theoretical contributions to the situations where all people could display their talents and find themselves the right careers, and get along with each other harmoniously.

Chapter 5

The Main Historical and Logical Line of China's Economic Transformation

China's 30 years of reform and opening up between 1978 and 2008 was a significant economic transformation. It was mainly constituted by the following four points: First, the transformation of the economic system, i.e., economic reforms that achieved a transition from a planned to a market economy; Second, the transformation of the economy's social formation, i.e., economic development that achieved a transition from a traditional to a modern form; Third, the transformation of economic openness, i.e., the integration into the global economy that achieved a transition from a closed to an open economy; Fourth, the transformation of the patterns of economic development, i.e., a transition from a material-oriented to a people-oriented form of development and the turn of economic growth from extensive to intensive mode. All of these transformations were both successful experiments and great practices of developing socialism with Chinese characteristics.

5.1 Exploring a Socialist Development Path with Chinese Characteristics in Accordance with the Conditions at the Primary Stage of Socialism

After the establishment of the Soviet Union as the first socialist country in 20th century, other nascent socialist nations successively implemented an economic system based on the classical Marxist vision of the socialist system in an attempt to lead their countries to communism. Starting after the socialist transformation in the 1950s, China also followed the Soviet Union's Stalinist model to build a socialist planned economy. However, practice has shown that after the stage of developing productivity, these relations of production and the economic system will not be successful. After the death of Joseph Stalin, the so-called market-based reforms, particularly those that were conducted in the Soviet Union and socialist countries in Eastern Europe from the 1970s and 1980s onwards, were not just an abandonment of the Stalinist model in general, but were in fact an embrace of capitalism. That being said, China's economic transformations since the Third Plenary Session of the 11th Central Committee of the Communist Party of China (CPC) have not duplicated the path of former Soviet bloc countries. Instead, China has started from the primary stage of socialism and explored the socialist road with Chinese characteristics.

Adjusting the relations of production to accommodate the development of productivity does not always continuously advance the relations of production; it may also be a retreat. When relations of production are artificial or adopted prematurely, the resulting conditions hinder, and even undermine, the development of productivity. Relations of production and economic systems that transcend levels of productivity development return to an earlier stage that is more conducive to productivity: this is a great change in the liberation and development of productive forces.

The period known as the primary stage of socialism refers to a specific time in which China must build socialism and face situations such as lagging productive forces and an underdeveloped market economy. Under such conditions, China needs to achieve industrialization, economic socialization, marketization, and modernization, namely all the conditions that are all achieved by countries in capitalist economies. At this stage, the principal social contradiction is that the level of productive forces cannot meet the ever-growing material and cultural demands of the population. Accordingly, the goal of socialism at this stage is to develop productive forces instead of eliminating private ownership, even employing forms of private ownership to develop productivity on a larger scale. In accordance with this great theoretical breakthrough, China's reform and opening up has realized the following four economic transformations over the past 40 years.

The first transformation concerns the economic system. There are two regulations involving the economic system in economics. The first is that it is a fundamental system that reflects society's true nature, which is the essential characteristic of the relations of production. The second defines the economic structure as a concrete form of certain social relations of production that pertain to the institutional arrangements in economic operations. In general, the goal of China's economic transformation has not been to change the socialist economic system, but instead to seek new institutional arrangements within the basic system of socialism such as turning to a market economy, changing the means of resource allocation, and so on. However, one must acknowledge that China is currently still in the primary stage of socialism, suggesting that its economic reforms will inevitably touch upon the established socialist economic system. That is to say, economic reform aims to tailor the socialist economic system beyond the stages of development to fit in with the characteristics of primary stage as well as the current level of productive forces. Therefore, the three decades of economic transformations on the institutional level have two distinguishing features: one is to build the basic economic system at the primary stage of socialism; the other is to establish the socialist market economic structure, a system of innovation, dynamism, and efficiency.

The second transformation concerns the stages of economic development. As a historical process, the primary stage of socialism gradually breaks away from conditions of underdevelopment to achieve basic modernization. The central task of this process is to develop the economy and transform society from a traditional to a modernized form. The modernization of an agricultural country involves industrialization, urbanization, the turn to advanced technologies and so on. It is necessary for a latecomer to abide by the general rules of modernization and to adopt the basic course taken by countries that have already modernized. Meanwhile, a newly emerging developing nation must also pioneer its own unique path to modernization, taking into account its own national conditions and the new economic, social, and political environments at home as well as abroad. Promoting the well-rounded construction of a moderately prosperous society as part of its modernization process, China has taken a path to modernization with Chinese characteristics. In light of this goal, the transformation of China's economic and political stage primarily includes the following four features: (1) the transition from an agricultural nation with a large rural population that was mainly dependent on manual labor to an industrialized country with a large, non-agricultural population and an economy comprising of modern agriculture and service industries; (2) the transition from a largely natural and semi-natural economy to a market economy with a higher degree of economic marketization; (3) the transition from a society with a large illiterate and semi-illiterate population and with development issues in science, technology, education, and culture to a society with an advanced approach in all the preceding areas; (4) the transition from a stage with large segments of the population living below the poverty line or at a low standard of living to one that features better living conditions for all of its people.

The third transformation concerns the shift from a closed and semi-closed economy to one that is well rounded and open. The development of productivity requires domestic and international resources. The founder of scientific socialism, Karl Marx, believed that socialism would proceed sequentially from capitalism. Of course, he was thinking about a future socialist economy that was non-existent in his time. In reality, capitalism and socialism have coexisted for quite some time. Although socialist countries are relatively young, they didn't grow out of developed, capitalist countries. However, within the hundreds of years of capitalist history, countries that had capitalist economies observed several significant industrial, scientific, and technological revolutions. They also gave birth to economic organizations and forms that represent advanced social productive forces. Therefore, socialist countries need to learn advanced technology and managerial experience from developed capitalist countries. By doing so, they will be able to develop social productive forces, especially those that involve advanced social productivity. They will also actively participate in international economic cooperation and competition in order to strengthen their own global competitiveness. It is essential for developing socialist countries to attract foreign investment through opening up and to adopt all economic forms — even those that are practiced in capitalist economies — as long as they are conducive to the development of productivity. Furthermore, China's economic opening up not only permits the importation of foreign capital and products, but also encourages the country's participation in international competition as well as its integration into the global economy.

The fourth transformation concerns modes of economic development. At the primary stage of economic growth, a developing country usually implements a "catch up strategy", hoping to catch up with other developed countries within a short period of time. This pursuit of "rapid" development succeeds at a certain stage, benefiting from an initial environment of development. For example, if the level of industrialization is generally low, then there is less drastic competition and any constraints involving the environment and resources will be relatively loose.

With comprehensive advancements in industrialization and more general economic development, this pursuit of "rapid", one-sided growth pattern will inevitably come to an end, prompting necessary transformations in the modes of development. Such a shift will transfer focus from the sole pursuit of economic growth to the pursuit of economic progress, and from the pursuit of quantity to the pursuit of the quality of development. These transformations could be categorized into four areas. First, economic growth will no longer be driven by investments and exports alone, but by the coordination among forces of consumption, investment, and exportation. Second, economic growth will no longer be driven by secondary industries but by the coordination among the primary, secondary, and tertiary industries. Third, economic growth will no longer be driven by an increase in the consumption of material resources, but by the coordination among technology, the quality of the labor force, and administrative innovation. Fourth, economic growth will no longer be driven by the traditional mode of industrialization, but by the new path of industrialization with Chinese characteristics: a path that seeks a sustainable harmony between humanity and nature. Practice has proven that the transformation of the patterns of economic development can be directed to a path of scientific development and social harmony.

The economic transformations during these 30 years of reform and opening up have been one of the substantial endeavors of developing socialism with Chinese characteristics. This is the direction for the quest to develop socialism with Chinese characteristics and the Chinese have sought to emancipate the mind in these practices of reform and opening up. The achievements of building a well-rounded and a moderately prosperous society along this path represent the fundamental interests of the people.

5.2 The Basic Economic System at the Primary Stage of Socialism Is the Concrete Embodiment of Socialism with Chinese Characteristics

Socialism with Chinese characteristics is a theoretical accomplishment of Sinicization Marxism. Its theoretical foundation proposes that the fundamental conditions of China will remain at the primary stage of socialism for a considerable time.

Acknowledging the fact that China is still at its primary stage of socialism has two implications. On the one hand, China has already become a socialist society and needs to uphold the basic principles of scientific socialism. On the other hand, China's socialist system has not yet fully developed and its socialist nature is not yet fully displayed in all manners of life, which can be demonstrated in the following two ways.

For one thing, China's socialist economic relations still remain at the primary stage and have not completely matured according to the standards of socialism. This fact is observable in two ways. First, the degree of public ownership of the means of production cannot be very high. Not only are there various forms of public ownership, but there are also many different forms of realization and modes of operation. Public assets, which do not have to be managed in full public ownership enterprises, can be operated in mixed-ownership enterprises with private elements. Second, the idea of distributing resources according to one's work cannot be fully realized. The "work" in this distribution system, whether it comes in the form of mobility, potentiality, or solidification, cannot fully reflect the labor contributions of the workers. Moreover, workers in different departments and enterprises cannot get equal pay for equal work. Third, the idea of common prosperity is incomplete. There are discrepancies between those who became prosperous "earlier" and those who did so "later" among different departments and workers. Obviously, in accordance with the characteristics of a socialist economy that still remains at the primary stage, one major aspect of reform will be adjusting the economic system. This process will make it a reflection of socialist relations of production at the primary stage rather than a reflection of socialist relations of production at some advanced stage in the future.

For another, the structure of socialist relations of production at the primary stage cannot yet be considered to be a "complete" form of socialism. That would entail multiple structures of diverse forms of non-public ownership. As opposed to other transitional countries, China's economic transformation has not completely abandoned public ownership or adopted comprehensive privatization. Instead, it has developed diverse forms of ownership, building the basic economic system in which public ownership plays a dominant role and diverse forms of ownership develop side by side. Within this basic economic system, a series of institutional arrangements are formed: the economic institution is a socialist market economy; the dominant system of income distribution proceeds according to one's work, and multiple forms of distribution also exist side by side. All of these institutional arrangements are the concrete embodiments of socialism with Chinese characteristics.

5.2.1. *In the basic economic system, public ownership plays a dominant role and diverse forms of ownership work alongside each other*

Within this institutional framework, one of the characteristics of socialism is the dominance of public ownership. More specifically, the joint development of diverse forms of ownership is characteristic of China at its present stage. This regulation has two distinct effects.

The first effect is the development of diverse economies of private ownership in terms of both breadth and depth. Although the privately owned economy was considered to be "outside the system" in the past, now it has become a part of the basic socialist economic system, being"within the system". The development of the basic socialist economic system has broken through institutional limits. In terms of breadth, foreign investment and private capital are now allowed to enter sectors that were once monopolized by state-owned enterprises, such as retail, foreign trade, finance, insurance, communications, and so on. Under this development trend, the non-public economy will be allowed to enter any area as long as it does not affect national security or violate Chinese laws. In terms of depth, public ownership can take the form of mixed-ownership. More specific examples can take the form of joint-stock systems, cooperative stock systems, joint ventures between China and foreign entities, as well as the joint capital and the joint operation of various sectors of ownership. This change permits private-property rights to enter the realm of public enterprise. Therefore, the co-development of public and non-public ownership systems does not only occur between enterprises but also within an enterprise itself. It follows that different types of ownerships can coexist in a single enterprise.

Another impact is represented by the changes to the dominance of public ownership. In the process of developing an economy with diverse ownership systems, one will inevitably encounter problems with maintaining the dominance of public ownership. Traditional theories focused on the absolute public ownership of enterprises defined the dominance of public ownership in terms of the dominant numbers of public enterprises. China's practices of reform have broken this dogma. The theoretical breakthrough in this reform is the redefinition of public ownership as publicly owned capital, including state-owned and collectively owned capital, rather than publicly owned enterprises. Thus, the dominance of public ownership has resulted in new implications: public assets are dominant when it comes to total social assets and the state-owned economy controls national economic lifelines and plays a leading role in economic development. This theoretical breakthrough provides the following significant guidelines to China's economic transition and reform. First, public assets do not have to be managed in enterprises that are entirely publicly owned; they can also be operated in mixed forms of ownership that involve private elements as well. The dominance of public ownership reveals itself through the controlling power of public assets in mixed-ownership enterprises. Second, the state-owned economy will concentrate on the fields where it should play a positive role. These areas include critical national economic sectors, such as railways, airlines, ports, post and telecommunications, finance, etc. Additional sectors include those essential industries that play a decisive role in the development of the national economy, but are relatively weak such as the energy and raw material industries. The state-owned economy should maintain its dominance in these fields, but give up its dominance in other fields that may be defined as competitive sectors. Even in the critical national economic sectors controlled by the state-owned economy, total state ownership is not required unless issues of national security are involved. It is feasible to grant partial equity to non-public capital through a shareholding system and secure their access to these sectors.

5.2.2. *The structure of the socialist market economy system*

The goal of China's economic reform is to establish a socialist market economy. Traditional theories have linked planned and market economies to different socioeconomic systems. Specifically, it is believed that socialism must have a planned economy while capitalism must have a market economy. One of the most important contributions of China's era of reform and opening up is that planned and market economies have both been categorized as a means of resource allocation and a mechanism of economic operation. Whether we are speaking of an economy that is planned or dictated by a market, the mechanisms of operating the economy do not necessarily reflect the nature of that economic system. In effect, capitalism may have some degree of planning, and socialism may have a "market". To improve the efficiency in the allocation of resources, it is necessary to establish a socialist market economy in which the market plays a fundamental role in resource allocation, while the government will strengthen its own macro control. Within this process, the government's continued macro control is a characteristic of the primary stage of China's socialism, representing China's unique qualities as well as the regulating role of the market's mechanisms. This regulation also has two distinct effects.

First, the mechanism of the market must play a fundamental role in adjusting resource allocation so as to guarantee its efficiency. In order for the market to function well, it is critical to enable four mechanisms for resource allocation. The first is the mechanism of equivalent exchange, a mechanism that is accepted by enterprises that pursue profits independently and that also allocate resources to different production fields according to the standards of socially necessary labor consumption. The second is the competition mechanism, which exerts external pressure on enterprises. It could also be called the survival of the fittest. Resources are allocated competitively with the principle of efficiency, enabling the flow of resources to more efficient areas, sectors, and enterprises. The third is the information mechanism in which sellers and buyers meet directly, creating direct feedback that enables the quick exchange of information and reduces administrative distortions. The fourth is the mechanism of risk and benefit. Real competition will not exist until competitors bear the risks. Economic agents in the market economy should take risks for their own behavior. They should not only receive the benefits of these actions but also bear the consequences. For instance, both investors and managers need to bear the risks for their investments and operations, and be responsible for their profits as well as their losses.

Second, even when a market economy is modified with the label "socialist", its basic regularity does not change. Rather, this act highlights the idea of national macro control, which not only serves to prevent the market from malfunctioning, but also meets the requirements of the socialist system, particularly the requirement for fairness and justice and the prevention of polarization.

5.2.3. *An income distribution system whereby distribution according to work dominates and multiple forms of distribution coexist*

In traditional theories of socialism, income distribution can only proceed according to one's work. This is because all the other factors were publicly owned with the exception of labor. At the primary stage of socialism, however, all the production factors are privately owned to different degrees, thereby legitimizing the coexistence of multiple distribution forms. Besides, although common prosperity is the basic principle of socialism, there is still an inevitable discrepancy between those who enjoy prosperity earlier and those who lag behind. It is necessary to acknowledge this discrepancy in order to promote efficiency and to allow some areas and some people to enjoy prosperity before others. In this system, the institutional characteristics of socialism are the distribution according to work and the emphasis on common prosperity. The characteristics that define China in the primary stage of socialism, on the other hand, are the coexistence of multiple distribution forms and the permission for some people to enjoy prosperity first. With the establishment of these theoretical regulations, the following two effects will proceed to appear.

First, in order to mobilize all factors to invest in the process of developing productivity, and to fully mobilize a vitality in the various ways of creating wealth, it is necessary to allow capital, technology, management, and other production factors to participate in income distribution according to their contributions. It is also necessary to allow people to attain not only the income from their labor, but also income from their properties and operations in order to achieve early prosperity.

Second, it is necessary to maintain fairness and justice in income distribution in order to accord with the principles of socialism. First, equal rights to income distribution must be guaranteed. It is necessary to prevent deals that exchange power for money or influence peddling, as well as to regulate profits from monopolies. Furthermore, a proper balance should be maintained between efficiency and social equity when it comes to both primary distribution and redistribution, particularly when it comes to equity in redistribution. Finally, those who have enjoyed early prosperity should be encouraged and guided to help those who have lagged behind so as to gradually achieve common prosperity.

After the 40 years of reform and opening up, China has accomplished the aforementioned three aspects of the economic system at the primary stage of socialism. This is the basic socialist economic system with Chinese characteristics. It both upholds the basic principles of scientific socialism and endows it with distinctive Chinese characteristics, reflecting the combination of basic principles of Marxism and Sinicization Marxism. What's more, it has demonstrated, and continues to prove, its advantages in promoting the development of productivity and the improvement of people's living standard.

5.3 The Construction of the Socialist Economic System with Chinese Characteristics

The goal of economic transitions is not just to break away from old institutions, but more importantly to construct new systems. The theoretical practice of the socialist economic system with Chinese characteristics also needs to be constructed. Deregulating the market is an indispensable process to develop diverse forms of ownership and transform from a planned to a market economy. However, the single strategy of deregulation is not enough to construct a socialist market economy or a socialist system with Chinese characteristics. Constructing the corresponding institutional systems is indispensable to realizing this economic transition.

5.3.1. *The construction of enterprise system*

The transformation of the enterprise system involves the construction of the micro-foundations of the socialist systems with Chinese characteristics. Now that we have confirmed that the shareholding system can become a major form of public ownership (be it in the reform of state-owned enterprises or the development of private enterprises) the basic direction for transforming the enterprise system is to establish a modern corporate system. Accordingly, the transformation of enterprise institutions can be divided into three categories. The first is the transformation of the system of property rights, i.e., the construction of a modern system of property rights. It features "clearly-designated ownership, well-defined rights and obligations, strictly-implemented protection, and smoothly-flowing circulation" based on the diversification of the corporate equity structure. The second is the transformation of the corporate governance structure. In modern corporations, the property rights of investors and of legal persons are separated. Hence, the core issue in the corporate system is the corporate governance of legal persons. These governance structures involve the relationships between enterprises and the government, between enterprise shareholders, between shareholders and operators, and between operators and employees, and so on. When establishing a set of effective institutional and contractual arrangements, corporate governance structures must be improved to achieve the investors' targets. More specifically, that would refer to maintaining and increasing the value of assets, especially to improve the mechanisms of supervision and motivations of operators. Third, it is imperative to strengthen the incentives and restraints on entrepreneurs, prompting the operators to be entrepreneurs institutionally.

For those enterprises that may struggle with low efficiency or poor overall quality, it may be impossible for all of them to emerge from difficult situations just by transforming their enterprise systems. Therefore, the transformation of enterprise systems must follow the rule of the survival of the fittest, thereby necessitating corporate reorganization. This may become a quick and efficient path for the transformation of the enterprise system. It can be achieved through the competitive merging of enterprises, the acquisition of weak ones, or through mutual mergers and acquisitions between enterprises of different ownership types. All these processes will involve the flow of property rights between different enterprises. Such corporate reorganizations can effectively solve the problem of the diversification of equity required by the corporate system, and may also improve the overall efficiency of the enterprises under this kind of economic transformation.

5.3.2. *The construction of a market system*

China may be a latecomer to the development of a market economy, but its starting point is actually quite high. That is to say, China should be a modern market economy that cooperates with socialism. In order to meet the standards of a modern market economy, the market system must be established with a consideration of the following three aspects.

The first is the establishment of a modern market. The modern sense of the word market is not merely a place for exchange, but more importantly it is a mechanism for connecting exchanges and making deals. Therefore, the key to market construction is strengthening its connections. That act may include training and guiding its mainstay, building a network for supply, production, and sales, and improving the means of disseminating market information. After decades of construction and development, the previous planned channels have already reached an advanced level and cannot be replaced by low-level markets. According to the standards of the modern market, it is imperative to focus on constructing various modernized wholesale, specialized, and futures markets, and establishing networks that make use of modern scientific methods. The more important moments in the transformation from a planned to a market economy is when the production factors gain entry to the market as well as when a sophisticated market system is formed. All of the production factors have to be fully involved in the market. Only when various factors enter the market system can the practical market economy be secured. Therefore, at the present stage, there is an urgent need for well-functioning capital and labor markets.

The second is the establishment of a sound market mechanism. The market's effective regulation of the basic allocation of resources depends on the efficiency of market mechanisms. Specifically, the linkages and movements of factors such as the market, competition, price, supply, and demand must accord with the law of value. In view of the institutional barriers that arise from the operation of various market factors, China needs to build a market mechanism that includes the following three aspects. First, the pricing mechanisms established by the government should be completely transformed into market-based pricing mechanisms. This will allow prices to follow the market and eliminate price rigidity. Second, restrictions on company budgets should be further imposed, forcing enterprises that are dependent on the government to rely on the market instead. Finally, it is necessary to break up monopolies and end government protection in order to intensify competition. Under a unified state policy, all enterprises will have to compete for profits solely based on their own strengths.

The third is to establish market norms. The free competition and independent management required by a market economy are by no means disordered or random. It is only when competitors abide by certain norms that the market economy can operate with order and efficiency. Establishing market norms mainly includes the following three principles. First, pricing norms should be established so that, after deregulation, the market determines prices. It is necessary to restrict monopolies, dumping, and profiteering so as to prevent any drastic price fluctuations. In addition, an open and competitive market must establish norms for competition, such as those involving the entry to, competition within, and withdrawal from the market. Meanwhile, rigid rules for market competition must be made to ensure it is fair and just to increase transparency. Finally, strict rules must be established in speculative markets. Such regulations must apply to markets involving risky and speculative securities, futures, foreign exchange, and real estate in order to secure the investors' legal rights and interests. These indispensable rules for all kinds of markets concern self-discipline, the unification of market laws and regulations, well-functioning law-enforcement systems, and norms for regulating market intermediaries.

5.3.3. *The construction of macro control mechanism*

After the transition to a market economy, the construction of macro control mechanisms clarifies the demarcation between the role of the government and that of the market. However, it also achieves a transformation in the macro control mechanisms as well as a turn from direct to indirect control in the three following ways. First, the object of macro control has shifted from the direct management of enterprises into market adjustments. Even for products in need of the state's direct control, the government no longer directly controls them through mandatory plans, but rather acts as a market participant, ordering and purchasing goods. Second, the content of macro control has changed from the direct pricing mechanism to the regulation of overall price level in order to maintain the order of competition. Third, the means of macro control have been improved from the past method of directly issuing quantitative plans and quotas to the current method of using policies and norms as constraints to make adjustment. These policies may include government regulations for the market as well as the fiscal and monetary policies that compose a total equilibrium of macroeconomics. The financial adjustment mechanism is an important macro control mechanism that should also be adapted to the market economy. China has set up a central banking system and a corresponding monetary-adjustment system based on the establishment of commercial banks and the commercialization of state-owned specialized banks. In addition, it has also founded various financial agencies such as the China Banking Regulatory Commission, the China Securities Regulatory Commission, and the China Insurance Regulatory Commission to supervise their financial activities.

Government transformations are of vital importance to the transformation of macro control mechanisms. It is widely believed that in a market economy, a "strong" market should be supported by a "weak" government so as to fully engage the market's function. However, China's practices of reform and development have resulted in a successful coordination between a "strong" market and a "strong" government as long as the two play their roles on different operational levels. In the past, the government focused mainly on economic construction, thereby producing conflicts between the role of the government and that of the market. Currently, government reform is essentially oriented to reducing its influence in economic construction and administrative intervention, gradually narrowing the focus of government at all levels to "economic adjustment, market supervision, social management, and public service". Correspondingly, we may observe two factors in the government transition. One is the financial transformation into a public financial system. The other is the transition toward a law-based government, i.e., the idea that governance should be secured primarily with the rule of law rather than with policies. These transitions are currently in progress in China and have achieved salient results.

To sum up, China has made substantial achievements over the past four decades of reform and opening up. China's economic transformation has demonstrated: (1) the scientific proposition of socialism with Chinese characteristics is based upon the national conditions at the primary stage of socialism; (2) the theory of socialism with Chinese characteristics has been established and enriched in the process of reform and opening up; (3) the feasibility of this theory has stood up to practical tests. Today, in commemoration of the 40th anniversary of China's reform and opening up, the Chinese should be even more determined to hold high the banner of socialism with Chinese characteristics aloft and to elevate the great cause of reform and opening up.

Bibliography

习近平:《关于中国特色社会主义理论体系的几点学习体会和认识》, 载于《求是》2008 年第 7 期. Xi Jinping. On some points of understanding and realization of studying the theoretical system of socialism with Chinese characteristics. *Qiushi* 7: 3–16, 2008.

洪银兴:《转型经济学》, 高等教育出版社 2008 版. Hong Yinxing. *Transition Economics*. Beijing: Higher Education Press, 2008.

Chapter 6

Deepening the Reform Comprehensively in the New Era

Over 40 years have passed since China's reform initiative was introduced in 1978 at the Third Plenary Session of the 11th Central Committee of the Communist Party of China (CPC). As a result, the subsequent economic progress enabled China to join the ranks of the middle-income countries. At this new historical point, General Secretary Xi Jinping developed a strategic plan to deepen reforms in all areas. To comprehend Xi Jinping deepening the reforms, we must first develop a basic understanding of the strategy of this reform within the overall and historical context. Xi Jinping deepening of comprehensive reform not only stays consistent with the reform in the past but also address new issues. It is also necessary to define the correct position for the myriad of reforms involved within the overall framework of deepening comprehensive reform. Only in this way can China promote its reform in the new era to a new, higher level.

6.1 New Development Tasks in the New Era

China's reform has achieved clear economic results in the past four decades. At this new historical turning point, the main task of development is no longer the pure pursuit of GDP growth, a development need at the low-income stage, but the aspiration for economic and social development in all areas to become a high-income country. At this new stage, China still counts on the reform to promote its development, but the content and the impetus are completely different from the past. Unlike the previous 40 years, the goal of the current reform has changed from overcoming structural barriers for development at the low-income stage to resolving emerging conflicts inside the system during development at the middle-income stage. The first round of reform focused on the solution of low efficiency, while the present round highlights efficiency and social fairness at the same time. The first round aimed at increasing competitiveness, while now both competitiveness and cohesiveness are emphasized. The first round was prominently market-oriented, but this round intends to let the government play its functions better, based on marketization. The first round underscored the efficiency of businesses, while the present one pays more attention to government efficiency. All these come down to the issue of national governance system and capacity, which is to say "to improve and develop the system of socialism with Chinese characteristics" and to "promote the modernization of the national governance system and capacity" at the same time. The modernization of the national governance system means to adapt to the change of times in both ways: On the one hand, it is necessary to reform the mechanisms and institutions, laws and regulations that fail to meet the requirements of practice; on other hand, the new ones need to be constantly constructed to create more scientific and complete systems in all areas and ensure the governance of issues about the party, the nation and the society in a systematic way by adopting due standards and procedures. The new goal of promoting the modernization of the national governance system and capacity should go hand in hand with the already promoted goal of improving socialism with Chinese characteristics. Together, they form the general direction of reform in the new era.

6.1.1. *Using reform to support economic development in the "new normal" phase*

With an average growth rate of nearly 10%, China's economy developed rapidly in general in the 40 years after the reform and opening up. Besides, in terms of the economy's impetus, it is the supply factors that have strongly boosted the economy. For example, demographic dividends have led to high savings and big investment; resources and environment were in loose supply; rural reform unleashed a lot of surplus labor, making it possible to actualize growth at low costs. After 40 years of rapid growth, along with the obvious increase of economic base to the second total GDP in the world, the supply-side impetus that has boosted the economy in the past is declining. Such is mainly reflected in the following four aspects: First, the tightening supply of resources and the environment turns hard to bear the load of massive economic growth. Second, since China is entering an aging society, demographic dividends are fading away. Third, the "Lewis turning point" for agricultural labor transfer is coming, during which the urban labor shortage and higher labor cost result in an increase in the cost of economic growth. Fourth, the improvement of residential living standards has gone beyond the stage of meeting the basic needs and has entered or is entering the stage of moderate prosperity. At this stage, the residents are concerned with education and health care and become aware of safeguarding their civil rights. They no longer tolerate the old model of economic development, which blindly pursued the growth of GDP at the expense of environment and ecology. Given the above background, China is leaving the "old normal" phase with a high speed of growth and entering the "new normal" phase with the medium-high speed of growth.

Faced with the "new normal" phase with the medium-high speed of growth, China needs to think about its new strategy. First, a medium-high speed of growth is not naturally obtained but requires hard work. When the impetus on the supply side is declining, it is necessary to seek and form new impetus as soon as possible to realize long-term, sustainable growth at a medium-high speed. Second, the medium-high speed of growth asks for improving the quality of development in terms of sustainability instead of lowering the standards of development. This involves a transformation from the old model of economic development at the low-income stage to a new one for the middle-income stage. The "new normal" phase with the medium-high speed of growth forces us to change the developmental strategy to offer space for accelerating the transformation of economic development model, especially in the following two aspects.

On one hand, the industrial structure needs accelerated transformation and upgrading. China is still using an economic structure at the low-income stage. Its characteristics include: First, the proportion of manufacturing, especially traditional manufacturing, in the current industrial structure is too high, while that of service industry, especially modern service industry, is too low, and often in manufacturing, high outputs bring low additional values. Second, in the technical structure, technologies that cause high consumption and high pollution are in the majority, resulting in the unsustainable resource supply, and the creation of large production overcapacity in the pursuit of high-speed growth. The industrial structure of this kind fails to fit in with the "new normal" phase with the medium-high speed of growth, so it is necessary to transform and upgrade it to promote the industries toward the medium-high end. To realize this, the following four aspects should be considered. First, increase the proportion of the service industry, the modern service industry in particular, and promote the structure of the tertiary industry to the medium-high end. Second, promote the industries measured by scientific and technological content toward the medium-high end, including strategic emerging industries. Third, promote the "made-in-China" part of high-tech products up to the medium-high end of the global value chain to change the situation of high outputs but low additional values. Fourth, adopt new technologies in all industries, such as information technology, Internet Plus, Intelligence Plus, and green technology, etc. An industrial structure up to the medium-high end requires transformation and upgrading based on industrial, scientific, and technological innovations. In short, reform is needed to break with the rigidity of low-end industrial structure, and market selection based on competition should be strengthened. Relevant reform measures need to address local governments' protection of excess capacity and pollution capacity, and resolve redundant construction and investment that lead to the early death of emerging industries.

On the other hand, the strategy of innovation-driven development should be implemented. Faced with the limitations caused by the unsustainable supply of resources and the environment, China's economic growth needs to change from being driven by the consumption of material resources to being driven by innovation. As the world's second largest economy now, China is capable and desperately in need of joining the developed countries at the same starting line, aiming at proceeding to the commanding height in the fields of world's technology and industry, and replacing comparative advantage with competitive advantage supported by innovation in global labor division. As for the innovation path, imitation and introduction should be replaced by independent innovation. This involves research, development, and use of green technologies as well as energy conservation and emission reduction to realize sustainable development; and the innovation of strategic emerging industry to increase additional values and strengthen China's overall competitiveness. Innovation-driven development highlights the transformation from new scientific discoveries to new technologies. It requires an emphasis on industrialized innovation, the collaboration through the joint efforts of enterprises, universities, and research institutes, the contribution of businesses as the real players, and public participation in innovation and entrepreneurship. The innovation-driven development needs to set up an incentive system to encourage innovation. As General Secretary Xi Jinping said, "if innovation is the new engine for China's development, reform is the indispensable igniter". The essence of reform is to systematically enable innovation to play its role as the driving force and start the innovation engine at full speed. By promoting the transformation and upgrading of traditional industries, it aims to form new growth points and driving forces as soon as possible.

6.1.2. *Using reform to go beyond the "middle-income trap"*

Globally, quite a few developing countries have fallen into the "middle-income trap" since their entry into the middle-income stage. This should be taken as a warning for China.

As the World Bank explains in *East Asian Visions: Perspectives on Economic Development* (2006), the so-called "middle-income trap" refers to what had happened to some emerging markets that already made their way into the middle-income countries in the 1970s but was still struggling at the stage of $3,000–5,000 of GDP per capita, unable to make a breakthrough to $10,000 or see the impetus and hope for any growth till 2006. The reason is that as economic development reaches this stage, the original growth mechanism and developmental model cannot effectively respond to systematic risks caused by the outbreak of conflicts accumulated in the past rapid development during a relatively long period. Strong fluctuation and stagnation may easily occur in those middle-income countries, leading to a long-time stay at the middle-income stage and little chance to grow into high-income countries.

China also confronts the threat of the "middle-income trap" after reaching the middle-income stage. This is reflected in the following three aspects.

First, the income gap is too large. China's reform in the past 40 years began with the cancelation of the "iron rice bowl" (permanent employment) and the "mess together" (indiscriminate egalitarianism) distribution system. The implementation of the policy of allowing some people to get rich first has achieved obvious effects in encouraging the input of key elements such as capital, technology, and management, and in increasing the labor efficiency. Nevertheless, it has also dramatically widened the income gap. According to the reports of the National Bureau of Statistics of China, the Gini coefficients of 2012 and 2013 were 0.474 and 0.473 respectively, close to or even higher than those of some developed countries though China's GDP per capita is far lower than theirs. The current income gap exists between the urban and rural areas, different regional areas, and different professions and different classes. If the growing income gap is not reversed in time, it will harm the efficiency and influence social stability by causing the polarization of wealth.

Second, corruption cases happen frequently. Recent years have witnessed the exposure of many striking corruption cases. Corruption can be attributed to economic reality. When the power of the government is too strong, especially in resource allocation, there is a much higher chance for power rent-seeking. Meanwhile, the rule of law is not sound and the government action lacks restraints, so the corruption of officials is unavoidable. In particular, the collusion between officials and businessmen makes the situation worse. Undoubtedly corruption will devastate the credibility of the government, costing it the leadership in guiding the public to overcome the "middle-income trap".

Third, environmental and ecological conditions are getting worse. The "forging ahead" strategy of going all out and going fast at the low-income stage unavoidably leads to a predatory mode of development. Environmental pollution culminates at the point when economic development reaches the middle-income stage. When people are enjoying the results of economic development, they also must pay for environmental damages, such as resource depletion, global warming, smog, hazardous chemicals in food, and so on, all of which threaten human existence critically. Meanwhile, as their basic living needs are met, people grow more concerned with environmental and health issues. Environment and ecology become two major facets of the right protection. The overcoming of the "middle-income trap" requires not only a change in developmental mode and the use of technologies for green development but also the governance of damaged environment and ecology in the past development.

Threats caused by the above three aspects of the "middle-income trap" give rise to the mission of using development to overcome the trap. Since all these threats are rooted in the system, the overcoming of the "middle-income trap" not only needs development but also structural reform to support the transformation of developmental mode.

6.1.3. *Using reform to get rid of the urban–rural dual structure*

The urban–rural dual structure is the sign of the low-income country. The developmental task at the middle-income stage is to enter the high-income stage by getting rid of this dual structure. This is also part of modernization for developing countries. The path of socialism with Chinese characteristics includes the path of modernization that aims at integrating the development of industrialization, IT application, urbanization, and agricultural modernization. However, real modernization is always led by industrialization, so it is unavoidable that agricultural modernization falls behind the process of industrialization. In the course of history, industrialization may concede the development of agriculture, rural areas, and farmers, but modernization based on industrialization should never do so. As General Secretary Xi Jinping said, even though the ratio of urbanization reaches over 70%, there are still 400–500 million people in rural areas, so the rural areas should never become bleak or left-behind places or hometowns in memory. Agricultural modernization and the construction of new rural areas should go hand in hand with urbanization so that they can reinforce each other.

According to the Cannikin Law, the overall level of modernization is determined by weaknesses in the end. As for the integration of the development of industrialization, IT application, urbanization and agricultural modernization, the development of agriculture, rural areas and farmers are the weaknesses. Therefore, the core issue of modernization is to get rid of any dual structure, including the urban–rural dual structure and industrial–agricultural dual structure, and to foster the growth of the unitary modern economy in agriculture and rural areas. At a new historic starting point, the modernization of agriculture, rural areas, and farmers should be promoted with agriculture, rural areas, and farmers as direct targets of development. As China is about to build a moderately prosperous society in all respects and start working on the basic realization of modernization, it is necessary to make up for the weakness.

A strong China must have good agriculture, so the realization of agricultural modernization is essential. Related institutional arrangements include the following three major aspects.

First, the cultivation of agricultural businesses. The most important thing in innovating structural systems for agriculture is to nurture new types of agricultural businesses on the basis of the existing household contract management and through land circulation and agricultural labor division. Such new-type businesses include large and specialized agricultural family operations, family farms, agricultural operatives, and agricultural enterprises, etc.

Second, turning farmers into market participants. The circulation mechanism for agricultural products needs reforming to lower the transaction cost of agricultural products. Since the reform of the contract responsibility system has been carried out in rural areas, farmer cooperative organizations are no longer producer cooperatives in the past but cooperative organizations that provide farmers with circulation and financing services, such as credit cooperatives and circulation cooperatives.

Third, the reform of the rural land system to ensure farmers' assets income. Full compensation should be guaranteed for the flow, transfer, and expropriation of land and house properties. Farmers should be encouraged to use commercialized assets to absorb modern production elements into agriculture, such as gaining assets income via land transaction and land pooling.

The essence of urbanization is the transformation of farmers to urban citizens, but it is mainly hindered by the urban–rural dual structure. On one hand, the development of the market economy in rural areas is far lower than that in urban areas. The proportions of the natural and semi-natural economies are still relatively large. Markets for all kinds of production factors are concentrated in urban areas rather than rural areas, as farmers are unlikely to enter these markets as equal participants. On the other hand, the long-existing household registration system that features rural–urban segmentation divides residents into urban and rural residents or urban and rural residences. Rural residents with rural household residences are usually considered inferior. Therefore, to overcome the gap between urban and rural areas, it is a basic initiative to promote urban–rural integration in the economic system and replace the urban–rural dual structure. To realize it, the first thing is to introduce the standards of marketization in urban areas to rural areas. This includes the elimination of various structural and policy-related obstacles to the free flow of factors between urban and rural areas, and the realization of equal pay for equal work, the equal price for equal land, and equal market and price for the same products in urban and rural areas. Second, the household registration system that features rural–urban segmentation should be canceled to allow free residence and flow between urban and rural areas. Whether a farmer can live in the city or an urban employee in the countryside depends entirely upon their own choices. All kinds of discriminatory policies should be canceled. The civil rights for farmers who have migrated to cities should be protected so that they can enjoy the same policy treatment and opportunities like urban residents. Third, basic public services of high quality need to be introduced in rural areas to build happy homes for them. They should be able to enjoy all kinds of civil rights without moving into cities, and with a lifestyle that is basically the same as that of urban residents.

6.2 Economic Structural Reforming Being Still the Focus of Deepening Reform Comprehensively

Though economic structural reform has been carried out for over 40 years, it remains the focus in the new era. The necessity lies in the fact that economic construction is still the central task of the party, and the major developmental obstacle is still largely caused by inadequate economic structural reform. The range of economic structural reform is very wide. Its foremost guiding importance in taking comprehensive measures to continue the reform is mainly reflected in the following three aspects.

6.2.1. *The decisive role of the market in resource allocation*

The Third Plenary Session of the 18th Central Committee of the CPC revised the market role from resource allocation to decision making. By highlighting the autonomy of the market, we return to the original definition of the market economy. The exercise of such autonomy includes not only making a decision on the direction of resource allocation by the market itself but also independently forming the signal of market regulation, i.e., price, in the market without any improper government interference.

The identification of the decisive role of the market in resource allocation means China's economic structural reform and marketization have taken a new step. The major orientation of reform is to drastically reduce the government's direct allocation of resources and encourage the maximization of effectiveness and optimization of efficiency through resource allocation according to market rules, market prices, and market competitions. The old definition about the basic role of the market in resource allocation involves acts of regulation at two different levels, i.e., national regulation of market and market regulation of resource allocation. However, the current statement of the "decisive role" of the market in resource allocation means there is no such a thing as two-level regulation anymore, and the market no longer regulates resource allocation under the regulation of the government; instead, it decides autonomously how resources should be allocated. The key to the effectiveness of the market's allocation of resources is the soundness of the market system and mechanism, so reform in these two aspects is surely necessary.

To begin with, the market system needs to be improved. China stepped into planned economy directly from natural economy, and then again transformed from planned economy to market economy, so at current stage the problem of market disorder is quite serious: the seeking of economic benefits by illegitimate means widely exists; sector protectionism and regional protectionism are ubiquitous due to the disunity of market rules; inadequate market competition hinders the natural selection of the fittest and the structural adjustment, etc. Due to such a disorder, the market's allocation of resources is never effective. The above problems largely originate from governmental actions: First, institutions and policies breed unfair competition; second, regional inequality and local benefits give rise to local protectionism; third, the remains of planned economy cause administrative monopoly. To deal with market disorders caused by governmental reasons, the reform to regulate the order should start with the regulation of governmental actions, including the abolishment against local protectionism, administrative monopoly of market and regional blockages as well as the realization of the nationwide free flow of goods and production factors to allow different market entities to enter all kinds of market transactions equally.

In the second place, a sound system for the market economy needs to be constructed and cultivated. The aims are to build a unified and open market system with the orderly competition, to build a good business environment ruled by law, to build a unified urban–rural market, and to implement a unified market access system and market exit mechanism. For example, financial system reform, i.e., promoting the building of a financial market system on the basis of the existing construction of financial organizations and the regulatory reform of financial markets. This includes measures like liberalization of interest rates, marketization of exchange rates, and the founding of financial organizations by private enterprises.

6.2.2. *Speeding up the transformation of governmental functions and corresponding reform of the governmental system*

The development of the socialist market economy requires that the market and government play their respective roles. Since the market decides the allocation of resources, it needs to be strengthened. However, that does not necessarily mean to weaken the government. Development still needs a powerful promotion of government. This involves two critical aspects: First, the boundary between the government's role and the market's role should be made clear; second, governmental actions must obey certain regulations. The responsibilities and functions of government are to keep the macroeconomy stable, strengthen and optimize public services, ensure fair competition, improve market supervision, maintain market order, promote sustainable development, encourage common prosperity, and make up for market failures. Also, the government is expected to set up a market information disclosure system to provide market participants with information concerning production overcapacity, technical standards, and market needs to lower information costs in the whole society.

Beside market resources that have already entered market, resources of the whole society also include public resources. The decisive role of the market in resource allocation cannot be extended to the allocation of public resources, because they are resources without defined private ownership. The allocation of public resources cannot be decided by the market. Resource allocation must obey the principles of equity instead of the principles of efficiency used in the market's allocation of resources. As the government decides the allocation of public resources, it is also necessary to avoid government failures based on structural defects other than government inability. The structural quality is shown from the following three things. First, government regulations. Government regulations reject the functioning of the market. For example, natural monopoly industries, such as water, electricity, and gas, are generally subject to state pricing or price-fixing but too often the results turn out to be a fall in the output, leading to the failure of supply to meet the demand. As for unnatural monopoly industries, government regulations usually intend to protect or provide favorable conditions to some or a few industries. These often lead to a lack of effective competition, resulting in the rise of cost and price. Second, rent-seeking. It means taking advantage of the power to seek "rent". Rent-seeking often relates to the power of government. The government officials make the direct use of power, or the enterprises borrow governmental power. In either case, certain rights of monopoly are created together with corruption. Third, the bureaucracy. Bureaucracy causes expansion of the government. The self-propagation mechanism of governmental agencies leads to more officials in the society and correspondingly, a larger chance for the increase of officials' accumulated wealth.

Thus, the reform of government should highlight three things. First, the scope of government regulations needs to be reduced, and even within the regulatory scope, incentive mechanisms need to be established. State pricing is limited to resources of public character and public interest. Second, it is necessary to construct a limited government with limited power and size to ensure effectiveness, and this is the only possible way. The limited government can interfere with limited issues using limited methods. For all economic activities that can be adjusted effectively via a market mechanism, government approval should be canceled. The government no longer participates in the allocation of market resources and changes its role from the distributor of market resources to the supervisor. Thirdly, effective institutions need to be empowered to restrict governmental actions, including rent-seeking actions, regulatory actions, and bureaucratic actions. The corresponding institutional restraints limit government actions through government size, finance and revenues, and rule of law, which includes especially the requirement that the power of government should be restricted by the Constitution. According to that, the government needs to make lists of rights and responsibilities, and a negative list as well. Then all market participants will be allowed to enter the fields outside the lists equally within the law.

6.2.3. *Upholding and improving the basic economic system*

China's basic economic system in which public ownership plays the dominant role and diverse forms of ownership develop side by side is determined by its development at the primary stage of socialism. The fundamental task at this stage is to increase productive forces instead of eliminating private ownership. China needs to utilize diverse forms of ownership including private ownership to strengthen productive forces. The goal is to make sure that the vigor of labor, knowledge, technology, managerial expertise, and capital keeps bursting forth.

China's significant advancement in reforming the basic economic system in the past is the rapid growth of diverse forms of ownership. One typical example is the private economy. Theoretically identifying the dominant role of the public sector of the economy and public ownership marks a breakthrough in the theory of public ownership. In the old days, the dominant role of public ownership was recognized according to the number of public sector enterprises; however, the practice of reform broke through this definition. The public sector of the economy does not refer to public sector enterprises but involves government capital and collective capital. Correspondingly, the dominant role of public ownership is no longer embodied in the number of public sector enterprises but the amount of public capital. As long as public capital dominates total social capital, public ownership is playing the dominant role. For the mixed-ownership enterprises, the dominant role of public ownership can be embodied in the dominance or controlling ownership of public capital in equity structure. Thus, the reduced number of public sector enterprises does not necessarily mean the decline of such a dominant role. So far, the reform has made strategic "given-and-take" adjustments to the state sector of the economy. As public capital can quit former public sector enterprises (mainly in competitive fields) through institutional transformation, a new development path for the non-public sector of the economy has emerged.

The current basic economic system is an important pillar for the system of socialism with Chinese characteristics and the foundation of the socialist market economy structure. Public and non-public sectors of the economy are both important components of the socialist market economy and the important foundation for the development of China's economy and society. Therefore, the reform of basic economic system should follow the direction of the "two unswervingly". Firstly, to unswervingly consolidate and develop the public sector of the economy, which includes upholding the dominant role of public ownership and the dominance of the state sector, and meanwhile, constantly enhancing the vigor, control, and influence of the state sector. Secondly, to unswervingly encourage, support and guide the development of non-public sectors of the economy to arouse its vitality and creativity. According to these requirements, the task of upholding and improving the basic economic system at the preset stage mainly involves the following three aspects.

First of all, the vitality and creativity of the non-public sector of the economy should be further stimulated. China's private enterprises grow up relying upon the vitality released from institutional gaps. At this moment, their further development is hindered by a series of institutional obstacles. Firstly, the fields that private capital has entered lack space for further development since there are many restrictions. Secondly, though an equal market participant, private capital cannot obtain production factors equally but suffer from difficulties and high costs in financing. Thirdly, the majority of private capital is committed to the sector of the real economy, which is greatly challenged by a virtual economy that accumulates sudden wealth through speculation regardless of risks. Meanwhile, the operation of the real economy needs to hire many employees, so they are confronted with heavy burdens, great responsibilities, and big risks. If such institutional problems are not solved, immediate consequences will be the flight of capital and assets or even the private entrepreneurs after private capital is scaled up. To deal with the above institutional issues, deepening reform comprehensively at the current stage needs to encourage, support, and guide the development of non-public sectors of the economy to arouse its vitality and creativity. The measures include: First, improving the property rights system. For both public and non-public sectors of the economy, property rights are inviolable. The nation not only protects state assets but also property rights and legal interests in all sectors of the economy. Residents should be granted property rights, provided with more channels for private investment and encouraged to set up their businesses, so their income from property can grow in many ways. Intellectual properties and income need protection. Employees are allowed to hold shares while entrepreneurs are encouraged to not only hold shares but also gain shares using technology investment. Famers can earn income from the land through land circulation. Second, implementing a unitary market access system based on a negative list. Private enterprises can enter all the fields outside the negative list. Unreasonable regulations in various forms against the non-public sector of the economy should be eliminated, so should hidden barriers of different kinds. Specific measures to permit the participation of non-public sector enterprises in franchising should be formulated. Non-public sector cultural enterprises are encouraged to grow by lowering the threshold for social capital. Social capital is allowed to take part in investing and operating urban infrastructure facilities using franchising and others. Urban public services or even monopoly industries can be run with private enterprises involved. Third, insisting on equal rights, equal opportunities, and equal access to rules. Speaking of policy treatment, ownership obstacles that hinder the access of private enterprises to market resources need to be removed. The nation should make sure that all sectors of the economy can use production factors equally within the law. They participate in open, fair, and just market competitions, receive legal protection equally, and operate under the same supervision according to the law.

Secondly, a mixed-ownership economy is an effective form through which China's basic economic system realizes itself. Such a kind of economy with cross-shareholding by and blending of state-owned capital, collective capital and non-public capital is an important way to materialize the basic economic system. It can improve the functions of state-owned capital, maintain and increase its value, and enhance its competitiveness. Given the purpose of maintaining the dominant role of public ownership under new circumstances, the development of a mixed-ownership economy is the most effective way and an inevitable choice to strengthen the vitality, control, and influence of the state sector of the economy. The identification of a mixed-ownership economy as an important form that a basic economic system should take to realize itself indicates the direction of deepening the reform of the basic economic system in all areas. Specifically speaking, the state sector and other ownership economies are given more chances to grow into a mixed-ownership economy. Non-state capital is allowed to take equity interests in projects invested by state-owned capital; mixed-ownership enterprises held by non-state capital are encouraged to grow; private enterprises are encouraged to take part in the reform and restructuring of state-owned enterprises as well as share and hold equity there; employees of mixed-ownership enterprises are allowed to hold equity so as to form the community of shared interests among capital owners and laborers. Non-public sector enterprises are encouraged to participate in the reform of state-owned enterprises. For sectors concerning the national lifeblood of the economy, the state sector needs to take control, not necessarily in the form of full ownership but also by holding the controlling stake while giving part of equity to the non-public sector. National monopoly industries, as well as infrastructure facilities and public utilities exclusively run by the nation, can all serve to promote market-based reform and absorb private and foreign capital. Also, assets securitization and listing for the public sector and non-public sector enterprises are important ways to develop mixed-ownership economy.

Thirdly, reform of state-owned enterprises and improvement of the management system of state-owned assets. In the past, reform of state-owned enterprises has long been a focus and has successively gone through several procedures including the strategic adjustment of the state sector, the restructuring of state-owned enterprises, the reform of public ownership form, and the transformation of the shareholding system. Now there are not many enterprises solely funded by the state. A majority of state-owned enterprises engaged in national welfare and people's livelihood have been transformed into state-holding enterprises. Thus, in general, state-owned enterprises have mixed with the market economy. Based on this, state-owned enterprises need to deepen reform in the following three major aspects. Firstly, the functions of state-owned enterprises should be identified to highlight their social responsibilities. State-owned capital should be invested more in key industries and fields concerning national security and the national lifeblood of the economy. It is expected to provide public services, develop important prospective and strategic industries, protect the ecological environment, support technological progress, and assure national security. The input of state-owned capital into non-profit enterprises should be increased so that it will make a greater contribution to the supply of public services. By doing so, state-owned enterprises no longer compete with private enterprises for interests but facilitate them in gaining profits. Secondly, the monopoly should be eliminated. In natural monopoly industries in which state-owned capital continues to hold controlling interests, reform should be carried out focusing on separation of government administration from enterprise management, separation of government administration from state assets management, franchise operation, and government oversight, separate network ownership from operation, and deregulate control over competitive businesses in light of the conditions of different industries. Thirdly, a modern corporate system should be established, which involves reforms concerning the construction of a modern property-rights system, the corporate governance structure, and a system of professional managers.

Having clearly defined the state sector of the economy as state-owned capital, people are getting more and more concerned with the reform of state-owned capital. There has been a process for China to reform its management of the state sector. In the beginning, state-owned enterprises were managed directly by the nation. Since the separation of government administration from enterprise management, the focus of government management has shifted from the state sector to state-owned assets. Here assets include capital plus debt. The Third Plenary Session of the 18th Central Committee of the CPC made the decision on perfecting the system of state-owned assets management via reform. China should reinforce the supervision of state-owned assets with an emphasis on managing the capital, reform the authorized operation mechanism for state-owned capital, set up several state-owned capital operating companies, and support the transformation of qualified state-owned enterprises into state-owned capital investment companies. This means another step forward in reforming the state-owned capital. The supervision of state-owned capital is simply the management of capital operation, which involves issues like investment orientation of state-owned capital, equity management, capital interests, and capital circulation. Meanwhile, it is currently the operating companies and investment companies that manage the state-owned capital instead of administrative agencies. This embodies the separation of government administration from state assets management based on the separation of government administration from enterprise management.

6.3 Cultivation of Impetus for Deepening the Reform Comprehensively in the New Era

Reform, in a certain sense, means an adjustment to the relationship of economic interests. If reform is regarded as institutional change, then its path has two directions: One is to reform from bottom to top, or the interest-induced reform; the other is to reform from top to bottom, or the compulsory reform, which is the adjustment of economic interests.

The reform launched more than 40 years ago was carried out from bottom to top. It was promoted by the people and induced by interests. As for the problem of low efficiency caused by the distribution system of egalitarianism, the focus was to increase efficiency, so the priority was given to efficiency with due consideration to fairness. The policy was made to allow some regions and some people to get rich first. The effect of the reform on development is obvious. Although prosperity came at different times and in different degrees, people's living standards generally improved in comparison with the old days when the "mess together" distribution system of indiscriminate egalitarianism was implemented. To seek development, people might tolerate an increase in the income gap. This kind of reform was characteristically induced by interests, which had aroused high enthusiasm among people in participating in and supporting it.

Based on the bottom-up reform in the past, deepening reform comprehensively in the new era is, to some degree, motivated from top to bottom. Therefore, it is necessary to find new impetus. In the new era, the impetus still needs to be born within a sound socialist market economy structure. People's leading role in reform remains the same, meaning that their participation and support are indispensable. Their enthusiasm, initiative, and creativity should be fully aroused. To breed new impetus, it is necessary to take the improvement of people's well-being as an important way of mobilizing them. If people can share the fruits of reform and development, they are willing to join and support the reform. People gain visible benefits and acquire more "sense of gain" as is mentioned in the talk of General Secretary Xi Jinping. Such is the origin of reform impetus. People's sense of gain is mainly correlated with two things: the promotion of fairness and justice, and the improvement of people's livelihood.

6.3.1. *Promoting social fairness and justice*

Socialism is a belief in a fair and just society. The primary establishment of the socialist market economy means the formation of economic democracy. Groups of different economic interests naturally take the initiative to take part in politics to protect their special interests. This has laid the economic foundation for the expansion of socialist democracy, including having more citizens from different levels and fields participate in politics in an orderly way. Such will lead to the formation of a people's democracy that is wider, fuller, and more vibrant. The basic requirement for expanding socialist democracy is to promote social fairness and justice.

The promotion of social fairness and justice needs to deal with the relationship between fairness and efficiency, which requires distinguishing the field of resource allocation from the field of the income distribution. The efficiency impetus for deepening reform comprehensively in the new era should firstly be aroused in these two fields.

In the field of resource allocation, since resources are limited, their allocation must consider efficiency. Now it has been made clear that having the market decide the resource allocation means following the goal of efficiency. As resource allocation is decided by the fair market, the strong impetus is provided for increasing the efficiency and later promoting economic growth. Here the market is regarded as a born leveler. In this sense, its allocation of resources by the goal of efficiency can reflect fairness and justice. Certainly, an unavoidable result of resource allocation by the market is the increase in the gap between the poor and the rich. This needs to be solved through fair distribution within the field of the income distribution.

In the field of income distribution, fairness and efficiency form a unity of opposites. The degree of fairness can influence efficiency. As Joseph Eugene Stiglitz, winner of the Nobel Memorial Prize in Economic Sciences in 2001, once said, distribution and efficiency concerns are inseparable, "In some cases, high degrees of inequality may reduce economic efficiency, while in other cases some inequality may enhance economic efficiency".[1] Two issues of understanding are involved here. First, equal rights in distribution and efficiency do not contradict with each other. For example, distribution according to work reflects equal rights and support the improvement of working efficiency. Similarly, distribution according to factors not only embodies equal rights but also supports the increase of factor efficiency. Under this principle of fairness, gaps in distributed income between different people surely exist. However, without these gaps, efficiency does not exist, either. Fairness and justice originally contain these equal rights. Second, social unfairness caused by the increase of gaps through income distribution must have a limit, because when social unfairness reaches a certain degree, the resulting social conflicts will reduce efficiency, which further harms the healthy and sustainable development of the whole society and economy. If people cannot share the fruits of economic development fairly and reasonably, they will stop supporting reform and development. So, it is necessary to bring up at a proper moment the requirements for fair distribution, such as equal opportunities, equal rights, and fair rules. Accordingly, the principle of fairness in the field of income distribution asks for both equal rights in distribution and reasonable distribution results within the limit of social fairness. These two aspects together promote social fairness and justice.

What causes the growth of the income gap lies in the inequality of rights. The symptoms include power abuse for personal gain and income monopoly, which has become intolerable for people. Related reform needs to be advanced in two aspects. To deal with power abuse for personal gain, the abusers should be punished through anti-corruption initiatives, but more importantly, institutional leaks that have enabled the occurrence of power abuses should be closed, which means no chance for power to set and seek rent. Then, the monopoly should be abolished. Currently, high-income industries are largely monopoly industries, especially administrative monopoly industries. Their high incomes are not gained through hard

[1]Joseph E. Stiglitz. *Whither Socialism?* (Cambridge and London: The MIT Press, 1994), p. 47.

work but a monopoly of natural and administrative resources. Only if such incomes are nationalized and redistributed can true fairness and justice be achieved.

6.3.2. *Improving people's livelihood*

The improvement of people's livelihood shares the same purpose as socialist production. It is also an important way for people to share the fruits of reform and development. Forty years ago, when reform was an advanced concept, promises could be made that the pains of reform would be returned by the gains. Currently, each reform is supposed to yield benefits. When the top priority is given to the most direct and realistic interests that the people care about the most, strong impetus to reform will be aroused among them.

Income is the source of people's livelihood. The existing reform has generally increased people's income but the income gap as well. As economic development enters the middle-income stage, people become unwilling to tolerate the ever-increasing income gap and inequality of rights that causes the income gap. Moreover, with the deepening of reform, if there are significant differences in sharing the fruits of reform, people's enthusiasm will be reduced to some degree. Under this circumstance, to bridge the income gap is important to the establishment of an income distribution system that focuses on the improvement of people's livelihood. The target of reform is the old income distribution system formed in the past reform with the foremost emphasis on efficiency. Speaking of policies, allowing "some people to get rich first" is turned into having most people get rich. In the past, the idea of allowing "some people to get rich first" aimed at seeking impetus to GDP growth institutionally. Now the issue of having most people become more affluent is essentially about sharing the results of economic growth fairly and reasonably. This also conforms to Deng Xiaoping's strategic thinking. On his tour of the South in 1992, he pointed out that after coastal areas realized the moderate prosperity in all aspects, people who got rich first should help the rest to get rich to achieve common prosperity. Related reforming measures include protecting legitimate incomes, regulating excessively high incomes, redefining and clearing away hidden incomes, outlawing illegal incomes, increasing the incomes of low-income groups, and increasing the proportion of the middle-income group in society. The income gap between urban and rural areas, different regions, and different sectors needs to be narrowed with great efforts to form an olive-shaped distribution structure step by step.

The reform of the income distribution system that focuses on improving the people's livelihood mainly intends to increase the income of low-income groups. The major approach is to establish a mechanism that helps to raise the proportion of wages and salaries in primary distribution. The guiding principle in the previous period was seeking efficiency in primary distribution and fairness in redistribution, and the corresponding mechanism of distribution featured a reliance on market regulation in primary distribution and government regulation in redistribution. Now efficiency is not the only concern in primary distribution and fairness should be highlighted as well. When the input of capital, labor, management, and technology is taken into consideration in primary distribution, it is essential to set up a mechanism that enables labor reward to grow in step with the improvement of labor productivity. Meanwhile, market regulation is not enough, and other regulatory mechanisms are needed, such as legal protections that guard labor rights and mechanisms of collective wage bargaining inside enterprises. Only by doing so will the share of labor reward in income distribution grow.

Employment is at the root of people's livelihood. The increase in residents' income is closely related to employment, and the life of many families is affected by this issue. Many factors influence employment, including the oversupply of labor, the carrying capacity of industrial structure, macroeconomic conditions at different times, and knowledge and skill structure of labor force. Reform that increases efficiency saves labor, thus causing great pressure on employment. Currently, in terms of employment, China faces considerable pressure in general, along with the prominent problems of structural labor inadequacy and talent shortage. If the issue of employment is not handled properly, serious social problems may occur. The solution, after all, lies in development. The fundamental way is to create more jobs, improve job markets, and increase employment quality through development and reform. At the institutional level, on one hand, employment opportunities need to be developed extensively to bring more jobs via economic development under diverse forms of ownership and promotion of business startups. Channels for circulation of urban and rural labor should be opened through unitary development of urban and rural areas and removal of the urban–rural separation system. On the other hand, human capital investment needs to be made to provide good vocational training and a sound service system. The purpose is to promote the transformation and upgrading of enterprises and guide employees to adapt themselves to related changes to alleviate structural unemployment.

Education has a fundamental bearing on people's livelihood. Other issues in a similar connection with it include public services like basic healthcare. Currently, the most important thing is the promotion of equal access to basic public services in urban and rural areas and different regions. The principles of equal access to education and equal access to basic healthcare aim at helping middle-income and low-income groups afford schools and hospitals. These involve both sides of supply and demand. On the supply side, the construction of basic public service facilities should be strengthened. On the demand side, when it comes to the use of paid public services like education, basic healthcare, and public transport, both horizontal equity (people who use the services pay) and vertical equity (people with affordability pay) should be realized, allowing low-income groups to use basic public services. In the previous reform, the scope of marketization was set too large, including the sector of public services, which cannot be market-oriented. For example, hospitals, schools, and public transport were privatized. Some local governments surrendered their function of providing public services. Now it's time for these public services to return to the takeover of government (private schools, hospitals, and transport entities as complements not excluded) so that low-income groups can also go to school, receive medical treatment, and take buses.

Social security provides reliance for people's livelihood. A social security system that is led by the government and covers both urban and rural residents should be improved to include the basic old-age insurance, health-care insurance systems, social assistance systems for low-income groups, and basic housing insurance. The leading role of the government in constructing a social security system should be made clear.

6.4 Political Courage and Wisdom as Necessities for Deepening Reform Comprehensively

Big countries like China are not allowed to make any subversive mistakes concerning fundamental issues during the reform, or the damage will be irreversible and irreparable. Fundamental issues here refer to the adherence to the correct direction of reform and the advancement of reform along the correct way. China's reform was launched 40 years ago and there was little experience to follow. The implementation was restrained by traditional theories, established bad habits and attitudes, and old systems. Under such circumstances, reform could emphasize nothing but emancipating the mind and respecting the people's pioneering initiative to make a way out. The major mode of reform was "put destruction first", meaning the abolishment of the old institutional structure that already held back the growth of productive forces. Such is the circumstance relatable to cross the river by feeling the stones.

After over 40 years of market-oriented reform, the direction is becoming clearer. China will "reject both the old and rigid closed-door policy and any attempt to abandon socialism and take an erroneous path", but adhere to socialism with Chinese characteristics. In other words, China will reform its national governance system within the framework of the socialist system with Chinese characteristics and promote the modernization of the national governance system and capacity. A direction decides a pathway. As the direction of reform has been identified, China should and can start top-level planning, in an all-round way and with a holistic approach under the guiding principle of "cross the river by feeling the stones".

During 40 years of reform, China adopted neither the radical way recommended by "Washington Consensus" nor the Russian Big Bang reform mode known as "shock therapy" but an incremental approach to launch its reform. Intending to make breakthroughs at key points, it progressed from easy to difficult, from "outside the system" to "within the system", from increment reform to stock reform, and from the part to the whole. Specifically, structural reform began with the economic system; ownership reform prioritized the development of diverse forms of ownership outside the institution; reform of state-owned enterprises dealt with operational mechanisms first; reform of regulatory mechanism began with the establishment of dual-track system. The advantage of such a strategy lay in the promotion of development stability. The process of reform did not harm productive forces and ensured the steady growth of the economy.

Over 40 years have passed, and reforms on easy issues, the increment and key parts outside the system have been completed. The rest is all difficult and challenging but also decisive to the final success of China's reform. Now it is time to target difficult issues, the stock and those within the system in the overall manners. This means China's structural reform has entered a deep-water zone where it needs to navigate treacherous rapids and take on difficult challenges. Conflicts of interest are intricate and complex and formed link by link, so reform at this moment needs to focus on the following two aspects. First, it is necessary to have the determination to take on difficult tasks and navigate treacherous rapids and the political courage to cut the wrist like brave warriors. Deep-rooted problems lasting for many years should be addressed with concrete measures to ensure the continuance of reform and opening up. Second, a wise and discreet attitude is needed to maintain the overall, systematic, and comprehensive nature of reform, so it can gain support from the people. This is what General Secretary Xi Jinping said: "Reform and opening up is a systematic project, which should be pushed forward in an all-round way with all kinds of reforms well-coordinated".

The reform in the new era is required to be carried out in a more systematic, holistic, and coordinated way and target at more important issues. These are brought up according to the process and strategy of China's reform. It is necessary to grasp the inherent law of deepening reform comprehensively, especially the major relations in this cause including those between freeing our minds and seeking truth from facts, between advancing on the whole and making breakthrough at key points, between top-level design and wandering across the river by feeling for the stones, and between bold attitude and safe action.

The focus of reform in the past 40 years can be summarized with one word "breaking". As an old Chinese saying goes, "there is no making without breaking". Indeed, for many institutions, the making of new rules occurs at the moment when the old ones are being abolished. Nevertheless, this does not happen automatically but under construction. Deepening reform comprehensively in the new era needs to deal with certain old institutions that have been broken in the past market-oriented reform but has not yet yielded any new outcomes. Constructive requirements should be highlighted, including developing a set of institutions that are well-conceived, fully built, procedure-based, and efficiently functioning to ensure that institutions in all aspects are more mature and well-defined. In particular, at the current stage, the reform of government itself is crucial. Here "breaking" means canceling and delegating administrative items that require government review and approval. At the same time, "making" is indispensable, reflected in who takes over those delegated items and how the market, including market intermediary agencies, is matched with enterprises to run the items that have skipped over government review and approval. These are all questions that need coordinating and planning; otherwise, institutional chaos may occur to destroy normal economic order.

In the relationship between advancing on the whole and making breakthrough at key points, institutions are set link by link and mutually restrained. Existing reforms that have chosen to make a breakthrough at key points are easy to be carried in some areas but as they are going deep, they will fail to coordinate with the whole structure. The progressing economic reform is exactly the case. Conflicts of interest have emerged but the reform of the social system still falls behind, resulting in serious social conflicts. In particular, too much social attention is paid to economic interests while social values are absent. Under these circumstances, reform as a whole requires putting the reform of the social system and the reform of the cultural system on the agenda. Besides, the ownership reform has focused on making breakthroughs in the non-public sector of the economy outside the system. With no corresponding changes in the reform of the state sector, the benefits of the state sector continue to drop and, more importantly, will probably lose its dominant role. Therefore, deepening reform comprehensively needs to nicely deal with the relationship between advancing on the whole and making a breakthrough at key points. At the current stage, reform is more focused on advancing on the whole.

As for the systematic quality of reform, take the relationship between market and government, for example. Since China's reform of the economic system follows a market-oriented way, the relationship between the market and government remains a core issue. The Third Plenary Session of the 18th Central Committee of the CPC National Congress recognized the decisive role of the market in resource allocation, so obviously, the government's role in resource allocation will be weakened. But this is by no means to say that the government is not asked to better perform its role. From the viewpoint of system theory, reform cannot do one thing but neglect others; instead, it is supposed to advance in a coordinated way and with the collaboration of all aspects of the institution as a whole. The purpose of transforming government functions is not to cancel the government but to solve the problems of it doing either too much or too little to form a law-based and service-oriented government with power and efficiency. First of all, China is facing many intrinsic and complex problems other than growth at the current stage of development, such as those concerning fair distribution, innovation, environment, and public services.

Second, in the development of large countries including China, important issues related to development like the transformation of industrial structure must involve the government instead of its sole dependence on the market. Third, to give more space for the functioning of market, a reasonable range should be defined for macroeconomy. Correspondingly, the system of macro control needs to be improved. If it can do nothing within the reasonable range, then macroeconomy can slip out of the range, which will lead to a loss of macroeconomic control altogether with heavy costs. All these prove that in a new system allowing market to play the decisive role is inadequate and it is also necessary to involve government in a better way. With the two roles complementing each other to eliminate conflicts, coordination is thus realized.

The ultimate goal of whatever kind of reform is to help people live better lives. Reform of the economic system is, in fact, an adjustment to conflicts of interest, which appear intrinsic and complex during the process of reform. Some people gain benefits from reform while others may have losses. It is also possible that the welfare of some people may drop relatively. In the past, reform has been implemented to allow some people to get rich first to promote development. The results are quite obvious, but the hidden problem is that the excessive increase in the income gap is starting to affect efficiency. Deepening reform comprehensively at this stage needs to improve people's well-being, promote fairness and justice, help the majority of the people to get rich, and nicely deal with the relationship between making the pie bigger and splitting the pie properly among a large number of people. Meanwhile, reform of the income distribution system should shift its focus from efficiency first to fairness and strive to narrow the income gap between urban and rural areas, different regions, and different sectors. However, it involves a number of fields and groups, so the seesaw effect is likely to happen since one change makes all changes in this situation. This requires the reform of the income distribution system to be performed in a systematic way and via an integrated approach. China should pay strong attention to the adjustment to conflicts of interest caused by deepening reform comprehensively and make an overall review on change of interests before, in the middle of, and after the reform. Also, it should form a holistic view of interests in different areas and at different levels to facilitate the implementation of targeted guidance and targeted handling.

The economic system is composed of diverse factors, which can be divided into fast variables and slow variables according to their changing speed. The existing reform changes fast variables because slow variables do not take effect through a single action but require time for cultivation and growth. For example, enterprises transforming their shareholding system is a fast variable while setting up modern corporate system is a slow variable; letting the market decide resource allocation and canceling administrative review and approval are fast variables while improving market system is a slow variable; urbanizing and removing restrictions on urban–rural household registration are fast variables while turning farmers into urban residents is a slow variable. Also, the economic system is a fast variable, but the political system is a slow variable; constructing governance system is a fast variable but improving governance capacity is a slow variable. It can be said that fast and slow variables coexist in institutional reform of all areas. The effect of reform is identified exactly when slow variables are in place. Therefore, the systematic quality of reform lies in the well-coordinated relationship between fast and slow variables. When the reform of fast variables gets results, attention should be paid to the reform of slow variables to ensure the achievement of real, overall effects.

Finally, to conclude this chapter I would like to quote a speech from General Secretary Xi Jinping in May 2015 when he hosted the 12th meeting of the Central Leading Group for Comprehensively Deepening Reform: Leading officials should be trained and guided to consciously use the Four-Pronged Comprehensive Strategy to seek unity of thinking. A correct, holistic view of reform should be adopted to look at the changes in conflicts of interest. As long as they facilitate the overall reform, the cause of the Party and the country, and the formation of sound structures and mechanisms in given systems and areas, officials should consciously comply with the interests of the whole and serve the overall situation with the courage for self-targeted revolution and confront challenges to comprehensively deepen the reform in all areas with joint efforts.

Bibliography

中共中央文献研究室:《习近平关于全面深化改革论述摘编》, 中央文献出版社 2014 年版. CPC Party Literature Research Office. *Extracts from Xi Jinping's Speeches on Comprehensively Deepening the Reform*. Beijing: Central Party Literature Press, 2014.

《中共中央关于全面深化改革若干重大问题的决定》, 人民出版社 2013 年版. *Decision of the CCCPC on Some Major Issues Concerning Comprehensively Deepening the Reform*. Beijing: People's Publishing House, 2013.

吴敬琏:《直面大转型时代:吴敬琏谈全面深化改革》, 上海三联书店 2014 年版. Wu Jinglian. *Facing the Big Transformation: Wu Jinglian's Talks on Comprehensively: Deepening the Reform.* Beijing: SDX Joint Publishing Company, 2014.

洪银兴:《市场秩序和规范》, 格致出版社、上海三联书店、上海人民出版社 2015 年版. Hong Yinxing. *Market Order and Norms*. Shanghai: Truth & Wisdom Press, Shanghai: SDX Joint Publishing Company, Shanghai: Shanghai People's Publishing House, 2015.

Chapter 7

The Political Economy Will Progress along with the Times

Among all the economic disciplines, the field of political economy is the oldest. Because its theories and methods are still progressing with the times, the political economy continues to have vitality today. As a science, the political economy must maintain its distinct status while progressing along with the times.

7.1 The Modern Development of the Marxist Political Economy

In the mid-19th century, Marx and Engels fundamentally reformed the political economy and founded the Marxist political economy, representing the interests of the proletariat who entered the stage of history as an independent force at that time. Their major contributions include the following: first, they proposed for the first time that the research object of political economy was the relations of social production between the people; second, they proposed the theory of the dual nature of labor in producing commodities and established the scientific theory of labor value; third, they established the scientific theory of surplus value and discovered the general laws and historical trends of the accumulation of capital; fourth, they revealed that capitalism would inevitably be replaced by socialism and formulated some basic characteristics of the future socialist and communist society. In the late 19th and early 20th century, capitalism entered the stage of imperialism; Lenin then established the theory of imperialism that was based on an analysis of the basic economic characteristics of the stage, particularly monopolies. His theory provided the theoretical weapons for analyzing the characteristics of the capitalist economy in the monopoly stage.

The Soviet Union was the first socialist country in the world. Stalin summarized a series of laws of socialist construction in the initial practice of building socialism, thus giving the shape to *Economic Problems of Socialism in the USSR*. Based on this book, The Institute of Economics of the Soviet Academy of Sciences published *Political Economy Textbook* in the 1950s. The book concerned both the capitalist and socialist portions of the political economy, which focus on the capitalist and socialist relations of production, respectively. The socialist economic laws that the book expounds upon spread to various socialist countries for a period of time including China. However, the Soviet Union model, or the Stalinist model, of the socialist economic system that developed from the theories expounded upon in the book were both proven to be rigid and inefficient in practice.

The Party's first generation of central collective leadership, with Mao Zedong at the core, identified the shortcomings of the Stalinist model early in the practice of leading China's socialist construction. They then began to explore the socialist path that would be suited to the national conditions. Since 1978, China has embarked on the road of reform and opening up. This great practice greatly promoted the development of the socialist political economy.

The emergence and development of the political economy has embodied the trajectory of the political economy as it has progressed along with the times. From Marx to Lenin, the fundamental task of the political economy was overthrowing the old society. Starting with Stalin, the basic task of the political economy has been to build a new society. However, in the progression from Stalin to Mao Zedong, the fundamental idea of building the new society has been centered on class struggle. Accordingly, class analysis and struggle have been taken as key links in the political economy. Since China's reform and opening up, the fundamental idea of the Party's two generations of collective leadership directed toward building the new society has been economic construction. Correspondingly, the political economy takes increasing social wealth as both its point of departure and its destination, thus determining the distinction between the modern and traditional political economies.

The ability for the political economy to progress with the times is related to research conducted in different eras. In turn, the progression is related to the stages of development. Under the conditions of capitalism, Marx and Lenin logically deduced the future of socialism based on an analysis of the contradictions of capitalism. This inevitably included some guesswork. The Stalinist model and its related political economy, on the other hand, went beyond reality and summarized the socialist economic relations into several dogmas. While these dogmas were put into practice, the model ultimately failed. A major theoretical breakthrough that marked the modern development of the political economy is the confirmation that the current stage of socialism is the primary stage. This stage began with the establishment of the socialist system and will end with socialism reaching the same or higher level of productive forces than capitalism does. This is a long-term historical process. Its significance lies in a shift of research focus from socialist economic relations to the socialist relations of production in the primary stage; the conclusion is that the fundamental task of socialism in the primary stage is not to eliminate private ownership but instead to develop productive forces. This conclusion was reached after an analysis of the contradictions between productive forces and the relations of production at this stage. Thus, there has been an establishment of the basic economic system of socialism in the primary stage, which suits the actual conditions.

Undoubtedly, the historical mission of the political economy is making socialism replace capitalism. The political economy in a capitalist society needs to reveal the basic contradictions of capitalism and seek its gravedigger. The political economy in the socialist society undoubtedly also needs to analyze capitalist economic relations. However, in addition to analyzing past capitalist relations, the political economy also needs to place increased focus on the forms of contemporary capitalism that coexist with socialism. The analysis of contemporary capitalism from the perspective of the political economy necessitates the adoption of a Marxist world outlook and methodology in order to reveal new contradictions. However, we must be aware of the mutual influence and competition between the two coexisting societies. If the revolution of the proletariat was relied on in Marx's time to replace capitalism, we should hope today that socialism could reach a higher level of productive forces than capitalism in order to realize this act of replacement. The present problem is precisely the fact that existing socialist countries were not formed on foundations of mature capitalism with developed productive forces. Therefore, while the systems of socialist countries may be advanced, their productive forces still are backward. The capitalist social system may be more backward than that of the socialist social system in theory, but its social productivity is more advanced in reality. The advanced social productivity is supported by systems including a mature market, modern enterprise system, effective macroeconomic regulation and control, well-developed financial system, and so on. Today's economic globalization includes the globalization of the market economy, as well as the globalization of modern economic organizations and the enterprise systems, which were originally established in capitalist countries and which are now related to advanced productive forces in society. Just as Marx and Lenin said that joint-stock ventures between companies and state monopolies were an entry point to socialism, these modern economic organizations and enterprise systems might be a step closer to socialism. It is for this reason that the analysis of capitalism from the perspective of the political economy does not exclude capitalism, apart from revealing its contradictions. There is no doubt that the purpose of studying capitalism is to develop the productive forces of the socialist countries. Therefore, while adhering to Marxism as its guiding principle, the modern political economy reflects two senses of the word "open". First, it should be open to practice. It should constantly study new practical problems, enrich the content of economics, and make theoretical generalizations based on new practices of contemporary capitalist and socialist economic development. Second, it should be open to Western economics to track the field's development and constantly absorb its latest scientific findings concerning the laws of social production and market economy. In order for the political economy to progress with the times, this ancient subject must be endowed with vitality so that it might explain new phenomena and problems at the present stage.

7.2 The Tasks of the Political Economy Will Progress with the Times

The basic framework of the Marxist political economy is analyzing the contradictory movements between productive forces and the relations of production. When the political economy takes capitalism as its research object, it analyzes such contradictions in order to reveal the hindering effect of the capitalist relations of production on the productive forces, seek out both the driving force and the gravedigger of such relations, and expound upon capitalism's inevitable replacement by socialism. When the political economy takes socialism as the object, it also needs to analyze these contradictory movements. However, the purpose in doing so is to seek methods to improve the socialist relations of production as well as to further liberate and develop the productive forces through the self-improvement and development of the socialist relations of production. In other words, when considering the research object, the task of the political economy is quite clear. It should be pointed out that the task of studying and teaching political economics under socialist conditions, whether the field analyzes capitalism or socialism, is to promote the development of society's productive forces. The political economy should study economic laws, the directions which advanced productive forces of society would take, and the adjustment of the relations of production to suit the development of the productive forces. This is the basic task of political economy.

Currently, the political economy is mainly criticized because lack of descriptions of economic phenomena means that it departs from reality. However, this view should be analyzed in more detail. The field of political economics is a science and its task is to explain, rather than describe, the world. To explain the world is to reveal the economic essence and the inherent inevitability behind economic phenomena. Revealing the essential connections among economic processes and the objective inevitability of their movements precisely means revealing the objective economic laws.

According to Marx's analysis, each economic movement has its own laws in every historical period. "One and the same phenomenon falls under quite different laws in consequence of the different general structure of the organisms, the variations of their individual organs, and the different conditions in which those organs function … With the varying degrees of development of production power, social conditions and the laws governing them vary too".[1] The scientific value of the research conducted from the perspective of the political economy is located in laying bare the unique laws that govern the origins, the existence, the development, and the disappearance of a given social entity as well as its substitution by another higher entity.

Economic laws are the inherent, essential, objective, and inevitable connections among economic phenomena and processes. Just like other

[1]Karl Marx. *Capital: A Critique of Political Economy.* Vol. 1 (London: Penguin Books, 1976), pp. 101–102.

natural laws, economic laws are objective and independent of human will. As Lenin stated, the economic formation of society is by no means "at the will of the authorities (or if you like, at the will of society and the government)" and emerges and changes causally. Its evolution was viewed as "a process of natural history", "governed by laws not only independent of human will, consciousness and intentions, but, rather, on the contrary, determining the will, consciousness and intentions of men".[2] It follows that people must act in accordance with economic laws. Economic behaviors as well as policies and decisions that are formulated by the state must meet the requirements of economic laws and conform to their development. This is the necessary underpinning that allows economic decisions, policies, and behaviors to achieve their expected effects. The practices of China's economic development have proven that when we act in accordance with economic laws, the economy develops. When we fail to act in accordance with economic laws and the will of the authorities, or when the subjective will that is divorced from the reality prevails, the economy will not grow. To the contrary, it will suffer serious losses and be punished by economic laws. This is true of countries as well as companies. This shows the importance of respecting objective economic laws and acting in accordance with them.

The premise of acting in accordance with economic laws is part of understanding their objectivity. We usually say that the people are not powerless when confronted with economic laws, meaning that people can understand them and then make use of them to serve the people. The task of the political economy is to reveal the objective existence of economic laws. The laws revealed by the political economy are people's understanding of the objective economic laws. They provide both the base and the methods for them to understand and solve problems. In a certain sense, the economic laws that people know and use are the economic laws that have been correctly revealed by the political economy.

Economic laws come into being and function under certain economic conditions. Such economic conditions include the levels of productive forces, relations of production, market conditions, and so on. When certain economic conditions do not exist, the relevant economic laws will disappear. There are three levels of economic laws that are defined by

[2]Vladimir Lenin. What the 'friends of the people' are and how they fight the social-democrats. *Collected Works*. 4th English edition (Moscow: Progress Publishers, 1972), p. 142, p. 166.

objective economic conditions the economic laws depend on. The first level consists of the economic laws that are shared by all social formations such as the law that the relations of production must suit the nature of the productive forces. The second level consists of the economic laws that are shared by several social formations. For example, the law of market economy that exists in several societies includes the law of value, the law of market competition, and other laws of market economy. The third level consists of the specific laws of a certain social formation, such as the law of surplus value, which works under capitalist conditions; the law of distribution according to work, which works under socialist conditions; and so on.

In reality, there are some economic laws that capitalism and socialism have in common. Capitalist society and socialist society are not only two societies that have appeared sequentially to each other; they have also coexisted and many of their economic organizations, modes, rules, and orders have tended to converge. Therefore, today's political economy must analyze the general principles of political economics including the economic laws that are common to all societies, especially the laws shared by both capitalism and socialism. In the particular analysis of the economic relations in socialism and capitalism, we should pay more attention to the specifics. When analyzing capitalism, we should focus on its modern characteristics, and when analyzing socialism, we should focus on the economic relations in the primary stage of socialism.

The task of the political economy when it comes to analyzing capitalism is to reveal the inherent contradictions of the capitalist economy as well as the historical inevitability that capitalism will be replaced by socialism. In this sense, the political economy provides the ideological weapons of class struggle. In accordance with this task, the study and teaching of political economics focus on the secrets of capitalist exploitation (revealed by the theory of surplus value), the historical trend that the proprietors will eventually be replaced (which is revealed by the theory of primitive accumulation of capital), the contradiction of reproduction in capitalist society (revealed by reproduction theory), excess capital, overproduction and the resulting cyclical crisis (revealed by the theory of the decline of the average rate of profit), the conflicts among different industrial capitalists (revealed by the theory of surplus value division), the analysis of the economic crisis under the condition of credit economy (described by the theory of the general process of capitalism), and so on. It should be pointed out that the contradictions inherent to capitalism that are revealed by traditional political economics have been eased in modern times. This is because capitalist countries have taken a series of measures to adjust the relations of production within the scope permitted by their system to ease the contradiction and avoid the intensification of social conflict. The political economy must face up to these new issues. If it does not, it will be difficult to explain why capitalism not only still exists, but is also still developing more than 100 years after Marx sounded the death knell of capitalism. The analysis of the capitalist economy from the perspective of progressing with the times necessitates the study of the new phenomena of contemporary capitalism, the revelation of its new laws, and the focus on new characteristics of capitalism under new conditions as well as its inherent contradictions.

In order to study modern capitalism, we must admit that several major scientific and technological revolutions have taken place in capitalist countries since the great crisis of the 1930s. Based on this fact, the modern enterprise system (characterized by the company system, mature capital market, modern banking system, and government intervention in the economy), scientific and technological innovation mechanisms, and others have become the new methods to promote the development of modern capitalism. These are also the major factors that have enabled the productive forces of modern capitalist countries to break through the shackles of the relations of production and further develop. When explaining these new phenomena, the present political economy should more seriously consider the fact that capitalism and socialism are two social systems coexisting in space. Therefore, the task of the economic analysis of modern capitalism can be divided into three parts. The first part is learning. With two coexisting economic systems, many economic activities and organizations are in the process of mutual learning and integration. For socialist countries, one form of learning is analyzing the economic forms and organizations in modern capitalist countries which are suited to advanced productive forces of society. This is pursued so that their productive forces can catch up with, and then surpass, those of the capitalist countries. The second part is competition. The coexistence of the two systems inevitably includes the competition between them. An analysis of the modern capitalist economy can provide counter-theories for the eventual victory of socialism over capitalism in economic competition. The third part is belief. In the modern stage of capitalism, it is difficult to explain the inevitable trend of its demise if we only rely on traditional political or economic theories. It is of great necessity to use the theories and methods that progress with the times to reveal new contradictions of capitalism so as to strengthen the belief that socialism will replace capitalism.

When it comes to analyzing socialism, although the task of political economy certainly includes strengthening of the belief that socialism will replace capitalism, it is not limited to this alone. In order to meet the needs of China's modernization and reform and opening up, the political economy should aim at reforming and improving the socialist economic system, promoting the development of advanced productive forces of society, and increasing national wealth. Accordingly, there should be two shifts to the conceptions of the research and teaching of political economics. The first shifts from class struggle to economic development. The political economy was once the weapon of class struggle in a confrontation with capitalist society and now it is the theoretical guidance of economic development in today's socialist society. The second shifts from taking the theories of political economy as dogmas to taking them as guides to action. When Marx criticized capitalism more than 100 years ago, he logically deduced certain characteristics of the socialist society. These should not be taken as dogmas for building socialism today, but instead as guides to action. We should not stick to some individual conclusions put forward by Marx at that time, but rather develop Marx's theory of socialism according to the practices of socialist social development.[3]

As it was representatively stated in *Capital*, the Marxist political economy takes capitalism as its research object. Some of its predictions and regulations concerning the socialist economic relations are also included in its analytical framework on capitalism. Today, an important and arduous task of the political economy is to clearly distinguish what parts of the Marxist political economy should be inherited and enriched according to the changed circumstances. The political economy should take the fundamental principles and methods of the Marxist political economy as its foundation, discard any unscientific understandings, and enrich and develop Marxism with theoretical innovations.

First, we need to reconsider the category of capital Marx uses in *Capital*. In the past, many textbooks stated that capital was a unique quality of capitalism. Using this logic, we should use other categories such as asset, money, and others instead of capital when analyzing the socialist

---

[3]Hong Yinxing. From critique to construction — On the shift in the idea of the researches on *capital*. *Journal of Nanjing University*, (4): 5–8, 1999.

economy. This view is limited. Capital, as a factor of production, is indispensable to any market economy. It also goes without saying that many connotations carried by the category of capital cannot be replaced with the words of "money" or "assets". For a long time, the low efficiency in the operation of China's state-owned assets has been related to actions that were not in accordance with the rules of capital operation. Undoubtedly, the concept of capital used under socialist conditions differs in its essence from the concept of capital under capitalist conditions in terms of the relations of production it reflects. There are no wage-labor relations in the denotations of capital used under socialist conditions.

Furthermore, Marx opposed certain categories and rules because they might produce the evil of capitalism. However, they do not have to be completely negated under socialist conditions. For example, competition and accumulation may cause polarization, but their capacity to promote economic and social development should also make them subject to approval. As another example, in the analysis of capitalism, personal property and private capital are both regarded to be tools of exploitation because they belong to the category of private economy and the proletariat is approved as the gravedigger of the society. However, in analyzing the socialist economy, we should not stick to this theory. As both the masters and builders of socialist countries, the proletariat is also able to become property owners. A judgment about whether one is politically advanced or backward should not be based on the criteria of whether one possesses personal property or in what amount.

Finally, some principles of the Marxist political economy require new developments. When Marx wrote *Capital* more than 100 years ago in a free capitalist society, the development of productive forces in the large-scale mechanized industry was still at a primary stage, the enterprise system was in the factory system stage, and the joint-stock economy was at the embryonic stage. More than 100 years later, major changes have taken place in the stage of capitalism, the level of the development of productive forces, and the enterprise system. Moreover, the development of socialist society is not the same as what Marx predicted at that time. For all of these reasons, the principles of the political economy should be required to develop along with current practices. For example, the theory of labor value is the theoretical cornerstone of the Marxist political economy. However, the economic conditions under which Marx founded the theory of labor value were quite different from those of the modern economy. In Marx's time, a decisive role in economic growth was played by labor, specifically workers' labor. However, in modern economic development, the effect of knowledge and technology on economic growth far exceeds that of labor. Accordingly, the content and scope of labor has also been further expanded; labor is not just provided by workers but also by technicians, administrators, service staff, and so on. Therefore, when analyzing the modern economy with the theory of labor value, we need to offer new explanations according to the changed situations. In regard to the current socialist economy, it is necessary to deepen the understandings of socialist social labor and the theory of labor value while taking into account the new reality.

7.3 The Methods by Which the Political Economy Will Progress with the Times

The methodologies of the political economy were established in *Capital*. As opposed to natural sciences, the field economics studies the actual social economy and has one important methodological feature: the economy cannot be tested in the laboratory, so it needs to seek scientific research methods. So far, there have been two main economic methods. One is the philosophical method and the other is the mathematical analytical method. The basic analytical method adopted by the Marxist political economy is the philosophical method, although it often uses the mathematical approach as well. Marx said: "In the analysis of economic forms neither microscopes nor chemical reagents are of assistance. The power of abstraction must replace both".[4] Marx explained his scientific method of abstraction in the preface to *Capital*: "The method of presentation must differ in form from that of inquiry. The latter has to appropriate the material in detail, to analyze its different forms of development and to track down their inner connection. Only after this work has been done can the real movement be appropriately presented".[5] From this quote, it can be seen that Marx's method of abstraction contains two interrelated processes of scientific thinking.

The first process transitions from concrete to abstract research. The procedure is as follows: analyze some pervasive and specific economic

[4]Karl Marx. *Capital: A Critique of Political Economy.* Vol. 1 (London: Penguin Books, 1976), p. 90.
[5]*Ibid.*, p. 106.

phenomena based on materialistic dialectics, seek the most fundamental and basic features among them while leaving aside secondary factors, explain economic categories and reveal economic laws while considering various forms of development and the inherent and inevitable internal connections among them. The whole process is similar to Marx's analysis of the capitalist economy. He resorted to abstraction when approaching various complicated capital formations and specific economic phenomena, abstracting basic economic categories such as commodity and use value, as well as abstract and concrete labor.

The second process transitions from abstract to concrete research. The procedure is as follows: take the results of the first process as a foundation, start from the most simple and basic categories, follow the thinking process from simple to complex, and construct a logical system. When Marx explained the capitalist economy in *Capital*, he started from the simpler category of the commodity. Then, he gradually expanded his analysis to more and more complicated economic categories such as currency and capital. The above two processes could be summarized as follows: "On the first road the rounded concept was dissolved into an abstract determination; on the second abstract determinations lead by way of thought to the reproduction of the concrete".[6]

It should be noted that the reason why Marx emphasized the method of abstraction is because he knew that the field of economics differed from natural sciences; it could not be tested in the laboratory. This conclusion might have been reasonable given the conditions of scientific experiments at that time. Marx's theories include the replacement of capitalism by socialism, but it was not at all possible for him to conduct such experiments under capitalist conditions. However, the emergence of computers and the development of information technology in modern times have enabled some (undoubtedly not all) economic principles to be simulated and tested by computer programs or other informational approaches. In fact, the 2002 Nobel Prize for Economics was awarded to two economists who contributed to experimental economics. Since China's era of reform and opening up, much of the theoretical progress concerning the socialist economy was achieved by drawing conclusions from the trials of reform and opening up. This indicates that the method of abstraction alone is not sufficient in revealing many economic principles or conclusions.

[6]Karl Marx. *Preface to a Contribution to the Critique of Political Economy* (Beijing: Foreign Language Press, 1976), pp. 31–32.

Experiments and trials can also be considered as possible methods of studying economics.

Although traditional models of political economics apply quantitative analysis and empirical methods, its basic analytical methods are qualitative analysis and normative analysis. The most fundamental method of the political economy is the philosophical approach used by Marxist economics that consists of dialectics and abstraction. In modern times, the methodology of that political economy has been challenged, indicating that economic methodologies should also progress with the times. Scientific research methods (including mathematics) should become its important research methods. Many people believe that a discipline can only be called a science when it utilizes mathematics. For this reason, the status of economics has been highly appraised in some Western economic literature: if mathematics is the treasure of natural science, economics is the treasure of social science. The field affirms that theories which can be tested mathematically are scientific, but the opposite is not true. There are two possible reasons why some theories could not be tested mathematically. One is that many actual economic relations are impossible to quantify. Similarly, while some relations can in fact be quantified in Western countries, they may not be quantified in China because of the country's economic transformations. The less normative an economic relation may be, the more difficult it is to quantify. The other reason is that many of these theories were proposed by experts in economics who were not basing their ideas on mathematics. It is the later generations that attempt to test their theories with mathematics. In fact, as an exact science, mathematics may sometimes limit innovative thoughts in social science disciplines.

Modern economics more commonly uses model analysis, which is also a quantitative method. Models are typically mathematical representations of the hypothetical relations among two or more variables. In fact, model analysis is also a type of abstract analysis. All models simplify real economic problems by eliminating unnecessary portions. In other words, models represent the important aspects of an issue in a concise manner. However, when utilizing them as tools of economic analysis, we need to be aware that both economic models and the theories that produce them have become detached from socioeconomic and political reality because of the methods of abstraction and simplification that are used in making the models. When using economic models to formulate actual political or institutional policies, we need to reintroduce the socioeconomic and political realities that had been disregarded in building them.

Normative analysis is a basic feature of a traditional analytical method of political economics. One of the important methodological advances in the modern political economy is combining empirical analysis with normative analysis on the premise of highlighting the former. According to the interpretation made by American economists Karl E. Case and Ray C. Fair in *Principles of Economics*, empirical analysis attempts to analyze the behaviors and operations of an economic system without making value judgments. It answers question about what an economic object is. Normative analysis examines the consequences of economic behaviors, judging whether they are good or bad and whether they can improve. Therefore, normative analysis includes the evaluation and regulation of the preferred course of action. It answers questions about what an economic object should be. Economics is divided into empirical economics and normative economics since it mainly adopts one of the two methods. However, in recent years, there is a growing sense that a combination of the two approaches could be more scientific.

7.4 Studying the Political Economy with an Attitude of Progressing with the Times

The political economy is one of the three components of Marxism. As the theoretical basis of the guiding principle of economic analysis, the Marxist political economy not only provides the ideological weapons for class struggle but also guides economic construction.

Both contemporary capitalism and socialism are undergoing new developments and changes. However, many new phenomena, features, and problems have also appeared. The new concerns of Marxist economics in the new historical stage consists of understanding modern capitalism and socialism in practice. These concerns will be answered by the developed Marxist political economy.

The first concern is the understanding of modern capitalism. The capitalist world has been relatively stable since the 1950s. Some new technological revolutions have taken place in developed capitalist countries, and new economic categories such as the information economy or the cybereconomy appeared after the 1990s. These new developments have all promoted the rapid development of productive forces. Thus, the average standard of living has also improved markedly, alleviating the contradictions inherent to imperialism to varying degrees. These new developments in capitalism cannot simply be explained by applying some readymade conclusions from traditional Marxist political economies; instead, they should be explained according to new findings. Admittedly, some individual conclusions of Marxist political economics may be outdated in the context of modern capitalism, but it is not outdated as a holistic scientific system that can be used to understand society. It can still provide a scientific world view and methodology for the understanding and research of modern capitalism, serving as the theoretical basis of the guiding principle for approaching the topic. In this way, the Marxist political economy can be further developed.

The second concern is the understanding of socialism in practice. Marx logically deduced some of the economic characteristics of the future socialist society when analyzing the contradictions of the capitalist economy. Marx made logical and scientific formulations concerning the future society after it had replaced capitalism in *Capital*. According to Marx's logic, these regulations are the economic characteristics of a mature socialist society established on the basis of a mature capitalist society. However, China is still in the primary stage of socialism. When implementing Marx's regulations on socialism, we should not carry them out dogmatically, but instead study them while taking into consideration the realistic conditions of China's current stage. This course of action is related to the adherence to and the development of the socialist theories in *Capital*. The development of such theories necessitates a careful study of *Capital*'s requirements for economic conditions. Based on this approach and the logic of *Capital*, one could conclude that it is impossible to fully meet the requirements of these regulations in the primary stage of socialism. An adherence to the theories necessitates a confirmation that Marx's regulations are still the goals of building socialism. According to Marx's thinking, the basic way to achieve these goals of socialism is to create certain economic conditions, especially by developing productive forces to create the material foundation for realizing socialist regulations. The fundamental theoretical progress of the socialist economy after the confirmation of the primary stage of socialism can be summarized into the following ways: (1) Acknowledge the existence of commodity relations under socialist conditions and then confirm the fact that the socialist economy is also a market economy. (2) Recognize that the basic economic system is public ownership, which will play a dominant role while diverse forms of ownership develop side by side; the corresponding distribution system that operates according to work is the main form while various other distribution methods also coexist. (3) Admit that the public ownership economy can be realized in a variety of forms, and further clarify the direction of the reform of public ownership enterprises — modern enterprise system on the basis of equity diversification. (4) Clarify that owners, operators, managers, and technicians of the non-public ownership economy should clearly be identified as builders of socialism with Chinese characteristics after taking into account the characteristics of the basic economic system at the present stage.

The third concern is to seek general economic theories that guide the operation of the market economy. The Marxist political economy provides the guiding principles for the actual socialist economy. These not only include a discussion of the characteristics of the socialist economy but also its general economic theories, among which the most important one is the theory of the market economy. Although *Capital* explores the theories of the market economy within the formation of capitalism, many of those theories can still play a significant guiding role in the current socialist economy after the regulations of capitalist economic relations have been removed. Since China's economic system has turned into a market economy, theories concerning commodity-money, competition, capital accumulation, organic composition of capital, capital circulation and turnover, the conditions for the realization of the aggregate product of society, the law of the average rate of profit, circulation costs, rent, credit economy, economic cycle and others shed light on both the economic research and practice of our country at the present stage.

People have often tended to study the political economy from the perspective of class analysis and class struggle. This approach was entirely understandable in the age of class struggle. However, now that it has been confirmed that China is in the primary stage of socialism, economic construction has become the central task. The up-to-date task of the political economy is highlighted in its theoretical contributions to the formulation of ideas and entrepreneurship mechanisms that adapt to the basic economic system in the primary stage of socialism. Accordingly, the function of the political economy has to be fundamentally changed. An analysis of the socialist economy should not provide a theory of class struggle, but rather one of class cooperation. In accordance with the situation in which all people do their best to play their proper roles, and coexist harmoniously, the political economy needs to propose and study the concepts related to the builders of socialism with Chinese characteristics, put forward the systems for protecting private property, introduce the contract theory in institutional economics, ensure that enterprises can participate in distribution according to their contributions based on the shares determined by various factors, including capital, labor and management, and seek effective methods for cooperating between labor and capital.

According to Marxist epistemology, truth is relative. "[W]e can only know under the conditions of our epoch and *as far as these allow*".[7] Marxist economics is no exception. In regard to the interpretation of socialist economic relations, we can only understand economic relations and laws in the primary stage of socialism. What's more, this understanding is also relative. With the increase and development of practice, our understanding will be deepened further, and many economic theories will be further developed.

[7]Karl Marx and Friedrich Engels. *Complete Works*. Vol. 25, Trans. Emile Burns and Clemens Dutt (London: Lawrence & Wishart, 2010), p. 521.

Chapter 8

The Theoretical and Methodological Innovations of the Political Economy in the Socialist Stage

There is another distinction of political economics when it is discussed in terms of stages. Specifically, there are differences in the political economies in capitalist and socialist stages, although both of them contain capitalist and socialist political economics. Compared to the political economy in the capitalist stage, the political economy in the socialist stage reflects the changes in the paradigm of political economics, highlighting the fact that its research objects, tasks, and methods are all progressing with the times. The political economy in the socialist society not only provides the theoretical weapons for class struggle, but it also serves as the guiding ideology for economic construction. Studying and learning about the political economy with the attitude of progressing with the times involves scientifically understanding modern capitalism and socialism in practice while using political economics as the guiding ideology for developing society's advanced productive forces.

8.1 The Missions of the Political Economy at Different Stages Determine Its Characteristic Progression with the Times

The political economy is one of the three components of Marxism. It is generally subdivided into capitalist political economy and socialist political economy. In fact, there is another distinction. Political economics could be classified by political economy in the capitalist stage and political economy in the socialist stage, both of which contain capitalist and socialist political economies. In order for the political economy to progress along with the times, we mainly rely on the theoretical innovations embodied in the political economy of a socialist society rather than those embodied in the political economy of a capitalist society.

The Marxist political economy, as represented by *Capital*, was founded in a capitalist society and its historical mission is undoubtedly to make socialism replace capitalism. Its task is to reveal capitalism's basic contradictions and to seek out the gravedigger of capitalism. The topic that currently needs to be studied is the mission of the political economy in a socialist society.

The current socialist society was born out of capitalism and also coexists with today's capitalist society. Therefore, it is not possible to change the political economy's function of expounding upon the nature of society and distinguishing socialism from capitalism or its mission to strengthen the belief that socialism will replace capitalism. However, socialism's ultimate replacement of capitalism depends on the development of productive forces and the building of the socialist society we have established. Thus, the function of the political economy in the socialist society is clear. As both a scientific economic system and the theoretical basis for the guiding ideology of economic analysis, Marxist political economics should not only provide the ideological weapons for class struggle, but also the guiding principle for economic construction.

The idea of Marx's *Capital* is basically based on class struggle, and its goal is to overthrow the old capitalist system. Now in the primary stage of socialism, China's goal is to build a new socialist society. Under such conditions, the study and research of the political economy necessitates a firm belief that socialism will replace capitalism. However, it is not confined to this belief. Adapting to the characteristics of the central tasks and economic background we face, the basic idea of studying the political economy is to shift from class struggle to economic development. Political economics was the weapon of class struggle when confronted with the capitalist society. Now it is the theoretical guidance for economic development in today's socialist society. This transformation in the political economy means that the focus of research should also alter from studying how to overthrow the capitalist society to studying how to build the socialist society. There should also be a change in thinking about how to adjust the relations of production, increase social productivity and social wealth, and enhance social welfare.

The history of the emergence and development of the political economy embodies its characteristic ability to advance with the times. The basic task of political economy established by figures from Marx to Lenin is to overthrow the old society. The basic task of political economy beginning with Stalin is to build a new society. However, soon after socialist countries were established, their political power needed to be consolidated. The basic idea was class struggle, and accordingly, class analysis and class struggle were taken as the key aspects of the political economy. Since China's reform and opening up, the fundamental idea of the Party's two generations of collective leadership in building the new society has been economic construction. Accordingly, both the point of departure and the destination of political economics are increasing social wealth. This then determines the distinction between the modern and traditional political economy.

For a long time, people have tended to study the political economy from the perspective of class analysis and class struggle. This approach was entirely understandable in the age of class struggle. The political economy founded by Marx under capitalist conditions was regarded as a weapon to criticize the old society, and its object of criticism was quite clear. However, in a socialist society the basic idea of studying *Capital* is not to play the role of a critic, using certain statements from *Capital* as dogmas to criticize some practice in reform and opening up. Instead, it should play the role of a builder, proposing suggestions about China's reform and opening up based on the logic and thinking in *Capital* and the basic theories expounded within it. In fact, as a historical materialist, Marx's scientific economic analysis in *Capital* also provides brilliant insights to guiding the construction of a new society today. Marxist political economics directly originated from classical economics represented by thinkers such as Adam Smith and David Ricardo. Representing the demands of the emerging bourgeoisie, they proposed theories that aimed to improve national wealth. When Marx reformed classical political economics, he did not abandon their theories, but instead developed them further. He reformed classical political economics in seeking both the sources and the creators of national wealth and value. The theory of increasing national wealth in *Capital* thus sheds light on China's construction of a new society.

The political economy in a socialist society still takes a specific society as its research object and is classified into capitalist and socialist divisions. The prominent contradiction in both teaching and studying political economics is revealing capitalist exploitation and criticizing the evils of capitalism in the capitalist part of political economy while also encouraging the development of diverse ownership economies (including the capitalist economy) based on the basic economic system of the primary stage of socialism and explaining the rationality of exploitation (even denying exploitation) in the socialist part of the political economy. This contradiction is the result of the vagueness of the guiding principle. This contradiction can be resolved by clarifying the fact that the political economy in the socialist stage meets the requirements of building a new society, focusing on the economic laws shared by both capitalist and socialist societies when analyzing capitalism. This process will thus strengthen the same economic laws in the relations of production. The fundamental reason this will happen is because there are common economic laws that capitalism and socialism share. Capitalist and socialist societies should not just be thought of as two societies that appear subsequent to one another. They coexist in space as well, and many of the economic organizations, modes, rules, and orders of both societies have tended to converge.

To meet the demands of China's reform and opening up, and modernization, the field of political economics should aim at reforming and improving the socialist economic system, promoting the development of society's productive forces, and increasing national wealth. The Marxist political economy, as it is represented in *Capital*, takes capitalism as its research object. Some of its predictions and regulations about socialist economic relations are also included within the analytical framework of capitalism. These should not be taken as dogmas for building socialism today, but rather as guides to action. We should not stick to a few individual conclusions put forward by Marx at the time in which he was writing, but rather develop Marx's theory of socialism according to the practices of socialist social development.

Therefore, the task of studying and researching the political economy under socialist conditions, whether the analysis concerns capitalism or socialism, is promoting the development of society's productive forces. Political economics should study economic laws, the directions that the advanced productive forces of society would take, and the adjustments to the relations of production that suit the development of productive forces. The categories and principles of the political economy drawn from such studies can serve as the theoretical guidelines of actual socialist construction.

8.2 The Evolution of the Paradigm of the Political Economy

The shift of political economics from criticism to construction has influenced changes to the paradigm of the political economy. This can be illustrated by the aspects of research objects, research fields, and changes to the methods of economic analysis.

First, the research object of the political economy is the relations of production. The production studied by Marx was limited to the production of physical materials alone. Marx said: "To begin with, the object before us is material production".[1] The Marxist political economy differs from mercantilism, which took circulation as its research object; physiocracy, which took the agricultural sector as its research object; and economic thought at that time, which took distribution as its starting point. Marx's research at the time in which he was writing was limited to the production of physical materials. His work shows that the production of physical materials serves as the basis for the existence and development of human society. Service was restricted by the level of productivity at that time, so it took up a very small proportion of production. In addition, it mainly belonged to the luxurious consumption of exploiters. However, in modern economic development, the expanded field of service takes up an increasingly larger proportion of social wealth and laborers are increasingly becoming consumers of the service industry. As a tertiary industry, the service industry ranks alongside industry and agriculture. Accordingly, service has become one of the research fields of political economics due to the rise of its status in the national economy. In today's political economy, production is also the starting point. However, it not only involves the production of physical materials, but also includes offerings in the field of service as well. Marx's logic and methods in analyzing the economic relations in the field of material production can also be applied to the study of the field of service from the perspective of the political economy. In this way, the research fields of the political economy can be said to progress along with the times.

Second, there are various levels of both productivity and relations of production in each society. Political economy is based on the dominant relations of production in any given society, that is, the relations of

[1] Karl Marx. *Preface to a Contribution to the Critique of Political Economy* (Beijing: Foreign Language Press, 1976), p. 9.

production, which Marx called the "general illumination". "In every social formation, there is a specific kind of production which predominates over all the others and whose relations therefore determine their rank and influence. It is a general illuminant tingeing all other colors and modifying their specific features".[2] Although there are various pre-capitalist relations of production in a capitalist economy, they are generally illuminated by capitalist relations of production and for that reason, they are not considered to be the research object of the political economy. After the socialist society was established, political economy attempted to take the pure socialist relations as the "general illuminant" to be studied; various non-socialist relations of production were excluded. The conclusion drawn from this kind of research resulted in incorrect practices due to the transcendence from the perspective of the stage. Now it has been confirmed that China is in the primary stage of socialism. Accordingly, public ownership plays the dominant role in the economy and diverse forms of ownership develop side by side. In this type of economy, the field of political economics should not only study socialist economic relations (such as public ownership), but also various kinds of ownership economies. In particular, now that the mixed-ownership economy has been confirmed, it may become the "general illumination" at the present stage and enter the field of political economics.

Third, political economics focuses on analyzing the contradictions of both socialism and capitalism. In accordance with the guiding principle of overthrowing capitalism, political economy in the capitalist stage analyzed the contradictions between labor and capital. The contradictions of socialism and those of capitalism are antagonistic. The political economy in the primary stage of socialism also needs to analyze and define the natures of various ownership economies. However, all of these economic components (including various private ownership economies) can be unified in socialist modernization. Although the ultimate goal of socialism is the replacement of private ownership by public ownership, the task of eliminating private ownership could not be put forward in the primary stage of socialism. To the contrary, we need to make use of private ownership on a large scale. The key point of political economics is not the struggle among different ownership systems, or a decision about which one wins. Instead, it is the search for an effective path for these ownership systems to develop side by side through equal competition.

---

[2] *Ibid.*, p. 39.

Fourth, the field of political economics reveals the essential connections among economic processes as well as the objective inevitability of the movement of these processes. That is to say, it exposes objective economic laws. According to Marx's analysis, every historical period and every economic movement has its own laws. "One and the same phenomenon falls under quite different laws in consequence of the different general structure of the organisms, the variations of their individual organs, and the different conditions in which those organs function ... With the varying degrees of development of production power, social conditions and the laws governing them vary too".[3] The scientific value of the research conducted from the perspective of political economics lies in its ability to expose the unique laws that govern the origins, existence, development, and disappearance of a given social entity as well as its substitution by another. The existence and development of socialism at the present stage relies on the development of productive forces. Therefore, a field like political economics that aims to reveal the laws of economic development should focus more on the laws of the development of productive forces as well as the manner in which the relations of production adapt to such development. Political economics can thereby ensure that our economic behaviors as well as various economic policies and decisions made by the state respect and act in accordance with objective economic laws.

Fifth, the field of political economics studies the contradictory movements of the productive forces and the relations of production. Traditional research attributes both the development and the backwardness of productive forces under socialist conditions to questions about whether such productive forces are capitalist or socialist. This theory has actually been denied by the reality of economic development. If the political economy aims to explain the economic reasons for the development and backwardness of productive forces, it must expand its research object. The analysis of the economic processes and relations within the political economy include research of the essence of the relations of production as well as economic operations and development. An analysis of the institutions within the political economy should not be limited to the nature of traditional relations of production. Instead, special attention needs to be paid to the mechanisms of economic operation as well as those of economic development. In fact, the aforementioned mechanisms of economic

---

[3]Karl Marx. *Capital: A Critique of Political Economy*. Vol. 1, Trans. Ben Fowkes (London: Penguin Books, 1976), pp. 101–102.

operations and economic development are also related to the relations of production. However, the difference is that they are concerned with the configuration and composition of existing relations of production including how to allocate and combine different ownership systems, how to allocate and coordinate market regulation and macro control, and so on. Because research objects have been added to the field of political economics, the political economy has then been enriched by the type of live content that is necessary for practice.

There are two major economic systems today: Marxist political economics and Western economics. The two systems differ both in terms of research objects and levels. Generally speaking, Western economics focuses on the descriptions of economic phenomena. According to Paul A. Samuelson, the top priority for Western economics is to describe, analyze, and explain production, unemployment, price, and other similar phenomena as well as to build the connections among these phenomena for systematic analysis. However, Marxist economics places particular emphasis on an analysis of the essence of economic relations. It studies social relations defining the men behind the relations between objects as well as the definition of the essence of economic systems, especially the laws pertaining to the movements of economic relations. The various economic categories it discovered all reflect certain social relations. While Marxist economics analyzes the essence of economic relations and problems in depth, Western economics analyzes the relations of economic variables and describes realistic economic phenomena. The field of Western economics, which places more emphasis on the analysis of economic operations, also analyzes economic institutions. However, it approaches economic system based on the premise of analysis, focusing on the relations among various economic variables in both microeconomic and macroeconomic operations. Political economics, which places more emphasis on the analysis of the relations of production, also involves economic operations. However, it focuses on the allocation and adjustment of various relations of production within economic operations.

It is generally believed that Western economics studies the effective allocation of resources and its efficiency target is *pareto optimum*. *Capital* also studies the allocation of resources, but it further abstracts resources into social labor. The allocation of resources is defined as the distribution of social labor in various sectors. The criterion of the efficiency of allocation is then the necessary social labor time. As Marx explained, the appointment of labor time "in accordance with a definite social plan maintains the correct proportion between the different functions of labor and the various needs of the associations".[4]

When analyzing the same economic phenomena and categories, Western economics and political economics have different research perspectives as well as varying levels. For instance, when it comes to the category of price, Western economics describes the relations among variables based on supply, demand, as well as the elasticity of both. It then illustrates the fact that price is determined by the relations between supply and demand and thus is therefore an equilibrium price. By contrast, political economics defines price as the monetary expression of value. It therefore states that the movements of prices exhibit the effect of the law of value and that prices will fluctuates around value. The price that balances supply and demand is the price that reflects value. This is actually the same as the idea of the equilibrium price; the difference lies in the varying levels of abstraction. As another example, Western economics regards the allocation categories of industrial profit, commercial profit, interest, and land rent as forms of the rewards of factors. By contrast, political economics defines them as forms of the divisions of surplus value, thus determining their respective limits in quantity. Obviously, in analyzing economic processes according to different research methods and levels, these two theoretical systems have different theoretical and practical significance, and they are irreplaceable. Because China's present socialist economy is a socialist market economy, we must make use of the theories and methods of these two theoretical systems. Simply excluding either of the theoretical systems will directly affect the scientific basis of the economic analysis. Because the Marxist political economy involves the analysis of both the essence and the system, it should undoubtedly be regarded as the theoretical basis for the guiding principles of economic analysis.

Generally speaking, because of the transformations and innovations of the content of political economics, its principles at the present stage (as they are defined holistically as opposed to in a specific textbook or a collection of them) are not as dogmatic as those of the traditional political economy. For that reason, many theoretical views have been both accepted and transformed into government decisions. Therefore, if there is no prejudice against it, the political economy has broken through the

[4] *Ibid.*, p. 172.

traditional theoretical paradigm on the whole. The reasons why it is still regarded as political economics are as follows: (1) Its research object is still the relations of production and its economic laws; (2) It focuses on the nature of the social system; (3) It mainly utilizes the basic categories and methods of Marxist economics. The main reasons why it breaks the traditional paradigm are as follows: (1) Although its research object is still the relations of production, its focus is not the comparison of the relations of production between socialism and capitalism, but instead on the adjustment and reform of the relations of production for the goal of developing productive forces, especially those of the Chinese economy; (2) Although it focuses on the nature of the social system, the political economy (within the framework of socialism in the primary stage) does not refuse to accept the effective systems and forms of the capitalist economy; (3) Although it mainly utilizes the categories and methods of Marxist economics, it has largely absorbed the categories and methods of Western economics; (4) Although it is a subject of theoretical economics, its basic function is to perform a theoretical analysis of practical economic problems. The scope of its analysis has been expanded from the economic system to economic operations, development, and policies. More and more people have realized that the political economy has become a theoretical discipline with strong applicability; (5) Although it still analyzes the capitalist economy, it is more concerned about the content that reflects the general laws of the market economy and socialized production. In summary, the political economy aims to study China's economic issues by using the basic categories and methods of Marxist economics.

8.3 The Political Economy and the Development of Society's Advanced Productive Forces

Marxist political economics is the field that analyzes the contradictory movements of both productive forces and relations of production. Traditional analysis, especially the analysis of the socialist economy, is mainly limited to the analysis of the relations of production. This may be related to Stalin's *Economic Problems of USSR*, published in the 1950s. At that time, Yaroshenko proposed that the main problem of socialist political economy was exploring and developing a scientific theory of the organization of productive forces in social production. Stalin sharply criticized him for deviating from Marxism and overstating the role of productive forces, thus making economic problems absent in political economy.[5] Under this guiding principle, the Soviet version of the political economy avoided the study of productive forces and, because of this influence, other socialist political economies have also followed this paradigm. The consequence is that political economics only studies the adjustments to the relations of production rather than the issues of the development of productive forces. However, the development of productive forces itself is governed by internal laws and the lack of research concerning productive forces has meant that the guiding role of the political economy in actual economic construction has ultimately been renounced. In particular, if the historical mission of the political economy is to replace capitalism with socialism, the biggest constraint in the present moment is the backwardness of the productive forces, rather than the backwardness of the relations of production. In this sense, the study of productive forces should be given priority in the field of political economics.

In terms of the political economy established by Marx, *Capital* indicates that productive forces should take up a large proportion of the analysis. Marx analyzed the development of the relations of production in accordance with the development of productive forces. For instance, he made a detailed and technical analysis of each mode of production, from simple collaboration to the division of labor in manufacturing and large-scale, mechanized industries. Likewise, the analysis of socialist economic relations should be based on similar methods. The primary stage of China's socialism is determined by the level of the development of society's productive forces. In addition, the development of socialist economic relations fundamentally depends on the development of productive forces.

In explaining the conditions for the realization of conscious and planned control of material production in the free association economy, Marx specifically pointed out: this "requires that society possess a material foundation, or a series of material conditions of existence, which in their turn are the natural and spontaneous product of a long and tormented historical development".[6] Here, Marx draws attention to the material foundations that are required for a socialist economy. Undoubtedly, what

---

[5] Joseph Stalin. *Economic Problems of Socialism in the USSR* (Beijing: Foreign Languages Press, 1972), p. 60.

[6] Karl Marx. *Capital: A Critique of Political Economy*. Vol. 1, p. 173.

China currently needs to do is not to abandon the basic definitions of socialism, but rather to create the material foundations for the realization of these regulations. To put it more specifically, the focus of the current development of socialist economy is not the pursuit of an advanced system, but instead the pursuit of advanced productive forces of society that will then promote the system's development.

Although the primary stage of China's socialism is determined by its low level of productive forces, this definition by no means implies that present productive forces should be developed according to the standards of backward productive forces. Instead, they should be developed according to the standards of advanced social productive forces. It is crucial to emphasize this point for the development of the current economy. The form of socialism in which public ownership plays a dominant role is not supported by administrative coercion but rather by the higher efficiency at higher levels of productive forces. According to Marx's generalization, the development in social productivity can be reduced "to the social character of the labor that is set to work, to the division of labor in society, and to the development of intellectual labor, in particular of the natural sciences".[7] Marx's analysis of machinery and large-scale industry in *Capital* sheds light on the manner in which society's advanced productive forces may be defined.

According to Marx, the means of production are the symbols that distinguish different economic eras, especially the instruments of production. As he said, "It is not what is made but how, and by what instruments of labor, that distinguishes different economic epochs".[8] According to Marx's historical analysis, the productive forces that capitalist economic relations depend on started from simple cooperation and went through the division of labor in manufacturing. Only machinery and large-scale industries established their own material and technical foundations. Large-scale industries were characterized by that fact that machines produced other machines. "Large-scale industry had to take over the machine itself, its own characteristic instrument of production, and to produce machines by means of machines. It was not till it did this that it could create for itself an adequate technical foundation and stand on its own feet". According to Marx's analysis, there are two functions of productive forces generated by

[7]Karl Marx. *Capital: A Critique of Political Economy*. Vol. 3, Trans. David Fernbach (London: Penguin Books, 1981), p. 175.

[8]Karl Marx. *Capital: A Critique of Political Economy*. Vol. 1, p. 286.

machines: "As machinery, the instrument of labor assumes a material mode of existence which necessitates the replacement of human force by natural forces, and the replacement of the rule of thumb by the conscious application of natural science".[9] Obviously, these two requirements of machinery and large-scale industries are precisely the frames of reference for the advanced social productive forces which China needs to develop at present. To sum up, a society's advanced productive forces are those that are based on modern science and technology.

As a matter of fact, the concept of a society's advanced productive forces is dynamic. As Marx stated, the technological foundations of a large-scale industry are revolutionary. The current level of productive forces in China may have far exceeded that of the capitalist countries where Marx lived. However, we have not yet reached the point where we can say that the material foundations of China's form of socialism have been well established. This is because developed, capitalist countries utilized the foundations of machinery and large-scale industries and constantly innovated them along with their technologies. For this reason, their productive forces have reached a higher level. Under such conditions, the society's advanced productive forces (those that we are currently discussing) should not be limited to the level of the machinery and large-scale industries that are described in *Capital*. Instead, the level of productive forces achieved by developed countries at the present stage should be considered to be the frame of reference. In each period, new content will be added to a society's advanced productive forces. The industrial structure is a comprehensive reflection of a society's level of development of productive forces. More than 100 years ago, advanced productive forces were related to machinery and large-scale industries; now they are related to the emerging high-tech industries represented by information industries.

In particular, we should note that at the end of the 20th century, the United States and other developed countries entered a new economic era defined by the development of advanced technology represented by information technology. The new emerging economy is a generalization of the information, network, and digital economies. Its effects have been, and in fact are still being, manifested and the productive forces may be dozens of times higher than those in the past. The productive forces reflected in this new economy can also be explained by *Capital*. If the large-scale

[9] *Ibid.*, pp. 506–508.

mechanized industry used machines to replace natural forces including human power, the new economy uses information and network technologies to replace brain power. This process might also change some of the axioms of the past economics. For instance, there may be an increased tendency to decrease the marginal revenues of scale; because the new economy is based on knowledge and information and the demand for tangible resources has been relatively reduced, the economy can maintain rapid growth for a considerable period of time without overheating and falling into a crisis; the growth period of enterprises may be shortened, but the decline period of enterprises may be sped up; the scale of an enterprise is no longer the main determinant of its competitiveness as small and medium-sized enterprises with information and network advantages may also have stronger competitiveness; the determinants of economic growth may no longer be labor and capital, but instead will be knowledge and technology. The last change will directly affect the methods of allocation.

We must admit that if China cannot keep up with the pace of the new economies in developed countries, the gap in productive forces between China and developed countries that had once narrowed may be widened even further. At the same time, this also gives China a clear frame of reference as well as the fundamental contents of the requirements in developing a society's advanced productive forces: the requirement of developing advanced productive forces must reflect the requirement of developing the first productive forces, that is, science and technology. China should truly rely on science and technology to promote the development of productive forces, striving to strengthen the awareness of modern science and technology among laborers.

The political economy's study of advanced social productive forces includes seeking out the sources of developing productive forces as well as ways to emancipate and develop them. This involves adjusting economic relations through reforming and opening up. The concrete measures include adjustments to ownership structures, the construction of enterprise systems, adjustments to the structure and system of distribution, the construction of the market economy system, and adjustments to the relations between the state and enterprises. Both the principles and methods of political economics can guide the research and analysis of these aspects. Given the confirmation that the basic economic system in the primary stage of socialism is a system in which public ownership plays the dominant role and diverse forms of ownership develop side by side, political economy needs to make theoretical contributions to the formation of corresponding ideological and entrepreneurial mechanisms. In accordance with the circumstances in which all people do their best, play their proper roles, and coexist harmoniously with one another, the political economy needs to propose and study the concepts related to the builders of socialism with Chinese characteristics, put forward systems for protecting private property, introduce the contract theory in institutional economics, ensure that enterprises can participate in distribution according to their contributions based on the shares determined by various factors, including capital, labor, and management, and seek effective methods for cooperating between labor and capital.

The field of economics is an empirical science. The practices of China's economic construction require Marxist economics to guide the country's economic reform and development as a theoretical economic discipline, endowing this field of theoretical economics with the characteristic of applicability. In the West, economists have provided the government with policy proposals based on Keynesianism, supplierism, monetarism, new institutionalism, and other theories for the government to choose from. The practices of China's economic construction need Marxist economics to perform this function as well. Therefore, we should focus on the major issues raised in the construction of modernization, study economic operational mechanisms, economic systems, and macroeconomic policies, as well as discuss strategic, overarching, and forward-looking issues, so as to provide the theoretical basis for the decision-making of the state and enterprises, contributing to the construction of a socialist society with high material standards.

Chapter 9

The Innovation and Development of the Marxist Political Economy

The Marxist political economy is the critical theoretical basis for socialist economy with Chinese characteristics. The formation of the theory of socialism with Chinese characteristics is inseparable from innovation and development of Marxist political economy under new historical, social, and economic conditions. Socialist practices, new changes in contemporary capitalism, and economic globalization all promote the development of the Marxist political economy. A series of important theoretical innovations made in the course of developing China's Marxist political economy have generated scientific theories as well as guidance for the building of socialism with Chinese characteristics.

9.1 Concerning the Research Objects of the Political Economy

There have been different views concerning the research objects of the political economy. The political economy, as it is represented in *Capital,* analyzes the capitalist economy's relations of production. This has essentially been recognized in academia. However, in a socialist society developing socialist economy requires the promotion of productive forces. Therefore, a question naturally arises: Can productive forces be the research object of political economy? The ongoing economic reform poses a vital problem to both the system and structure of the political economy. Although these are mainly issues concerning the relations of production, they will inevitably involve the superstructure as well as some problems in economic operation. Therefore, the question becomes: Which part of the superstructure should be the research object of the political economy?

As a traditional economic subject, political economy has been clear in identifying its research object since its very foundation. Confronted with socioeconomic relations in a given society as well as the basic social contradiction between productive forces and the relations of production, political economy is devoted to studying the relations of production as well as the laws by which they emerge, develop, and grow to be extinct. Because productive forces play a decisive role in the emergence, development, and extinction of the relations of production, political economy will necessarily study them in order to understand the relations of production. In this case, the research object of political economy would generally involve the relations of production based on a certain level of productive forces, or the mutual relationship between productive forces and the relations of production in a given society. When analyzing capitalist economic relations, Marxist economics aims to reveal that their relations of production have blocked the development of productive forces. When it comes to the analysis of economic relations in the primary stage of socialism, Marxist economics needs to reveal that the development of productive forces has promoted socialist economic relations.

The Marxist political economy takes production as its starting point for study because it has included both productive forces and the relations of production. It is necessary to point out that production and its consequent exchange and distribution of products form the basis of all socioeconomic systems. Nevertheless, Marx's study of the issues of production was confined to the production of material goods; the service industry was limited to the continuation of the productive process in the field of circulation including transport, packaging, storage, etc. In the modern economy, however, service industry is developing rapidly, the range of services is expanding, service products are becoming an increasingly important part of social wealth, and services have been included in the sphere of consumption with greater frequency. Therefore, service industry is a tertiary sector that, together with industry and agriculture, has become part of the gross national product and entered the horizon of the political economy. The logic and approaches adopted by Marx to analyze the economic relations in the field of material production could then be applied equally to the study of the service industry.

Although the political economy views the relations of production as its research object, it does not reject productive forces. Instead, the field studies how they interact with the relations of production. Marx points out that "[w]hatever the social form of production, workers and means of production always remain its factors. But if they are in a state of mutual separation, they are only potentially factors of production. For any production to take place, they must be connected".[1] From this perspective, production is a kind of structure that combines the workers and the means of production in a natural or technical way if the social forms of various social productions are not taken into consideration. The political economy therefore examines the issue of the productive forces that could exert decisive influence on the relations of production. Two aspects of the current research on productive forces are worth noting.

The first concerns the driving forces that promote the development of productive forces. Key aspects of these productive forces include the laborers, means of labor, subjects of labor, etc. The level of the development of the productive forces is reflected in the quality of these factors. Of these, the quality of laborer is the primary, most dynamic, and the most active factor. In reality, however, science and technology are considered to be the primary productive forces. Herein lies the question: Are there any contradictions between these two views? Answering this question requires a distinction between the key factors of productive forces and the driving force that develops productive forces. Cooperation, the division of labor in society, and science and technology are not factors of productive forces, but they are instead the driving force and impetus to promote their development. As Marx states, the development of productive forces "can always be reduced in the last analysis to the social character of the labor that is set to work, to the division of labor in society, and to the development of intellectual labor, in particular of the natural sciences".[2] When it comes to social and economic development, there has been a change in the status of the driving force that plays a decisive role in promoting the development of productive forces. For example, the division of labor in society once played a decisive role and is still playing a vital role in promoting the development of productive forces.

[1]Karl Marx. *Capital: A Critique of Political Economy.* Vol. 2, Trans. David Fernbach (London: Penguin Books, 1978), p. 120.

[2]Karl Marx. *Capital: A Critique of Political Economy.* Vol. 3, Trans. David Fernbach (London: Penguin Books, 1981), p. 175.

At present, science and technology are playing an increasingly important role in the development of productive forces, thereby becoming primary productive forces. Science and technology not only promote the quality of factors of productive forces such as labor and the means of labor, but they also serve as the internal factors that will directly improve the level of productive forces.

The second concerns advanced productive forces. At different stages of social development, there are multiple levels of productive forces that are distinguished by differences in both time and space. In terms of time, the development level of the productive forces at a certain stage will be more advanced than that of the previous one while simultaneously lagging behind that of a subsequent stage. In terms of space, there are substantial differences among countries and regions to the extent that they develop productive forces. Therefore, there is a difference between advanced productive forces and backward ones. The political economy studies multiple levels of productive forces, especially those that are dominant in a given society and thus exert influence on the nature of the relations of production. Due to the fact that every society has multiple levels of productive forces, a particular set of social relations of production must provide adequate space for the development of multiple productive forces, especially those that are more advanced. Establishing the relations of production that represent advanced productive forces could help emancipate and develop them, further releasing the potential and energy of advanced productive forces.

China's economic reform could be regarded as the adjustment and improvement of the relations of production. Both the system and structure of the economy, as the concrete forms of the relations of production, have become the research object of the political economy. Furthermore, the study of the economic system and structure will expand the range of the political economy's research object.

First, the superstructure is not the research object of the political economy. However, according to Marx's analysis of the relationship between the economic base and superstructure, when the political economy is studying the total relations of production, it will include the superstructure within a certain range, namely the economic base. In particular, the extent to which the economic system fundamentally reflects the nature of society largely concerns the superstructure. Certainly, the adjustments to the economic system that have been motivated by economic reform essentially reflect the attributes of the relations of production, although they will also affect the changes to the superstructure. This could be best illustrated by China's basic economic system in the primary stage of socialism. On the one hand, when China implemented the basic socialist economic system, the essential attributes of the relations of production did not change. On the other hand, China is still in the primary stage of socialism. The basic economic system in this stage has been constructed, which is a local adjustment to the relations of production in order to accommodate the development of productive forces. Meanwhile, the superstructure studied by the political economy mainly concerns the protection of property rights that influence the relations of production, the legal system, industrial policy, public financing that standardize economic operations, and macro control policies that intervene in the market.

Next, the economic structure and operations enter the vision of the political economy. Generally speaking, the measures of economic efficiency, which are related to the development of productive forces, are bound to the relations of production. In this case, economic inefficiency can be attributed to the fact that the relations of production do not accommodate the development of productive forces. However, economic efficiency reflects both the efficiency of resource allocation and the quality of economic operations. In this way, economic efficiency is not completely determined by the relations of production; it is also determined by the economic structure. The economic structure refers to the concrete form of the relations of production in a given society, which is mainly the realistic economic form established by resource allocation rather than the economic system. Therefore, the reform of the economic structure needs to reflect not only the essential demands of the economic system, but also the efficiency and quality of its operations. As far as the former is concerned, the economic structure must be reformed according to the needs of the basic economic system in the primary stage of socialism. The quality and efficiency of the operation of the economy is not completely relevant to the economic system but is instead related to resource allocation to a great extent. Hence, even though the economic system is built to accommodate the development of productive forces, it still needs to be adjusted and reformed in a timely manner. At present, an effective method to promote the efficiency and quality of economic operations is to establish the socialist market economic structure, which takes market mechanism as the basic means of resource allocation. To reflect the essential demands of the socialist economic system, the market economy structure needs to combine with the socialist economic system. This is a new institutional arrangement of the mechanism of economic operation, which begins with the premise of upholding the basic socialist system.

9.2 Concerning the Class Features and the Task of the Political Economy

In the previous era, some people have been influenced by supposedly "universal values" that tone down the class features of economics and instead emphasize a more general theory that transcends class. However, political economy that takes relations of production as its research object would necessarily have a class feature because it would address economic relations and interests.

Marx has identified the class features of the Marxist political economy since its very foundation. He points out that political economy represents the interests of the bourgeoisie and "[t]he peculiar nature of the material it deals with summons into the fray on the opposing side the most violent, sordid and malignant passions of the human breast, the Furies of private interest".[3] The political economy founded by Marx publicly claims and maintains the interests of the proletariat, serving its revolutionary cause as well as that of the entire human race. Based on the theory of labor value, Marx established the scientific theory of surplus value, discovered the secret of capitalist exploitation, and thus became the gravedigger of capitalist society that sounded the death knell of capitalism. The class features of the Marxist political economy are not only reflected in its criticism of capitalism, but also in its portrayal of an ideal society for the proletariat. This is the socialist society and communist society that Marx calls "the Community of Freemen". In the process of criticizing capitalist economic relations, Marx logically deduces the basic economic characteristics of the future society, reflecting the proletariat's yearning for a future society as well as their determination to fight for it. After the foundation of a socialist society, the Marxist political economy provides the theoretical weapons for building a new society and reflecting the fundamental interests of the overwhelming majority of people.

The essential attributes of the political economy differ in different historical periods. In the previous society, it was a weapon for criticizing

---

[3]Karl Marx. *Capital: A Critique of Political Economy.* Vol. 1, Trans. Ben Fowkes (London: Penguin Books, 1976), p. 92.

and burying social evils; in the new society, it serves as a guiding star for building society. Due to the fact that socialist and capitalist countries coexist in reality, the political economy is determined by its class feature and still functions as a critique of capitalism.

In order to understand the task of the political economy, one needs to pay attention to what Marx says: "No social order is ever destroyed before all the productive forces for which it is sufficient have been developed, and new superior relations of production never replace older ones before the material conditions for their existence have matured within the framework of the old society".[4] There are two implications here. First, the emergence and development of any relations of production depend on material conditions, namely the level of the development of the productive forces. This implies that the relations of production must accord with the nature of productive forces. Second, the relations of production in a given society are relatively stable and will continue to exist and take effect as long as they accommodate the development of productive forces. According to this important principle proposed by Marx, one could understand modern capitalism and socialism as they are currently practiced. Particularly, it is a starting point to understand the arrangement of the relations of production in the primary stage of socialism.

The Marxist political economy is a constantly evolving science. "In every epoch, and therefore also in ours, theoretical thought is a historical product, which at different times assumes very different forms and, therewith, very different contents".[5] The Marxist political economy not only keeps pace with the times, but also reaches different levels of development in different countries.

Marx perceived socialism and capitalism as two sequential social systems. Accordingly, the political economy founded by Marx originated from capitalist society and its research objects included the existing capitalist economy as well as a future socialist economy. At present, capitalism and socialism are two social systems that coexist in the same space. Thus, the political economy studies the socialist economy in practice, while the capitalist economy involves not only the pre-socialist economy but also that of the modern capitalist market with which it coexists.

---

[4]Karl Marx. *Preface to a Contribution to the Critique of Political Economy* (Beijing: Foreign Language Press, 1976), p. 10.

[5]Karl Marx and Frederick Engels. *Marx & Engels Collected Works*. Vol. 25, Trans. Emile Burns and Clemens Dutt (London: Lawrence & Wilshart, 2010), p. 338.

The task of political economy is to reveal the intrinsic contradictions of the capitalist economy, the hindering effect of capitalist relations of production on the development of productive forces, and the historical certainty that capitalism will inevitably be replaced by socialism. In this sense, the political economy provides the ideological weapons for class struggle. Ever since Marx founded the political economy, the capitalist economy has also been developing for more than a 100 years. In that period of time, there have been a lot of new phenomena that have emerged in contemporary capitalism. Thus, the political economy must keep pace with the times when analyzing the capitalist economy. This requires that the political economy not only reveals the inevitability of the extinction of capitalism, but also focuses on its new phenomena and problems, exposing the new laws of the contemporary capitalism.

First, there should be scientific explanations as to why the capitalist economy continues to exist and develop. This question could also be explained through the paradoxical movements between productive forces and the relations of production. On the one hand, several significant scientific and technological revolutions have taken place in advanced capitalist countries since the first industrial revolution, thereby promoting the level of the development of the productive forces to an unprecedented height. On the other hand, in order to ease class contradictions, capitalist countries have taken a series of measures to adjust the relations of production, which, to a certain extent, has accommodated the development of productive forces. The establishment of the modern corporate system, the formation of the developed capital market, the reasonable intervention of governments in the economy, and the improvement of innovative mechanisms of science and technology are all adjustments of economic forms that accommodate the development of modern productive forces.

Next, the emerging contradictions of the capitalist economy should be addressed to strengthen the belief that socialism will inevitably replace capitalism. Generally speaking, the level of productive forces in developed capitalist countries is higher than those in socialist countries. However, the trend that socialism will replace capitalism will not change. There are two reasons why this is true. First, the substitution of capitalism for socialism is a long, tortuous, and arduous process. Confronted with the objective requirements of developing productive forces, capitalism has made some adjustments and improvements in order to save itself from extinction. They are in fact much closer to the relations of production of the future society that was envisioned by Marx. Second, even though there is still a large space for the capitalist relations of production to accommodate the development of productive forces, the basic contradiction between the socialization of production and the private ownership of the means of production, which is inherent to the mode of capitalist production will never change. No matter what adjustments capitalism might make, it will inevitably go extinct if it is only concerned with private ownership. The political economy should not only focus on the economic forms that correspond to the relations of production that have been adjusted within capitalism. It also needs to pay more attention to the new contradictions emerging in the private ownership of capitalism. Since the second half of 2007, the world financial and economic crisis derived from the U.S. subprime mortgage crisis has shown the drawbacks inherent to capitalism.

Third, the economic forms and organizations that accommodate socialized mass production in the developed capitalist countries should be studied. Under the circumstance in which capitalism coexists with socialism, many economic activities and organizations need to learn from and combine with each other. In order to catch up with, and eventually surpass, the level of the productive forces of modern capitalist countries, socialist countries need to borrow from the capitalist countries' effective economic forms and organizations that were adopted to accommodate socialized mass production. Although these economic forms and organizations both appeared and matured in capitalist countries, they represent the common wealth of humankind, which can then be borrowed and utilized by socialist countries.

9.3 On the Sinicization of the Marxist Political Economy

It should be mentioned that the visions or regulations of the basic attributes of the future society given by the political economy that was founded by Marx have provided guidance for the practices of the latter socialist countries. However, there are two reasons for China to make innovations. On the one hand, there are sharp differences between the socialist economic system once envisioned by Marx and the real-world socialist practices now. Founded on the basis of a semi-colonial and semi-feudal society, socialist China could not mechanically copy those principles when implementing Marx's demands for socialism. On the other hand, Marx only formulated some basic characteristics for the future society at the moment; he did not make concrete regulations for the economic structure of the future society. These also require innovation on the part of China. Therefore, the course of China's innovation of the actual socialist economic system and structure will involve the combination of the basic principles of Marxist socialism with Chinese practices; this is also the task of modernizing and Sinicizing the Marxist political economy.

First, one must establish an economic theory of the new society with the goal of developing social productive forces. The previous teaching materials concerning the political economy identified the aim of socialist production as meeting the people's ever-growing material and cultural demands to the utmost extent. At present, the problem still remains that the level of the development of the productive forces cannot meet the demands of the people. This principal social contradiction cannot be overcome by the development of productive forces. Undoubtedly, developing productive forces requires a constant improvement of the relations of production and their corresponding superstructure. However, in practice, merely adjusting the relations of production is not sufficient. After entering socialist society from a semi-colonial and semi-feudal one, China faced the reality that the level of development of the productive forces could not meet the demands of socialism. Therefore, the basic approach to practicing the regulations of socialism proposed by Marx is to create the correct economic conditions. More specifically, this is achieved by laying a material foundation through the development of productive forces. Thus, the socialist part of the political economy is the form of economics focused on economic development. This not only reforms and improves the socialist economic system and structure, but it also studies productive forces in addition to seeking methods to develop advanced productive forces and increase national wealth. Accordingly, the political economy should shift its focus from class struggle to economic development, while simultaneously serving as its theoretical guide. Therefore, it has become a research mission for the political economy to emancipate and develop productive forces, to increase national wealth, and to achieve a common prosperity.

Second, one must proceed from reality and explore the economic system in the primary stage of socialism. The classic socialist economic system was built on the basis of a developed capitalist society. The corresponding socialist political economy focused on the socialist economic system characterized by public ownership. However, in practice, socialism does not originate from a developed capitalist society. Instead it is still in the primary stage with a low level of productive forces, immature socialist relations of production, as well as coexisting, diverse forms of ownership. Therefore, the historical task of the political economy is to perform an economic analysis of the primary stage of socialism based on the basic theories and methods of the Marxist political economy. It aims to explore the basic economic system and its forms in which public ownership dominates while diverse forms of ownership coexist in the primary stage of socialism.

Third, one must summarize the experiences of socialist economic development and build the theoretical system of the socialist economy with Chinese characteristics. Socialist practices with Chinese characteristics need to be guided by socialist theory with Chinese characteristics. Since 1949, China's practices for developing the socialist economy have experienced several twists and turns. Since the Third Plenary Session of the 11th Central Committee of the Communist Party of China (CPC) in 1978, China has shifted the focus to economic development, carrying out socialist practice for more than 40 years. The guiding principles that have been adopted during this period include Deng Xiaoping Theory, the important though of the "Three Represents", and the scientific outlook on development; these have constituted the theoretical system of socialism with Chinese characteristics and they were all produced by applying Marxism to China's existing conditions. Using this theoretical system, one may comprehensively summarize the experience of China's socialist construction, especially the successful practices since reform and opening up. Doing so will further build the theoretical system of socialist economy with Chinese characteristics that has become a task for political economy.

In fact, the aforementioned work of the political economy involves adapting Sinicization of Marxist economics. There are no readymade theories or experiences of constructing socialism in a large, developing country like China. Thus, the basic theories of Marxism need to be combined with the actual practices of China's socialist construction, constantly adapting Sinicization of Marxism to. In turn, these actions will guide the great cause of socialism with Chinese characteristics. In summary, the theoretical accomplishments of Sinicization of Marxism are mainly reflected in the following four aspects.

The first aspect is the theory of the basic economic system that constitutes the primary stage of socialism. Developing socialism with

Chinese characteristics requires an adaptation of the country's fundamental conditions, meaning that it will remain in the primary stage of socialism for a long time. At this stage, the principal social contradiction lays between the people's increasing demands and the backward nature of social production. The historical tasks of the primary stage of socialism gradually eradicate underdevelopment, essentially realizing socialist modernization, and transforming China from an agricultural country with a large rural population that is mainly dependent on manual labor into an industrialized country with a large non-agricultural population and an economy comprising both modern agriculture and service industries. Building socialism with Chinese characteristics does not involve changing the socialist system or lowering the requirements of socialism. Instead, it adapts the present institutional arrangements to the level of the development of productive forces. Furthermore, these actions must benefit the development of productive forces and the promotion of the development of socialist cause. In addition, it is an institutional innovation to start from the primary stage of socialism and build the basic economic system. Its meaning lies in discovering the new impetus and factors to promote the development of productive forces, which would in turn mobilize the diverse economy and the multiple factors that exist in the primary stage of socialism. Doing so thus gives full play to all sources that can create social wealth. With these actions, the basic economic system established in the primary stage of socialism not only sticks to the basic principles of scientific socialism but also endows it with distinctive Chinese characteristics according to the actual conditions and features of contemporary China. This process reflects the combination of the basic principles of Marxism with adapting Marxism to Chinese conditions, the combination of the basic system of socialism with the market economy, as well as the combination of the improvement of efficiency with the promotion of social equality.

The second aspect is the theory of the socialist market economy. Developing socialism with Chinese characteristics in a country like China that implements a long-term planned economy requires emancipating the mind, pushing reforms forward, and building systems and mechanisms that are full of both vigor and efficiency. As opposed to other transitional countries, China's reform process does not mean abandoning forms of public ownership or adopting an overall policy of privatization. China is still in the primary stage of socialism, which suggests that the goal of reform is to build the economic structure of a socialist market and to allow it to play a fundamental role in resource allocation. The aim of the reform corresponding to it is therefore to develop diverse forms of ownership, to enable various factors such as capital, technology, and management to participate in income distribution, to allow people to obtain property income, and to open and constantly improve the market for factors represented by the stock market. All these measures have become powerful driving forces in the development of productive forces while simultaneously enriching the content of socialism with Chinese characteristics.

The third aspect is the theory of economic development under socialist conditions. The task of developing socialism with Chinese characteristics in a backward country requires resolving issues concerning development, maintaining the central position of the task of economic development, and using the scientific outlook on development as a guide. Promoting the building of "a moderately prosperous society in all respects" as part of its modernization process, China has taken a path to modernization with Chinese characteristics. In addition, in order to build a form of socialism based on an agricultural country, China must push forward the modernization process that is centered on industrialization and urbanization. China's practice of economic development has created new paths of industrialization, agricultural modernization, and urbanization with Chinese characteristics. Furthermore, because this is a form of economic development in a backward country, there must be an outlook on development that coordinates between the growth rate and overall quality. The scientific outlook on development that originates from the practices of economic development confirms that development is the top priority, putting people first is the core requirement, pursuing a comprehensive, balanced, and sustainable development is the basic requirement, and taking the holistic approach is the fundamental method. Under the guidance of the scientific outlook on development, the mode of economic development has been transformed into a scientific one that is both sound and quick. Practice has proven that socialism with Chinese characteristics serves as a banner of development and progress in contemporary society, setting the goal and providing directions for China's development. China's reform and opening up, as well as the cause of building a moderately prosperous society in all respects, are both great practices of building socialism with Chinese characteristics.

The fourth aspect is the theory of opening up to the outside world under socialist conditions. Building socialism with Chinese characteristics in a country that has a long history of being closed and then semi-closed requires the establishment of an open economy. In addition, China needs international resources and markets to develop its productive forces. Therefore, in order to develop social productive forces, especially advanced ones, socialist countries need to learn advanced technology and managerial experience from developed capitalist countries and to take active part in international economic cooperation and competition; these actions will strengthen their global competitiveness. It is essential for them to attract foreign capital through opening up and to adopt all economic forms — even those that are practiced in capitalist economies — as long as they are conducive to the development of productive forces.

9.4 Comprehensively Deepening the Innovation and Development of Economics at the Stage of Reform

In different eras, the political economy has had different historical tasks. When the Marxist political economy is confronted with the socialist economy in practice, it needs to study new problems, reveal new laws, summarize new theories, and constantly make theoretical innovations according to the mission of the times. Beginning from a new historical starting point, China has entered a new phase of establishing "a comprehensive well-off society" and building a modern socialist country. The 18th National Congress of the CPC and the Third Plenary Session of the 18th Central Committee of the CPC decided to take comprehensive measures to deepen the reform of the economic structure, embodying theoretical innovation and further enriching and developing the theory of socialist economy with Chinese characteristics.

9.4.1. *The innovation and development of the theory of the basic economic system*

The core of Marxist economics is the theory of ownership and the structure of ownership constitutes a society's basic economic system. In this case, the essential requirement of socialism is eliminating private ownership. The People's Republic of China was founded on the basis of a semi-colonial and semi-feudal society. Therefore, the development of socialism needed to go through a primary stage when it entered socialist society. According to the basic tenets of Marxism, the relations of production must accommodate and promote the development of productive forces. Therefore, the aim of establishing the theory of the basic economic system in the primary stage of socialism is exploring the new impetus and factors that could promote the development of productive forces and socialism, thereby giving full play to all sources that can create social wealth. Therefore, the basic economic system in which public ownership dominates while diverse forms of ownership coexist is established. After public ownership becomes dominant in the economy, Marxist economics does not intend to eliminate private ownership; instead, in accordance with the mission of building a new society, it seeks to make diverse forms of ownership cooperate and develop harmoniously, and to make all kinds of factors such as labor, knowledge, technology, management, and capital coexist harmoniously.

The Third Plenary Session of the 18th Central Committee of the CPC identified this basic economic system in which public ownership dominates while diverse forms of ownership coexist as an important pillar of the system of socialism with Chinese characteristics as well as the foundation of the socialist market economy structure. In so doing, a variety of non-public economies such as the individual economy, the private economy, and the economy of foreign investment have transformed from "within the system" to "outside the system", being granted the same status as the public economy. In order to give full play to their energies, the framework of the basic economic system needs to create a market environment for fair competition among economic entities under diverse forms of ownership, further breaking up monopolies or barriers from the state-owned economy. Such breakthroughs are reflected in two aspects. First, while it has been emphasized that it is necessary to maintain the dominant role of public ownership and develop the non-public economy, a further requirement needs to be clarified. The property rights of both the public and non-public economy should not be infringed upon. Second, a unified market access system should be implemented on the basis of a negative list, allowing non-public economies to enter those sectors that were once monopolized by state-owned enterprises, such as foreign trade, finance, insurance, communications, and railways.

In the process of reform, a breakthrough in the theory of ownership is to confirm that the public economy could have various forms. For example, the shareholding system could be a form of public ownership. Furthermore, the Third Plenary Session of the 18th Central Committee of the CPC claimed that the structure of mixed-ownership in which government, collective, and non-public capital have cross shareholdings and mix together could be an important form of the basic economic system. Therefore, the mutual development of public and non-public forms of ownership not only occurs between enterprises but also within an enterprise itself. Identifying mixed-ownership as an important form of the basic economic system thus provides wide space for the adjustment of the structures of ownership and the strengthening of enterprise competitiveness. The measures taken are as follows: allowing more state-owned economies and other economic forms to transform into mixed-ownership, allowing non-state capital to participate in investment projects held by the state capital, encouraging the development of mixed-ownership enterprises in which private capital holds a majority of shares, encouraging private enterprises to participate in the reform, transformation, and shareholding of state-owned enterprises, and allowing employees to have shareholdings in mixed-ownership to form a community of shared interests between the owners of capital and the laborers.

9.4.2. *The innovation and development of the theory of socialist market economy*

The economic structure is constructed on the basis of the basic economic system. The mutual development of diverse forms of ownership is an essential requirement of developing the market economy. One of the significant marks of progress of the political economy is including the field of economic operations in the research concerning China's post-reform economy. The basic problem and aim of economic operations are to improve the efficiency of resource allocation. After China brought forward the reform goal of building the structure of the socialist market economy in 1992, the market began to play a fundamental role in resource allocation, thus increasing economic energy and improving the efficiency of resource allocation. At present, China has initially built the structure of socialist market economy and is constantly improving its ability to identify and grasp market principles. On this basis, the Third Plenary Session of the 18th Central Committee of the CPC further confirmed that it needed to enable the market to play a decisive role in resource allocation and to make the role of government more extensive. This is a new breakthrough in the theory of the socialist market economy.

In this case, the market now autonomously takes effect and plays a decisive role in resource allocation. This is distinct from a system that operates under the macro control of the state where the market plays a fundamental role in resource allocation. The fact that the market determines resource allocation means that the market's rules, price, and competition jointly regulate the allocation of resources. Guaranteeing the market's decisive role in resource allocation requires two essential conditions. First, an effective market must be built. This includes the fact that the market system is unified and open, its rules are fair and transparent, its prices are autonomously formed, and competition is effective and orderly. Second, all the productive factors such as capital, land, labor, and technology should be able to enter the market and allow the free flow of factors, enterprises, products, and services. However, enabling the market to determine resource allocation does not mean allowing unrestrained freedom; instead, the government must play a better role in reducing the direct allocation of resources, on one hand, and playing a leading role in building market system and mechanism, on the other.

Clearly, after the market is confirmed to play a decisive role in resource allocation, the role of the government must be given full play. However, allowing the market to play a decisive role in resource allocation does not mean that it can determine the allocation of public resources. As opposed to the market's allocation of resources, which follows the principles of efficiency, the allocation of public resources needs to follow the principle of equity. A new economic project is guaranteeing that the function of government will not be in conflict with that of the market which determines resource allocation. Instead, the government needs to play a role in the following three aspects. First, when carrying out the principle of fair allotment the government should enter the field of income distribution rather than resource allocation. Second, the government needs to abide by the market rules and utilize its mechanisms when providing public services. Third, some of the public services that must be provided by the government do not necessarily need to be produced and operated by the government. The government could purchase the services produced and operated by the private sectors, which could endow the public services with higher quality as well as increased efficiency. For example, environmental protection projects could adopt methods such as charges for pollution and emission trading.

Identifying the market's decisive role in resource allocation means that the market will no longer function under the macro control of the state. However, the government should not abandon the methods of macro control under these circumstances. It is necessary to point out that macro control aims to balance the aggregate equilibrium. In this case, the original intention of the state's macro control is to ensure that the market regulation could carry out the macro planning of the state. However, this has not been a success. For example, the state continuously regulated the real estate market in previous years, but the price of real estate continued to increase, implying that there have been failures in regulating the market. Therefore, it should be clarified that in the system in which the market determines resource allocation, the government should not directly regulate the market. Instead, it needs to monitor macro effects such as the overall levels of prices and employment. This means that the government needs to determine the lower limits of the rate of inflation and the upper limits of the rate of unemployment. If the inflation rate and unemployment rate have exceeded their limits, the government should carry out deflation or stimulus policies, respectively. If not, the government should not regulate the market at random, instead preserving a larger space for the market to function autonomously. In recent years, such practices of macro control have proven to be successful.

9.4.3. *The innovation and development of the theory of income distribution*

Efficiency not only stems from resource allocation but also from the stimulus of income distribution. Both the economic subject and the efficiency of the input of various productive factors are stimulated by an effective mechanism of income distribution. Over the last 40 years, China's economic development has not only relied on the market's participation in resource allocation, but also on the establishment of a distribution system in which the distribution according to one's work is dominant while multiple forms of distribution exist side by side. This has eliminated a distribution system based on egalitarianism.

In the process of reform, the incentive function of income distribution has been reflected step by step. First, the principle of distribution according to one's work has stimulated the efficiency of work. Second, it has improved corporate governance. In a corporate system that is characterized by the separation of ownership and management, building an incentive mechanism that allows the managers to share residual claims could avoid opportunistic behaviors caused by informational asymmetry. Third, it has both established and improved reward mechanisms. In the future society envisioned by Marx, income could only be distributed according to one's work because labor was the only factor that was privately owned while all the other factors were publicly owned. After the establishment of the basic economic system in the primary stage of socialism, the private ownership of non-labor factors such as capital, knowledge, technology, and entrepreneurship have also been acknowledged. Thus, the system of distributing income needs to not only stimulate work efficiently but also encourage the input of factors such as capital, technology, and management. Accordingly, the distribution system allows these non-labor factors such as capital, technology, and management to be paid according to their contributions, aiming to stimulate their energies in creating social wealth. According to the requirement that the market should determine resource allocation, the Third Plenary Session of the 18th Central Committee of the CPC further proposed that the payment of capital, knowledge, technology, and management should all be determined by the market for factors of production. This means that the factors of production need to match up with their market allocation when being paid according to their contributions. This case must reflect the relationship between the market's supply and demand, thereby conserving factors that are scarce and making full use of those that are abundant.

The distribution of income under socialist conditions not only needs to promote efficiency, but also eliminate polarization. The reform over the past 40 years has provided a distribution mechanism that allows certain areas and people to get rich first. Regardless of the positive effects of this process, the negative effects have begun to emerge; the gap between the poor and the rich has been widening and the resulting social contradictions have in turn blocked the further improvements to efficiency. This indicates that China has entered a stage in which those who get rich first should help those who have lagged behind so as to gradually achieve common prosperity. Under the circumstances in which the market plays a decisive role in resource allocation, the key to maintaining both equity and justice is to raise the income of laborers. To begin with, equal rights in income distribution should be safeguarded. It is necessary to prevent the abuse of power for personal gains as well as to regulate monopolies. Furthermore, there should be an emphasis on primary distribution. Primary distribution should not only highlight efficiency, but also balance equity and efficiency as well. In particular, the proportion of labor pay in the primary distribution should be raised, ensuring that labor-based earnings grow in step with improvements in labor productivity. Third, conditions for residents to earn more property income should be created in order to solve the problem of inequity in property possession. Finally, a particular emphasis should be placed on equity in redistribution, requiring that the government should ensure equitable access to basic public services. To sum up, all the above measures have reflected the demands for social equity and justice.

In conclusion, theoretical innovation and creation are necessary when answering questions about what kind of socialism should be constructed and how that process should work in a country whose economy and culture are relatively backward. The economics founded by Marx envisioned the economic system and development in the future society, while the practice of developing socialism with Chinese characteristics has turned that vision into reality. The new progress in the economic theory after the 18th National Congress of the CPC and the Third Plenary Session of the 18th Central Committee of the CPC has reflected this economic mission at the new stage of economic development, which will guide China's reform and development at this new stage.

Chapter 10

The Advanced Social Productive Forces and the Scientific Labor Theory of Value

China's market-based reform will inevitably touch upon a range of new issues, all of which involve an understanding of advanced social productive forces, including the evaluation of the value of personal property and private capital, the scope of the current social labor, the evaluation of the role of various labor forms, the value judgment of various non-labor income, the role of various productive factors, the relationship between distribution according to factors and value production, and so on. The scientific judgment of these issues is related to the scientific understanding of Marx's labor theory of value, the application of which depends on two methods of thinking. First, in order to offer a scientific answer to those issues, one should have a comprehensive and accurate understanding of the labor theory of value. If one carefully examines *Capital: A Critique of Political Economy*, one can find that Marx had analyzed the positive and negative sides of the capital and the value increment when he expounded on the labor theory of value. In particular, one should pay attention to the analysis of the positive side that has long been ignored. Second, the current economic condition differs greatly from that in Marx's time when he put forward the labor theory of value. Therefore, it is necessary to apply the labor theory of value in conjunction with new practices in the new stages of development to study and elucidate new issues.

10.1 Private Property and Private Capital

The power of Marxism lies in its progress with different practices at distinct times. Marxist labor theory of value is no exception. The development of socialism consists of two stages: First, the replacement of capitalism with socialism; second, the construction of socialism. Correspondingly, the Marxist labor theory of value has distinct research tasks and goals during different historical periods. It is originally a weapon to criticize capitalism and is used to reveal the laws of economic operation under the capitalist condition. It aims to seek the gravediggers of capitalism by revealing the source of surplus value. However, in a socialist society, if one continues to study and apply the labor theory of value, one needs seek the factors and ways of building a new society.

Under capitalism, the laborers are separated from the means of production. The free laborer owns nothing and if he wishes to adopt the means of production in his work, he has to become the wage-laborer of capital owners. The surplus value he produces is thus possessed by property owners, including capitalists, and what he receives simply equals to the sale of labor in his labor value. The personal consumption of laborers is also a link in the capitalist reproduction, and their labor productivity indeed belongs to the productivity of capital. Therefore, laborers simply obtain labor income rather than property, let alone property income, and become proletarians to whom this society does not belong. It is through these analyzes that Marx discovered that the proletarians would be the gravediggers of the capitalist society and would initiate the most thorough revolution.

The status of laborers has changed fundamentally in the new society as they have become the builders of the society. As a builder, one is no longer a proletarian but a property owner who shares the fruits of construction. In *Capital*, Marx pointed out that the negation of the capitalist ownership gave rise to the "co-operation and the possession in common of the land and the means of production produced by labor itself".[1] The private ownership mentioned here was understood as the ownership of means of subsistence; however, it should include private property according to Marx. If a laborer is still a proletarian in the new society, what is the point of his overthrow of the old society? The traditional theory

---

[1]Karl Marx. *Capital: A Critique of Political Economy*, Vol. 1. Trans. Ben Fowkes (London: Penguin Books, 1976), p. 929.

explains that the laborer has become the master of productive means of public ownership. Yet the issue is that the means of production have not been occupied by the whole society at the present stage of socialism, and inequality does exist in the possession of the means of production. Moreover, in the current system, laborers have not become the masters of the means of production. Then, it is in line with Marx's thinking to confirm private property and private possession of means of production, and to establish the relationship of joint labor on that basis.

The ultimate goal of socialism is to make people prosper, not only to increase their income, but also to increase their property. The laborer then will not necessarily be a proletarian who is separated from the labor condition, and he might become a part of the production process as the property owner, and that explains that every laborer has his property. His income consists of not only the income from labor but also that from property. Yet the ownership of private property never means the individual possession of the same amount of property. In the primary stage of socialism, it is simply possible to guarantee the equal rights of obtaining private property.

Private property comprises financial assets, real estate, and in particular assets such as stocks, corporate bonds, and equity, influencing the value judgment of the property as the source of income, that is, private capital. According to Marx, the separation of labor and the ownership of the labor condition (capital) is historically and logically the starting point of capitalism, which is created by the primitive capital accumulation. That is what Marx cursed in *Capital*, "capital comes dripping from head to toe, from every pore, with blood and dirt".[2] That value judgment is made in terms of the primitive capital accumulation, and we should not crystalize this starting point or simply restore this logic abstraction to reality. At the present stage of socialism, some private corporations indeed face the problem mentioned in the curse in the primitive accumulation, but most corporations do not have that problem. In reality, the laborer might be the owner of the factors and he not only can obtain income from labor, but also from the equity he holds, the technology he invests, and his management abilities. On the contrary, the capital owner may also invest in labor through the investment of management and technology, and some capital owner might directly invest in labor. Therefore, we should not simply curse the capital accumulated through legal businesses

[2] *Ibid.*, p. 926.

and entrepreneurship; instead, we should encourage their efforts because the scarcest factor of production at the present stage is not labor but capital.

In response to the long-standing tradition of treating individual investors as a different category, Jiang Zemin's "July 1 Speech" in 2001 clarified that one should not simply use the possession and the amount of property as a criterion to judge a person's political advancement or backwardness. That is a recognition of private investors whose purpose is to achieve property increment. The construction of a new society not only needs labor, but more importantly, it asks for private investment. Thus, property income, like the income from labor, should also be acknowledged in China's market economy.

Income and property play different roles in promoting economic development. The previous system refused to acknowledge private interests, giving rise to the lack of motivation in laborers. The existing reforms not only acknowledge the private interests of laborers but also link them with productions and corporate interests, thus mobilizing the enthusiasm of the laborers and arousing their concern for productions and corporate interests. Nowadays, the acknowledgment of private property impels laborers to care for the increase of national wealth as it is related to their own property interests. The increase of private property not only increases personal wealth, but also national wealth, which is a requirement of building a new society. Recognizing personal property not only increases its share in the market economy but also fuels the creation of wealth from property assets. Future classes will be defined not only by their income but also by their property holdings. The issues of fairness and efficiency will arise and will need to be addressed at a new level. For instance, the progressive personal income tax is adopted to bridge the gap of income distribution, and the estate tax is used to narrow the gap of property.

10.2 Social Labor and Advanced Productive Factors

The Communist Party of China represents the demand of advanced social productive forces and one of its important roles is to seek advanced productive factors to develop productive forces. The Marxist labor theory of value indeed studies advanced productive factors. Nevertheless, it has overly emphasized the role of labor in the production of value and neglected the role of capital, land, technology, management, and other factors in the creation of wealth. The unilateral understanding of the labor theory of value equates the production of value with the creation of wealth, thus limiting the productive factors to labor and hindering the exploration and utilization of advanced productive factors. That can be explained on the basis of a comprehensive understanding of the labor theory of value.

In order to scientifically recognize the role of various factors in the development of productive forces, it is necessary to acquire a comprehensive and accurate understanding of the methodology Marx employed to establish his labor theory of value. Marx abstracted commodity from numerous economic phenomena: value from commodity and labor from value, thus formulating the labor theory of value. Following the logic of abstraction and concreteness, to arrive at reality, we need to add in the factors that have been abandoned. For instance, the labor that produces value not only includes manual labor, but also mental labor such as technology and management. The production of commodity is not simply the production of value but also the creation of wealth that contains use value and involves labor factors and non-labor factors such as capital.

First, we must consider the scope of social labor.

In Marx's analytical framework, social labor consists of productive labor and unproductive labor. It is necessary to clarify that productive labor differs from unproductive labor in the production of value, not in necessity or significance.

Productive labor produces value while unproductive labor does not produce value. In Marx's era, productive labor was limited to labor in the field of material production. Therefore, Marx categorized the labor in the service industry as unproductive labor, although he believed that much labor was socially necessary. That might explain the long underdevelopment of the service industry in China. Economic practices have broken through their theoretical frameworks. Modern socialist societies, including China, have already included the income of the service industry into the gross national product in the name of the tertiary industry, and the labor in the service industry is also recognized as productive labor.

It is impossible to state that all labor is productive labor that produces value, since the labor of civil servants and teachers is considered as social labor but not as productive labor that produces value. However, the labor that does not produce value cannot be deemed insignificant as it is a requisite in society and can provide the environment and condition for productive labor that produces value.

Many people simply regard productive labor that produces value as the labor of laborers, excluding the labor of technicians and management personnel, which disobeys the theory of labor value. The theory of labor value does not attribute the source of value to direct labor, and in its framework, management, and technology also participate in the production of value. In *Capital*, Marx put forward the concept of "the collective laborer", that is, "With the progressive accentuation of the co-operative character of the labor process, there necessarily occurs a progressive extension of the concept of productive labor, and of the concept of the bearer of that labor, the productive worker. In order to work productively, it is no longer necessary for the individual himself to put his hand to the object; it is sufficient for him to be an organ of the collective laborer, and to perform any one of its subordinate functions".[3] This means that the labor that produces value is not simply direct labor but also labor engaged in technology and management. Productive labor means all the labor that has been added to the production of commodities (the production mentioned here includes the commodity's circulation from the primary producer to the consumer), whether the labor is manual or non-manual (labor related to science). Correspondingly, managers and engineers can become members of the collective laborer who produce value as long as they are in their specific division of labor. The theory of labor value also points out that the value produced by complex labor is many times more than that by simple labor, and the tendency of modern economy is that the proportion and role of managers, engineers, and technicians in the production of value will be greater than those of direct laborers. Nowadays, most private entrepreneurs may participate in the production of value through the investment of management and technology, and the expansion of market; hence, they also participate in the production of value in this sense. If further consideration is given to the fact that the technical and managerial labor is complex labor, the value produced by it may be many times more than that by simple labor of direct laborers.

Second, we must analyze the distinction and connection between value production and wealth creation.

The labor theory of value distinguishes value production from wealth creation: value production cannot replace wealth creation as it is simply a further abstraction of the latter. Social products (wealth) are a product of

[3] *Ibid.*, pp. 643–644.

value and use value. Wealth creation is related to various productive factors, and value production is only related to labor. However, the labor process of creating value cannot be carried out in isolation and must be combined with the entire process of wealth creation. Marx abstracted the process of value production from that of wealth creation in order to reveal the source of surplus value through the analysis of value relations and value production. Yet one needs to study the process of wealth creation if one wants to study the role of various productive factors. When we apply the labor theory of value, we must not replace the process of wealth creation with the process of value production abstracted from wealth creation. In *Critique of the Gotha Program,* Marx and Engels respond to the statement "Labor is the source of all wealth and all cultures" in the Gotha program of the German Workers' Party. Labor is not the source of all wealth. Nature is just as much a source of use value, of which material wealth is composed. Labor is but a manifestation of the natural power, that is the human labor power. The above statement is right only when it means that labor owns the corresponding object and materials. However, a socialist program should not tolerate this bourgeoisie statement or evade the conditions that make the statement meaningful.

Third, we turn to the decisive factor of wealth creation.

Non-labor productive factors fail to become factors of value production, but they can become factors of wealth creation. The creation of wealth requires the combination of labor and various productive factors, including capital, land, technology, management, and so on. Marx once stated famously that labor is the father of material wealth, and the earth its mother. This means that the production of wealth requires production conditions such as land. Non-labor productive factors such as capital and land participate in the creation of social wealth although they do not produce value, and various productive factors, including labor, contribute to the creation of social wealth. Here, the role of capital in wealth creation and value production is particularly emphasized. According to Marx, various productive factors, including labor and land, are incorporated into the production process by capital. "By incorporating with itself the two primary creators of wealth, labor-power and land, capital acquires a power of expansion".[4] Capital also incorporates science and technology into the production process of wealth. "Science and technology give capital a power of expansion which is independent of the given magnitude of the

[4] *Ibid.*, p. 752.

capital actually functioning".[5] Just as they are the primary productive forces, science and technology cannot turn into productive forces without the involvement of capital. Otherwise, advanced science and technology can only be a castle in the air.

Capital also plays a certain role in the production of value. The value of wealth is composed of C + V + M, where V + M is the newly produced value and C is the transferred value. This transferred value is not passive to value production and can function dynamically. Marx's analysis of the relationship between labor productivity and value theory points out that capital, technology, and other factors will affect the value of unit products by affecting the gross use value produced in a certain period of labor time. With the improvement of the quality of the capital, the advanced machinery and equipment may produce more products and affect the amount of value. He states, "An immense difference exists between the value of the weekly product of the Englishman, who works with a mighty automatic machine, and that of the Chinese, who only has a spinning-wheel".[6] Moreover, labor is not homogeneous. It is also introduced into the value production process by capital. The more qualified the living labor employed by capital is, the more value it can create.

Fourth, we need to consider the advanced production sector.

Since value is produced by labor, can it be concluded that labor-intensive sectors produce more value and therefore are the most advanced? The answer is "no". According to the labor theory of value, the value produced by labor is related to the market. That is to say, the amount of value is determined by the social necessity of labor time. Whether the labor consumed can produce value depends on the recognition of the market, and the labor consumption that exceeds the socially necessary labor time is not recognized by the society. When an enterprise adopts some new factors such as new techniques or technology to improve labor productivity, it reduces the individual labor time of producing products and obtains excess profits. When the whole society employs these new factors, the labor productivity overall will increase and a new socially necessary labor time will be formed. That is also the case of labor-intensive sectors, and the amount of value produced is irrelevant to the intensity of labor. The law of the average rate of profit not only averages profits but also allows capital and technology-intensive sectors to obtain excess profits.

---

[5] *Ibid.*, p. 754.

[6] *Ibid.*

Therefore, in the advanced production sector, it is not the labor-intensive sector but the capital- and technology-intensive sectors that produce higher value.

The labor theory of value analyzes not only the role of labor productivity but also capital productivity, land productivity, the productivity of division of labor, and productivity generated by management and technology. In Marx's analysis, these factors play a far greater role than labor productivity does in the creation of wealth. Therefore, in terms of value-producing labor, advanced productive factors are complex labor, and with regard to wealth creation, advanced productive factors are not labor but technology and knowledge, and the role of capital is to incorporate these advanced productive factors into the production process. Whether capital is an advanced production factor depends on the quality of the productive factors that have been incorporated into the production process.

10.3 Distribution According to Work and Distribution According to Factors

The labor theory of value naturally deduces the inevitability of distribution according to work under socialist conditions. When we establish the role of various non-labor productive factors in wealth creation, this includes the necessity of the coexistence of distribution according to work and distribution according to other factors in the current structure of China.

Here it is necessary to clarify that the distribution structure is not a passive distribution of products; instead, it plays an irreplaceable role in production. The function of the distribution mechanism is to improve labor efficiency and the efficiency of resource allocation, and to stimulate the input of labor by the labor factor owner and that of capital, technology, and management by owners of other factors. Institutional innovation also aims to encourage the owners to consciously put factors into the improvement of productivity, and then it is essential to obtain remuneration according to factors which means remuneration according to labor input, capital input, technology input, and the input of entrepreneurs.

The theoretical hindrance to the factor distribution mechanism mentioned above is Marx's critique of the "trinity" formula of capital interest, labor wages, and land-ground-rent. If we examine Marx's labor theory of value from two aspects, we can recognize the difference between distribution by factors and the "trinity" formula. First of all, in Marx's view, the vulgarity of the "trinity" formula is that capital, labor, and land are equally regarded as sources of value. However, he did not deny that land ownership, capital and wage labor were sources of income. Second, income distribution and value production are two different issues, and the theory of income distribution is not necessarily explained by the theory of value production. According to Marx, the production of value is related to labor, but distribution is related to factor ownership. Capital, labor, land, technology, management, and other factors belong to different owners; the distribution process is the realization of factor ownerships; and, just as Marx stated, land rent is the realization of land ownership. The analysis of the division of surplus value in *Capital* explains the positive role of the realization of factor ownership in distribution in improving productivity and increasing social wealth.

In the general theory of price, people regard interest rates, wages, and rents as the prices of productive factors such as capital, labor, and land, which are formed in their respective factor markets. That has a positive effect on the distribution and use of factors in an efficient way. Moreover, the labor theory of value never denies the participation of factors in distribution. Nevertheless, people have always treated the labor theory of value simply as the role of labor, thereby further limiting the distribution mechanism under socialist conditions to distribution according to work and resulting in the inefficiency of the entire factor distribution.

In practice, the limitations of distribution simply according to work are readily apparent. First, the distribution according to work that Marx envisaged is only related to consumer goods, but distribution in actuality is tied to income distribution. One part of income is used for consumption, and the other part is used for saving, which means that income distribution is beyond the scope of the distribution of consumer goods. In order to mobilize residents to invest their savings, it is necessary to introduce other ways of distribution apart from distribution according to work. Second, the production process is a combination of multiple productive factors, and labor is only one of them. The main constraint to the development of productive forces in the primary stage of socialism is the insufficient supply of capital, technology, and entrepreneurs, and it is impossible to mobilize factors other than labor by relying solely on distribution according to work.

Nowadays, China needs to address the following three issues with regard to the mechanism of obtaining remuneration according to factor inputs.

First, encourage the input of knowledge and technology. The reward represents the value of their input in distribution, and pays off the costs for the advancement of technology. Its goal is to mobilize the enthusiasm of technological personnel and promote technological progress. The labor that includes technology in the production has to address the issue of remuneration. The reason for the long-term low remuneration of technological and managerial staff is revealed in Engels's work *Anti-Dühring*. As he explains, the value produced by complex labor is higher than that by simple labor, and as individuals have paid for the education and training fees to form complex labor under capitalist conditions, they should obtain higher remuneration than the simple laborers. However, under socialist conditions, as the education and training fees are provided by society, the complex laborers should not demand higher income, and the higher value they produce ought to belong to society. Yet that is not the case in true socialist societies. The society has provided part of the education and training fees for technical and managerial staff; nevertheless, another considerable part is paid by the individuals themselves, not to mention the opportunity cost they incur. Therefore, it is reasonable for technological and managerial staff to ask for higher income.

Second, stimulate capital input. The possession and the amount of property should not be criteria to judge a person's political advancement and backwardness. However, the source of property and the use of property should become criteria to judge a person's political advancement and backwardness with regard to promoting economic growth. Subsequently, distribution according to input are reasonable and legal, and should be encouraged. Citizens can use some income that is not for consumption to buy stocks to obtain dividends, to buy corporate bonds to obtain debts, and to invest in enterprises to obtain capital revenues.

Third, encourage operators to become entrepreneurs. As a productive factor, an entrepreneur represents the abilities in management. According to Marx's labor theory of value, management is the labor involved in the production of value and the function of capital. As Marx stated, "all directly social or communal labor on a large scale requires, to a greater or lesser degree, a directing authority, in order to secure the harmonious cooperation of the activities of individuals, and to perform the general functions that have their origin in the motion of the total productive organism, as distinguished from the motion of its separate organs".[7] As a function of

[7] *Ibid.*, p. 448.

capital, management input should be involved in the distribution of capital income (profit), not just labor income. In the third volume of *Capital*, capital consists of the interest-bearing capital as ownership and the capital of executive function, and the profits generated are correspondingly divided into interest and business owner income. According to Marx, the capital of executive function may mean that the functional capitalists simultaneously perform the duties of supervision and management, or they hand over the duties of supervision and management to others. In the first case, the income of the business owner includes the reward for his supervision and management, while in the second case, the reward for supervision and management is separated from the income of the business owner. Apparently, to represent the operators' management abilities and input, the entrepreneurs participate in profit sharing through the distribution of annual salary and shares, which can encourage more operators to become entrepreneurs. That then will help prevent the corruption of operators and promote their innovation in management.

Considering the role of factors in wealth creation, capital, knowledge, and technology are scarce productive factors at the present stage of China. The owners of those factors will become the center of wealth creation, and it is natural for distribution (income and property) to be tilted toward them.

Therefore, in order to adapt to the transformation from an old society to a new society, Marxist theories have shifted from weapons of criticism to tools of construction. The dynamic nature of Marx's labor theory of value lies in its not being a solidified dogma. In order to fulfill the requirements of constructing a new society, we can further study the labor theory of value to find the theories and methods that can guide our reform at the stage of development in socialism.

Chapter 11

Marx's Theory of Wealth Creation and Its Practical Significance

One significant task of studying *Capital* in the context of building socialism with Chinese characteristics is to seek Sinicization of Marxism's entry point. The political economy represented by *Capital* puts forward the theory of value production and the theory of wealth creation, and the Marxist theory of value reveals the inevitability of socialism's replacement of capitalism. At the present stage of socialism, economic construction has turned into a central task, and the increase of national wealth has become the goal of economic development. Considering the goal and task, the theory of wealth elucidated in *Capital* might become a vital entry point into the study of modernization and Sinicization of Marxist political economy. However, compared with the study and analysis of Marxist theory of value, we have focused little on Marxist theory of wealth. Therefore, we need to explore the theory of wealth creation in *Capital* in a comprehensive way, and to extract it from that ideological system.

11.1 The Theoretical Distinction between Wealth and Value

In order to apply Marx's political economy to the explanation of economic development, we need to pay attention to his theory of wealth. We used to employ the theory of value to illustrate wealth creation; however, with a careful examination of Marxist political economy, we can find that value production and wealth creation have common rules and evident differences as well. The theory of wealth can address the issue of the full flow of various sources of national wealth, but the theory of value alone is unable to fully explain the creation of wealth.

With regard to the definition of wealth, the founder of classical economics, Adam Smith's *An Inquiry into the Nature and Causes of the Wealth of Nations* reflects the demands of the emerging capitalist class on their rise, and stresses the significance and methods of increasing national wealth. He defined wealth as, "yet in representing the wealth of nations as consisting, not in the unconsumable riches of money, but in the consumable goods annually reproduced by the labor of the society".[1] Marx approved that definition, and pointed out that with the abstract generality of the activities of wealth creation, there exists the generality of the object defined as wealth, and that is the product in general. Thus, political economy indeed examines the achievements of human beings' economic activities.

The wealth in Marxist political economy refers not only to the wealth of human beings, but also to wealth within the scope of human's economic activities, specifically social wealth. Resulting from economic operations, social wealth is the product created by human labor to have use value for human beings. According to Marx, wealth is only expressed as human activities. Anything that is not the result of human activities or the result of labor is nature, and nature is not social wealth. In a market economy, commodities are the social form of wealth. Therefore, "the wealth of societies in which the capitalist mode of production prevails appears as an 'immense collection of commodities'; the individual commodity appears as its elementary form".[2]

The commodity is a unity of use value and value. In Marx's view, "regardless of the social form of wealth, use value always constitutes the material content of wealth". "It is therefore the physical body of the commodity itself, for instance iron, corn, a diamond, which is the use value or useful things".[3] Then, wealth is separated from value, and although both of them belong to one element of the commodity, they are two different concepts, and wealth is categorized as the use value.

---

[1]Adam Smith. *An Inquiry into the Nature and Causes of the Wealth of Nation.* Ed. Edward Cannan (Chicago: University of Chicago Press, 1977), p. 902.

[2]Karl Marx. *Capital: A Critique of Political Economy.* Vol. 1, Trans. Ben Fowkes (New York: Penguin Class, 1976), p. 125.

[3]*Ibid.*, p. 126.

Marxist value analysis begins with the commodity, and scientific abstraction is adopted to divide the commodity form of wealth into use value and value. It abstracts value from the commodity and clarifies that labor is the sole source of value. Apparently, Marxist analysis of value is in-depth and abstract, and the theory of value he created is indeed the result of the gradual abandonment of factors related to wealth. According to Marx, when we examine wealth, we must reverse the process of Marxist value analysis, and as the value analysis is a process from concreteness to abstraction, the wealth analysis should be process from value to reality, i.e., from abstract value to concrete wealth.

Moreover, according to Marx's definitions of wealth and value, the wealth analysis and the value analysis are two aspects of the same process. Whether political economy is expanded from the value analysis or the wealth analysis is subject to its goals and tasks. Marx's political economy starts from the analysis of value as its goal is to eventually reveal that the surplus value produced by living labor is appropriated by the capitalist, that laborers or the proletarian is the gravedigger of capitalist society, and that capitalism will inevitably be replaced by socialism. Hence, the value analysis is also a process that reveals various contradictions of the capitalist society. Wealth analysis was not fully expanded when Marx analyzed the contradictions of the capitalist society, and that was consistent with Marx's aim of research. Nevertheless, in a new society where the laborers are the masters of the country and their own destiny, the aim of political economy is to increase national wealth and to seek the builders of the society and the impetus for wealth increase, and then it is necessary for us to expand the analysis of wealth. Although this analysis was not fully made by Marx, we can still follow his logic to study the formation and increase of wealth and to establish a scientific Marxist theory of wealth to guide our economic development.

In fact, Marxist value theory encompasses the wealth analysis. Value production and wealth creation are two aspects of the same production process. Abstract labor produces value, while specific labor produces use value (wealth). When we establish the Marxist theory of wealth, we need to follow the logic of value analysis to sort out wealth theory. Afterward, we can discover the differences between wealth creation and value production.

First, the difference between the source of value production and that of wealth creation. Labor is the sole source of value production; yet it is not the sole source of wealth creation although the creation of wealth is inseparable from labor. Material factors, such as capital and land, and intangible factors represented by technology and management, are sources of wealth creation. Consequently, wealth analysis needs to study various factors and their combinations in the creation of wealth, and to study the historical features and dynamics along with the alteration of the mode of production.

Second, the difference between the measurement of value and that of wealth. The amount of wealth consists of both labor value transferred from specific labor (C) and the new value produced by abstract labor (V + M), meaning that the existing wealth is involved in the creation of new wealth through concrete labor, and the previous labor produces not value but wealth. Hence, the theory of wealth focuses on the total value of the commodity, and the means of production possess a significant position in that theory as the material conditions of labor play an important role in the creation of wealth.

Third, the difference between the distribution principle of value and that of wealth. The distinct sources of value and wealth give rise to different modes of distribution in value and wealth. Value distribution refers to the distribution of newly created value between the necessary labor value and surplus value, and the division of surplus value within the capitalists; while the distribution of wealth is the distribution according to the factor owners' individual contributions to wealth creation.

Fourth, value and wealth alter in an opposite direction to labor productivity, as is explained from the duality of labor itself. As Marx said, "By 'productivity' of course, we always mean the productivity of concrete useful labor; in reality this determines only the degree of effectiveness of productive activity directed towards a given purpose within a given period of time. Useful labor becomes, therefore, a more or less abundant source of products in direct proportion as its productivity rises or falls". Instead, "The same labor, therefore, performed for the same length of time, always yields the same amount of value, independently of any variations in productivity".[4] The amount of value is only related to labor-time, and the living labor with higher productivity can produce more use value within the same labor-time. However, this does not mean higher productivity of living labor can produce more value as the increase of labor productivity only means more use value produced in the same labor-time, and the total amount of value within the same labor-time is the same.

[4] *Ibid.*, p. 137.

Labor productivity is proportional to the use value of a commodity and is inversely proportional to the amount of value of a commodity. Similarly, the alteration of the organic composition of capital caused by the increase of social labor productivity impacts the value and wealth in an opposite way. In terms of value production, the increase in the organic composition of capital means a relative decline in the proportion of living labor, thus leading to the decline of the amount of value produced and the general rate of profit. Nevertheless, with regard to wealth creation, the increase in organic composition of capital means the increase of the proportion of materialized labor, i.e., the material factors of labor, the increase of the social labor productivity, and the increase of the production of use value, or in other words wealth.

Marxist value analysis points out that the amount of value is inversely proportional to the increase of social labor productivity, and the alteration of the amount of value has different effects on capital and laborers. The productivity generated by the increase of labor productivity rate is possessed by capital because value distribution refers to the distribution of value produced by living labor between the necessary labor value and surplus value. The increase of social labor productivity results in the decline of labor value (necessary labor value), and "relative surplus value, however, is directly proportional to the productivity of labor".[5] Meanwhile, the increase in the organic composition of capital gives rise to the decrease in employment. Then, the conclusion of value analysis is that the increase of social labor productivity conflicts with the interests of laborers, which is in line with Marx's intention of revealing the grave-digger of the capitalist society.

The amount of wealth is inversely proportional to the amount of value and is proportional to social labor productivity, and the analysis of wealth creation can be fully applied to the theory of building a new society. This theory can be explained as wealth increase being consistent with the increase of social labor productivity in a new society. The participants of wealth creation or the factor owners share common interests, and wealth distribution refers to the distribution of wealth among factor owners, and all the builders, that is factor owners, are likely to share the fruits of the increase of social labor productivity. Therefore, the aim of wealth analysis is to seek ways to improve social labor productivity, to increase national wealth, and to give full play to the vitality of wealth creation.

---

[5] *Ibid.*, p. 436.

11.2 The Source of Wealth Creation and Increase

In Marxist value analysis, the sole source of value production is labor or abstract labor. The way to increase value is either to extend labor-time, to increase labor intensity, or to reduce necessary labor value (depending on the increase of social labor productivity). It is evident that the value theory alone cannot explain issues of economic development related to wealth increment. Different from value theory, which seeks the gravedigger of capitalist society, wealth theory seeks the source of and impetus for wealth increase and the builders of society. In Marx's view, the process of wealth creation is the labor process itself, which "is purposeful activity aimed at the production use values. It is an appropriation of what exists in nature for the requirement of man. It is the universal condition for the metabolic interaction between man and nature, and the everlasting nature-imposed condition of human existence".[6] Thus, wealth increment is involved in the role and mobilization of various productive factors.

First, the source of wealth creation. With regard to the misconception that "labor is the sole source of wealth" in *Critique of the Gotha Program*, Marx explained that "labor is not the sole source of all wealth. Nature is just as much the source of use value (and it is surely such that material wealth consists of labor, which itself is only the manifestation of a force of nature, human labor power ... Labor becomes the source of wealth and culture only as social labor, or what is the same thing through society".[7] It can be concluded that apart from labor, nature can also be a source of wealth, and that labor alone cannot create wealth and needs to combine with other factors through social labor process, that is, the combination of man and nature.

The reason why labor is not the sole source of use value or material wealth it produces can be explained from Marx's analysis of the labor process. The creation of wealth, that is, use value is a specific labor process. The factors of a labor process comprise labor, the means of labor, and the object of labor, and labor is not the sole factor of wealth creation. Capital, land, technology, and management are also the factors that can create wealth. Unlike the focus of value production, wealth creation not only focuses on the role of labor, but also on the role of factors other than

---

[6] *Ibid.*, p. 126.

[7] Karl Marx. *Capital: A Critique of Political Economy*. Vol. 3, Trans. David Fernbach (London: Penguin Books, 1981), p. 13.

labor. According to Marx, factors that determine labor productivity include the "workers' average degree of skill, the level of development of science and its technological application, the social organization of the process of production, the extent and effectiveness of the means of production, and the condition found in the natural environment".[8] Specifically, with the advancement of science and technology, the factors other than labor will play an increasingly important role in the creation of wealth and directly influence labor productivity.

With regard to the role of natural forces in the creation of wealth, Marx believed that human beings and nature go hand in hand. Human beings "often rely on natural forces" in the labor process, and "As William Petty says, labor is the father of material wealth, the earth is its mother".[9] External natural conditions are divided from the economic point of view into two great classes by Marx. One is natural wealth in the means of subsistence, i.e., a fruitful soil, waters teeming with fish, etc. The other is natural wealth in the instruments of labor, such as waterfalls, navigable rivers, wood, metal, coal, etc. Those two classes of natural wealth play different decisive roles at different stages of development. "At the dawn of civilization, it is the first class that turns the scale; at a higher stage of development, it is the second".[10] The creation of wealth apparently cannot depend on nature. It also does not mean that the more abundant the nature is or the more advanced the economic development is, the more wealth will be created. On the contrary, "where nature is too prodigal with her gifts, she 'keeps him in hand, like a child in leading-strings'".[11] In terms of the role of natural wealth in wealth increase, "It is not the absolute fertility of the soil but its degree of differentiation, the variety of its natural products, which forms the natural basis for the social division of labor, and which, by changes in the natural surroundings, spurs man on to the multiplication of his needs, his capacities, and the instruments and modes of his labor. It is the necessity of bringing a natural force under the control of society, of economizing on its energy, of appropriating or subduing it on a large scale by the work of the human hand, that plays the most decisive role in the history of industry".[12] The utilization of natural resources

---

[8] Karl Marx. *Capital: A Critique of Political Economy*. Vol. 1, p. 130.

[9] *Ibid.*, p. 134.

[10] *Ibid.*, p. 648.

[11] *Ibid.*, p. 649.

[12] *Ibid.*

in the increase of wealth creation analyzed here by Marx is still meaningful even today.

Considering the role of technological advancement in wealth creation, the increase of social labor productivity brought about by technological advancement may result in the decline in the amount of value and the increase in wealth. First, with the increase of labor productivity, the number of products that can reflect the certain amount of surplus value will also increase. For instance, "The value of a week's products by British people who adopt a powerful automaton strikingly differs from that by Chinese people who simply use a hand spinning wheel". Second, with regard to the renewal of machinery, "the old machines, tools and apparatus, etc., will be replaced by more efficient and (considering their increased efficiency) cheaper ones".[13] Third, in terms of its effect on the objects of labor such as raw materials, technological advancement not only increases the quantity and use of useful substances, but also expands the fields of investment, and "teaches capital how to throw back the waste from the processes of production and consumption into the cycle of the process of reproduction, and thus, without any previous outlay of capital, it creates fresh materials for it".[14] This is what we call circular economy today. Therefore, science and technology equip the capital of executive function with the ability of expansion that is not influenced by its certain amount. Unlike the confrontation between technological progress and the capitalist system highlighted by the value analysis, wealth analysis may highlight the support of technological progress for wealth increment.

Second, the combination of wealth creation factors. The various factors do not work in isolation. Instead, they work in collaboration to generate productivity that creates and increases wealth. According to Marx, the combination of factors and their functions are inseparable from two types of factors.

On one hand, it is the role of capital. Marx used the primary driving forces to explain the role of capital as a binder in the collaboration of factors. According to Marx, various productive factors, including labor and land, are capitalized into the production process. "By incorporating with itself the two primary creators of wealth, labor-power and land, capital acquires a power of expansion".[15] Capital also incorporates science and

---

[13] *Ibid.*, p. 753.

[14] *Ibid.*, p. 754.

[15] *Ibid.*, p. 752.

technology into the production process of wealth. That is because technological productivity not only can be the productivity of capital, but also can enable capital to achieve higher productivity. The role of capital in wealth creation, as suggested by Marx, not only lies in its own input, but more importantly, lies in its being the binder of factors to improve productivity in the allocation of different factors. The capital's input in the quantity or the quality of factors exerts a different influence on the increase of productivity, and that also reflects the difference in the ways of growth.

On the other hand, it is the role of management. Marx pointed out that "[a]ll directly social or communal labor on a large-scale requires, to a greater or lesser degree, a directing authority, in order to secure the harmonious cooperation of the activities of individuals, and to perform the general functions that have their origin in the motion of the total productive organism".[16] Hence, management supervises "the process of the value increment of capital", and also "the social labor process of product manufacturing".[17] Distinct from the management of surplus value production, the management of wealth creation not only supervises labor, but more importantly, organizes and allocates the factors and their input in the production process. The total factor productivity discussed is based on the management system and its efficiency, which will directly affect the level of wealth creation and increment.

With social progress and economic development, the combination of different factors of wealth creation manifests in two trends. The first is that with the concentration and socialization of capital, "the conscious technical application of science, the planned exploitation of the soil, the transformation of the means of labor into forms in which they can only be used in common, the economizing of all means of production by their use as the means of production of combined, socialized labor".[18] The other trend is that productive factors that play a decisive role in wealth increase transfer from the tangible material factors to intangible factors such as management, technology, and knowledge. The owners of those factors will become the center of wealth creation, and it is natural for distribution (income and property) to be tilted toward them. It is also the inner need to maximize national wealth at the present stage.

[16] *Ibid.*, p. 448.
[17] *Ibid.*, p. 450.
[18] *Ibid.*, p. 929.

11.3 Wealth Possession and the Sharing of Surplus Value

Wealth possession is closely related to income distribution. In addition, the wealth analysis and the value analysis of income distribution have distinct goals. The value analysis based on Marxist labor theory of value is indeed the theory of the possession of surplus value, while wealth analysis starts from the participation of the owners of productive factors in wealth increment, and studies the issue of whether wealth can achieve better development in this or that form of property. That involves the institutional arrangement of wealth possession, of which the core issue is who possesses surplus value.

Marxist value analysis divides the value produced by living labor into the necessary labor value and surplus value. The income distribution is in fact the issue of the possession of surplus value. The increase of the amount of surplus value is based on the absolute extension of labor-time and relative reduction in necessary labor-time under the conditions of improved social labor productivity, reflecting the conflict between capital and labor. Then, the distribution is the division of surplus value among industrial capitalists, landowners, commercial capitalists, and money capitalists. The theory of the segmentation of surplus value aims to demonstrate that the proletariat is faced with the exploitation of the entire capitalist class. It is evident that the research conclusions of value distribution fail to address the issue of a better realization of wealth increment and development.

When Marx criticized Smith's faith, he pointed out the essence of the distribution relationship. As he stated, "in dealing with the relations of distribution, it is usual to start from the ostensible fact that the annual product is divided into wages, profit, and ground-rent, but expressed in this way, that is wrong. The product is divided into capital on the one hand and revenues on the other. One of these revenues, wages, only ever assumes the form of a revenue, the revenue of the worker, after it has previously confronted the same worker in the form of capital. The confrontation between the produced conditions of labor and the products of labor all together as capital, and the immediate producers, gives the material conditions of labor right from the start a specific social character *vis-à-vis* the workers, and hence sets up a specific relationship which the workers enter into, in production itself, to the owners of these conditions of labor and to one another … but this is a completely different distribution from what is understood by relations of distribution when a historical character is claimed for these, in contrast to the relations of production. What is meant under this rubric are the different titles to the part of the product that falls into individual consumption. The former relations of distribution, on the other hand, are the foundation of particular social functions which are ascribed to specific agents of production within the relation of production itself, as distinct from the immediate producers".[19] Marx's analysis indeed mentioned two forms of distribution: One is the distribution of social production conditions (i.e., C + V) which reflects that the material conditions of labor are given a specific social character *vis-à-vis* the workers[20]; the other form is the distribution of value products (i.e., V + M), which refers to "the different titles to the part of the product that falls into individual consumption.[21] Strictly speaking, Marx's analysis of those two forms aims to clarify that "the distribution relation and distribution method are only expressed as the back of productive factors", and "the structure of the distribution is completely determined by the structure of production". Thus, "the former relations of distribution give the actual conditions of production, and their representatives, a specific social quality", "they determine the whole character and movement of production".[22]

Marx's above statements suggest that the distribution of wealth must first address the issue of the distribution of production conditions. In other words, "any distribution whatever of the means of consumption is only a consequence of the distribution of the conditions of production themselves. The latter distribution, however, is a feature of the mode of production itself".[23] Under capitalist conditions, the distribution of production conditions is the social arrangement of C and V, reflecting the opposition of labor and capital. In the future society that Marx envisioned, "material conditions of production are the collective property of workers" and the distribution of productive means, namely C, should be the direct

[19] Karl Marx. *Capital: A Critique of Political Economy*. Vol. 3, pp. 1018–1019.

[20] *Ibid.*, p. 1018.

[21] *Ibid.*, p. 1019.

[22] *Ibid.*

[23] Karl Marx and Frederick Engels. *Karl Marx Frederick Engels Complete Works*. Vol. 3, Tran. Jack Cohen, Richard Dixon, Clement Dutt, Alex Miller, Martin Milligan, Barbara Ruhemann, Dirk J. Struik, and Christopher Upward (London: Lawrence & Wilshart, 2010), p. 19.

deduction of total social products. That is to say, "first, cover for the replacement of the means of production used up. Secondly, additional portion for expansion of production. Thirdly, reserve or insurance funds to provide against accidents, dislocations caused by natural calamities, etc.".[24] The deduction that enters the production process forms the distribution of the production process. It is the distribution of production tools, and the distribution of members of society among various forms of production (individuals are subject to certain production relations). The distribution included in the production process is not income distribution, but it determines income distribution.

After wealth is deducted from the means of production for reproduction, the remaining portion is used for income distribution. This is the object of distribution — the gross social income minus the value of the means of production (or the value of materialized labor) — the social net income, or (V + M). The distribution of this part of income can be analyzed from the perspectives of value distribution and wealth distribution.

The value analysis of income distribution is based on value theory, which believes that income distribution is the distribution between V and M. The income earned by various non-labor factors is the income of exploitation, as it exploits the surplus labor of workers. The distribution of M among industrial capitalists, commercial capitalists, loan capitalists, and landowners are the division of surplus value.

The wealth analysis of income distribution is based on the goal of increasing wealth. It is believed that the aim of income distribution is to obtain remuneration according to factor contribution. The gross income of each factor owner is also new creation value (V + M). The total amount of wealth distribution and that of value distribution are the same, which is different from value analysis. The aim of wealth analysis is to propel each factor owner to provide factors of production to increase wealth. As Marx said, the real wealth is the high productivity of all individuals. The mechanism or institutional arrangement for wealth increment lies in the arrangement of "property form" to give full play to the productivity of all factors.

The realistic production conditions are a collection of factors such as labor, land, capital, technology, and management. The wealth increment requires the full flow of all factors of wealth creation, and the different ownerships of factors give rise to the possession of wealth, which in turn

---

[24]Karl Marx and Frederick Engels. *Karl Marx Frederick Engels Complete Works.* Vol. 3, p. 16.

fosters the concept of property. Property is wealth with a clear ownership, and manifests itself as a right under the protection of certain rules and regulations since its birth. The possession of wealth, as is suggested by Marx, is the distribution of wealth in the form of property ownership among factor owners. That solves the theoretical and practical problem of the participation of non-labor factors in income distribution, which cannot be explained by the value theory.

Specifically speaking, factor ownership is actually the property possession of different factor owners, such as the property rights of capital owners and landowners. Consequently, wealth is distributed according to the ownership of factors. When criticizing the "trinity" formula of bourgeois vulgar economics, Marx clearly pointed out that the forms of income distribution such as wages, profits, and land rents were the realization of corresponding factor ownerships, such as capital ownership, land ownership, and labor ownership. Therefore, it is reasonable for each factor owner to participate in wealth distribution, and that is also a realization of the appeal of all the factor ownerships.

It is necessary to achieve the effective realization of property ownership in income distribution in order to establish a mechanism to give full play to wealth creation factors and their owners, and that is to obtain remuneration according to factor contributions. Once that mechanism is established, it can effectively give full play to all sources that can create wealth, and can stimulate the vitality of various factors such as labor, capital, technology, and management.

From the perspective of wealth distribution, income distribution cannot be limited to the allocation of V. When we talk about income distribution in the phase of socialism, we simply refer to distribution according to work, which is incomplete, at least in the primary stage of socialism. Income distribution involves not only the allocation of V, but also the sharing of the remaining, i.e., the allocation of M. M is the value of the remaining product, or profit. People often believe that M is the reward for capital factor, which is denied by Marx's theory of the division of surplus value. Landowners, commercial capitalists, and loan capitalists all participate in the division of M, and its necessity lies in the realization of ownership, and the proportion of its division depends on each owner's contribution. If we apply that theory to the factor remuneration theory, we can clarify that each factor owner participates in the allocation of M according to his input and contribution, including the remuneration of capital owners and all the factor owners such as landowners.

In terms of the participation of factors in the sharing of surplus M, we should not solely focus on the participation of factors such as capital and land, but more importantly, we should pay close attention to the participation of the human factor. The human factor refers to not only the living labor as the general labor force or general labor, but also the role of the intangible factors embodied by human beings, including technology or management in increasing the surplus value. Moreover, it should include the increase of labor productivity that gives rise to the increase in surplus M. In Marxist value analysis, technological and management personnel are considered as complex labor whose value production is many times more than that of simple labor. The remuneration that complex labor obtains should be higher considering the higher education and training fees they have paid, and that is reflected in V, not in the distribution of surplus value. That is also the case of the improvement of laborers' efficiency. The human factor that increases the surplus value is possessed by capitalists as the productivity of capital, while efficient laborers who provide technology and management take nothing from the remaining M. The above claim is clearly in line with the goal of value analysis as capitalism itself is the hindrance to technological progress and the improvement of efficiency.

In the wealth analysis, the institutional arrangement of income distribution mentioned above severely hinders and affects the increase of wealth. Factors such as technology, management, and labor efficiency that directly affect the increase of surplus value can help increase wealth only when they participate in the sharing of the remaining M. The higher value produced by complex labor should get reward from the distribution of the remaining M, and that can be considered as the reward for the human capital. Then, the participation of laborer factor in the distribution should not be limited to the distribution of V to obtain the income of laborers; rather, the laborer factor should participate in the distribution of M, that is the sharing of the remaining M, such as bonuses for the improvement of labor efficiency, dividends for managers and technicians, and returns for intellectual property. With the social and technological progress, the role of human capital factor in the increase of surplus value will become more and more significant, and correspondingly, the human capital factor will take a larger share in the remaining M in the structure of obtaining remuneration according to factor contributions.[25]

---

[25] The capital category in wealth analysis and that in value analysis carry completely different theoretical functions. The wealth analysis studies the material and human factors in

It is clarified that factor remuneration is the sharing of the remaining M, and that the human factor (human capital) remuneration accounts for an increasing share. Nowadays, some people oppose the concept of factor remuneration, and one concern is that factors such as capital and land will account for too large a share in the factor remuneration structure to affect the interests of workers. However, as long as the corresponding institutional arrangement is made, the factor remuneration will be conducive to the wealth increment, and "distribution according to work" will also be fully reflected.

In order to ensure the full flow of various sources of wealth creation and to keep the effective functioning of various factors of wealth creation, an effective institutional arrangement is needed. First, seek a factor property system that is suitable for the development of wealth. Second, establish the system of factors allocation in which the market mechanism plays a fundamental role. Third, establish a distribution system in which each does its best and has its own place. As long as the various sources of wealth creation flow in full, the social wealth that Marx expected will spout like a spring.

The duality of labor is Marx's great discovery and is key to the understanding of political economy. The duality of labor explains the formation and production of value and also the creation and development of wealth. According to Marx's labor theory of value, the comparison between wealth and value and the comparison between the process and form of economic movement can clarify the differences among wealth creation, value production, wealth possession and surplus value possession, and they further clarify the means and significance of the increment of national wealth.

The examination of the dialectical relationship between wealth theory and value theory highlights the duality of the study of political economy. Starting from the materialist conception of history, political economy reveals the character of social production and the laws of development movement, which is the demand of the critical political economy. Moreover, it also regards the wealth increment as its goal, which is the

---

the economic process in a broad sense. According to that analysis, the "human capital" in political economy is abstracted on the basis of the "material capital" in Marx's *Capital: A Critique of Political Economy* and the new development form of historical production practices — modern commodity production. Thus, it is also a category that reflects the objective appeal of the alteration of the modes of production in a modern society.

demand of the constructive political economy. Guided by the theory of building socialism with Chinese characteristics, the practices of socialist market economy put forward the scientific demand for constructing an outlook for the development of the gross wealth of human beings. The socialist political economy has confirmed wealth increment as the research topic of economics, and expanded the content and form of the research on Marxist political economy, thus enabling the exploration of the unity of wealth production and development in the broadest sense and greatly rejuvenating the vitality in development.

Bibliography

Karl Marx. *Capital: A Critique of Political Economy*. Vol. 2, Trans. David Fernbach, London: Penguin Books, 1978.

Karl Marx. *Theories of Surplus Value*. Moscow: Progress Publishers, 1969.

Chapter 12

The Attributes of Private Capital and Its Income Under Socialist Conditions

At the present stage of socialism, an important aspect of further enriching the research on social labor and labor value is deepening the study of Marxist capital theory. Its practical significance is to provide the appropriate value judgments to private capital that is in urgent need of development under socialist conditions. In addition, there is a need to further evaluate the attributes of income allocated according to capital input.

12.1 The General and Particular Qualities of Capital

Over 100 years ago, Marx established a scientific theory of capital based on the scientific theory of labor value in *Capital*. He defined capital in two ways: capital in general terms and capital in particular terms.

Marx used *Capital* to put forward a general definition of capital. Capital in general is an abstraction, "but not an arbitrary abstraction but one which grasps the *differentia specifica* which distinguishes capital from all other forms of wealth or modes in which (social) production develops. These are determinations which are common to every capital as such, or which make any particular sum of values into capital".[1] According

[1]Karl Marx and Friedrich Engels. *Marx & Engels Collected Works*. Vol. 28, Trans. Ernst Wangermann (London: Lawrence & Wilshart, 2010), p. 378.

to Marx's analysis, the general definition of capital is determined by the following two factors.

First, it is determined by the regulation of the relations of production. In *Capital*, Marx clearly defines capital as one of these relations of production. Obviously, he discusses capital in the context of capitalist production relations. It is noteworthy that the capital defined by Marx is therefore related to the relationship between wages and labor. It is precisely because of the relationship between capital and wage labor that it is possible to rely on capital ownership to occupy the surplus labor relationship without compensation. Capital income is income from exploitation; its value entity is surplus value.

Second, it is determined by function. Capital can generate added value. That is to say, only when value brings about profits (surplus value) can it be counted as capital. In order to maximize profits, enterprises need to constantly transform profits into capital so as to achieve capital growth through accumulation. In addition, the life of capital lies in its movements. According to Marx, once capital stops moving, it will cease to be capital. Capital movement in Marx's analysis falls into two categories. One is the rotation and turnover of capital, meaning that it continuously realizes the transformation from money capital to production capital then to commodity capital and finally back to money capital. The other is the flow of capital from one sector to another. In sum, the general feature of capital is to flow, reward, grow, and add value.

As for capital in particular, Marx is referring to specific forms of capital. Marx's definitions of both capital in general and capital in particular provide us with approaches to capital at the present stage of socialism. In China, capital can be divided into the categories of public and private capital. These divisions could be interpreted from the perspectives of capital in general and capital in particular. The current classification of capital in China demonstrates profound value in both theoretical and practical terms. Both public and private capital, being particular forms of capital, also represent the general features of capital. However, their respective representations are somewhat different.

The definition of capital in the socialist economy is also the definition of public capital. According to Marx's definition of the kind of capital that is related to productive forces, capital only exists in capitalist economies. Therefore, socialist economics uses the concept of assets instead of the concept of capital. However, economic analysis shows that concepts like assets and funds only underline certain aspects of capital. They fail to convey the meaning of capital comprehensively. This is especially true when it comes to the activities of the real economy: assets and funds take the form of value movement, which does not necessarily accord with capital movement. That inevitably leads to economic inefficiency in public enterprises including activities such as disregarding profits, ignoring value proliferation, and noticing few investment returns. Since China's reform and opening up, there has been a great breakthrough in the socialist economy: the acknowledgment of capital. Some relevant concepts like state-owned capital, capital market, and capital management are widely used in socialist economics. Once there has been acceptance of the notion of public capital (including state-owned and collective capital), the value movement of funds and assets of public enterprises should meet the requirements of capital movement. The concept of public capital, developed from Marx's analysis of the function of capital in general, comes into widespread usage in terms of capital increase and return. What's more, the concept does not indicate the kind of wage labor that is determined by the relations of production. In this sense, it is capital in particular, i.e., there is no capital concerning the relationship between wages and labor. It does not belong to private capital, but instead to the capital of the whole people or the collective.

According to Marx's definition of capital in general, the funds and assets of state-owned enterprises are clearly also capital. This perspective is not only conducive to the growth of state-owned capital but also to its effective flow. In this regard, the following are most conspicuous aspects. First, in the strategic adjustment of the state-owned economy, the direction of such adjustments should be determined according to the requirements of value proliferation. State-owned capital will gradually withdraw from the enterprises that fail to realize value proliferation and go to those that are capable. Enterprises in certain industries, however, will be exceptions. Second, the current diversification of equity and the reform of private ownership will be carried out after the concept of public capital has been clarified. Third, the financing structure of enterprise should be adjusted. The enterprise not only conducts debt financing through the bank, but also enters the capital market for equity financing. Finally, the corporate governance structure will be established according to capital requirements and it will go on to seek institutional arrangements for capital personalization.

Under socialist conditions, private capital also falls into two categories from the perspective of capital in general and in particular: One is the capital that performs the function of wage labor and the other is the capital that does not hire labor but instead enters the market in the form of credit. The former is the capital that belongs to private enterprises. It contains the complete content of capital, especially the definition of the relations of production. At the present stage of socialism in China, the private sector is not only permitted to exist, but also encouraged to develop vigorously. This includes a large number of private enterprises with private ownership and hired labor. As Marx pointed out, private capital in these private enterprises is the embodiment of capital relations. According to the definition of capital, wage labor would direct our attention to the surplus labor that is appropriated by capitalists. It follows that capital income comes from exploitation. We cannot deny that capital income, by its very nature, is still exploitative, although private capital is indispensable at present. The act of admitting its exploitative nature, however, is not meant to eliminate capital income. The private economy is legal, so its income, though exploitative, is legal.

In the private sector, capital mobilizes and cooperates with other production factors such as labor. Capital integrates various production factors into the process of production, even though there are different owners of production factors. According to Marx's theory, capital determines the pattern of the relations of production that are determined by wage labor. Therefore, capital occupies a position of dominance over other productive factors. That is what Marx means when he said capital involves other factors when value is created. "[B]y incorporating with itself the two primary creators of wealth, labor-power and land, capital acquires a power of expansion [...]"[2] The productivity of other factors such as labor and land are incorporated into capital productivity.

Past research has cited Marx's statement in *Capital* that capital expands itself as a way to explain the function of capital. These studies, however, seem to misunderstand Marx who actually merely refers to capital forms (G–G'). This is not the case in reality. The self-expanding value of capital is mainly related to capitalist entrepreneurship. Profits (or surplus value), therefore, are not so much the outcome of capital self-expansion but rather the self-proliferation of the human capital of both capitalists and entrepreneurs. To be more precise, they are the outcome of cooperation between capital and entrepreneurs.

---

[2]Karl Marx. *Capital: A Critique of Political Economy*. Vol. 1, Trans. Ben Fowkes (London: Penguin Books, 1976), p. 752.

According to Marx's analysis, capital can function according to two methods. On the one hand, industrial capitalists may supervise and administrate simultaneously. On the other hand, they may delegate supervision and administration to others. In the former case, the entrepreneurs' profits include the reward for both supervision and management, while in the latter case, the reward for supervision and management should be divided from the entrepreneurs' profits. Marx pointed out that entrepreneurs' profits then include the reward for their supervisory and administrative work. In this way, "[h]e obtains surplus-value not because he works as a *capitalist* but rather because, leaving aside his capacity as a capitalist, he *also* works. This part of surplus-value is therefore no longer surplus-value at all, but rather its opposite, the equivalent for labor performed".[3] It is almost the same case with private business owners at the present stage in China. They invest capital as well as other production factors such as technology and management. They also work and therefore actually participate in creating value. In this sense, though they may be exploiters, private business owners also provide other production factors such as labor.

Private capital under socialist conditions has distinct features relative to private capital under capitalist conditions. Capital income from wage labor is a source of exploitation. However, private capital under socialist conditions cannot simply be judged to be exploitative — as it was once suggested by Marx's curse on private capital. According to Marx, the historical and logical starting point of capitalism is the fact that the conditions of capital ownership separate workers from their working conditions. The original accumulation of capital started the process of separation. In a response to the cruel deprivation of producers at the time in which workers experienced in the transformation of arable land into sheep-walks, Marx made the condemning statement that "capital comes dripping from head to toe, from every pore, with blood and dirt".[4] It is undeniable that at this stage in China, there are indeed private enterprises that have engaged in such reprehensible exploitation during their early accumulation of capital. Not all kinds of private capital, however, can be characterized in this way. When it comes to sources of capital, entrepreneurs' capital can come from honest work and legal means, from buyouts,

[3]Karl Marx. *Capital: A Critique of Political Economy*. Vol. 3, Trans. David Fernbach (London: Penguin Books, 1981), p. 506.

[4]Karl Marx. *Capital: A Critique of Political Economy*. Vol. 1, p. 926.

fund-raising, and bank loans, to technology or patents invested as capital stock. Some people become business owners through purchasing stocks in the state-owned enterprises. As for wage laborers, they may be laid-off workers of state-owned enterprises, peasant workers, or employees taking advantage of buy-out offers from state-owned enterprises. Therefore, neither the process of accumulating capital nor the wage laborers themselves are the outcome of deprivation. They are instead the result of reform. Moreover, these private enterprises play an increasingly important role in creating opportunities for jobs and social welfare. Although exploitation exists in private enterprises, their contribution to social welfare cannot be completely eliminated.

12.2 Functioning and Non-functioning Capital

In the modern economy, capital is closely associated with credit. In the analysis of the relationship between the two, Marx made a distinction between functioning and non-functioning capital, clarifying the nature of their yields.

According to Marx, functioning capital refers to the capital that operates in the process of reproduction, while interest-bearing capital does not perform that function. Therefore, interest-bearing capital "does not have wage-labor as its opposite but rather functioning capital".[5] Marx regards non-functioning capital, without engaging wage labor as the capital of sole property.

The transformation of capital ownership into capital begins with the separation of ownership of enterprise from its actual operations. However, certain types of capital do not perform this function even when they are separated from the operations. Only the stocks and bonds people purchase in the capital market and their bank deposit slips can be counted as the capital of ownership on its own. The reason why this kind of capital does not function in this way is that, as Marx describes, it is actually used by credit. To be more specific, enterprise operators or substantial shareholders mobilize it. "[C]redit offers the individual capitalist, or the person who can pass as a capitalist, an absolute command over the capital and property of others, within certain limits, and, through this, command over other people's labor. It is disposal over social capital, rather than his own,

[5]Karl Marx. *Capital: A Critique of Political Economy.* Vol. 3, p. 503.

that gives him command over social labor".[6] As it can be observed, social capital consists of private capital in the form of stocks, leading to a scenario Marx describes, in the following way: "a great part of the social capital is applied by those who are not its owners".[7]

Marx defined the type of capital that is transformed from a pure state of ownership as virtual or fictitious capital: "[t]he formation of fictitious capital is known as capitalization. Any regular periodic income can be capitalized by reckoning it up, on the basis of the average rate of interest, as the sum that a capital lent out at this interest rate would yield".[8] This part of fictitious capital is composed of bonds and stocks. They exist as ownership titles and circulate on the market.

The movement of fictitious capital (non-functioning capital) is separated from the movement of actual capital (functioning capital). This is reflected in the separation of their value movements from each other. As Marx maintains, the capital value invested in stocks does not exist twice over, "once as the capital value of the ownership titles, the shares and then again as the capital actually invested or to be invested in the enterprises in question".[9] The movement of capital value only exists in the latter form. The circulation of bonds and shares representing ownership titles is not the circulation of real capital value. Rather, it is a movement of fictitious capital, pointing to the shift of legal claims for profits.

The reason why stocks are used as title certificates and that they do not perform capital functions is because stock holders have "no control over this capital. The capital cannot be withdrawn. They give only a legal claim to a share of the surplus-value that this capital is to produce [...]. For the actual capital exists as well, and in no way changes hands when these duplicates [or these titles] are bought and sold".[10]

The same can be said about the market circulation of bonds. Within a certain period of time, creditors cannot require debtors to cancel their contracts. Instead, the creditors can sell the bonds representing the certificates of ownership. These bonds "[represent] paper duplicates of annihilated capital, function for their owners as capital in so far as they are

---

[6] *Ibid.*, p. 570.

[7] *Ibid.*, p. 572.

[8] *Ibid.*, p. 597.

[9] *Ibid.*

[10] *Ibid.*, p. 608.

saleable commodities and can therefore be transformed back into capital".[11]

Although non-functioning capital does not perform the function of wage labor, it is still necessary to perform the function of proliferating as capital. As opposed to the real capital movement, the value of stocks and bonds as ownership titles is unique both in terms of its movement and its determination: "[O]n the one hand their market values fluctuate with the level and security of the receipts to which they give a legal title", and on the other hand, "[t]he market value of these securities is partly speculative, since it is determined not just by the actual revenue but rather by the anticipated revenue as reckoned in advance".[12] Changes in various market variable factors such as the exchange rate, quantities of circulated bonds, risk-taking mentality, and market manipulation would lead to the mismatch between the market value of fictitious capital with that of real capital. The value of these paper copies is not determined by the fluctuation of real capital value that they are entitled to. Instead, it is determined by their transactions in the stock exchange. The main predictors of the ability to proliferate these non-executive forms of capital include the capability to obtain information, the willingness to take risks, the rationality of expectations, and the ability to optimize portfolios.

Fictitious capital is not really fictitious. The term just means that private capital enlarges its coverage instead of directly working on wage labor. Marketable securities can be counted as private capital and the holding of them is considered to be a form of private investment. While private capital does not have to set up enterprises and employ laborers in order to increase value, it can invest in the capital market to realize its valorization. Marx and Engels observed and commented on this tendency. According to Marx's analysis, because of the decline of the general rate of profit the minimum capital limit has been raised, and a large amount of capital has entered the speculative field such as stock investment. Such small amounts of capital operate directly as speculative capital in the capital market, not as venture capital. This means that a considerable amount of capital operating on the stock exchange market can be said to have no capital movement into reality as a real capital. When Engels revised the third volume of *Capital*, based on the findings at the time, a financial company established solely to buy and sell a type of interest-bearing

[11]*Ibid.*, p. 608.

[12]*Ibid.*, p. 598.

securities appeared in the market. Engels pointed out, "[t]his duplication and triplication of capital has been taken very much further in recent years".[13] These finance companies then solely invested in stock market rather than in the real economy.

In the present stage, fictitious capital has immensely enlarged its scope within the economy. To be more specific, capitalized revenue not only includes the forms that Marx has mentioned such as bonds and stocks, but also foreign currency and financial derivative instruments such as financial futures, stock index, options and so on. In addition, the amount of fictitious capital has greatly increased. As one can observe in the relevant data, the amount of fictitious capital daily transacted on various capital markets is dozens of times as much as that of real capital. Today, businesses solely operating fictitious capital have greatly outnumbered those kinds of financial trust companies that Engels wrote about.

Fictitious capital obscures enterprise ownership. Because most current investments take the form of bank deposits and stock purchase on capital market, bond financing and equity financing provide enterprises with their main channels to raise capital. In modern companies, not only are the shareholders scattered, but the investors are also unfixed. As James Tobin says, an investor could sell the equity of a railroad company he holds and convert it into an airline instead. According to portfolio theory, an investor often holds shares in multiple companies. When it comes to investors, they mostly prioritize the price of assets rather than the ownership of a particular enterprise or capital function in the enterprise. Therefore, in an enterprise with dispersed ownership, the awareness of business ownership becomes increasingly vague.

The practical significance of the theory of the separation of private capital from the employment relationship lies in that in China's current primary stage, the development of the private capital economy is not limited to private investments or the operation of an enterprise. Private purchases of stocks and bonds or private ownership of equity also provide methods to increase private capital. Looking ahead, with the development of shareholding economy, we can predict that this part of private investment will have an upward trend.

---

[13] *Ibid.*, p. 601.

12.3 Incomes from Exploitation and Ownership

Based on the theoretical analysis of functioning and non-functioning capital, we can decide whether the income from private capital in joint-stock companies is exploitative. In the above analysis, the capital income concerned with wage labor was already assumed to be exploitative, so it is not part of the following discussion.

Observing the formation of joint-stock companies during his own time, Marx pointed out that the separation between capital ownership and capital function leads to "[t]ransformation of the actual functioning capitalist into a mere manager, in charge of other people's capital, and of the capital owner into a mere owner, a mere money capitalist", and the latter's profit (or interest) is "a mere reward for capital ownership".[14]

According to the theory of factor compensation, capital income, like other factor incomes, is income from ownership. Judging whether capital income is exploitive is determined by its nature. The difference between capital that performs capital functions and capital that does not perform capital functions indicates that capital can be decoupled from employment relations. Further analysis will show that capital income is not necessarily exploitative.

In the third volume of *Capital*, Marx divided the profit from industrial capitalists into two parts: interest and the business owner's income when the surplus value was distributed: "In relation to him, in other words, interest appears as the mere fruit of property in capital, of capital in itself, abstracted from the reproduction process of capital in so far as it does not 'work', i.e., function; whereas profit of enterprise appears to him as the exclusive fruit of the functions he performs with the capital, as the fruit of capital's movement and process".[15] This distinction has implications for our methodology for distinguishing whether capital income is exploitive.

According to Marx's theory of capital, the question of whether capital income is exploitative is related to whether it performs capital functions. The capital income that derives from wage labor is obviously exploitative. However, the surplus income that residents deposit in banks in the form of interest-bearing capital is not exploitative because it does not perform a function. As Marx believed, if a functioning capitalist does not own capital and the lender has the property in capital, then the interest that the

---

[14] *Ibid.*, p. 567.

[15] *Ibid.*, p. 497.

functioning capitalist pays the lender is the fruit of property in capital and the functioning capitalist's income is enterprise profit, "as the fruit of merely functioning with capital, as the fruit of capital as capital in process".[16] Obviously, Marx defines interest as the fruit of pure capital. Although it is actually the result of the process of functioning capital, the interest is not exploitative for the lender. If that is the case under capitalist conditions, then why is the interest of household savings considered to be exploitative? We note that the provider of interest-bearing capital that does not perform its functions referred to here is the borrowing capitalist. At this stage, it is basically ordinary residents who provide interest-earning capital.

Research on the manner in which residents hold wealth has found that different people choose methods based on their risk tolerance and their expectations for their economic prospects. "Those whose main concern is for funds to be immediately and assuredly available for unusual expenditures can hold bank deposits or easily marketable securities. Those whose interest is in long-run capital appreciation, even at some risk, can be the owners of specific tangible assets".[17] According to the statistics released by the Chinese National Bureau of Statistics, as of October 2001, the total amount of individual financial assets in the People's Republic of China has exceeded 10 trillion yuan. This figure includes 7 trillion yuan of personal savings, nearly 80 yuan billion of personal foreign currency deposits, and over 1 trillion yuan of private-owned stocks and bonds. Residents can hold wealth in the form of bank deposits, treasury bonds, insurance policies, stocks, and equities. That is why interests, debt services, dividends, and incomes from stock transfers can be regarded as capital income. This kind of income can also be considered as risk returns of different risk levels. If all types of capital income are exploitative, as some have asserted, then isn't everyone an exploiter?

At present, residents' investments in capital market are the most active. Their investments in the stock market rather than enterprises demonstrate that the movement of fictitious capital, rather than the movement of real capital. There are two types of income that allow residents to purchase stocks in the securities market: one is to obtain dividends; the other is to obtain income from the transfer of stocks. Investing in stocks in order to obtain dividends is, in fact, just like bank savings. Investors simply

[16] *Ibid.*, p. 498.

[17] James Tobin. *Money, Credit, and Capital* (Boston: Irwin/McGraw-Hill, 1998), p. 6.

obtain capital income as a pure capital owner. Income from stock transfers is related to asset prices. Securities income is not determined by actual income, but by expected income, so this type of income is speculative. As Marx said, "credit gives these few ever more the character of simple adventurers. Since ownership now exists in the form of shares [...]".[18] Asset prices reflect the supply and demand of capital market assets. The relationship between supply and demand depends on individual preferences for assets. These preferences are not related to specific assets, but instead to the prospects and risks that these assets have. Clearly, the income from securities transfers is not so much exploitive income as it is risk income.

As for the income from private capital invested in enterprises, it is not necessarily exploitative. Only when capital mobilizes other production factors is the income considered to be exploitative. If capital is mobilized by other factors, then the income from property in capital may not be exploitive.

At each stage of development, various factors do not perform the same or equal role. One factor must play a decisive role over other attached factors. For instance, capital ranks among the factors that contribute to economic growth. At different stages, the role of capital varies with its place in the combination of production factors. It can be the dominant factor and integrate with other factors. It can also be integrated with other factors and become an attached factor.

Today, various production factors play dramatically different roles in economic development. Knowledge, technology, management, and entrepreneurship tend to become decisive factors in economic growth. In many ways, capital does not play the leading role in integrating production factors. It might be mobilized by other production factors rather than the opposite. In particular, it is not only the capital invested, but also the technology stocks and operator stocks that constitute the equity structure of the enterprise. Income from capital and other production factors are yielded from ownership instead of from exploitation.

In a modern enterprise represented by a joint-stock company, the investor and the legal person's property rights are separated. The investor can neither withdraw capital nor dispose of it at will. It is the corporate manager who then has control over the dispersal of capital. Although these managers may not hold shares, they can manage investors'

[18]Karl Marx. *Capital: A Critique of Political Economy*. Vol. 3, p. 571.

considerable amount of capital. In Chandler's *The Visible Hand: The Managerial Revolution in American Business*, the separation between the management and ownership of the enterprise is described as follows: The ownership becomes so dispersed that shareholders can hardly participate in making decisions about an enterprise. It is under the complete control of paid managers. For enterprise owners, it merely constitutes the source of income, far from being a manageable enterprise as it was before.[19] This kind of enterprise in which entrepreneurs make use of capital clearly differs from a traditional system in which entrepreneurs are employed by capital. In this sense, capital income from ownership is not so much exploitative as it is risky. The reasons are as follows. First, because corporate investors do not participate in managing and controlling the enterprise, its investment in the enterprise is risky. Second, for investors, the decision about whether to invest capital in the enterprise or in the bank itself is risky. If the bank's interest is in the opportunity cost of its investment, capital income in the enterprise will be opportunity income.

In Marx's analysis, capital income that does not perform capital functions and income that performs capital functions belong to the division of surplus value (hence being exploitative), and industrial capitalists play a leading role. Before considering whether Marx's analysis establishes a proper theoretic basis for evaluating property with income from private capital, we need to study the features of the modern enterprise system.

In the modern economy, factors such as capital, technology, and entrepreneurs who invest in the enterprise will actually participate in income distribution as part of a corporate equity structure. Therefore, an enterprise is actually a collection of various factors. The income distribution is in proportion with investments of various factors and their corresponding effects. That is what American economist Eugene Fama meant when he writes, "Each factor in a firm is owned by somebody. The firm is just the set of contracts covering the way inputs are joined to create outputs and the way receipts from outputs are shared among inputs".[20] From this contractual relationship, the income from one production factor actually is yielded by the ownership of corresponding factors. Capital income is no exception. Institutional economic theory understands an enterprise to be

---

[19]Alfred D. Chandler Jr. *The Visible Hand: The Managerial Revolution in American Business* (Cambridge: The Belknap Press of Harvard University Press, 1977), pp. 491–493.

[20]Eugene F. Fama. Agency problems and the theory of the firm. *The Journal of Political Economy* 88(2): 288–307, 1980, p. 290.

"a nexus for contracting relationships and which is also characterized by the existence of divisible residual claims on the assets and cash flows of the organization which can generally be sold without permission of the other contracting individuals".[21] This means that the distribution proportion is prescribed by a contract, and the agent (or manager) in reality plays a decisive role in the distribution of capital income.

Of course, the use of capital by entrepreneurs (and also by operators) generally refers to situations in which corporate companies disperse equity. In a firm with concentrated equity or a monopoly, however, things are different. Although it may not be accurate to generally say that entrepreneurs make use of capital, "big capital" still employs "small capital". In the listed companies in today's China, private investments in corporate stocks are actually employed by a substantial shareholder that is mostly state-owned capital. Therefore, it is unreasonable to regard private capital as exploitative.

As for venture capital, it promotes high-tech industrialization. In the modern economy, the founders of technology companies may have patents or other scientific and technological achievements, but they often lack venture capital. For this reason, venture capital emerges when needed. Accelerations in high-tech industrialization have the following features. First, venture investment aims to incubate advanced and new technology directed at scientific and technological enterprises. Second, it takes the form of equity investment. Third, rather than holding shares for a long period of time, it withdraws from the invested scientific and technological firm once it is running on track so that the money can be reinvested in new projects. In terms of the relationship between venture capital and technology companies, who is actually in the dominant position? Clearly, venture companies differ from traditional businesses that mobilize labor and technology through capital. In venture businesses, knowledge and technology mobilize capital. This means that knowledge capitalists employ money capitalists. Although the success rate for venture capital investment is still only 20%, even in the United States, a higher return for higher risk is characteristic of high-tech investment. Therefore, venture capital income is actually risk income. Moreover, apart from financial support, venture investors also assist with consultation and

[21]Michael C. Jensen and William Meckling. Theory of the firm: Managerial behavior, agency costs and ownership structure. *The Journal of Financial Economics* 3: 305–360, 1976, p. 311.

management services. Venture income returned by scientific and technological startups from their profits thus contains the reward for its management services and the compensation for its undertaking uncertainties and risks. This income is also not exploitation income. In addition, venture capital takes funds from a variety of sources including governments, enterprises and residents who would entrust their money to professional investors for financial management.

At the present stage in China, multiple methods of income distribution coexist. The basic distribution principle accords with the contributions made by production factors that vary with fundamental changes of enterprise ownership structure. Ownership is now not only gained from investing money, but also from providing technology, entrepreneurship, or other intangible assets. The proportion of material capital equity within corporate equity has decreased significantly. It is difficult to clearly distinguish which kind of income is exploitation income from the income formed in this equity structure.

With the economic development and evolution of the enterprise system, it may become a trend for capital to be mobilized by other production factors and then integrated into the economic process. Productive forces develop from other factors such as human resources and knowledge rather than from capital. A bigger part of revenue is allocated to human capital and knowledge capital, signaling social progress.

When taking a historically specific approach to Marx's theory of capital, we can reach the following realistic conclusions: The income from private enterprises may be exploitive, but the owners' contribution to social welfare cannot be ignored; private investment ranges from labor employment to the purchase of securities; under the conditions in which capital is employed by other production factors, the revenue it yields is from pure ownership instead of from exploitation. Therefore, we can rightfully mobilize more private capital into the economic process at the present stage in China.

Chapter 13

The Transition of the Ownership Structure in Accord with the Current Basic Economic System

According to China's affirmed basic economic system at the primary stage of socialism, an important aspect of improving the socialist market economy is to deepen the reform of ownership. In the reform of the ownership system, we must not only develop a variety of ownership economies, but also improve the realization of public ownership and build a modern property rights system.

13.1 Transformation of the Ownership Structure

According to Marxist theory, the ownership structure should be subject to the development level of productive forces. Some of the routes, guidelines, and policies that we formulated in the past have not been successful, mainly because they outpaced the development of productive forces at the time. Taking productivity as the standard for research and development, we might say that each society has its own material foundations. Manual labor cannot produce capitalism; only mechanized industrialization can produce capitalism. When it comes to socialism, its material basis is supposed to meet or exceed that of capitalism. The problem, however, is that no socialist country in the world has established the required material foundation yet. In this context, China puts forward the concept of the primary stage of socialism. This refers to the stage in which socialism is established and the level of productive forces has not yet reached that of the capitalist stage. In China's primary stage of socialism, it is necessary to complete the tasks of industrialization and modernization that other countries have accomplished under capitalist conditions. Therefore, it is impossible to propose eliminating private ownership in the initial stage of socialism. The fundamental task is to develop productive forces.

The fundamental task of the primary stage of socialism has clearly been to develop productive forces, which has proven to be incomplete in practice. It is also necessary to enrich the people. Although the enrichment of society is based on the development of productive forces, on many occasions the latter does not necessarily result in the former. In reality, development should not occur for the sake of development alone. People's living standards may not be simultaneously improved along with the development of productive forces. That is why the 16th National Congress of the Communist Party of China (CPC) claims that building a moderately prosperous society in all respects requires that people share the fruits of economic growth at every stage of the development of productive forces. When it comes to enriching people, they not only need to experience an improvement in their income but also in their ownership of property.

Enriching the people is part of developing the non-public economy. This can be proved when different regional income levels are compared. The extent to which the non-public economy is developed in a certain area determines the speed of growth of the residents' income there. When it comes to the policies that have allowed some people to get rich first, this initial wealth does not depend on labor income but on non-labor income. This is also related to the development of a non-public ownership economy.

Based on the knowledge of the basic tasks at the primary stage of socialism, it is necessary to deepen our understanding of the current basic economic relations in China. In the past, we established the fact that public ownership is the basis of the national economic system. At present, we regard public ownership to be the main body of the national economic system, with diverse forms of ownership developing side by side. This means that non-public ownership has become an important part of the basic economic system at the present stage in China. Non-public ownership is within the system instead of being outside. The relationship between public and non-public ownership is defined by competition and cooperation, rather than a life-or-death struggle.

The key to the transformation of the ownership system lies in a clear and proper understanding of the public economy as well as the establishment of its status as the mainstay of the economic system. In the past, public ownership was defined as the number of publicly owned enterprises. The practices of recent economic reform, however, have broken this definition. At present, the public ownership economy is not defined by publicly owned enterprises, but rather by state-owned and collective capital. Accordingly, the fact that public ownership is the main body of the national economic system is demonstrated by the quantity of public capital instead of the number of publicly owned enterprises. As long as public capital is dominant over gross social capital, ensuring the leading role of the state-owned economy, then public ownership could take the lead in the national economic system. This could guarantee that lifelines of the national economy are under the control of public capital.

It is meaningful to interpret public ownership economy in this way and regard it as the main form of the economic system. If the main path of developing multiple ownership economies that are not publicly owned during the early stage of reform was developing non-public ownership of enterprises outside of public ownership enterprises, then it would be necessary to withdraw public capital in enterprises that do not need to maintain public ownership. First of all, in the economic fields that do not affect the lifelines of national economy, the state-owned economy can withdraw steadily and achieve the same progress and retreat. In sectors that are not related to the lifeblood of the national economy, the private economy must be the main body. Secondly, even in the economic sectors that are related to the lifelines of national economy, the state-owned economy can be controlled through the holding shares, a small portion of which can be transferred to non-public sectors of economy. Third, some industries in which the state retains a monopoly can also take in more private capital through shareholding and other forms. For instance, market-oriented reforms can be promoted in fields such as infrastructure and public utilities that were once exclusively operated by the state. Non-public forms of capital such as private capital, foreign capital, and so on would enter these sectors so as to break up state monopolies. Public ownership refers to the assets of the enterprise, not the enterprise itself. Since the public ownership economy is not the equivalent of public enterprises, the auction and sale of public enterprise is natural. According to the basic theory of the Marxist political economy, any commodity has two factors: value and use value. The auction and sale of state-owned enterprises take away their use value, and what is recovered is its value that could be reinvested later. The auction and sale of state-owned enterprises point to the change in the material bearers of state-owned capital. Simply stated, this refers to the flow of state assets. What matters is not the quantity of state-owned or private enterprises but rather the quality of assets. The leading role of the state-owned economy lies in its capability to control the lifelines of the national economy.

13.2 Transformation of Public Ownership

In the past, public ownership was realized in the form of state-owned and collective enterprises. It is now clear that the public ownership economy does not refer to public ownership enterprises, but instead to state-owned and collective capital. Therefore, public ownership can take diverse forms. In particular, various types of mixed-ownership enterprises that include private property rights can also become part of public ownership. For example, the existing Sino-foreign joint ventures, joint-stock enterprises, and joint-stock cooperative enterprises reflect the common development of public and non-public capital within the same enterprise.

The key to realizing public ownership in a mixed-ownership economy lies in building a diversified ownership structure that contains the most competitive forms of private ownership. That is to say, the mixed-ownership enterprises that contain instances of private ownership are more vigorous in realizing public ownership in comparison to state-owned and collective enterprises. The essence of the mixed-ownership economy is represented by its emphasis on private equity and diversified ownership. As opposed to the private economy, the private equity economy refers to a mixed-ownership economy with diverse private property rights. Why is the private equity economy competitive? There are three reasons. First, it clarifies all relevant responsibilities and rights, makes property rights clear, and promotes the mobility and appreciation of property rights. Second, it effectively ensures a separation between the government and enterprises. Third, private property rights could provide a way to prevent losses. In the past, state-owned enterprises claimed to be responsible for their own profits and losses, but, in reality, they could not afford such losses. With private equity, this problem can be solved. In order to illustrate the significance of private equity, economists researching property rights put forward the example of the tragedy of the commons and point out the fact that public property is often undervalued when the same amount of public equity and private equity are engaged in transactions on the market.

The core of the reform of property rights is introducing private property rights, developing a mixed-ownership economy in the framework of a modern enterprise system, and transforming state-owned enterprises into corporations. To borrow the expression Marx mentioned in *Introduction to the Critique of Political Economy*, the study of economic relations in a given society requires grasping the "general light". In a period of economic transition, the economic relations of the "general light" are based on a mixed-ownership economy with the shareholding system as the main body. In accordance with a mixed-ownership economy, the basis of the market-oriented reform of state-owned enterprises is introducing private property rights, rebuilding the governance structure, and improving their competitiveness through new arrangements of the property right system.

At present, there are three major dynamic economic forms: private enterprises, corporations with foreign capital, and listed companies. They are significant because they are fit into the private property rights economy. Therefore, the direction of the reform of the state-owned economy should be in line with the three main dynamic economic forms, including the following three aspects. First, state-owned enterprises absorb private equity. For instance, state-owned enterprises can be listed and raise private equity on the capital market. In addition, the enterprise staff or operators can also hold shares. These private investments can provide state-owned enterprises with more channels to absorb capital and also propel them to be restructured through the introduction of private equity. Second, state-owned enterprises and private enterprises merge with each other. More specifically, the structure of the property rights of state-owned enterprises as well as that of private enterprises would be integrated with each other. For example, state-owned enterprises can hold shares in private enterprises and vice versa. In the process of mutual shareholding, it is not necessary to maintain the state's control of holdings. Third, state-owned enterprises cooperate and build joint ventures with foreign capital. Against the background of economic globalization and China's admission to the World Trade Organization (WTO), foreign investors entering China are characterized by their mergers with and acquisitions of Chinese enterprises or their purchase of the property rights of those enterprises. In this regard, state-owned enterprises should adopt a positive attitude and take the initiative to accept mergers and acquisitions.

The various methods that state-owned enterprises can use to draw private equity, as they were described above, actually represent the withdrawal of state-owned capital. It can be expected that, in the future, it will become normal to adjust and integrate the ownership of enterprises, hold mutual shares between public and non-public capital, conduct acquisitions and mergers between enterprises, and change their controlling shareholders. Although it is difficult to avoid disorder in these processes, these changes and integrations are conducive to the formation of a highly efficient enterprise structure.

The most typical organizational form of a mixed-ownership enterprise is a joint-stock system. State-owned enterprises also resort to this system so they can carry out ownership reform by absorbing private property. In this sense, the joint-stock system constitutes the main way to maintain public ownership. The shareholding system is a form of organizing property rights. It can include diverse investments and combine multiple types of equities. Investing public capital in a joint-stock enterprise means that public ownership is realized to some extent, regardless of whether public capital holds the shares or not. Even if public capital does not have a controlling stake, it has the right to derive profits, i.e., to claim the residuals; if public capital does hold shares, it would participate in making decisions about the enterprise. Realizing public ownership in joint-stock enterprises, however, does not necessarily require shareholding. Both the necessity and the proportion of shareholding will vary according to the circumstances. As for the industries and sectors that are considered the lifelines of national economy, it is essential for public capital to hold shares. Otherwise, it would be unnecessary to hold shares. However, in the lifeblood of the non-national economy, some state-owned enterprises have good benefits and asset quality. They have the ability to absorb other capital into a joint-stock system and there is no need to give up their controlling position.

The joint-stock system provides a method of restructuring enterprises, but it may not get instant results once it is implemented. The key to the success of these joint-stock enterprises lies in the improvement of the property rights system. Property rights are the core and main content of ownership. They involve real rights, creditor's rights, stock rights, intellectual property rights, and so on. The system of modern property rights establishes a foundation for the standard joint-stock system, and the joint-stock economy should respect and protect all these property rights. The standard joint-stock system must be established on the basis of the system of modern property rights. The Third Plenary Session of the 16th Central Committee of the CPC made a clear statement about the connotations of this system of modern property rights, i.e., "a system of modern property rights characterized by clear ownership, specified rights and responsibilities, strict protection and smooth circulation".[1] It is a breakthrough to hold that property rights are the core and main content of ownership. In the past, the modern enterprise system was called the corporate system. It aimed to separate enterprise from the government, clarify property rights, specify powers and responsibilities, and conduct management in a scientific way. At present, the modern system of property rights has been elaborated further in the new and clear definition. This clarification of the system of modern property rights specifies both the structure and the standards of the joint-stock economy, contributing to the present ownership restructuring in both public and non-public enterprises. Clarifying property rights is conducive to clear ownership. Specifying rights and responsibilities points to the well-defined rights and responsibilities of investors and legal persons. Providing strict protection means that property rights, both public and private, should not be violated at will. As for smooth circulation, it demands that the capital invested in an enterprise flows smoothly, rather than stay static, in order to maintain and increase value. Establishing this type of property right system not only guarantees the dominant position of public ownership, but it also supports the development of various forms of non-public economies. It is noteworthy that many enterprises have been transformed into a joint-stock system through restructuring. If the established joint-stock system fits within modern enterprises, the requirements of the modern system of property rights should be invoked in order to evaluate them.

13.3 The Promotion of the Private Economy

The basic characteristic of the private economy is private ownership, or to put it another way, the enterprises that do not have public or foreign investments fall into the scope of the private economy. The denotation of the concept is often limited to private enterprises and self-employed

---

[1]Decision of the Central Committee of the Communist Party of China on some issues concerning the improvement of the socialist market economic system. *Guangming Daily*, Oct 15, 2003, p. 1.

entrepreneurs; this would underestimate the contributions the private economy has made to China's economic development. The private economy, however, not only refers to private enterprises and self-employed entrepreneurs; it also points to private investments and shares. Privately held enterprises and those that have been transformed from state- or collectively owned enterprises can also be included within the scope of private economy. Now that the reduction of state-owned shares is under way, a considerable number of listed companies will not be held by public capital and will instead fall into the scope of the private economy.

At present, what matters in the development of the private economy in China is scale and quality rather than quantity. The fact that the quality of private enterprises needs to be improved is manifested in three ways. First, there are not many large enterprises. Second, there are not many private enterprises with an internationally competitive edge. Third, private enterprises are concentrated in the low-grade industrial sector. The main goal of the development of a diversified ownership economy is to expand the scale of private enterprises, strengthen their competitiveness, and improve their industrial level at China's present stage.

The Third Plenary Session of the 16th Central Committee of the CPC provides all-round policy support for the expansion and strengthening of private enterprises. The basic position is to remove institutional obstacles, i.e., to revise and even eliminate the laws, regulations, and policies that restrict the development of the non-public economy. More specifically, this process involves two parts. One is about market access. Removing various policy barriers for private enterprises to enter the market will permit domestic private capital to have greater market access. In addition, non-public capital will be allowed to enter the zones that are not restricted in laws and regulations. The second is to ensure equal treatment with other enterprises such as state-owned and foreign enterprises in terms of investment, financing, taxation, land use, and so on. Private enterprises can enter the market of production factors and obtain various production factors without discrimination.

Private enterprises need to be expanded. To be more exact, expansion does not emphasize the size of private enterprises but rather the economic scale. The expansion of economic scale depends on an increase in investments. Private enterprises rely on internal financing alone, and it is difficult to form economies of scale in a short period of time. Therefore, financing constraints remains one of the biggest obstacles to the development of private enterprises. Research on the early development of the private economy in Zhejiang province found that when private enterprises develop rapidly, they largely depend on underground bank loans. In other regions, there are no such underground banks, and regular banks are unwilling or afraid to lend money to private enterprises. Under the circumstances, the expansion of private enterprises is bound to rely on endogenous financing, i.e., on its own capital and accumulation. This will become an obstacle to their development. The above-mentioned guidelines and policies set up during the Third Plenary Session of the 16th Central Committee of the CPC proposes comprehensively cleaning up and revising laws, regulations, and policies that restrict the development of non-public economic sectors. It states that private enterprises should enjoy equal treatment with other enterprises (such as state-owned enterprises and foreign-funded enterprises) in terms of investment, financing, taxation, land use, and so on. They can enter all kinds of production factor markets without any discrimination. This has largely solved the problem of factors restricting the development of private economy.

Enhancing the competitiveness of private enterprises also requires institutional innovation. At present, there are three major disadvantages in private enterprises. First, economies of scale cannot be achieved. Second, private ownership alone cannot build a modern enterprise system. Third, they run on family-based management, which determines that the enterprise system does not have continuity. In this sense, the private enterprise system cannot be regarded as the direction of reform. Instead a mixed-ownership economy that includes private property rights should be the direction of economic transformation. The joint-stock system also points to a proper method that private enterprises undergoing the process of restructuring should follow. As a form of organizing property rights, it fits in with public, as well as private, ownership. Private enterprises can establish a diversified ownership structure with multiple equities by absorbing other equity subjects. The modern enterprise system will be built through corporations. It is an economy that contains multiple private property rights. Whether it is a public or non-public economy, its development is the same. All enterprises will adopt the corporate system. Every reform leads to the corporate system. That is to say, all enterprises will follow the corporate system. The institutional innovations of private enterprise also involve the issue of professional management. In their initial phase, private enterprises are largely operated by the family system and now they are faced with the problem of choosing more professional operators. Keynesian economic theory solves the problem of state intervention, and Schumpeter's innovation theory stresses the significance of entrepreneurship in economic development. The development trend of private enterprises is to run the business by professional managers (entrepreneurs).

In the 21st century, the development of private enterprises has entered a new stage. They expand rapidly through operating capital and restructuring instead of mainly through their own accumulation, as they did before. If in the previous stage, the expansion of private enterprises mainly relied on accumulating capital; now it mainly relies on capital operation and the reorganization of assets. The participation of private capital in the reform of state-owned enterprises would bring about double benefits simultaneously. On the one hand, quite a number of state-owned enterprises can be reinvigorated when their assets are optimized. On the other hand, private enterprises can scale up instantly, since participation serves as a shortcut for private enterprises to become bigger and stronger. While state-owned enterprises have enjoyed advantages in technology, equipment, and human resources, they do not have institutional advantages. Private enterprises with institutional advantages control state-owned enterprises so that their advantages can be brought into full play, thus realizing the integration of advanced production forces into society. The entry of private economic factors into state-owned and collectively owned enterprises would assist private enterprises to develop and help state-owned enterprises to reform.

The basic methods by which private enterprises merge and acquire state-owned enterprises are as follows. First, both state-owned and state-holding enterprises could diversify property rights by selling state-owned property rights or assets. Mature enterprises can be transferred as a whole; if the overall transfer is difficult, then they can be transferred in parts. Private capital, foreign capital and the capital of legal persons are encouraged to obtain state ownership and assets by way of whole purchases, partial purchases, and purchases after or with a lease. Second, listed enterprises controlled by state-owned capital should reduce the proportion of shares that the state is holding by actively transferring these shares to foreign capital and other legal person capital. By renewing assets and stocks, the equity structure of state-holding listed enterprises could be adjusted to restore and then improve their capacity to re-finance. Third, as for these major state-owned enterprises with good asset quality, outstanding main businesses, and sustainable profitability, they could, in accordance with relevant state provisions, attract investments from foreign capital, domestic natural person capital, and legal person capital, transfer property rights, increase capital investment for equity participation, and conduct joint ventures in corporation to accomplish the diversification of equity subjects.

Another important aspect of developing the private economy is the issue of remunerating production factors based on their contributions. Originally, this was regarded as an income distribution issue. Production factors are justified in participating in this distribution process for their private ownership. A considerable part of non-labor factors such as capital, technology, and information remain in private hands. That is to say, they are privately owned. In the past, we did not pay enough attention to the ownership of factors; instead, we only focused on the ownership of factors of production. At present, the ownership of production factors should be worthy of our attention as well. The reason why Marx emphasized labor was because the labor in communist society was private and other factors of production were public. At this stage, individuals provide most of the education and training costs in order to realize private ownership or partial private ownership of the elements. Therefore, income distribution must be conducted according to the ownership of production factors. In terms of capital, economic growth not only depends on social investment but also on personal investment. This also determines the two institutional problems that should be tackled. One is to admit and accept private ownership, and the other is to distribute income in accordance with the contribution of production factors.

Distributing income in accordance with the contribution of production factors involves evaluating their contributions. According to the theory of economic growth, the weights of different production factors will vary with each economic development stage. More specifically, in the stage in which there is a resource-based economy, natural resources play a key role in economic development. In the stage in which there is simple cooperation and handicraft workshops, labor plays a key role in economic development. In the stage in which there is large-scale mechanized industry, the capital invested in machine and equipment plays a key role in economic development. In the stage in which there is a knowledge economy, knowledge and management play a key role. In the primary stage of socialism in China, these stages coexist in economic development with various production factors occupying different places in diverse economic forms. In the market economy of the socialist primary stage, capital, technology, and management constitute advanced production factors. For the sake of fairness, their contribution to economic development should be fully rewarded in the distribution process.

Income distribution is not only fair, but also has the function of stimulating the efficiency of resource allocation. In the past, we emphasized distribution according to work, which also has the function of incentivizing the allocation efficiency of labor factors. At this stage, we must not only encourage the allocation efficiency of labor factor, but also the allocation efficiency of other advanced production factors such as capital, technology, information, and knowledge. In the current development of the market economy in China, there are three kinds of incentives for advanced production factors. First, when it comes to incentives for capital elements, income distribution according to capital in various forms needs to be acknowledged. These may include personal income from running private enterprises, stock yields, and interest revenues. In developing countries, capital factor plays a key role in economic growth, and the amount of one's wealth should not be viewed as an attribute of individual class. Second, knowledge and technological innovation should be fostered through a system of income distribution. Because knowledge and technology are factors that are promoted through innovation, they play a key role in modern economic development. Third, there is an incentive for entrepreneurship. The entrepreneur himself is a factor of production who represents a certain spirit: innovation and adventurousness. During the course of developing China's state-owned enterprises, the critical issue is making the operator an entrepreneur, and the entrepreneur must run the enterprise. Being an entrepreneur requires innovation, meaning that the entrepreneur should be capable of weighing both the profits and the risks brought about by innovation. Personal qualities or capabilities do not account for the fact that state-owned enterprise managers are at a disadvantage when they are placed in competition with private enterprise owners. The problem is that state-owned enterprise managers lack both innovative and adventurous spirit. Private enterprise owners, facing risks, bear the costs and the fruits themselves. However, state-owned enterprise managers may yield nothing from taking risks because the capital of human resources they invested cannot participate in income distribution. In order to turn the operators of state-owned enterprises into entrepreneurs, the institutional problems must be solved by rearranging the system. The key is to form a reasonable income distribution system and give full play to the role incentives have in the distribution system of resource allocation. For another thing, a reasonable income distribution system is conducive to preventing corruption in state-owned enterprises. For example, the phenomenon of the "corruption of the 58-year-old" in state-owned enterprises is largely a product of the problems in the distribution system. Therefore, in order for income to be distributed, the operator's equity must be resolved. In turn, in order for the operator to become an entrepreneur, the equity must be resolved. This system has two major functions: addressing risks and addressing the corruption of operators. In addition, the system ensures that operators of state-owned enterprises will take the enterprises' residual claims. According to the team production theory, laziness will be created under the conditions of team production. In order to solve the problem of laziness and prevent the supervisor corruption, there should be an incentive mechanism that allows them to enjoy residual claims through operator equity.

The fulfillment of rewarding production factors entails studying and solving specific methods of realizing it. On the issue of factor distribution, it is necessary to deal with the relationship between the distribution of production factors and the theory of labor value. Marx's theory of labor value states that new values are created by labor. However, the theory of labor value also shows that new values are the object of distribution. What is distributed in $c + v + m$ is $v + m$ rather than the total value of the product. Distribution according to production factors is based on their contribution to the total value, i.e., their contribution to $c + v + m$, instead of based on their contribution to new values.

The following aspects deserve our attention when realizing the distribution according to production factors: First, the distribution of labor factors. This refers to the distribution of v in $v + m$. The participation of labor factors in the distribution of m depends on whether laborers hold the shares of enterprises and own their own property. The reason why contemporary capitalism has developed steadily mainly lies in the fact that problems concerning the property rights of laborers have been solved. Second, the distribution according to the factors of technology, capital, and entrepreneurship. The laborer who provides the technology or management can also be the owner of human capital in the enterprise. As a worker, the technology and management elements must participate in the distribution of v. As the owner of the human capital of the enterprise, he has to participate in the distribution of m. It is essential to emphasize that equity should be based on the ownership of production factors in order to allow technology or management factor to participate in distribution. Third, the determination of factor equity distribution based on the ownership of production factors. The marketization of production factors is a precondition for determining the proportion of equity distribution. On the market, the price of various factors is determined through supply and demand so that the process of determining equity based on the ownership of production factors is combined with their marketization. Marketization measures the scarcity of production factors. Determining equity based on the ownership of production factors involves considerations for the contribution of production factors.

Chapter 14

A Political-Economic Analysis of Virtual Economy and the Ensuing Financial Crisis

The global financial crisis caused by the American subprime mortgage crisis has been the gravest economic crisis since the Great Depression in the 1930s. The field of political-economics studies the nature of economic processes. Therefore, a political-economic analysis of the crisis can illuminate its essential causes, shed light on its cyclical indicators from the perspective of economic laws, and identify a fundamental approach to prevent and overcome such crises.

14.1 A Modern Financial Crisis Born Out of the Virtual Economy

In the context of tradition — meaning the past — an economic crisis basically occurred in the real economy as a symptom of overproduction. Since the 1990s, the crises in the capitalist world have been financial crises. One might use Marxist monetary theory to discuss the possibilities of objectivity.

In *Capital* Marx points out that because money functions as a means of circulation and payment, it is likely to create a crisis; this means of circulation can break through all the temporal, spatial, and personal barriers imposed by the direct exchange of commodities. When the amount of paper money in circulation exceeds its limits, there is a possibility of credit sweeping as well as inflation. Money as means of payment may create a chain of credits and debts. When this chain is disturbed, a crisis of currency payments can occur. Marx explicitly states that for the development of probability into reality "a whole series of conditions is required".[1] "Such a crisis occurs only where the ongoing chain of payments has been fully developed along with an artificial system for settling them".[2] Following the lead of Marxist logic, we can explore the institutional causes of the financial crises ranging from the aspects of "an artificial system" to "a whole series of conditions".

What Marx calls "an artificial system" is primarily the capitalist system. The basic contradictions produced by the capitalist system are in fact the fundamental reasons behind such crises. This observation has been confirmed by the series of economic crises in the capitalist world. The global financial crisis caused by American subprime mortgage crisis is by no means an exception. Now we need to start from this point to research the mechanisms of this financial crisis.

Marx points out that a crisis caused by the circulation of money requires a "complete series of conditions". According to the logic of Marxism and the practices of economic operation, this series of conditions can be attributed to the economic relations of the market. Commodity and monetary economies are both distinct embodiments of a market economy, and the best embodiment of the modern market economy is a credit economy. In advanced market economies, Marx suggests that the entirety of the relations of the reproduction process rest on credit. In regard to the financial structure of modern enterprises, internal financing, namely entity capital, occupies a relatively small proportion compared with external financing. The latter includes bank loans and financial entities on the capital market. In this sense, the market economy is a credit economy. A credit economy is essentially a financial economy, meaning that financial issues turn out to be overall issues concerning the macroeconomy. A credit crisis or a financial crisis thus becomes a major manifestation of an economic crisis. "As long as the social character of labor appears as the monetary existence of the commodity and hence as a thing outside actual production, monetary crises, independent of real crises or as an

---

[1]Karl Marx. *Capital: A Critique of Political Economy*. Vol. 1, Trans. Ben Fowkes (London: Penguin Books, 1976), p. 209.

[2]*Ibid.*, p. 236.

intensification of them, are unavoidable".[3] This fact has been demonstrated in the Southeast Asian financial crisis in 1997 as well as by crises happening in other countries.

Marx discovered that "it lays open, in the form of speculation and the credit system, a thousand sources of sudden enrichment".[4] The sudden enrichment stems from the various forms of speculation that take advantage of the artificial credit system. This situation is the subjective factor responsible for the eruption of modern financial crises. The mechanism of speculation occurs in the virtual economy.

First, virtual capital is generated in the form of credit. By that I am referencing capital produced by the repeated use of the same monetary capital. Credit includes commercial credit as well as banking credit. As Marx illustrates, the role of commercial credit is to enable economic and transaction expansion to break from the limits of present capital. This is because the commercial market cannot purchase all commodities and sell them. That being said, commercial credit makes the above situation possible. The mechanism is as follows: commodity transactions take bills of exchange as a means of payment, meaning they are a bond to pay at certain date. "Until (the bills of exchange) expire and are due for payment, these bills themselves circulate as means of payment and they form the actual commercial money".[5] The circulation of bills of exchange replaces money, which means mutual advances by producers and merchants "are not based on monetary circulation, that of metallic or government paper money, but rather on the circulation of bills of exchange".[6] Virtual capital is generated through the creation of this simple means of circulation.

Bank credit is also capable of expanding the economy, allowing the same currency to act as a tool on many occasions and repeatedly performing the function of lending capital. Bank credit also takes the form of bills of exchange, check, bank notes, loans with interest-bearing securities, national bond securities, stocks as collateral, deposit overdraft, and undue discounts on bills of exchange. The repeated use of the same amount of monetary capital produces virtual capital. Virtual capital arising from the circulation of credit would result in credit inflation, perhaps best

---

[3]Karl Marx. *Capital: A Critique of Political Economy*. Vol. 3, Trans. David Fernbach (London: Penguin Books, 1981), p. 649.

[4]Karl Marx. *Capital: A Critique of Political Economy*. Vol. 1, p. 741.

[5]Karl Marx. *Capital: A Critique of Political Economy*. Vol. 3, p. 525.

[6]*Ibid.*, p. 526.

exemplified by Japan's bubble economy during the 1980s. At that time, the so-called low-cost expansion and debt management created a credit bubble in Japan. In the case of unrestricted loans and the inability to return capital, the credit economy could not be sustained. Eventually, the bubble economy collapsed, resulting in a 10-year recession.

Second, virtual capital can be generated in the form of income capitalization. As Marx comments: "The formation of fictitious capital is known as capitalization. Any regular periodic income can be capitalized by reckoning it up, on the basis of the average rate of interest, as the sum that a capital lent out at this interest rate would yield".[7] Income from securities such as bonds and stock shares can all be capitalized according to a certain interest rate and thus become virtual capital. The capital raised by these securities is involved in the operation of enterprises and further involves the operation of the real economy. However, it would exist as a certificate of ownership, representing the right to claim future yields, which means it can enter the market. Real estate also shares this same feature. In the securities and real estate market, the prices of shares, bonds, and real estate have unique movements that are specifically set. "On the one hand their market values fluctuate with the level and security of the receipts to which they give a legal title". On the other hand, "the market value of these securities is partly speculative, since it is determined not just by the actual revenue but rather by the anticipated revenue as reckoned in advance".[8] Changes in interest rates, the amount of securities entering the market, speculative psychology, false information, manipulation of markets, and so on would possibly cause the market value to deviate from the value of their real capital. Therefore, the securities market is actually a speculative market and excessive speculation will produce a bubble economy. The Southeast Asian financial crisis in 1997 was basically a result of excessive speculation in the securities and real estate markets. The Wall Street credit crisis in 2001 is due to the fact that Enron, WorldCom, and other companies took advantage of mechanisms of speculation, practiced fraud, and manipulated stock prices.

Third, virtual capital can be generated in the form of financial derivatives. Marx discovered that virtual forms of capital such as stocks and bonds are all capable of multiplying. "In all countries of capitalist production, there is a tremendous amount of so-called interest-bearing capital or

---

[7] *Ibid.*, p. 597.

[8] *Ibid.*, p. 598.

'moneyed capital' in this form. And an accumulation of money capital means for the most part nothing more than an accumulation of these claims to production, and an accumulation of the market price of these claims, of their illusory capital value".[9] The mechanisms of virtual capital, which increase the multiplication of money, create a strong temptation to create even more virtual capital. The forthcoming financial innovations are mostly based on the creation of virtual capital. When Engels revised the third volume of *Capital*, he noticed that there were financial companies set up for the sole purpose of purchasing certain interest-bearing securities: "This duplication and triplication of capital has been taken very much further in recent years, e.g., through the financial trusts".[10] These financial companies simply invested in securities rather than investing in the real economy, thereby further inflating virtual capital. This made the market value of virtual capital deviate even further from that of actual capital. Especially since the 1990s and the development of informatization, the speed of financial innovations in Western countries led by the United States of America has accelerated. A series of financial derivatives were produced such as financial futures, stock indexes, and share options. The total amount of virtual capital significantly expanded and, as relevant data has revealed, every day the amount of virtual capital transacted on the entire capital market is 10 times that of actual capital.

In modern times, the main method of innovating financial instrument is to create financial derivatives. They are, to a certain degree, speculative instruments. Trading these derivatives is the act of transferring risk. The direct cause behind the 2007 American subprime mortgage crisis was an excess of financial innovation and the creation of derivative instruments. At that time, financial innovation had actually virtualized the real economy. For example, when the supply of real estate increased, financial institutions provided mortgage loans even to people with weak credit. Financial institutions then transferred these claims into securities and sold them. To purchase these claims, companies would once again use bank credit and loans. Thus, the chain of buying and selling was long and the accompanying speculation produced a significant increase in virtual capital. In this way, once a certain link (paying debts and loans) was interrupted, there was an ensuing global crisis; the entire financial system was destroyed because there was too much inflation. This can be illustrated by

---

[9] *Ibid.*, p. 599.

[10] *Ibid.*, p. 601.

the bankruptcy of the Lehman Brothers in 2007, one year after the subprime mortgage crisis and the global financial crisis.

The subprime mortgage crisis that began in the real estate financial sector rapidly spread to the entire financial system in the United States This is not only related to unregulated lending from financial institutions but also the capital structures of banks. Marx discovered that "[T]he greater part of banker's capital is therefore purely fictitious and consists of claims (bills of exchange) and shares (drafts on future revenues). … this capital's money value, as represented by these papers in the banker's safe, is completely fictitious".[11] This also illustrates why banking sectors were affected immediately after the subprime mortgage crisis happened, pushing large corporate banks such as Citibank to the verge of bankruptcy. The capital structure of banks is dominated by virtual capital. It would be inevitable that excessive speculation in the virtual economy would not increase bank's risk resistance but instead be contaminated by virtual capital, resulting in hazards to the entire financial sector.

The financial crisis that began in the United States soon spread to the entire world, not even sparing countries with healthy economies. This could be discussed in terms of financial globalization. As early as the end of 19th century and the start of 20th century when capitalism entered the stage of imperialism, Lenin discovered: "Imperialism is the epoch of finance capital and of monopolies, which introduce everywhere the striving for domination, not for freedom".[12] Financial capital has strength over all other forms of capital, meaning "a small number of financially 'powerful' states" stand out "among all the rest".[13] After nearly a century of development, the economy entered the stage of globalization, characterized by financial globalization. The specific manifestations of this stage include the free exchange of money and the globalization of capital, the globalization of financial market (money and capital markets), the globalization of the virtual economy, the free flow of capital, and the global payment relationships produced by trade and globalization. Since the United States is a country with financial strength, when it has a crisis, it will spread globally through channels of financial globalization.

[11] *Ibid.*, p. 600.

[12] V. I. Lenin. *Imperialism, the Highest Stage of Capitalism* (Moscow: Progress Publishers, 1966), p. 112.

[13] *Ibid.*, p. 54.

14.2 The Essence of the Modern Financial Crisis Is Still a Crisis in the Real Economy

The above analysis discusses the direct cause of financial crises in terms of the excessive speculation and fraud in the virtual economy. It is now necessary to conduct a further study of the deeper causes of financial crises, which is to say their essence. Marx has a clear judgment about the economic crisis of capitalism by which he means the relative surplus of production. The fundamental reason is the basic contradiction between capitalist private possessions and socialized mass production. This basic contradiction has led to the unlimited expansion of production and a relative contraction of people's consumption needs. When these contradictions continue to evolve, they create an economic crisis. As we have observed, the fundamental cause of the series of crises in the capitalist financial sector still can be discussed according to Marx's visionary judgment.

First, in using an analysis focusing on the relationship between the virtual and real economies, it is clear that the direct cause of the financial crisis is the undue separation of the former from the latter. There is a limit to the amount of credit-generated virtual capital and an overflow of this limit is likely to cause a crisis. Virtual capital in the form of credit is not limited to producing positive effects by enabling the production and circulation of goods; it also produces negative effects such as economic bubbles. Due to the existence of the virtual economy in the form of credit, "(market's) relationships and the conditions governing them assume ever more the form of a natural law independent of the producers and become ever more uncontrollable".[14] The volume of capitalist production "is determined by the scale of this production and its needs for constant expansion, and not by a predestined ambit of supply and demand, of needs to be satisfied".[15] In mass production, as long as commodities are sold, everything normally goes to the producer although direct buyers can be big merchants rather than consumers. "As long as the reproduction process is fluid, so that returns remain assured, this credit persists and extends".[16] The delay of capital flow-back would create a surplus of

[14] Karl Marx. *Capital: A Critique of Political Economy*. Vol. 3, p. 353.

[15] Karl Marx. *Capital: A Critique of Political Economy*. Vol. 2, Trans. David Fernbach (London: Penguin Books, 1978), p. 156.

[16] Karl Marx. *Capital: A Critique of Political Economy*. Vol. 3, p. 614.

commodities and a reduction of credit. "A crisis must evidently break out if credit is suddenly withdrawn and only cash payment is accepted".[17] This is the case with the US subprime mortgage crisis. Forms of credit such as subprime mortgages cause a sense of false prosperity in the real estate market. Once the limits of the support from the real economy are exceeded, credit ceases and then a crisis erupts.

Second, one might analyze the motives behind financial innovation. Although financial innovation aims to adapt to the modern market's economic development, its basic goal is for financial capital to seek monopoly profits. As Lenin describes, "finance capital, concentrated in a few hands and exercising a virtual monopoly, exacts enormous and ever-increasing profits from the floating of companies, issue of stock, state loans, etc., strengthens the domination of the financial oligarchy and levies tribute upon the whole of society for the benefit of monopolists".[18] Now methods to earn high amount of profits include immoderate loans and financial derivative instruments. Marx discovered that several economic crises in the United Kingdom in the 19th century were related to bank credit. The attractive high profits enabled people to extend beyond the limits of capital flow and allowed excessive expansion activities. Credit could be utilized because it was easily accessible and cheap. Moreover, the easier it is to obtain loans with unsold goods, the more such loans increase. Under such conditions, no one would let go of the profitable opportunities, "(which) could lead only to a massive flooding of the markets and a crash".[19] Financial innovation not only provides financial capital with chances to pursue high profit, it can also be used by some proprietors. For example, in order to stimulate the financial innovation of the operator, an option stimulus is designed to link the operator's compensation with the company's market value. This explains why CEOs of Enron, WorldCom, and other companies committed fraud by falsely reporting profits, purposely driving up the shares of stocks, and creating a crisis in the stock market as well as great losses to ordinary shareholders.

Third, one might analyze the relationship between production and consumption demands. Production and consumption can be distinguished in terms of both time and space. The tension between the two is due to the

---

[17] *Ibid.*, p. 621.

[18] V. I. Lenin. *Imperialism, the Highest Stage of Capitalism*. pp. 49–50.

[19] Karl Marx. *Capital: A Critique of Political Economy*. Vol. 3, p. 535.

purpose of production. "Since capital's purpose is not the satisfaction of needs but the production of profit, and since it attains this purpose only by methods that determine the mass of production by reference exclusively to the yardstick of production, and not the reverse, there must be a constant tension between the restricted dimensions of consumption on the capitalist basis, and a production that is constantly striving to overcome these immanent barriers".[20] In the capitalist economy, production is only limited by social productivity and large industrial production has expanded by leaps and bounds. The market is restricted by the proportion between a society's powers of production and consumption. In terms of society's power of consumption, Marx thinks it "is determined neither by the absolute power of production nor by the absolute power of consumption but rather by the power of consumption within a given framework of antagonistic conditions of distribution, which reduce the consumption of the vast majority of society to a minimum level, only capable of varying within more or less narrow limits. [I]t is further restricted by the drive for accumulation, the drive to expand capital and produce surplus-value on a larger scale".[21] The contradiction between the conditions of production and the conditions of realization indicates that the limitless expansion of production also requires the limitless expansion of the market, yet "its relationships and the conditions governing them assume ever more the form of a natural law independent of the producers and become ever more uncontrollable". Therefore, "the more productivity develops, the more it comes into conflict with the narrow basis on which the relations of consumption rest".[22] The result is a crisis of overproduction.

Financial innovation can intensify the contradictions between the limitless expansion of production and the relative shrinking of consumer demands both in terms of production and consumption. With regard to production, "credit, under every special stimulus, at once places an unusual part of this wealth at the disposal of production in the form of additional capital".[23] In the face of unrestricted expansion of production, the only way to prevent and overcome possible economic crises is to expand consumption. Theoretically, the most reliable approach to expand consumption is changing the adversarial mode of distribution and

---

[20] *Ibid.*, p. 365.

[21] *Ibid.*, pp. 352–353.

[22] *Ibid.*, p. 353.

[23] Karl Marx. *Capital: A Critique of Political Economy*. Vol. 1, p. 693.

increasing the income of laborers. Doing so would improve the social power of consumption. However, this approach is impossible to adopt under capitalism because it goes against its very nature. Capitalist countries can create market demands through financial innovation. The following analysis will argue that financial innovations alleviate the tensions between production and consumption through creating market demands while also leading to even more devastating crises.

The expansion of credit for production to credit for consumption may greatly increase the power of consumption so that production extends beyond the limits of current spending power. The issuance of credit cards can be said to be one of the financial innovations that encourage early consumption. The implication is that current consumption is not limited by current income levels, and that tomorrow's income can be used for today's consumption. When the supply of real estate increases rapidly, and when there is a bubble of consumer demands, banks and financial institutions provide home loans, even to subprime applicants with low credit. Superficially, mortgage loans thus help to increase the market's purchasing power. The financial institutions that issue mortgages will then securitize these debts, split the debt portfolio, and generate a variety of financial products, which will be sold to speculators (mainly banks and other financial institutions), thereby releasing a huge amount of liquidity (currency in circulation). All of these financial innovations have created false prosperity in short-term markets. At the same time, various risks also accumulate. As more and more homebuyers find it increasingly difficult to repay their loans, the risk of subprime mortgages increases, and the outbreak of a subprime mortgage crisis is inevitable. The reason why subprime loans are issued and sold is that this kind of financial innovation can stimulate the market and make the real estate market prosper. The essence of this issue lies in the greediness of Wall Street and those people who pursue a high amount of profit at any cost and are morally bankrupt. Economic laws are not subject to man's will. Ultimately, the virtual economy cannot withstand the real economy and a crisis occurs in the latter. As Marx described, "in fact a great part of the commodities has only apparently gone into consumption, and are actually lying unsold in the hands of retail traders, thus being still on the market".[24] Streams of commodities follow one another, flood the market and vie with each other for space. The late comers have to be sold below the valued price in order to

[24]Karl Marx. *Capital: A Critique of Political Economy*. Vol. 2, p. 157.

be sold at all. The earlier streams have not yet been converted into cash, and yet the payment for them is coming due. "This sale, however, has absolutely nothing to do with the real state of demand. It has only to do with the demand for payment, with the absolute necessity of transforming commodities into money. At this point the crisis breaks out".[25]

Finally, the crisis in the United States is the best case illustrating the law of the decline in average profit rate and its impact as it was described by Marx. The so-called average profit margin decline refers to the diminishing marginal income of capital. The reverse is the increase in capital required to increase the profit per unit. As Marx argues, the fall of average profit rate would lead to surplus capital. This is best illustrated by the increase of the minimal capital quota into real economy. "The mass of small fragmented capitals is thereby forced onto adventurous paths: speculation, credit swindles, share swindles, crises".[26] Since the 1980s, the United States has engendered a new economy represented by information technology, thus sustaining economic growth and prosperity that has lasted over 20 years. During the 21st century, however, there have already been signs of an economic recession, i.e., the break of IT bubbles at the turn of the millennium. This is in and of itself a reflection of the influence of the law of falling average profit rates. To prevent this decline, entities including the government and financial institutes are all using speculation and credit mechanisms. The Federal Reserve implemented a policy of loosening monetary regulations while financial institutions came up with innovations that aimed to create demands in the virtual economy. They issued large amounts of consumer credit, encouraged debt consumption, issued a variety of financial derivatives, and created a significant bubble in the capital market in an attempt to delay economic recession and stop the fall in average profit rate. Marx described the consequences of all of these actions, saying they "paralyze[s] the function of money as a means of payment, which is given along with the development of capital and depends on those presupposed price relationships. [T]he chain of payment obligations at specific dates is broken in a hundred places, and this is still further intensified by an accompanying breakdown of the credit system, which had developed alongside capital".[27] Marx thus illuminates the mechanisms for the outbreak of the financial crisis in the United States.

---

[25] *Ibid.*, p. 157.

[26] Karl Marx. *Capital: A Critique of Political Economy*. Vol. 3, p. 359.

[27] *Ibid.*, p. 363.

14.3 Overcoming Market Failure with Effective Government Interference and Institutional Adjustment

The emergence of an economic crisis exposes the contradictions between productivity and relations of production. Therefore, government anti-crisis measures not only involve emergency control measures to rescue the economy, but also include institutional adjustments against such exposed contradictions. For capitalist countries, it is precisely such institutional adjustments that help the economic system survive and develop. An analysis of measures taken by governments confronted with world financial crises can thus shed light on methods to overcome market failure in modern economies.

The Great Depression in the 1930s proved the implausibility of the long-standing, dominant liberal theory that the economy can adjust itself according to market mechanisms. The broad recognition of Keynesian theory recognizes the need for state intervention in the macroeconomy. In following Keynesian theory, the US government had adopted state intervention measures to get the United States and the world economy out of a major crisis. However, in the following decades, capitalist countries entered a relatively stable phase. For that reason, there was a revival of a form of neoliberalism that opposes national intervention in market adjustment and exerts a great deal of influence, even on Chinese economic scholarship. In the 21st century, the United States and other Western countries bore staggering pressures because of economic recession. A series of financial innovations in the US virtual economy were actually attempts to use the market's self-regulation mechanisms to overcome macroeconomic imbalance, thereby prevent an economic recession. Not until 2007 when the subprime mortgage crisis occurred in the United States did the government take immediate measures to intervene, causing the global financial crisis in 2008. The outbreak of the financial crisis once again illuminated the bankruptcy of the form of neoliberalism that simply believes in the market's self-regulation, proving that relying on market self-regulation cannot solve issues with the macroeconomy and economic recession.

In the face of the failure of the market's adjustment mechanisms after the world financial crisis, the governments of various countries quickly adopted substantial intervention measures to come to its rescue. For example, the US government implemented a $700 billion stimulus plan and a nationalization project for large banks facing bankruptcy while the central banks of Western Europe implemented a plan to cut interest rates. Such governmental efforts to stop the economic downfall were positive and avoided a long-term depression similar to that of the 1930s. Judging from the effects of these government intervention policies, it is clear that such measures are both necessary and effective. One of the major strategies the US government adopted was to nationalize some financial institutions on the verge of bankruptcy. One example is the acquisition of the shares in Citibank. Some criticized this nationalization as an act of "socialization". In fact, this is not the case. This is a tactic to save bankrupt corporations by making use of national capital. Once these corporations have survived the crisis, government would *denationalize* them once again by selling equity. In essence, this is state monopoly capitalism. As Lenin revealed in his past work, "state monopoly in capitalist society is merely a means of increasing and guaranteeing the income of millionaires in some branch of industry who are on the verge of bankruptcy".[28] Obviously, although the "nationalization" promoted by the US government had the effect of controlling the spread and depth of the financial crisis, it is undeniable that these actions also protected the income of bankrupt financial capitalists.

The fact that a sequence of financial crises has repeatedly occurred in the United States has not only proven that market self-regulation is a failure, but it also challenges the idea of using macroeconomic theory as the basis of government intervention theory, thus affecting the breakthroughs in this field.

First, the macroeconomy should be expanded to include the total level of asset prices on the capital market.

Ever since the 1990s, economic crises around the world have been manifested as financial crises. This fact challenges traditional theories about the macroeconomy and its relationship with government intervention policies. Previous economic crises, especially the Great Depression in the 1930s, were directly generated in the real economy and manifested as a symptom of overproduction. Corresponding theories about the macroeconomy analyze the issue of macroeconomic equilibrium with regard to three markets in the real economy (the commodity market, employment market, and monetary market). The theory of government intervention is also mainly limited to the balance of the total supply and aggregate demand in the real economy. The aggregate indicators adjusted by the

[28] V. I. Lenin. *Imperialism, the Highest Stage of Capitalism*, p. 35.

government initiatives are mainly the total price level in commodity market, the total employment level in the employment market, and the total interest rate in the monetary market. Even the related financial issues mainly concern the supply and demand in the monetary market, and its research perspective is limited to its impact on the overall level of commodity prices and the total level of employment.

Currently, most of the economic crises around the globe, especially those happening in capitalist countries, are taking place in the virtual economy. The factors influencing macroeconomic equilibrium not only include the general prices in the commodity market, the total employment in the employment market, and the interest in monetary market, but also include the general level of asset prices in the capital market. The latter not only has relatively independent determinants, but is also capable of changing macroeconomic equilibrium, expanding the asset price inflation caused by excessive speculation, and forming a bubble without the support of the real economy. Once the bubbles are broken, asset prices shrink rapidly and deflation and economic recession quickly follow as a consequence. Therefore, the capital market and the virtual economy must be considered as part of the research scope of the macroeconomy. The asset price level should become an indicator of macro-monitoring. The virtual economy must become the target of government monitoring, especially the degree of financial innovation in the virtual economy.

Second, the virtual economy has become the main aspect determining market failure, and thus is the main target of government regulation.

Traditionally, market failures happen in the real economy. Examples include failures that occur because of externalities or monopolies. As a result, government intervention was also concerned with the real economy. A series of economic crises in recent years have been triggered by the virtual economy, reflecting the lack of trust and excessive speculation that occur there. These issues cannot only be overcome through market adjustments, but also through the operation of market mechanisms that may have self-enhancing functions. This is because the value of virtual capital from Marx's perspective is "the accumulation of ... their illusory capital value".[29] The problem is not only the fact that virtual capital is divorced from physical capital because of excessive speculation, but also that a tremendous number of these bonds and financial derivatives in circulation "represent purely fraudulent deals, which now come to light and

[29] Karl Marx. *Capital: A Critique of Political Economy*. Vol. 3, p. 599.

explode; as well as unsuccessful speculations conducted with borrowed capital, and finally commodity capitals that are either devalued or unsellable, or returns that are never going to come in".[30] Issues that Marx revealed over a hundred years ago are common in the modern virtual economy, therefore necessitating an intensification of the government's financial supervision. For a long period of time, the virtual economy has been a blind spot for financial supervision.

As early as 2002, Enron's fraud and bankruptcy led to the collapse of the stock market, indicating that many problems in the virtual economy can be attributed to lack of integrity and moral risk taking. The credit mechanisms of the capital market cannot solely rely on self-regulation; they must also depend on outside regulation. The latter means government intervention and intensified legal regulation and supervision. The basic content of the Sarbanes–Oxley Act passed by the US government was to impose regulation over the action of every market entity and to intensify the punishments for dishonest conduct on the capital market. This would be achieved by means of stricter accounting and auditing systems. The introduction of this law coincides with the decline of the competitiveness of the US financial system. This situation, along with the liberalism that the United States has long espoused, facilitated the loosening up of financial supervision and the introduction of Financial Services Regulatory Relief Act of 2006. To some extent, the breakout of American subprime mortgage crisis in 2007 and the global financial crises in 2008 are both consequences of the relaxation of financial regulation in the United States.

The outbreak of the ensuing crises forced the US government to issue the "Financial Regulatory Reform — New Foundation: Rebuilding Financial Supervision" bill in June 2009. It establishes the central position of the government in dealing with financial crises, attempts to enforce comprehensive monitoring without bind spots, and aims to solve the problems of coordination and checks and balances between financial regulatory agencies. In light of the United States' loss of control and excessive financial innovations, the crucial part of financial regulation should concentrate on financial derivatives. The innovation of financial derivatives has a significant leverage effect on the creation of virtual capital and also on the real economy's support for the virtual economy. The global financial crises triggered by the subprime mortgage crisis are directly related to this. Therefore, the state must regulate the creation of

[30] *Ibid.*, p. 621.

financial derivatives, strictly control such innovations within the manageable range, and control the scope of support coming from the real economy.

Third, mechanisms of the virtual economy should be used to counter financial crises.

Although the direct trigger of this world financial crisis is excessive speculation in the virtual economy, the existence of this mechanism can be used by the state to regulate the macroeconomy.

Financial crises born out of the virtual economy have resulted in the real economy's devastation as well as economic recessions. Confronted with such crises, governments should undoubtedly focus on saving the real economy, preventing economic recession by securing growth, and reducing unemployment by securing employment. It is worth noting that there are already mechanisms for the virtual economy in the modern economy. These mechanisms have led to economic crises, and yet they can still be used to tackle them. In the face of the declining market demand in the crisis stage, the government's important intervention is to implement tax cuts and increase government demand. Enterprises and consumers either lack the confidence in investment and consumption or lack the capability to invest and consume due to a decrease in spending power during the crisis. The government's implementation of this positive fiscal policy not only directly increases investment and consumption demand, but also serves as a model and orientation to drive social demand, thereby playing a role in maintaining growth and ensuring employment. During the Great Depression, Keynes even came up with the remedy of deficit financing to grapple with the grave deficiency of effective market demand. Practically, both positive financial policy and loose monetary policy would use financial mechanisms that involve the virtual economy.

On the one hand, credit mechanisms could be utilized. Credit plays a crucial role in Marx's analysis of economic cycles. "The great regulator of the velocity of the currency is credit".[31] During a prosperous phase, credit expands and capital from loans is relatively ample. During a crisis, credit abruptly stops and borrowing capital is therefore lacking. Therefore, during an economic recession, there is deficiency of credit more than there is an insufficiency in demand. By virtue of this cyclical system, the main approach to counter a crisis and expand demand is to expand credit.

---

[31] *Ibid.*, p. 653.

Marx illuminates this point in saying "as long as a bank's credit is not undermined, it can alleviate the panic in such cases by increasing its credit money, whereas it increases this panic by contracting credit".[32] Increasing and activating credit and idle industrial capital are measures that can drive an economy out of a crisis. This round of financial crises broke out along with a sudden contraction in market demand, a substantial lack of liquidity. Consequently, there was a break in the capital chain of many companies. In this case, relaxing credit regulations and increasing the issuance of credit can save a number of companies. At the same time, the expansion of demand also requires the support of credit.

On the other hand, the virtual capital market is also useful. In the operation of the market mechanisms, those that concern capital do not entirely accord with those of the commodity market. Since the demand for commodities arises for the purpose of consumption, the prices in the commodity market change in reverse proportion with demand. A demand for capital arises for the purpose of increasing value. Thus, the prices of the capital market change in proportion with its demand, meaning that we tend to buy stocks and real estate when they are on the rise. Now as the financial assets of the virtual economy are taking an increasing proportion of the asset portfolios of both enterprises and citizens alike, the market conditions of the virtual economy would produce evidence of the effects of wealth. To some extent, the virtual economy is an economy of confidence, revealing that capital market is the most sensitive to the real economy and would even serve as a driving force in its cyclic changes. When the real economy maintains a positive growth, excessive speculation in capital market may cause a bubble economy and thus prosperity in the virtual market. Once the bubbles break, asset prices plunge. Then, the substantial depreciation and contraction of investors' assets directly, and significantly reduces the market's demand on the real economy. In the critical phase when demand in commodity market is depressed, it is of the utter importance to boost confidence in the virtual economic market, to activate the real estate and stock markets, to stimulate consumption and investment demands with the wealth effect, and to excite the market of the real economy. In examining the counter measures used against several economic cycles in China, when the real economy is depressed, the demands in real estate market have an evidently propelling effect.

[32] *Ibid.*, p. 649.

The last thing to point out is that Alan Greenspan, the ex-chairman of American Federal Reserve, claimed that Western capital markets, especially those in the United States are premium models. However, that mythical claim was broken by the credit crisis in Wall Street around the beginning of the new millennium, the subprime mortgage crisis in 2007 as well as the consequential global financial crisis in 2008. In the meantime, the international impacts from China's economy have been on the rise and Chinese economic patterns are receiving increasing attention. This should drive us to further reflect on the political economy concerning economics.

Bibliography

中国社科院金融研究所课题组:《美国金融监管改革最新进展》, 载于《金融论坛》2009 年第 26 期. Institute of Finance, Chinese Academy of Social Sciences. The latest development of American financial regulation reform. *Finance Forum*, 26, 2009.

Chapter 15

Market's Determination of Resource Allocation and Improved Role of the Government

The Third Plenary Session of the 18th Central Committee of the Communist Party of China (CPC) confirmed that the market plays a decisive role in resource allocation. This is a significant breakthrough in China's socialist market economic theory as well as an important achievement in the Sinicization of Marxist economics. This theoretical breakthrough involves a major adjustment to the relationship between the government and the market. In order to realize the mechanism of resource allocation, the government shall not only play a decisive role through its own reform, but also better fulfill its functions.

15.1 From the Market's Fundamental Role to Its Decisive One

The study of the trajectory of China's reform and opening up shows that each major reform takes place after a breakthrough in the theory of the market economy, with the orientation toward adjusting and optimizing the relationship between the government and the market.

Since the 14th National Congress of the Communist Party of China in 1992, a ground-breaking theory has been developed. It states that the market plays a fundamental role in resource allocation under the state's macroeconomic regulation and control. This principle has been the theoretical basis for guiding the market-oriented reform of China's economic system from the 15th to the 18th National Congress of the CPC in 2013. The Third Plenary Session of the 18th Central Committee of the CPC clearly stated that the market plays a decisive role in resource allocation, revealing the fact that China's socialist market economy theory has made ground-breaking progress. The new positioning of market will be a novel guide for dealing with the role of the government and market in the economic system.

The decision made by the Third Plenary Session of the 18th Central Committee of the CPC concerning comprehensively deepening reform clearly stated the core issue of economic reform: managing the relationship between the government and the market so that the latter can play a decisive role in resource allocation and the former can better fulfill its functions. This is a major breakthrough in the theory of the socialist market economy, indicating that China's economic system will usher in major reforms. The key here is to clarify the underlying connotative difference between what is "fundamental" and what is "decisive".

First of all, the original definition of the fundamental role of the market encompasses two levels of regulation: the state regulates the market and the market regulates resource allocation. In this way, the market has a fundamentally regulatory effect. However, these two levels no longer apply to the present decisive role of market. The market does not exert a regulatory effect under the regulation of government; instead, it has a decisive role in terms of self-independence.

Second, in the past the fundamental role of the market was to achieve macro, governmental goals through the state's regulation of the market. When the market plays a decisive role, the government is not regulating the market mechanism — which in turn determines resource allocation. Instead, it regulates the overall levels of price, employment, and interest rates, which then influence the stability of the macro economy. Without any interference in the market's resource allocation, the government regulates its macro result.

Third, according to the previous definition that determined that the market plays a fundamental role, the government needs to regulate the market consistently and in advance. When it plays a decisive role, macro or minor regulations are deployed whenever the inflation and unemployment rates exceed the upper and lower limit, leaving sufficient room for the market to function in the macro economy.

The original aim of the state's macro control of the market is comprised of two aspects. First, the state ensures that the market's adjustment of resource allocation can implement the socialist goal of fairness. Second, it achieves a balance in the macroeconomic equilibrium. What are the actual outcomes? For one, it is difficult for the market to implement the goal of fairness. Second, the macro economy can still be out of control from time to time. This is then coupled with the obvious subjectivity and limited rationality embedded within the state regulation of the market, resource allocation, the fact that it is subject to interference, and failures in fulfilling the aim of efficiency. In view of the governmental failure, de-regulation of the market seems much more sensible than its macro control.

In effect, the decisive role of market in resource allocation returns to the original meaning of the market economy. The field of economics not only studies efficiency, but more importantly the mechanisms behind it. The general conclusion, whether it originates from Marxist or Western economics, is that under the conditions of a market economy, only the market mechanism can effectively allocate resources. Marx explains that the standard to determine the effective allocation of social labor-time in various departments is that the total amount of labor-time spent by each department is socially necessary. Its realization depends on the full effect of the law of value, which applies to the market mechanism. Competition, and the fluctuations in market price which correspond to fluctuations in the relationship of demand and supply, constantly seek to reduce the total quantity of labor applied to each kind of commodity to this level".[1] In comparison with Western explanations, the law of welfare economics shows that each competitive form of economics has Pareto efficiency, and each mode of resource allocation with Pareto efficiency can be realized through a market mechanism. The market allocates resources in a competitive manner according to the principle of efficiency. In turn, this can promote a highly efficient flow of resources to regions, departments, and enterprises. China's economy has already passed the stage of relying on resource investment, and now the problem of an unsustainable supply of environmental resources has become prominent. It has indeed reached the stage of deriving value from efficiency. Therefore, it is more urgent than ever to hand over the task of resource allocation to the market.

There are two major functions of the market's determination of how resources are allocated. The first mechanism is the selection criteria that

[1]Karl Marx. *Capital: A Critique of Political Economy*. Vol. 3, Trans. David Fernbach (London: Penguin Books, 1981), p. 294.

the fittest will survive. The second mechanism incentivizes reward and punishment. The basic meaning of the market's resource allocation is allocating resources according to market rules, prices, and competition in order to maximize benefits and optimize efficiency. In reality, the market decides what should be produced, how it engages with production, and for whom resources are produced. This system is premised upon consumer sovereignty, equal opportunities, free competition, enterprise management, and a flow of resources. Obviously, a series of reforms will be affected by the shift to a system and mechanism in which the market determines resource allocation.

The fact that the market decides what it should produce denotes that consumers' currency determines what products are to be produced. To fulfill its decisive role, the market not only requires that the producing enterprises operate and make decisions independently but also demands that consumers have sovereignty and free choice. By taking the needs of market and consumers into account, producers can truly provide the products that society needs. Accordingly, it is necessary to overturn the government's absolute decisions over enterprises' production.

The idea that the market will decide how it engages with production denotes that enterprises will have their own manner of operating completely with independent technical improvements and choice. In a fully competitive market environment, producers will choose the most advanced technologies, the most scientific management methods, and the cheapest production methods. The more complete the competition is, the higher the efficiency of resource allocation will be. The corresponding institutional arrangement is to break with various forms of protection and monopoly. With the deployment of the concept of the survival of the fittest, producers truly become risk-takers.

The idea that the market will decide for whom it is producing refers to the distribution of the fruits of production among key owners. This in turn depends on the relationship between the supply and demand of the various production factors in the market. The resources allocated to the market include labor, capital, technology, management, and natural resources. Replacing or supplementing each other, all of these resources are involved in supply–demand relations and the corresponding prices. Therefore, an important aspect of the efficiency of resource allocation is the following: the scarcest resources are used most economically and can increase the effective supply while the most abundant resources are utilized to the fullest advantage. This goal is manifested by the regulation of the prices formed by the supply–demand relations in each essential market. Key users compare the costs and benefits of input factors according to the prices of production that are determined by the market. They then employ production factors at the lowest cost. Next, key suppliers can make adjustment to the supply. The corresponding institutions make arrangement so that key factors enter the market: their prices are shaped by its influence and can accurately reflect the scarcity of the production factors by simultaneously adjusting their supply and demand. Accordingly, the institutional arrangements ensure that all the production factors enter the market.

The idea that the market determines resource allocation highlights the autonomy of the market, finding its expression not only in the market's autonomous decisions about the direction of resource allocation, but also in the market regulation signals. By this I mean that market prices are formed independently, without the improper intervention of the government. Marxist economics has explicit specifications about the formation of prices in the market. Only when they are formed in a competitive market can the prices accurately reflect the system of supply and demand and the requirements of the law of value. Marx once pointed out that the market "acknowledge(s) no authority other than that of competition".[2] Hence, there is no need for the government to directly fix prices. Since the reform period, prices in the competitive sector have essentially been liberalized and rendered subject to the market. It is now necessary to promote price reforms in monopolized areas such as water, oil, natural gas, electricity, transportation, and telecommunication. The general theory of economics points out that monopolies severely cut off the vitality of the market, thereby reducing the efficiency of resource allocation. The prices, income, and quality of service provided by monopoly sectors are all essentially institutional issues. According to the governmental regulation theory, natural monopolies do not require the government to regulate every department. The forward and backward links that are part of a natural network-type monopoly can be used for competition, and their prices should be liberalized in the market. The government's pricing range is mainly limited to important public utilities, public welfare services, and natural network-based monopolies. Any price that can be formed by the market is handed over and the government should not intervene

[2]Karl Marx. *Capital: A Critique of Political Economy*. Vol. 1, Trans. Ben Fowkes (London: Penguin Books, 1976), p. 477.

improperly. In this way, the signal of market price becomes more accurate, and the range of market adjustments becomes more extensive. Moreover, the formation of market prices does not only involve commodities, but also includes the price systems of various production factors. According to the above market requirements, signals of market regulation such as price, interest rates, and exchange rates, should be formed in the market and reflect the market's supply–demand relations.

Obviously, for the purpose of ensuring the efficiency of resource allocation, the top priority for the government to better fulfill its role is to grant the market a decisive role through its own reform.

15.2 Improving the Market Mechanism that Determines Resource Allocation

The market determines resource allocation based on a mechanism that includes prices, competition, and rules. Obviously, the effectiveness of market resource allocation is premised on the improvement of market mechanism.

According to definitions from neoclassical economics, effective resource allocation should be completely based on the market. The classic Arrow–Debreu model exemplifies the standard of a complete market: any commodity, in any time, place, or natural state (any risk state), is in a fully competitive market. A large number of manufacturers, pursuing a maximization of their profits or values, interact with the consumers who rationally pursue the maximization of utility. The model has several basic rules for a complete market: all commodities must enter the market. each market should be completely competitive, and market entities (vendors and consumers) should rationally pursue maximization.[3] That is to say, the most effective market resource allocation identified by economics conforms to these standards for a complete market. The theory claims that a complete market does not exist in reality, but it instead serves as the standard for building and improving the market.

In real situations, the market fails to meet these qualifications of what is considered to be complete competition. The sense in which it is incomplete can apply to the competition, market system, or information. Under this incomplete regulation of the market, it is difficult for the economy to

[3] Joseph E. Stiglitz. *Whither Socialism?* (Cambridge: The MIT Press, 1994), p. 5.

be entirely efficient. The existing theories about market economy, encompassing the practice of a developed form, proves that in reality the market system is not perfect. The unbalanced market theory points out that a rigidity of prices, lack of flexibility in supply and demand, and insufficient competition can lead to market imbalance. The incomplete information theory points out that, for one thing, incomplete market information may lead to adverse selection, moral hazards, free rides, unpaid debts, and other opportunistic behaviors. For another, it may lead to the bad money in the market expelling the good. Since China's market economy has undergone its transformation from a planned economy, the chaos of market system has been more serious than ever. In reality, the excessive "shopping competition" in the market can cause a serious waste in social resources, destabilizing society. Pinpointing the incompleteness and imperfection of the above-mentioned market is not intended to eliminate its decisive role in resource allocation. Instead, it requires the construction and improvement of the market through a series of institutional arrangements. In this way, the market will more effectively determine resource allocation.

Most importantly, the degree to which the market allocates resources effectively depends on the sense of order. From Adam Smith to Hayek, theorists have advocated for natural order. The basic idea is that full competition naturally results in a particular order. Accordingly, promoting competition is fundamental for the establishment of a market's order. As long as there is sufficient competition, this order will naturally take shape. The theory of modern institutional economics emphasizes that competition must be orderly, and market order is not completely contingent upon self-regulation. It is not formed spontaneously; instead, it is necessary to consciously establish an order of competition, hence, an orderly competition. The commanding power of the invisible hand needs to be sought in the visible order, which constitutes an important aspect of the government's improved functioning. With regard to China's present stage, the construction of market order is prominent in the following aspects.

First, the market order is evident in the standardization and protection of property rights. The definition of property rights is premised on market transactions. A commodity can only be traded if property rights are clearly defined. The market order should be built upon an effective contract and property rights system. Protecting the legitimate rights and interests of market participants is fundamentally tantamount to protecting their property rights. Marx has said that both parties "contract as free persons, who are equal before the law. Their contract is the final result in which their joint will finds a common legal expression".[4] "This juridical relation, whose form is the contract, whether as part of a developed legal system or not, is a relation between two wills which mirrors the economic relation. The content of this juridical relation (or relation of two wills) is itself determined by the economic relation".[5] Obviously, ownership is the premise and foundation of the market economy. Without ownership rights, there is no legal relation in the form of contract. The property rights system established within the framework of the basic economic system of socialism with Chinese characteristics must clarify that the property rights of the public and non-public ownership economies are equally inviolable. The definition and protection of property rights are functions of the state. China should not only protect state-owned assets, but also all kinds of economic property rights and legitimate interests. In particular, it should achieve a clear definition and protection of the property rights of economic entities in terms of their legal and institutional areas, which include the regulation of the transfer of property rights and transactions, the market's adherence to equivalent exchanges, and equal competition, etc. After an innovation-driven mode of economic development takes hold, the object of property rights protection encompasses both material and intellectual assets.

Second, the market order is also evident in the establishment of fair, open, and transparent market rules. Any game has rules, and market trading is no exception. Establishing market rules means regulating the market order, which is an important path to stimulating the effect of market regulation and reducing its operation costs. The reason why the market mechanism has the effective function of resource allocation lies in its adherence to the principle of fairness, including equal rights and opportunities as well as fair trade and rules. In a fair market, enterprises are free to enter and exit, consumers are free to choose, elements are free to flow, and exchanges can proceed at equal prices. By allocating resources in such a free and fair environment, the market can achieve goals of efficiency. The unfairness of China's current market competition can be observed in three ways. First, different ownership economies are treated unequally: the non-public ownership economy is actually subject to various forms of discrimination. Second, there are market monopolies.

---

[4] Karl Marx. *Capital: A Critique of Political Economy*. Vol. 1, p. 280.
[5] *Ibid.*, p. 178.

A considerable number of administrative monopolies are left over from the planned economy. Enterprises with monopoly status can manipulate the market and obtain a monopoly over incomes. Third, there are a variety of preferential, skewed policies introduced by state and local governments. With preferences must come prejudices and discrepancies remain in these preferential policies. Some enterprises in certain regions receive preferential treatment, resulting in unfair competition opportunities and diminishing the regulatory effect of the market mechanism. Building a fair and competitive market requires establishing a law-based business environment and implementing a unified market access and exit system. On the basis of the formulation of negative lists, various market entities can enter the field outside the list in accordance with the law. Here, the key is that the government's formulation of negative lists should truly reflect the requirements of fairness, openness, and transparency. The openness and transparency of the market requires establishing a market information disclosure system. If the market information is incomplete, then the party that enjoys the information could monopolize and manipulate the market and its transactions would not result in a win–win situation. Therefore, the economic value of information comes to present itself. Market participants need to pay for the acquisition of information. From a societal perspective, it is necessary to force market participants to disclose information through certain institutional arrangements. The government must also establish a market information disclosure system to provide market participants with information about overcapacity, technical standards, market demand, and so on, thereby reducing the cost of information for the society as a whole.

Third, the market order is evident in establishing a unified and open market. The unification of the market can be observed from multiple angles. First, in terms of liquidizing products and essential factors, unifying the market means allowing for the free flow of elements, enterprises, products, and services. Second, from the perspective of the positioning of various market entities, unification refers to the different types of entities that enter markets and acquire production factors. Third, in terms of the market rules, the systems and policies in each region are unified and the market in each region operates in accordance with uniform rules. China has directly entered the planned economy stage from that of the natural economy, undergoing a transformation. Therefore, China's unified market has not yet been formed. The reform of the fiscal and taxation system and policies about regional development that both exist in the reform process have strengthened local interests. The resulting market barriers to protectionism have hindered the effective and free-flowing allocation of elements. At present, building a state market that is unified and open is highlighted in three respects: First, local protection must be broken. Local governments protect local, disadvantaged industries and enterprises, which would not in turn withdraw from the market, only leading to inefficiency and non-optimization of resource allocation. Second, it is necessary to break administrative monopolies and regional blockades of the market, realizing the free flow of commodities and various production factors across the country and making all the market entities enter the market transactions on an equal basis. The third is to put an end to the urban and rural market segmentation and build a unified urban and rural market. This path involves raising the level of rural marketization, improving the mechanism of agricultural product prices in the market, and building a unified urban and rural factor market.

Finally, the market order is evident in improving the market system. The market system is the carrier of the effective allocation of resources. Shifting to the decisive role of the market is characterized by the entry of capital, land, labor, technology, and other production factors into the market. Only if various factors are allowed to freely enter the market system might there be a market that determines resource allocation in real life. By monitoring the prices of various factors in the market, the relation between supply and demand can readjust the rewards of the owners of production factors. In this way, resource allocation can be effective.

The market economy is a credit economy. Resources are essentially allocated through channels of credit. Therefore, it is especially important to improve the financial market system. In *Capital*, Marx makes it clear that the necessary condition for full market competition is that capital has greater mobility, which makes it easier to move from one department to another. In addition to the existing, complete commercial freedom within the society, this premise involves the development of the credit system, which has gathered a large amount of scattered and available social capital. As the Third Plenary Session of the 18th Central Committee of the CPC has pointed out, the improvement of the financial market mainly involves three areas. First, all kinds of ownership economies will have equal access to financial resources, and qualified private capital is allowed to initiate the establishment of financial institutions like small and medium-sized banks. Second, when it comes to the marketization of interest rates that reflect and regulate the supply and demand of the capital market, the signals of financial market regulation need to be improved. Third, financial innovation should be encouraged, promoting the levels of financial market and multiple kinds of products. Fourth, using financial markets as a channel for opening up will bridge the domestic and international markets.

In effect, the government's improved functioning benefits from the above-mentioned four aspects of improving the market mechanism, which then pave the way for the market to have a decisive role. Expecting a better performance from the government will inevitably require the reform of the market supervision system. Market supervision means maintaining order and guaranteeing fair trade, thus ensuring that the market plays a decisive role in resource allocation. At present, the reform of the market supervision system is focused on tackling excessive government intervention and inadequate supervision. During the process of supervision, the government must abide by the rule that it should withdraw from the sports field, so to speak, refusing to be "athletes" or to blow the "black whistle" in the course of fairly enforcing the law.

15.3 Government Allocation of Public Resources out of Respect for Market Law

The discussion above has actually illuminated the government's role in making the market determine resource allocation. First, the government's own reform allows the market to play a decisive role. Second, the government promotes the construction and regulation of the market order. In the socialist market economy, the government's role is not limited to this alone. It should be made clear that the decisive role of the market in resource allocation cannot be promoted to the extent that the government's role is then abandoned, as is the case with neoliberalism. Nor can the determining role of the market be extended to the allocation of public resources.

The role of the government and the market does not mean that a strong market must accompany a weak government. The role of the government and that of the market are not necessarily oppositional. For example, in the southern part of Jiangsu Province, there is a strong driving force originating from both the government and the market. The reason is that they do not function at the same level, and the former does not have too much intervention in the latter. The government's strength lies in the creation of a positive environment for the effective operation of the market, which can include the legal system, harmonious social conditions, critical infrastructure, financial resources, a lack of exploitation of people's interests, guidance and assessment of the overall well-being and basic modernization of varying levels of government. Such governmental assets actually support the market as it fully fulfills its role. Therefore, the important symbol of a strong market is the fact that the world's top 500 enterprises and large-scale private enterprises flock to China in great concentrations. Of course, as the theory of the market's decisive role in resource allocation is confirmed, the cooperation between a strong government and market also needs to be transformed.

In terms of the decisive role the market has over resource allocation, everything that it can do that improves upon what the government can do shall be relegated to the market. Nevertheless, this does not mean that the government should never intervene in the economy. Apart from the resources that flow into the market, those that belong to the whole society include public resources. Public resources are unspecified and privately owned, including natural resources without explicit private ownership, the government's legal and policy resources, investments provided by public finances and consumer demands, and so on. Because they should meet public needs and follow the principle of fairness, the allocation of public resources can only be determined by the government and not the market.

Economists have different formulations concerning the government's role in determining how the market determines resource allocation. Neoclassical economists believe that the government needs to function in situations when market failures take place, including overcoming situations in which there is a polarization between the rich and the poor or when there are external problems like environmental pollution. Institutional economists point out that the government (state) is a significant cornerstone of institutional change, protecting the structures of property rights that contribute to efficiency. Macroeconomics clearly points out that when the market determines resource allocation it essentially achieves microeconomic benefits. To balance an aggregate macro economy and overcome macro unemployment and high inflation, one should rely on macroeconomic regulation and control.

Based on the theoretical definitions above, under the conditions in which the market plays a decisive role in resource allocation, the government's improved allocation of public resources needs to be facilitated by the establishment of boundaries between the government and the market.

This process can be roughly defined in the following way. Matters that the market cannot determine, such as issues of national and ecological security, should be handed over to the government. Market failures, such as problems with fair distribution and environmental protection, should lead to government intervention. Issues the market cannot cope with, such as projects involving major national productivity or the strategic development of resources and public interests, should be arranged by the government. Matters in which enterprises are reluctant to participate under conditions of market regulation, such as public welfare projects, should also be arranged by the government. In engaging such areas, the government should also act to the full extent to which its powerful role allows. The government's allocation of public resources is mainly conducted through policies such as promoting social equity through income distribution policies, using industrial structures and negative lists to guide transformations and upgrades, and regulating macroeconomic operations through fiscal and monetary policies.

In a country such as China, which still remains in the primary stage of socialism, development is still absolutely necessary. In theory, promoting development is an important function of the government. However, the government's promotion is not sufficiently efficient or qualified. The main reason for this lies in the GDP assessment of all levels of government and the unilateral pursuit of GDP growth. This has prompted the government to employ administrative means to allocate resources, which means it has not fully exerted the efficient function of the market in resource allocation to the extent that it has suppressed it. Now China has clearly redressed the bias toward simply assessing political achievements according to the growth of the economy. Simultaneously, it has requested abolishing preferential policies and substantially reducing the number of examination and approval projects. In this way, room can be made for all levels of government to get rid of the original mode of development and to fully engage the market's decisive role in resource allocation. Under this premise, all levels of government also need to undertake necessary tasks to promote development. These tasks may include, for instance, promoting the integration of urban and rural development, developing an innovation-driven economy, restructuring the economy, constructing ecological and environmental projects, and bolstering an open economy. Fulfilling the development tasks above and overcoming market failure requires the promotion and realization of the allocation of the government's public resources.

After the market plays a decisive role in resource allocation, following the market order is an important sign of the government's improved functioning. Mistakes in the government's functions or the abuse of its power can lead to confusion in the market order. When the government oversteps its authority and directly intervenes in the micro business activities of enterprises, it can distort corporate behavior mechanisms. Additionally, the government could malfunction, which would mainly be represented by instances of bureaucracy, rent-seeking, and administrative monopolies. What's more, "The government failure can also be caused by the cognitive difficulties of policy makers".[6] The basic path for an improved governmental performance in these issues is to connect the mechanisms of government to those of market, joining the government's allocation of public resources with the market's allocation of its own.

First of all, the government's role of in promoting development cannot be carried out in isolation: it needs to combine with the mechanisms of the market. The present state of economic development can be highlighted by two aspects: structural adjustments and innovation. Structural adjustments to the economy, especially industrial ones, mainly rely on the market. The striking problem with China's industrial structure is that overcapacity is becoming more and more serious. An important mechanism of the market's effective resource allocation is the idea of the survival of the fittest. As long as local protection is broken, production capacities that are backward or that produce surplus can be effectively eliminated by means of the market's mechanisms to adjust industrial structures. However, in a large developing country like China, adjustments to the economic structure cannot solely rely on the market. Transformations and upgrades to the industrial structure require the guidance of national industrial policies. In particular, the forward-looking cultivation of strategic, emerging industries still calls for guiding investments from the government. When it comes to driving forces, market competition can fuel innovation and the technological sectors need the orientation of the market. However, while the market allocates existing resources, innovation-driven forces need creative elements from non-material resources, or even the creation of new ones. Alone, the market cannot foster innovation: the state should join in. First, the state must implement major plans for scientific innovation. Second, the state must

[6]Hamid Hosseini. Underdeveloped countries' government failure caused by indeterminacy and lack of authentication. *Comparative Economic and Social Systems* 02, 2004, p. 97.

integrate the technological systems with innovations in knowledge. Third, the state must provide guiding investments for new, incubating technologies. Fourth, the state must establish systems and mechanisms for both motivation and innovation.

Second, when it comes to overcoming market failures, the government should respect market decisions. Under the system in which the market plays a decisive role, resources must be allocated to highly efficient regions, departments, and enterprises. Adhering to the market's rules for fair competition can guarantee efficient results rather than fair ones. The resulting polarization between the rich and the poor reflects a market failure. The operation of the socialist market economy pursues both efficiency and fairness as goals. In order to meet the requirements of socialism, the government has the responsibility to promote social fairness and justice and to overcome any malfunctions in the market. In order to ensure that the market allocates resources efficiently, the government's reason for implementing the goal of fairness should not be to enter the same level as the market. That is to say, it should not enter the field of resource allocation that is determined by the market, but instead enter the field of income distribution, regulating the initial distribution of enterprises according to the law and dedicating more efforts to deal with fairness through redistribution and social security. Even if the government seeks to coordinate regional development, it will use its own financial and public resources to transfer payments on an equitable basis. This will be done without changing the flow of resources determined by the market. The same might be said when constructing major infrastructure projects to attract enterprises from developed regions and entering underdeveloped ones to create external conditions.

Third, when it comes to providing public services, the government must resort to the market's mechanisms out of respect for its laws. Public services that must be provided by the government are not necessarily produced and operated by governmental departments themselves. When it comes to quite a few aspects, the private sector's production and operation can be more efficient. The manner in which the government purchases services from the private sector may make public services more efficient and qualified. For example, the important aspect of the integration of urban and rural development is promoting an equality in their basic public services. Basic public services provided in rural towns that are not wholly undertaken by the government can also be purchased. The same holds true for the gathering of public resources. Funds for urban construction can be led by the government to establish a transparent, standardized investment and financing mechanism including expanding the financing channels through various means like issuing bonds from local governments and allowing social capital to participate in the investment and operation of urban infrastructure through franchising or other means. For example, government interventions for the sake of environment protection can also take advantage of market activities such as charging for sewage and trading emissions.

Fourth, when it comes to maintaining market order, the government must strengthen the construction of the social credit system. To establish the market order, we must attach great importance to constructing ethical standards and resolving integrity issues: the ethical foundation of the market order. All of the market regulations will come into effect if traders act with integrity. The construction of the social credit system involves two aspects. First, institutional credit aims to establish a sound credit system through various statutory and non-statutory means, cracking down on fraud and other acts of dishonesty through legal actions. Second, moral credit promotes honesty and castigates those who break promises in order to form ethics and values observed by the whole society. Complementing each other, the two aspects will overcome any opportunistic behaviors and enable honest ones. In this same way, the market order can be preserved.

To summarize, in the socialist market economic system where the market plays a decisive role in resource allocation, it is necessary to distinguish between the role of government and that of market. Based on this premise, the government and the market each have fully effective roles. It is unreasonable to place the role of government in opposition to that of the market. We must not think that a strong market must be part of a weak government, or vice versa. The key point is that they never work in the same field of resource allocation or at the same level: therefore, the government and the market will not clash and there will be contradictions between them. Of course, as the theory of the market determining resource allocation is confirmed, two things will happen. First, in order to put the market's decisive role into practice, the government should stop allocating resources as directly as possible through its own reforms, promoting the improvement of the market system and establishing regulations to ensure the efficiency of its resource allocation. Second, all these governmental roles should dovetail with the market mechanism which demands more attention.

Bibliography

Joseph E. Stiglitz, *The Price of Inequality: How Today's Divided Society Endangers Our Future*. New York: W. W. Norton & Company, 2012.

洪银兴:《市场秩序和规范》, 格致出版社、上海三联书店、上海人民出版社 2015 年版. Hong Yinxing. *Market Order and Norms*. Shanghai: Truth & Wisdom Press, Shanghai: SDX Joint Publishing Company, Shanghai: Shanghai People's Publishing House, 2015.

Chapter 16

Theoretical Analysis of the Participation of Production Factors in Income Distribution

The income distribution system is a basic institutional arrangement in economic and social development. Efficiency not only comes from resource allocation, but also from the incentive of income distribution. The successful development of China over the past 40 years has been achieved not only by market allocation of resources but also by breaking the egalitarian distribution system, and establishing a distribution system in which distribution according to labor is dominant and multiple forms of distribution exist side by side. These multiple forms of distribution mean non-labor factors participate in income distribution. In this regard, the Central Committee has been gradually clarifying its formulation. The 14th National Congress of the Communist Party of China (CPC), while confirming the new socialist market economy, proposed that production factors like individual capital should be allowed to participate in income distribution. At the 15th National Congress of the CPC, it was proposed to allow and encourage production factors, such as capital and technology, to help determine income distribution, introducing the technological factor. The 16th National Congress of the CPC put forward the principle that production factors including labor, capital, technology, and management should participate in distribution according to their contributions, introducing the management factor. The 17th and 18th National Congress of the CPC proposed to refine the system in which production factors like labor, capital, technology, and management participate in distribution according to their contributions, which highlighted the corresponding problems in the existing system's construction. Based on the above-mentioned principle whereby production factors participate in distribution according to their contributions, the Third Plenary Session of the 18th Central Committee of CPC resolved that the reward of the production factors should be determined by their respective markets.

Since non-labor factors of production belonging to individuals were proposed to participate in distribution, theoretical research and debate on that issue has never ceased. Some major questions are: Is the participation of production factors in income distribution contradictory to Marx's theory of labor value? Is the participation of private production factors in income distribution inconsistent with socialist distribution principles? How can one accurately measure the contribution of production factors? Is this system a reproduction of John Bates Clark's theory of marginal productivity?

Since the production factors' participation in distribution, the gap between the rich and the poor has increased. This raises new issues, such as: How can we effectively implement a policy in which supply and demand in various factor markets determine the rewards of those factors? How can we achieve fairness and justice in this distribution system? Particularly, how can we improve labor compensation? If these questions are not clear, it will be difficult for the reform of the distribution system to be further promoted, and for the objective drawbacks to be effectively overcome. All the research concerning distribution systems should to be based on Marx's distribution theory. Meanwhile, the reality of China at the present stage has to be considered to reflect the localization of Marx's distribution theory in China.

16.1 Theoretical and Institutional Compatibility of Production Factors' Participation in Distribution

The participation of production factors in income distribution first involves the question of how to understand enterprises. Eugene Fama, winner of the 2013 Nobel Prize in Economics, makes it clear: "Each factor in a firm is owned by somebody. The firm is just the set of contracts covering the way inputs are joined to create outputs and the way receipts from outputs are shared among inputs".[1] That is to say, the participation

[1]Eugene F. Fama. Agency problems and the theory of the firm. *The Journal of Political Economy* 88(2): 288–307, 1980, p. 290.

of production factors in income distribution is an objective existence. However, the implementation of this distribution system at the present stage of socialism involves three aspects of compatibility in theory and system: first, compatibility with the theory of labor value; second, compatibility with the socialist distribution system; and third, compatibility with the goal of fairness.

16.1.1. *The compatibility of production factors' participation in distribution with Marx's labor theory of value*

Some scholars, based on Marx's criticism of labor wage, capital interest, and land rent, think that production factors' participation in distribution violates the labor theory of value. We can evaluate this issue according to Marx's theory. The evaluation will take place on two levels.

First, distinguish between value distribution and value creation. The participation of factors other than labor in income distribution undoubtedly means they participate in the distribution of the newly created value. But they cannot be regarded as the source of value creation just because of their participation in value distribution. Some people believe that the recognition of production factors' participation in income distribution will then necessarily lead to the deduction that production factors can create value. This is what Marx criticizes. In the so-called trinity formula of capital interests, labor wages and land rents, "capital, land and labor appear respectively as sources of interests (instead of profits), rents and wages, the latter being the formers' yields or fruits".[2] Marx thinks that various forms of income distributed from distinctive factors in the social production process is still derived from the value created by labor.[3] Obviously, the confusion of the form of value distribution and the source of value creation violates the theory of labor value. Confirming production factors' participation in income distribution does not mean that non-labor factors of production are the source of value creation.

Second, distinguish between value creation and wealth creation. Labor is the only source of value creation, but it is not the only source of wealth creation. As Marx explains in his *Critique of Gotha Programme*, "labor is not the source of all wealth". Nature is just as much the source

---

[2]Karl Marx. *Capital: A Critique of Political Economy*. Vol. 3, p. 955.

[3]*Ibid.*

of use values (and it is surely of such that material wealth consists!) as labor, which itself is only a manifestation of a force of nature, human labor power.[4] The production process is a combination of various factors of production, and labor is only one of them. The creation of wealth requires the combination of labor and various factors of production, including capital, land, technology, management, and so on. Marx quotes a famous saying: Labor is the material wealth's father and land its mother. It means that the production of wealth requires production conditions, such as land. Although non-labor factors of production such as capital and land do not create value, they participate in the creation of social wealth and contribute to the increase of wealth. For example, capital is one of such factors. According to Marx's analysis, various factors of production, including labor and land, are merged into the production process by capital: "by incorporating with itself the two primary creators of wealth, labor power and land, capital acquires a power of expansion".[5] As for the technology factor, "the productivity of labor … does develop continually, owing to the uninterrupted advance of science and technology".[6] Marx also mentions the management element. All direct large-scale social work or joint work requires more or less some command to coordinate the activities of individuals and to carry out the gross product. Since various factors of production contribute to wealth creation, they are to participate in the distribution of wealth, thus forming the income of capitalists, landowners, and workers. Undoubtedly, in Marx's theory of distribution, the distribution of wealth creation among various factors is not the distribution of all wealth, but the distribution of newly created value. He attributes the income of the capitalists and that of the land users to the division of surplus value, and technology to labor reward as complex labor in many cases. In this way, the participation of production factors in wealth creation is consistent with their participation in value creation. This indicates that the participation of production factors in distribution is compatible with Marx's labor theory of value.

[4] Karl Marx and Frederick Engels. *Marx & Engels Collected Works*. Vol. 24, Trans. David Forgacs, Rodney and Krystyna Livingstone, Peter and Betty Ross, Barrie Selman, Joan and Trevor Walmsley (London: Lawrence & Wilshart, 2010), p. 81.

[5] Karl Marx, *Capital: A Critique of Political Economy*, Vol. 1, p. 752.

[6] *Ibid.*, p. 753.

16.1.2. *The compatibility of production factors' participation in distribution with the basic economic system at the primary stage of socialism*

Based on the institutional principle of distribution according to one's work, some scholars believe that the participation of non-labor factors in income distribution is incompatible with China's socialist system. An analysis of this viewpoint needs to start with the relationship between production and distribution in Marx's theory. Marx believes: "The structure of distribution is entirely determined by the structure of production. Distribution itself is a product of production, not only with regard to the object, [in the sense] that only the results of production can be distributed, but also with regard to the form, [in the sense] that the particular mode of participation in production determines the specific forms of distribution, the form in which one shares in distribution".[7] The core of production structure is ownership structure. At the primary stage of socialism, the basic economic system is clearly defined as that in which public ownership plays the dominant role and diverse forms of ownership exist side by side. The ownership structure is reflected in the co-existence of various modes in the distribution system. Distribution according to work as the main principle is the embodiment of public ownership as the main body in the distribution. The participation of capital, technology, management, and other factors in the distribution reflects the side-by-side development of diverse forms of ownership, and thus becomes an important part in the distribution system at the primary stage of socialism.

According to Marxist economics, the factor participation in distribution is actually the economic realization of factor ownership, i.e., the distribution of the newly created value among the owners of various factors. "One part of this value as belonging or accruing to the owner of labor power, one part to the owner of capital and a third part to the owner of landed property. These are thus relations or forms of distribution, for they express the relationships in which the total value newly produced is distributed among the owners of the various agents of production".[8] Obviously, wages, interests, and rents are each the economic realization of the ownership of labor, capital, and land, respectively.

[7]Karl Marx and Friedrich Engels. *Marx & Engels Collected Works*. Vol. 28, Trans. Ernst Wangermann (London: Lawrence & Wilshart, 2010), pp. 32–33.

[8]Karl Marx. *Capital: A Critique of Political Economy*. Vol. 3, p. 1017.

In Marx's vision, the means of production in an ideal future society would be publicly owned. The workers own their labor power, but all other factors such as capital, labor, technology, and enterprises are publicly owned. Accordingly, there is only distribution according to work. In such a society, with a single public ownership, it will obviously be incompatible for other factors of production to participate in income distribution.

At the primary stage of socialism in reality, labor power belongs to individuals, and capital, technology, management, and other factors belong to different owners (including individuals). Income distribution is the realization of this ownership of various factors. In order to encourage various factors to take part in the process of economic development and create wealth with vitality, the income distribution system must reward the owners of these factors. The income distribution system should not only promote work efficiency but also stimulate the factor owners to invest their capital, technology, management, and various other factors. The way to achieve this goal is to implement a reward according to the input and contribution of various factors in the production process, like capital, labor, resources, technology as well as entrepreneurs.

Some people believe that the participation of production factors in income distribution only stresses efficiency but not fairness, and therefore is contrary to the objective of socialist fairness. It is necessary to clear this issue according to Marx's analysis of the relationship between fairness and efficiency. Generally speaking, the improvement of efficiency depends on the principle of fairness in two aspects. One is that in the field of resource allocation, the market economy is inherently egalitarian; the other is the principle of equity in the field of income distribution. Distribution according to work and getting reward according to the contribution of factors are both principles of fairness in promoting efficiency. In this respect, equity and efficiency are consistent, which can be concluded from Marx's analysis of distribution according to work. The reason why distribution according to work can improve efficiency lies in its fairness. "The equality consists in the fact that measurement is made with an equal standard, labor".[9] More work more reward, less work less reward. "The same principle prevails as that which regulates the exchange of commodities, as far as this is exchange of equal values".[10] Similarly, for the

[9]Karl Marx and Frederick Engels. *Marx & Engels Collected Works*. Vol. 24, p. 86.
[10]*Ibid.*, p. 86.

contribution of factors, the scale of measurement is also fair: the more the factor contributes, the more it is rewarded, and vice versa. This is the equity of rights.

There is no doubt that fairness can only be relative, and equal rights imply inequalities. "This *equal* right is an unequal right for unequal labor".[11] The reason is that measuring different individuals with the same measurement will produce different results. Different laborers have their unique physical strength and ability, and they have different number of family members to support. "Thus, with an equal performance of labor, and hence an equal in the social consumption fund, one will in fact receive more than another, one will be richer than another, and so on".[12] Marx calls this kind of distribution according to work "bourgeois rights", which implies fairness in form but unfairness in fact. However, he still believes this form of distribution conforms to the principle of socialist fairness. Accordingly, there is a similar inequity in the present principle of distribution in which distribution according to contributions of various factors coexists with distribution according to work. Factor reward cannot be equally taken into consideration for different people with unique intelligence and opportunities. It is probable that multiple factor rewards are superimposed on the same person and the unfairness in income distribution will be more notable. "Right can never be higher than the economic structure of society and its cultural development conditioned thereby".[13] The goal of fairness in the socialist economic system is different from the principle of fairness at the primary stage of socialism. Although the fair right of factor reward is inferior to that of distribution according to work, it is still consistent with the economic structure and culture at the primary stage of socialism.

16.2 Institutional Arrangement for the Participation of Production Factors in Distribution

How can we realize the participation of various factors of production in income distribution? The 16th, 17th, and 18th National Congresses of the

[11] *Ibid.*

[12] *Ibid.*, p. 87.

[13] *Ibid.*

CPC respectively proposed the principle and system wherein production factors including labor, capital, technology, and management should participate in distribution according to their contributions. At the Third Plenary Session of the 18th Central Committee of the CPC, it was further proposed that the reward mechanism determined by the factor market, such as capital, knowledge, technology, and management, should be improved. The implementation of these distribution systems needs proper theoretical guidance.

16.2.1. *Incentive mechanisms for the input of production factors*

At the primary stage of socialism, the main constraining factor for the development of productive forces is the insufficient supply of capital, technology, and entrepreneurs. It is impossible to mobilize factors other than labor if there is only distribution according to work. Due to incomplete information and other reasons, there will probably appear problems such as opportunism, hitchhiking, and laziness. Therefore, it is necessary to establish effective incentive mechanisms to encourage the investment of non-labor production factors.

First, encourage capital investment. The development of economy needs sufficient capital input. The main sources of capital input stem not only from the state, but also from enterprises and individuals. Now, it is theoretically clear that whether one has personal property and how much one has cannot become the criteria of evaluation in political performance. In this way, private property is recognized, and it can be invested in two ways. One is that the individuals start enterprises and employ laborers and individual entrepreneurs receive capital income. The other is that residents can use surplus income to buy shares for dividends, bonds for interests, and they can acquire capital gains by holding equity in enterprises (including private enterprises). Recognizing all the different sources of capital ownership income and providing channels for private investment with varying degrees of risks and returns means providing sufficient incentives for private capital investment.

Second, encourage technology input. Technology input includes not only direct R&D (research and development) activities of the technicians, which can create value, but also intellectual property rights such as materialized or informationized patents and industrialized scientific and technological achievements. Therefore, encouraging technology investment involves two aspects: on one hand, direct R&D of technicians is complex labor, and these technicians should get more rewards than those whose labor is simple. On the other hand, the value of innovative achievements such as patents created by scientists and technicians should be scientifically evaluated. In reality, the value of scientific and technological achievements is often underestimated. According to Marx, "The product of mental labor — science — always stands far below its value, because the labor-time needed to reproduce it has no relation at all to the labor-time required for its original production. For example, a schoolboy can learn the binominal theorem in an hour".[14] The key to solving this problem is to establish a strict system for the protection of intellectual property to ensure the income of its owner. Thus, the ownership of technology investment is reflected in the distribution of factor rewards, and the cost of technology development is compensated and rewarded correspondingly.

Third, encourage managers to become entrepreneurs. Management is a kind of production factor, which generally reflects managers' quality and ability. Management investment includes the direct management labor, and more importantly, the managers' entrepreneurship and talent, which can be regarded as human capital. According to Joseph Schumpeter, entrepreneurs are related to innovation. Only those who can constantly innovate in product, technology, market, and organization systems can become entrepreneurs. In addition to full autonomy of management, the key for a manager to become an entrepreneur is to undertake the risks and benefits of innovation within the existing distribution mechanism, i.e., an independent management reward. For a long time, state-owned enterprises have been less innovative than those of private entrepreneurs. One of the important institutional reasons is that the state-owned managers do not have relatively independent economic interests. They cannot obtain the benefits of innovation success nor shoulder the risk of innovation failure. If managers are rewarded with stock rights in the distribution system, i.e., entrepreneurs can share profits through annual salary, stock shares, and other distribution forms to reflect their management talent and investment, then encouraging management innovation can help promote more managers to entrepreneurs.

---

[14]Karl Marx. *Theories of Surplus Value*. Part I (Moscow: Progress Publishers, 1969), p. 353.

16.2.2. *Getting rewarded according to contributions of production factors*

According to Marx's theory of distribution, the process of income distribution concerns two aspects: first, the distribution of newly created value ($v + m$) between laborers' income (v) and surplus value (m), and then the division of surplus value (m), meaning distribution of surplus value (m) among production factors other than labor. While analyzing the division of surplus value (m), Marx not only points out the profits and land rent result from participation of capital and landowners in distribution but also specifies the division of profits between the income of the entrepreneur and the interest. The income of enterprise owners, as they carry out the role of capital management, ends up being management income. Marx indicates these means for the factors like capital, land, and management other than labor participating in income distribution. Though Marx's methodology has provided us important guidance to study the rewards of production factors according to their contributions at present stage, we should notice the abstract method Marx uses here: assuming that laborers do nothing but work while asset owners do not work.

It is generally believed that the so-called participation of production factors in income distribution means that the laborers get rewards (v) and the owners of other factors share surplus value (m). The premise is that the laborers do not hold assets, and the owners of other factors are not laborers. This is not consistent with the reality of the primary stage of socialism. At the present stage, laborers may have assets, including capital and intellectual property rights, while asset owners may also participate in work by means of management. So, the participation of production factors in distribution means that they both participate in the distribution of all the newly created value ($v + m$).

The first part is that labor rewards (v) from distribution according to work. According to Marx's concept of the "collective laborer", labor input participating in distribution according to work includes not only the work of laborers in the direct production process, but also the work of technicians and managers who are not on the production site, as well as the work of enterprise managers. In this way, technology and management may participate in the distribution of income by way of labor rewards. In fact, technicians and managers may be better rewarded for their complex work.

The second part is the sharing of surplus value (m). In general, surplus value (m) is capital income, and the equity structure is the structure of capital invested in the enterprise. In reality, an enterprise is a combination of various factors. The increase of surplus value (m) not only comes from material capital, but also from technology and management. The effective incentive for technology and management input can be realized through their participation in distribution of surplus value (m). The specific path is that technology and management, combined with capital, can take hold of equity ownership. In this way, the ownership of the factors in equity structure is achieved, and sharing the surplus according to equity structure reflects the rewards of factor ownership in distribution. In the case that capital serves as the unit of equity structure, technology, and management are converted into capital shares according to their contributions, respectively. Therefore, besides material capital equity, technology equity, and entrepreneur equity are established in the equity structure of enterprises, and technicians and managers are allowed to purchase a certain proportion of equity. The corresponding rewards are capital income, technician income, and entrepreneur income. On this basis, it is necessary to further study the issue of laborers' participation in the distribution of surplus value (m). In addition to receiving corresponding rewards (v) through labor input, laborers can also participate in the distribution of surplus value (m) through shareholding, thus forming a real incentive for laborers to work for the interests of the owners of enterprises. If laborers have technology input, there will surely be additional dividends of technology shares.

16.2.3. *Markets determine factor rewards*

What proportion should knowledge, technology, and management account for in the allocation of v and m according to their contributions? The key is how to evaluate contributions. Under the condition of market allocation of resources, the market evaluation of factor contributions is the most feasible approach. The so-called market determining the allocation of resources means that the market not only determines where resources flow, but also the most effective combination of various elements (resources). What works here is the price determined by supply and demand in each factor market. In a general sense of price theory, people regard interest rates, wages, and land rent as the price of using capital, labor, land and other production factors, and factor price is factor reward. This is what the Third Plenary Session of the 18th Central Committee of the CPC has proposed to do: improve the reward mechanism determined by the market factors, such as capital, knowledge, technology, and management. The factor reward mechanism determined by market has the following functions.

First of all, factor prices are formed in their respective markets, which regulate the effective allocation and use of various factors of production. The prices of various factors in the market reflect the relationship between supply and demand of those factors. An accurate reflection of the scarcity of production factors is shown in the proportion of factor rewards. The enterprise compares the cost and the benefit of factor input according to the factor price determined by the market, and uses the production factor at the lowest cost. Meanwhile, the factor supplier adjusts its supply according to market price. The result is that the scarcest resources are used most economically and effectively, and the most plentiful resources are used most adequately.

Secondly, the market evaluation of various factors serves as the reference for factor rewards. What works here is the scarcity of certain factors and their high quality and high price. For instance, technology and management cannot only be rewarded as labor input, but also share the surplus. In reality, the values of technology and of management are not mean, and the needs of each enterprise for these factors are also different, so consequently there will be different rewards. Objective evaluation criteria can only be provided by competitive factor markets. As for technology, the most reliable evaluation of knowledge capital and intellectual property rights is performed by the technology market. And in terms of management, the most reliable evaluation is the stock of human capital owned by professional managers in the entrepreneur market. These evaluations will become the market criteria for enterprises to divide the surplus or provide labor rewards to technicians and managers.

The factor rewards determined by the market should be based not only on the relationship between the supply and demand of various factors, but also on the qualitative evaluation of the contributions of various factors, which involves the weights of various factors in economic growth and consequently affects the proportions of income distribution. In general, especially in the capital-driven growth stage, various factors are driven by capital and aggregated into the production process, and capital (material capital) plays a dominant role in economic growth. This tilts the distribution of capital toward the owners of said capital. However, in a more modern economy, knowledge capital and human capital play an increasingly important role, and the corresponding shares in income distribution will increase. In an innovation-driven economy, knowledge capital and human capital are more powerful than material capital. Capital proliferation results more from the function of knowledge capital and human capital than from the proliferation of capital. This conclusion will directly affect the manner of distribution, and income distribution will obviously be tilted toward knowledge and technology. This situation will be more obvious in technological innovation and the creation of businesses.

16.3 Implementation of the Socialist Distribution Principle under the Condition of Production Factors' Participation in Distribution

Marx clearly points out that in the future socialist system, "society's productive power will develop so rapidly that … real wealth is the developed productive power of all individuals".[15] This means that common prosperity is the essential requirement of socialism. In China, since the implementation of production factors' participation in income distribution, both efficiency and wealth have been increased significantly. The income of all social strata has been improved to varying degrees, but the income gap between different strata has been conspicuously expanded. The Gini coefficient, released by the National Bureau of Statistics, was 0.481 in 2010, 0.474 in 2012, and 0.473 in 2013. In China, a country that is pursuing common prosperity, the income gap is close to or even exceeds the level of developed capitalist countries. This problem must be paid attention to. Against this background, it is necessary to deeply study the implementation of the socialist distribution principle under the condition of production factors' participation in distribution.

According to the classical writers of Marxist economics, there are mainly two principles in socialist distribution. One is to promote social equity and justice, and the other is the principle of "from each according to his ability, to each according to his work".

[15] Karl Marx and Frederick Engels. *Marx & Engels Collected Works*. Vol. 29, Trans. by Ben Fowkes and Emile Burns (London: Lawrence & Wilshart, 2010), p. 94.

16.3.1. *The implementation of social equity and justice*

In recent years, Simon Smith Kuznets' inverted U-shaped curves have been used to illustrate the trend of income gap: income inequality peaks when per capita GDP reaches middle-income level; then Gini coefficient begins to decline and income inequality begins to rise. In *Capital in the Twenty-First Century*, Thomas Piketty, a French economist, revises Kuznets inverted U-shaped curve, extending the cut-off period of the curve (1949) to 2010. According to the data he collected, the average income level of the top 10% wealthy families, whether in the United States or Europe, has shown a clear upward trend, resulting in a marked increase in income inequality. According to Piketty, there are two main reasons why the income gap continues to widen. First, the rate of capital return is much higher than that of economic growth. Piketty writes, "it is almost inevitable that inherited wealth will dominate wealth amassed from a lifetime's labor by a wide margin, and the concentration of capital will attain extremely high levels".[16] Second, there is a surge in executive income in big companies. "One possible explanation of this is that the skills and productivity of these top managers rose suddenly in relation to those of other workers. Another explanation, […] is that these top managers by and large have the power to set their own remuneration […]".[17]

At the present stage in China, the per capita income in 2013 was close to $7,000, which was higher than the average level of middle-income countries, but there were no signs of decline in income inequality. This situation can be explained from the above analysis. The enlarged income gap in China has resulted from the substantial increase of urban and rural income. Distribution according to work itself can result in distribution inequality, but the principle of distribution according to work by itself will not produce such a large gap. Ignoring the possibilities of a monopoly in some industries, reward according to contribution is the main reason for the wide income gap. Different people possess different factors. Those who are more skillful or better at saving or managing are also more capable of creating wealth. In addition, the reform and opening up policy provided more opportunities for development. In *Capital: A Critique*, it says, "it lays open, in the form of speculation and the credit system, a

[16]Thomas Piketty. *Capital in the Twenty-First Century*. Trans. Arthur Goldhammer (Cambridge and London: The Belknap Press, 2014), p. 26.
[17]*Ibid.*, p. 24.

thousand sources of sudden enrichment".[18] Some people can seize the opportunities, and consequently the rich are getting richer.

If the issue of widening income gap in China is approached from the perspective of fairness and justice, there exists a limit for tolerance of income inequality. In order to seek development at the low-income stage, people may tolerate a widening income gap. Once economic development reaches the level of middle-income countries, the widening income gap not only occurs in different regions but also among different strata. There are also obvious discrepancies in sharing the fruits of the reforms. At the same time, the civil consciousness of rights protection has been significantly enhanced, and the demands for fair development are also more intense. People will not continue to tolerate the increasing income gap caused by unequal rights. Economic growth will be resisted by those relatively poor groups and strata. The subsequent social contradictions will damage efficiency, and hence the whole process of sustainable and healthy social and economic development is affected. If people cannot share the fruits of economic development in a fair and reasonable way, they will not continue to support reform and development. Therefore, the fair distribution proposed at the new stage of development refers to the fair and reasonable sharing of the fruits of economic development.

In view of the above reasons for the widening income gap and the socialist principles based on common prosperity, some people tend to ask for a decrease in or even the abandonment of the system for the participation of various non-labor factors in income distribution. Other people propose prioritizing fairness instead of the previous prioritization of efficiency with due consideration to fairness. We have to have a clear distinction between right and wrong about these viewpoints.

Egalitarianism is not socialism, and polarization of wealth is not either. This is what Deng Xiaoping clearly pointed out: "We permit some people and some regions to become prosperous first, for the purpose of achieving common prosperity faster. That is why our policy will not lead to polarization, to a situation where the rich get richer while the poor get poorer. To be frank, we shall not permit the emergence of a new bourgeoisie".[19]

---

[18] Karl Marx. *Capital: A Critique of Political Economy*. Vol. 1, p. 647.

[19] Deng Xiaoping. Replies to the American TV Correspondent Mike Wallace (Sept. 2, 1986). *Selected Works of Deng Xiaoping*. Vol. 3 (Beijing: Foreign Languages Press, 1994), p. 172.

Common prosperity does not mean equal wealth, and fairness does not mean equal income. "Making a big cake" is the basis of distribution. The purpose of production factors' participation in income distribution is to make the cake bigger. To narrow the income gap is not going back to the former indiscriminate egalitarianism, but to make the sharing of the cake more reasonable. Although the GDP of China is the second largest in the world, per capita GDP is still at the middle level. The contradiction between individuals' growing material and cultural needs and backward social production is still the main social contradiction. Social wealth has not yet begun to "flow like a spring". In order to encourage the vitality of labor, capital, technology, management, and other factors to create wealth, we must rely on the institutional arrangements of income distribution among various production factors.

In face of the widening income gap, people generally attach importance to the equality of results. The inequality of results in reality makes people question the necessity of factor rewards. On the surface, inequality in distribution is largely caused by the participation of factors in distribution. However, a deeper analysis shows that the fundamental reason for the income gap lies in the significant disparities among factors possessed by different individuals. Therefore, the key to addressing income inequality is to narrow the disparities in the factors participating in distribution. Consequently, we can not only make a bigger cake, but also promote equality of results. We can promote this in two ways: through fairness at the starting point, and fairness in process.

The first aspect to discuss is fairness at the starting point, the core of which is property equity. According to Marx's theory of capital accumulation, the widening of the income gap will not lead to polarization; rather, only in the context of private investment and accumulation there will be bipolar accumulation — the accumulation of wealth and the accumulation of poverty. According to this idea, the fundamental way to avoid polarization is to realize equality in property possession. Income from private property participating in income distribution can be categorized as property income. The participation of production factors other than labor in income distribution can contribute to equity in property possession. However, the disparity in property possession and the subsequent disparity in property income have become an important reason for the widening gap of income distribution. At the primary stage of socialism, we should not follow the old way of depriving private property. What is feasible is to provide the residents with the means of increasing their property, as well as their property income. This includes providing more opportunities and channels for private investment, encouraging individuals to start business, protecting intellectual property rights and their income, improving the ownership structure of enterprises, allowing employees to hold shares, and encouraging entrepreneurs to hold and buy technology shares. Farmers can also gain land income through the transfer of homestead and land contract rights. In addition to capital, factors including knowledge, technology, and management can also be regarded as properties. When knowledge and technology participate in income distribution and share a higher proportion in income distribution, it is necessary to provide residents with equal opportunities to accumulate knowledge capital and human capital. A basic approach is to promote education equity, especially the popularization of higher education, and to increase investment in human capital for low-income people. Education's significance lies in the overcoming of inequalities caused by unfair starting points. As *Capital in the Twenty-First Century* puts it, "Over a long period of time, the main force in favor of greater equality has been the diffusion of knowledge and skills".[20]

The second aspect to discuss is fairness in process, the core of which is equal opportunities. It mainly involves two aspects: one being the equality of development opportunities including investment and employment; the other being the equality of competition opportunities, which include fair competition environments, standardized market orders, and fair access to market resources and information. The reform of the market economy system that China is carrying out has made it clear that the market determines the allocation of resources, which means that all producers can obtain market resources equally. On this basis, there is a need for building and improving a unified, open, competitive, and orderly market system. In particular, any kind of monopoly, either in market or in administration, should be strictly opposed. If these reforms are fully executed, a fair market environment with equal opportunities shall appear.

The implementation of the aforementioned two aspects of fairness will definitely affect the results of distribution. The decreasing disparity in factors owned by each distribution subject as well as fairness in opportunities can narrow the Gini distribution results. On this premise, recognizing the inequality in distribution resulting from factor rewards. "This is consistent with the important role of income differences in providing

---

[20] Thomas Piketty. *Capital in the Twenty-First Century*, p. 22.

incentives to invest in education and physical capital, to work, and to take risks".[21]

16.3.2. *The implementation of the principle of "from each according to his ability, to each according to his work"*

In the situation that various production factors participate in income distribution, there still exists distribution according to work through the form of labor rewards, though the proportion of labor reward in income distribution has an obvious downward trend. According to *Blue Book of China's Society: Society of China Analysis and Forecast* (*2013*) by the Chinese Academy of Social Sciences, the proportion of wages in China's GDP is relatively low and tends to decline. The proportion of workers' rewards in GDP fell from 50.7% in 2004 to 44.9% in 2011. Corresponding to the downward trend of labor rewards is the increase in the rewards of other production factors. On the surface, the decrease of the proportion of labor rewards is related to the decline of labor's contribution to income growth. It is essential to implement socialist distribution principles with distribution according to work as the main body in the structure of income distribution in which various other factors participate.

First, it concerns the realization of distribution according to work. At the present stage of China's development, distribution according to work is inevitably imprinted with the characteristics of the primary stage of socialism. Distribution according to work cannot solve many problems. First, it cannot completely solve the problem of equal pay for equal work. In Marx's vision, in a future ideal society, the labor that everyone provides to society can be directly calculated. Under the conditions of a commodity economy, it is impossible to directly calculate the social labor provided by each person. Whether the labor provided by each person is social or not has to be tested in the process of social recognition through market exchange. Because of the law of value in the market, the labor provided by individuals is not necessarily accepted by the market or recognized by society, which results in a situation where equal labor provided by different industries and enterprises will not get equal rewards,

---

[21] *World Development Report 2006: Equity and Development* (Washington DC: The World Bank and Oxford University Press, 2005), p. 3.

or "unequal reward for equal work". Disorder in the real market may further increase this inequality. Second, distribution according to work also cannot completely solve the problem of work efficiency. The work defined in distribution according to work has multiple forms. Distribution according to the flowing form of labor (work time) cannot avoid some people loafing on the job instead of working. Distribution according to the solidifying form of labor (the fruits of labor) can make up for the above defects, but not all labor can be counted by pieces in actual socialized production. In distribution according to the potential form of labor (labor capacity), the value of complex labor can be properly evaluated, but, in reality, it is impossible to avoid the problem of incompatibility between the high-income of some individuals and their labor contribution. This indicates that it is not enough to measure work with a single labor standard. Third, it is impossible to implement the principle of "from each according to his ability" in collective work. Under the conditions of socialized production and collective work, it is difficult to accurately measure the labor contribution of each laborer, and it is also impossible to eliminate the case of laziness in collective work. If one person is lazy, and others follow, it leads to the inefficiency of collective work. The above defects of distribution according to work show that distribution according to work needs improvement and reform. For example, regarding the question of which "labor" should be regarded as the basis for distribution so as to achieve higher efficiency — the flowing form, the solidifying form, and the potential form — it may be feasible to combine them together as the basis for distribution. Concerning how to overcome laziness in collective work, we can implement an economic responsibility system in each production unit and distribute the fruits of collective work on the basis of the accurate evaluation of labor.

Secondly, it concerns the realization of "from each according to his ability". The premise of distribution according to work is that we should do our best. Nowadays, the rewards of labor generally refer to the rewards of workers in the forefront of production, or the rewards of simple workers. If this is the case, the decrease in the proportion of labor rewards is inevitable. According to Marx's definition of productive labor: "In order to work productively, it is no longer necessary for the individual himself to put his hand to the object; it is sufficient for him to be an organ of the collective laborer, and to perform any one of its subordinate functions".[22]

[22]Karl Marx. *Capital: A Critique of Political Economy*. Vol. 1, pp. 643–644.

According to this definition, the work of technicians and managers belongs to productive labor, and the income they earn are labor rewards. It is in this sense that Marx separated the manager's salary from profit as a reward for management and supervision.[23] Based on this analysis, in the structure wherein production factors participate in income distribution, the reward of technology and management can also be regarded as the reward for complex labor. If this part of the labor reward is recognized, the present conclusion that the proportion of labor reward declines is not entirely accurate. Consequently, we come to the question of how to understand the principle of "from each according to his ability". It is not only a matter of not being lazy in work, but also a matter of giving full play to one's talent and obtaining higher reward on the basis of improving one's ability. This situation will also affect workers' ability to do their best. Because of the different roles of technology and management, the improvement of productivity and the transformation of economic structures can be regarded as a great achievement of organization and technology in the work process, and ultimately to the improvement of work efficiency. Workers in the production line should also share the outcome of growth in a fair and reasonable way. It should be embodied in the increase of labor reward consistent with the improvement of work productivity. The confrontational distribution of capitalism, revealed by Marx, is characterized by reducing labor rewards to increase surplus value. Increased labor productivity, for instance, is included into the productivity of capital and thus should be possessed by capitalists. Socialist countries must safeguard the rights and interests of workers and protect their earnings, especially those gained in the process of improving efficiency.

Third, it concerns the realization of labor as a means of livelihood. Marx indicated that the premise of the principle of distribution according to work in socialist society is that labor is still a means of livelihood. As a means of livelihood, the growth of labor rewards is e not only related to labor contribution, but also to the requirements of livelihood. While comparing national wages, Marx points out that the determinants of wage levels include: "The price and the extent of the prime necessities of life in their natural and historical development, the cost of training the workers, the part played by the labor of women and children, the productivity of labor, and its extensive and intensive magnitude".[24] The requirement of

[23]Karl Marx. *Capital: A Critique of Political Economy*. Vol. 3, p. 567.

[24]*Ibid.*, p. 701.

labor reward should not be met only through redistribution by the government, but rather at the primary distribution stage.

For a long time, there has been a misunderstanding in the distribution theory that the realization of fairness is separated from the realization of efficiency. It is held that the primary distribution method stresses efficiency and the secondary method stresses fairness. The corresponding distribution mechanism is that the primary distribution relies on market regulation and the secondary one relies on government regulation. As a result, there is no fairness in the primary distribution. The 17th and 18th National Congress of the CPC pointed out "[a] proper balance should be struck between efficiency and fairness in both primary and secondary distribution, with particular emphasis on fairness in secondary distribution".[25] In primary distribution of national income, there are three forms of income: the income of laborers, the income of enterprises, and the tax revenue of the state. The participation of production factors in income distribution is basically carried out in primary distribution, thus the problem of low labor rewards cannot be solved until the redistribution stage. It is necessary to establish a mechanism to increase the proportion of labor rewards in primary distribution, especially since capital, management, and technology are involved in primary distribution, meaning owners of these factors have strong negotiation ability and play a leading role in distribution. In terms of income distribution in enterprises, laborers are always those to be arranged, and their labor rewards are often artificially depressed. Needless to say, the labor–capital gap in private enterprises is widening, and even the income gap between chief executives and workers in state-owned enterprises, especially central ones, is surprisingly huge. This means that the increase in the proportion of labor rewards in initial distribution can be realized not only through market regulation, but also through other institutional arrangements, such as legal norms for protecting labor rights and interests, collective negotiation mechanisms for wages within an enterprise, mechanisms for pay raises, a safeguard system for minimum wage and wage payment, and so on. In addition, restrictions on the income of senior executives are also necessary. An important reason for the decline in the proportion of labor reward is the

[25] Hu Jintao. Full text of Hu's Report at 18th Party Congress. *Chinadaily.com.cn.* Nov 18, 2012. https://www.chinadaily.com.cn/china/19thcpcnationalcongress/2012-11/18/content_29578562.htm.

overestimation of the contributions made by senior executives and the excessive growth of their income.

As for further fairness in the redistribution dominated by the state, it is less an issue of labor rewards in primary distribution, than an issue concerning the social problem of excessive income disparity. Apart from rationally adjusting high incomes through the progressive income tax system, it mainly aims to solve the problem of low incomes for those low-income workers in underdeveloped areas and rural areas, urban workers in difficult sectors and unemployed people. Further discussions about this problem need to be made in the future.

Bibliography

Joseph E. Stiglitz. *The Price of Inequality: How Today's Divided Society Endangers Our Future*. New York: W. W. Norton & Company, 2012.

逄锦聚:《论劳动价值论与生产要素按贡献参与分配》，载于《南开学报:哲学社会科学版》, 2004 年 第 5 期. Pang Jinju. On the labor theory of value and participation of productive factors in distribution according to their contributions. *Nankai Journal (Philosophy, Literature and Social Science Edition)* 5: 1–4, 2004.

卫兴华:《论社会主义共同富裕》，载于《经济纵横》2013 年第 1 期. Wei Xinghua. On common prosperity in socialist countries. *Economic Review Journal* 1: 1–7, 2013.

Chapter 17

New Political Economic Issues in the New Era

China's reform and development have been promoted on the basis of the major theoretical achievements of the socialist political economy with Chinese characteristics. The most prominent among these accomplishments include the following: the theory of the primary stage of socialism; the declarations that the essence of socialism is to develop social productivity and that poverty is not socialism; the basic economic system in which different types of ownerships coexist and develop with the public ownership serving as the main form; the socialist market economy and its corresponding orientation of reform; the idea that public ownership can be realized in diverse forms; the major principle of distribution according to one's work, supplemented by other distribution forms, and so on. These major theoretical breakthroughs have promoted the great cause of socialism with Chinese characteristics. These theoretical accomplishments have been confirmed by both theory and practice, although they could certainly still continue to develop. As they currently stand, they can become the basic theoretical prerequisite to study the socialist political economy with Chinese characteristics.

The cause of socialism with Chinese characteristics is still ongoing and the socialist political economy with Chinese characteristics remains under construction. Since the 18th National Congress of the Communist Party of China (CPC), deep-seated problems have continuously emerged with the deepening economic reform and development. Some of these problems need to be tackled according to new conditions and challenges.

Others require us to reread or find new understandings in familiar theories at the new development stage. According to epistemology, these problems are not isolated but are instead interconnected, meaning that the innovation and development of the socialist political economy with Chinese characteristics needs to address the following major economic relationships.

17.1 The Relationship Between the Dominant Public Ownership and Mixed-Ownership

The basic economic system at the primary stage of socialism is the development of public ownership as a dominant form with diverse forms of ownership alongside it. It should be noted that the dominance of public ownership does not refer to the dominance of public-owned enterprises within this framework. Instead, it means that public capital remains dominant in the total social capital and that state-owned enterprises (hereafter SOEs) maintain their control over the lifeline of the national economy. This major theoretical breakthrough of socialist public ownership plays an important role in the development of the non-public sector as well as in the strategic adjustment of SOEs for "development amid withdrawal".

The Third Plenary Session of the 18th Central Committee of the CPC has further identified that the final realization of the basic economic system should be a mixed-ownership economy that combines government capital, collective capital, and private capital. This assertion should be regarded as a new breakthrough of socialist political economy with Chinese characteristics. People used to define the basic economic system as the external coexistence of public enterprises and diverse, non-public enterprises. Today, it is thought of as the internal integration of public and non-public capital within the same enterprise. The reform within the framework of the basic economic system allows more SOEs and other forms of ownership to be combined as part of the mixed-ownership sector. State capital investment projects allow non-state capital to participate in equity and encourage development of mixed-ownership enterprises in which private capital can be the dominant stockholder. Accordingly, a new issue arises in the way in which public ownership plays a dominant role within the framework of the basic economic system. In the past, research has focused on the public sector's dominant position among the diverse forms of ownership that are simultaneously being developed, but at present it is necessary to study how the public sector embodies its principal status within the framework of the mixed-ownership economy.

Today, a majority of public capital is invested in mixed-ownership enterprises. It is necessary to analyze two aspects of the dominant status of public ownership within these mixed-ownership enterprises. Currently, SOEs can be divided into two categories: commercial SOEs and public welfare SOEs. These different categories have their own unique requirements.

Since commercial enterprises are mainly involved in competitive fields, their public capital aims to increase its values (just like any other kind of capital would). Capital flows wherever it has the potential to multiply. This means that public capital in mixed-ownership enterprises will pursue a capacity to multiply rather than a capacity to be dominant. Thus, public capital with its still larger overall quantity is distributed among enterprises with higher multiplication capacities. Even if public capital doesn't hold a majority of shares, it still plays a dominant role in general.

Public welfare SOEs ensure public interests and are generally managed by public enterprises. However, it is impossible for public capital to monopolize everything. In public welfare SOEs, there can also be a mixed-ownership system and non-state capital can be allowed to participate in equity and become a shareholder. Meanwhile, it is necessary for public welfare projects to attract private capital. The dominant role of public ownership is mainly reflected by the fact that they hold a status in mixed-ownership enterprises. Actually, as long as public capital sustains its controlling power over the mixed-ownership enterprises, it can dominate not only its own capital but also the non-state capital which participates in and shares equity. The control and dominance of public ownership is embodied not only in its holding status, but also in the attractive manner in which it equally treats other forms of ownership and shares interests with them. Hence, the dominant role of public ownership is apparent.

17.2 The Collaborative Relationship Between the Market and the Government

The key issue in economic structural reform is handling the relationship between the government and the market. The theory of neoliberalism sets the government and the market in opposition to each other, proposing that the government cannot play a role in engaging a market economy, and a government with a strong role will not have a sufficient market. The socialist political economy with Chinese characteristics instead theorizes that there should be a collaborative relationship between a powerful market and a powerful government.

The established theory of the socialist market economy has solved the problem of combining the socialist economic system and a market economy. The Third Plenary Session of the 18th Central Committee of the CPC has further confirmed that the market should have a decisive role in resource allocation and the government should play an enhanced role more generally. These are the major theoretical breakthroughs of a socialist market economy. The confirmation of the market's decisive role in resource allocation is actually a return to the original connotations of a market economy. When the market determines resource allocation, its own autonomy is highlighted. This autonomy is not only manifested in the market's decisive role in resource allocation, but also in the market adjustment signals. Namely, the market price is autonomously formed in the marketplace without any improper interventions on the part of the government.

The perspectives on what role the government should play in the market's allocation of resources vary from one economist to another. According to theories of neoclassical economics, the government needs to play a role when the market fails. These failures may include the polarization between the rich and the poor or external forces such as environmental pollution. From the perspective of institutional economics, the government (state) is the cornerstone of institutional change. Its essential function should be protecting the property-rights structure that is conducive for efficiency. Macroeconomics makes it quite clear that the market's determination of resource allocation mainly concerns microeconomic benefits. However, we are supposed to depend on the government's macro-adjustments to balance the overall amount of macroeconomy and to prevent macro failures such as high inflation and high unemployment.

Clarifying the decisive role of the market in resource allocation also clarifies the "strong" function of the market in this field. However, the developing socialist economy should not conform to theories of neoliberalism which propose that it is unnecessary for the government to play its role. Instead, the premise is that the role of the government should be enhanced, while there are still clear boundaries between the functions of the government and the market. Anything the market can do better than the government should be handed over to the market. In reality government agencies have decreased or canceled the need for administrative approvals, which has been proven extraordinarily effective in ensuring the autonomy of the market.

Identifying the strengths of the market does not necessarily mean defining the government's role as weak. Strong markets can be matched by strong governments. The so-called indispensable role of the government refers to the decisive role that the government should play in situations in which its role is critically needed. The first of those situations would be creating an environment for the efficient operation of the economy. It is not only necessary for the government to provide a rule of law-based business environment; it is also critical to exert powerful macro-control to enable the macroeconomy to be within a reasonable range. The second scenario concerns the allocation of public resources. The market determines the allocation of resources, excluding those that are public. The reason why the market cannot determine public resource allocation is that this process needs to meet public demands and follow the principles of equity, which can only be determined by the government. The third scenario concerns preventing market failures. The government should intervene in, and bring the full strength of its role to bear on, those projects that are involved with national security, ecological security, environmental protection, major national distribution of productive forces, exploitation of strategic resources, and significant public interest. The fourth scenario concerns promoting development. For a developing country like China that is still in the primary stage of socialism, development is still a primary concern. Therefore, promoting development should become one of the most important government functions. This task may involve promoting the integration of urban and rural development or urbanization, developing an economy driven by innovation, making adjustment to the economic structure, undertaking ecological or environmental construction projects, developing an open economy, and so on. The promotion and realization of all of the initiatives mentioned above depends on the allocation of public resources. The government mainly allocates public resources through policies such as promoting social equality and justice through the policy of income distribution, guiding the transformation and improvement of industrial structures through industrial policies and negative lists, and regulating the macroeconomy's operations through fiscal and monetary policies.

After identifying the decisive role of the market in the allocation of resources, there is an additional question: how does the government better play its role? The basic requirement for the government is to obey the market order. In order to better play its role, the government should basically coordinate its mechanisms with those of the market, integrating the allocation of public resources with the market's resource allocation. In this form of coordination, the strength of the government should not restrict the strength of the market.

17.3 The Relationship Between a Distribution According to Work and a Distribution According to Contributions and Supply and Demand

Distribution according to one's work is the principle of socialist distribution. After the establishment of the basic economic system at the primary stage of socialism, public ownership plays a dominant role and diverse forms of ownership develop side by side. In this system, it has also been confirmed that the main form of distribution that allocates income according to one's work coexists with other, multiple forms of distribution. The basic economic system and the basic distribution system are significant theoretical breakthroughs in socialist political economy with Chinese characteristics.

The participation of production factors in income distribution is based on the background of private (or different owners') ownership. This system was proposed to ensure that the vitality of labor, knowledge, technology, managerial expertise, and capital compete to fully engage all sources of social wealth. In terms of the multiple production factors that participate in distribution, reform is constantly deepening. The 14th and the 16th National Congress of the CPC established the principle that production factors such as labor, capital, technology, and management should participate in a form of distribution according to their own contributions. The 17th and 18th National Congress of the CPC proposed to refine this system. Based on that idea, the Third Plenary Session of the 18th Central Committee of the CPC proposed that the rewards of these production factors should be determined by their respective markets. Such statements indicate that income distribution depends not only on the input of each production factor but also on its contribution as well as the market's supply and demand. Thus, the dominant system in which income is distributed according to one's work has been a major research topic.

In terms of the impact, the supply and demand of factor markets have on distribution, each factor is divided according to its contribution. The remuneration of production factors such as capital, labor, technology, and management should be determined by their respective markets. The supply and demand of factor markets are objectively reflected in the proportion of factor prices. Consequently, the rarest factors can be used the most economically, contributing to an increase in the effective supply. Meanwhile, the most abundant factors can be used the most frequently. The positive role of this distribution system is quite noticeable in the effective allocation and use of production factors. Obviously, the participation of production factors in distribution is generally in accordance with the essential demands of socialism to develop social productivity. Multiple production factors are fully engaged to increase social wealth, significantly increasing the workers' absolute income, which accords with their interests.

Furthermore, when it comes to the contributions of various production factors, their involvement with income distribution varies significantly when they are possessed by different people. Allowing some people to get rich first implies that they have strong saving capabilities, a high standard of skills, and excellent operation abilities. With the superposition of these factors, the gap between labor compensation and the income of non-labor factors has significantly expanded. Therefore, the theoretical issue that is raised is the following: how one might reflect the dominant role of distribution according to one's work. First, it must be clarified that this situation is not like what some scholars have thought: namely that distribution according to one's work should be carried out in public enterprises, and distribution according to non-labor factors should be limited to non-public enterprises. It should instead be clarified that the so-called distribution according to work references the fact that labor remuneration is the dominant amount of disposable income, or it is the larger part of income in various distribution methods according to one's work. This situation exists in both public and non-public enterprises.

Socialist expectations for distributing income according to one's work are reflected in the elimination of the exploitation of workers. In clarifying the distribution structure according to the current stage of socialism, it is necessary to clarify that just as there might be mixed-ownership of production materials, there might also be mixed production factors.

That is to say, the types of labor input may include the labor of workers in the direct production process, the labor of technicians and managers who are absent from the production site but are still indispensable for production, and the business activities conducted by enterprise operators. When it comes to direct workers, they may also provide technical assistance besides their basic labor. Generally speaking, Marxist economics uses the phrase human capital to refer to this kind of complex labor. Based on such considerations, two principles should be upheld when it comes to the principle of distribution according to one's work. First, the higher rewards should be given to complex labor to reflect such contributions. Second, the rewards for labor should grow in step with the improvement of productivity. Therefore, it is possible to reflect the principle of distribution according to one's work as the main form in the total amount of distribution.

In reality, the principle of distribution according to one's work as the dominant form should not be confused with narrowing the income gap. In fact, the significant decline in the amount of front-line workers' reward in the distribution of national income has drawn public attention. Strictly speaking, this issue is not related to the principle of using a distribution according to one's work as a dominant form but is rather related to demands for social equality and justice as well as an interest in narrowing the income gap. The following three aspects should then be clarified further. First, in the primary stage of distribution, we need to handle the relationship between equity and efficiency according to the demands of socialism. The contributions workers performing less complex labor make in improving business efficiency should not be ignored. Second, according to the principles of Marxist economics, the reason why distribution according to one's work is carried out in a socialist society is that labor is still a means for a livelihood. For this reason, the growth of labor remuneration as a way of making a living should not be limited to the laborers' contributions but also should be coordinated with the requirement for earning a living. The scope of what that means to a livelihood is also that of the necessary labor, which has both historical and moral factors. As society progresses and the culture develops, the scope of necessary labor is continuously expanding and the corresponding remuneration for that work tends to increase. Third, in consideration of the equity of socialism, the gap in labor income is mainly caused by the differences in various factors one possesses, including things like technology. Therefore, one needs to take approaches to issues such as educational equality to bridge the gap among the qualities possessed by various owners in order to create equal opportunities and narrow the income gap.

17.4 The Relationship Between Demand Side and Supply Side Economics

Supply and demand are two inseparable aspects of economics. They are not just balancing issues. Since both the supply side and the demand side have their distinctive laws and mechanisms of operation, the political economy needs to study the two sides respectively.

In different stages of China's development, the focus of reform has changed. For more than 30 years, the reform of the market economy has shifted to the demand side including strengthening the mechanisms of market competition, highlighting the demand-oriented market, canceling the mandatory plan, and so on. Moreover, under the circumstances of the buyers' market, the growth of the macroeconomy has been promoted by the troika of investment, export, and consumption. Macro-control has been shifted towards the gross demand control of fiscal and monetary policies.

Practice has proven that in developing countries, relying on demand in isolation cannot effectively promote economic growth even if such nations adopt a market economy. On the basis of many years of demand side reforms as well as their significant results, we need to move from a development approach prioritizing scale and speed to one that emphasizes quality and efficiency. It is necessary to promote economic growth on the supply side, particularly in two respects. First, the supply side should improve the efficiency of the supply. A shortage in structural supplies is characteristic of developing countries. This might be reflected by issues in product quality, technical grade, efficiency, service, food hygiene, and product safety. At the same time there are ineffective and low-end supplies. Those supply side problems need to be solved by structural reforms, more specifically through cutting overcapacity and reducing excess inventory. Second, the supply side should provide an impetus for growth. We should not assume that the impetus for economic growth in the market economy will be transformed from a supply-driving force to a demand-driving force. Consequently, the driving force of the supply side is underestimated. Growth is not only driven by demand but also by supply. Supply factors may include technology, structure, efficiency, and system apart from the input of material factors. Once the supply drivers for material resources and low-cost labor dissipate, there still are other drivers on the supply side. Innovation, structural adjustment, and the promotion of efficiency can all become new driving forces for supply. Especially when the demand-driven development fails to have enough impetus to prevent economic downturns, it is essential for the supply side to provide the driving force for economic growth.

One of the crucial principles of both the socialist political economy with Chinese characteristics and supply side structural reforms is persisting in liberating and developing productive forces while keeping all participants motivated. In accordance with this requirement, the focus of supply side structural reform is economic development: enhancing the vitality of the supply side market. Because the objectives of the supply side reform are either to increase the efficiency of the supply system, to improve its quality and efficiency, to enhance the adaptability and flexibility of the supply structure in the face of changes to demand, or to improve the total factor productivity, it is necessary to mobilize the enthusiasm of the various parties on the supply side in order to reinforce their vitality. Therefore, the corresponding reforms include reducing various corporate tax burdens, reducing administrative intervention, cultivating entrepreneurs and artisans, and strengthening system construction in terms of refined management.

Emphasizing structural reforms on the supply side does not deny the function of the demand side; instead, both sides need to work together. In face of inefficient and low-end supply, cutting overcapacity, reducing excess inventory, deleveraging, and lowering costs, the demand side depends on the competitive market system, while the supply side adopts the method of resolving and optimizing reorganization. For another example, when confronted with the pressures of an economic slowdown, the demand side can adopt an expansionary monetary policy, while the supply side cuts taxes and burdens to mobilize enthusiasm for economic enterprises. If there is no demand in the market, even a strength in the supply side will not help.

In this way, when it comes to the study of the supply and demand of the socialist political economy with Chinese characteristics, the former highlights the development of dynamic research while the latter emphasizes the pressures of development; the former underlines the study of incentive mechanisms while the latter stresses the study of selective mechanism.

Based on the above analysis of the significant progress achieved by the socialist political economy with Chinese characteristics, we can find that the cause of socialism with Chinese characteristics is well underway and its theories have also been developing. New practices generate new theories and new theories illustrate new practices. Therefore, these theoretical achievements adapt to the conditions of contemporary China and the characteristics of the times. They not only provide guidance for the practices of China's economic development but also open up new horizons for Marxist political economics.

Chapter 18

The Major Innovations of Chinese Economic Development Theories in the New Era

Economic development is indispensable for building up socialist political economy with Chinese characteristics. Political economy mainly focused on relations of production in the past years, through connecting the research with productive forces. Therefore, it was generally believed that development was an issue of development economics, not of political economy, which is a misunderstanding of the latter. China's economic development should be guided by no other theories of economics than socialist political economy with Chinese characteristics. Its necessity lies in two aspects. First, China has its unique development conditions. Any development theory from abroad will find it difficult to correctly guide and clarify development problems in a socialist country, such as the huge population and the extreme imbalance between the urban and the rural and among regional developments. Second, the problems of China's economic development cannot be solved without the analysis of the relations of production. Only political economy studies both the relations of production and the productive forces, and only a theory combining both can correctly guide China's economic development, which especially needs to be promoted by taking advantage of the socialist economic system. Therefore, the first and foremost principle for socialist political economy with Chinese characteristics is to insist on liberating and developing productive forces.

Since the reform and opening up, the major theoretical contributions to economic development from socialist political economy with Chinese characteristics can be summarized from the following aspects. First, the theory of socialist modernization with Chinese characteristics, the theory of an all-round construction of a moderately prosperous society, and the theory of integrating the development of new industrialization, IT application, urbanization and agricultural modernization; second, the theory of economic development mode and its transformation; third, the theory of science and technology as the first productive force; fourth, the theories about the scientific outlook on development, new industrialization, urbanization, and so on. These are the theoretical contributions of the socialist political economy with Chinese characteristics promoted by the practices of the reform and opening up. Since the 18th National Congress of the Communist Party of China (CPC), a series of major contributions have been further made by development theories, including: (i) the economic "new normal" phase theory; (ii) the innovation-driven economic development theory; (iii) five new visions for development; (iv) the theory that lucid waters and lush mountains are invaluable assets and the ecological civilization theory; and (v) the theory of supply side structural reform.

At present, China's economy has entered the "new normal" phase with the transformation of development stage from low-income to middle-income. Accordingly, there appear a series of innovations in development theories. Innovations involve creative destructions. Therefore, innovative development theories at the present stage either deny the prevailing principles of development economics, or deny the theories that once effectively guided development at the low-income stage, or even sublate some of the development polices that were propelled and proved effective at the beginning of the reform and opening up. The fundamental reason is that, as the development stages evolve, there occur new development tasks, new periodical characteristics, and new laws of development.

18.1 The Change of Disciplinary Tasks from Guiding Economic Take-off to Guiding Modernization

Development economics, which originated in the 1940s, takes former colonial and semi-colonial countries as its research targets. These newly independent countries were faced with the tasks of eliminating poverty, promoting development, establishing an autonomous industry system, and realizing economic take-off. So the then development economics was aimed at getting rid of poverty and pushing economic development and take-off. Objectively speaking, this type of development economics did once have positive guiding effects on China's economic development, including establishing catching-up and overpassing strategies for boosting GDP, supporting economic growth at high accumulation and high investment rates, transferring surplus agricultural labor force, realizing urbanization, and industrialization, following developed countries to make innovations in science, technology, and industry, relying on the radiations of the core in the core–periphery circle, participating in international division of labor based on comparative advantage and implementing export-oriented foreign policies, and so on. These mentioned theories have once guided economic development policies in developing countries, including China, for a rather long time. Meanwhile, these theories have also worked as theoretic bases for traditional economic development mode, giving a positive guidance for China's transformation from a low-income country to a middle-income one.

Since 2010, China has ranked second in the world in terms of GDP and has become the world's largest exporter of goods, the largest foreign exchange reserve country and the world's second largest manufacturing country. This indicates that China has made major progress in its status in the world economy, and more importantly, the construction of China's modernization has entered a new historic starting point. First of all, with the apparent improvement in people's living conditions, the poverty-stricken population has conspicuously declined. Second, the proportion of agriculture has descended to 10.1% while that of industry has risen to 46.8%; besides, the rate of urbanization has reached beyond 50%. This means that China has transformed itself from an agricultural country to an industrial one. The all-round construction of a moderately prosperous society to be accomplished soon has marked the take-off of China's economy and the beginning of China's modernization. At this new historic starting point, economic development theories need to innovate themselves to guide economy. Namely, the development economics needs to shift its focus from eliminating poverty to bringing affluence to people, and from guiding economic take-off to guiding modernization.

As China's total amount of GDP ranked second in the world, its GDP per capita reached $5,414 in 2011. This marks China becoming one of the middle-income countries, which requires its economic development theories to account for the process and law of a country's development from a middle-income stage to a high-income one. A middle-income country is confronted with the biggest risk of the "middle-income trap". This trap mainly indicates: first, as a country develops from a low-income stage to a middle-income one, it has no competitive advantages either over the low-income country in terms of salary or over the wealthy country in terms of sophisticated technology research and development; second, in the process of reaching high-income level, it is difficult to get rid of the original low-income development pattern; third, the contradictions accumulated at the low-income stage due to the rapid economic development promoted by the original growth mechanism and development pattern will experience concentrated outbreak at the middle-income stage. The poignant social contradictions arising therefrom may seriously hinder economy from sustainable development, and the economy may easily slip into drastic fluctuation or stagnation and be long stuck at the middle-income stage.

It is crucial to provide theoretical guidance for jumping over the "middle-income trap" at the new starting point of the middle-income stage. It mainly involves three aspects. First, the economic development modes need transformation. The development mode originally used in the transforming process from the low-income stage to the middle-income stage should no longer be adopted at the middle-income stage. The goal should be to compete with the wealthy countries in terms of sophisticated technology research and development. The second is to make people affluent. Enriching people at the middle-income stage not only means increasing people's incomes, but also involves the following two aspects. On one hand, inhabitants' family properties should witness apparent increases and their incomes increase correspondingly; on the other hand, inhabitants should share more public wealth, especially the enlarged cover of social welfare and the equal access to the basic public services both in the urban and rural areas. Third, efficient growth should shift to equitable growth, overcoming social contradictions based on the principles of equity and justice and gradually realizing the goal of common prosperity. The abovementioned have become the innovative contents of the economic development theories at the middle-income stage.

18.2 Shift of Development Engine from Overseas Demand to Domestic Demand

In the existing development economics textbooks and development theories, it is generally believed that foreign trade and foreign investment are the major economic development engines for developing countries. Compared to the past closed economy model, the open economy model, export orientation, and a heavy introduction of foreign capital have been working as engines to motivate China's economic development. At present, China's development engine needs to shift from the outward to the inward due to the following two major reasons. First, a change has occurred in terms of international market circumstances. Export-orientated development strategy constructs the industrial and trade structure and makes the international competition strategies according to the demands of exports, which are dependent upon the international market. The 2008 world financial crisis hit the open economy directly and till now the world economy is still in recession, making a great increase in the demands of exports impossible. From 2013 to 2017, the annual average contribution rate of the final consumption expenditure was 56.2%, and that of gross capital formation was 43.8% while that of the net exports of goods and services was nearly zero. This, of course, is merely on the surface and could have only a temporary impact. More importantly, the open economy based on the existing opening up strategy is weakening its impetus for economic growth, which might have a long-term impact. Its main indicators are as follows. The international production overcapacity of many of China's exports (especially those labor-intensive products) has become increasingly serious; due to the increase in land and labor cost, both the competitiveness of the exports and the appeal of foreign investments in manufacturing are in decline; due to protectionism and deglobalization trends prevailing in some developed countries represented by the United States, international trade frictions become increasingly frequent. All of these indicate that the export-oriented development strategy is hard to sustain.

Second, the status of Chinese market has risen. The globalized economy is structured with the center and the periphery, so the developed countries such as the United States, Germany, and Japan have been the center of the world economy for a long term. China as a developing country stood in the periphery all along, but since it rose to the world's second largest economy, China has been moving from the periphery to the center. The so-called center here refers to the economic growth center within a certain area of the world on one hand, and on the other hand to the facts that Chinese market has leaped into the front rank of the world market in terms of its total scale and that it will become an innovation center of the market. The increasing international impact of the Chinese market implies that it has become and is becoming an important world market, which indicates that entering Chinese market means as well entering the world market. The economy based on domestic demand has lower transaction costs due to the shorter market distances and the more convenient channels for information acquisition and so on.

Third, the demands made by imbalances among regional developments need coordination. For a rather long time, China's export-oriented economy has merely been promoted along the coastal areas. The economy driven by overseas market demand has only pulled development in these coastal areas while the large central and western areas at the margin of the export-oriented economy can gain impetus neither from overseas demand, nor from the eastern areas due to their overseas targets. Therefore, there has been a further increase in the regional gap. At the present middle-income stage, not only have the eastern coastal areas already integrated into globalization obtained powerful development capacities, the central and western areas will also surely provide tremendous domestic demand and development opportunities due to their own intense demand for development and the coordinated efforts made to balance the eastern and western areas.

As the export-oriented economy can no longer serve as the engine for China's development at the present stage, domestic demand for economic development is becoming a new engine. Joseph E. Stiglitz points out in the 1990s that "as its economy grows and as the global economic environment changes, China will no longer be able to rely as fully on the export- and Foreign Direct Investment (FDI) oriented model that has so far driven its reform-era growth. At the same time, China faces the challenge of continuing to improve resource allocation and productivity". To cope with the challenges, China has to "make the domestic economy the engine of growth and equity".[1]

The strategy that domestic economy works as the engine of growth is based on the expansion of domestic demand as the strategic focus of economic development. The expansion of domestic demand refers to the investment demand and consumer demand fueled by domestic economic development. The commitments to construct an all-round moderately prosperous society and to realize modernization will yield tremendous

---

[1]Joseph E. Stiglitz. *China: Forging a Third Generation of Reforms* (Lecture at Peking University, July 23, 1999).

demands, mainly involving the following four aspects. First, with the widespread rapid increase in the people's incomes, consumer demand will become a strategic focus to expand domestic demand; second, with the process of urbanization and the integration of urban and rural areas, both investment demand and consumer demand will constitute a large-scale domestic demand; third, with the transformation and upgrading of domestic industrial structure, striving in particular to develop the emerging industries on the same start line of innovation with developed countries will not only enhance supply capacity, but also serve as an important aspect of expanding domestic demand; fourth, solving the problem of regional imbalances will produce multilayered domestic demand. All the expanded domestic demand will directly promote the overall scale of the Chinese market to join the front rank of the world market. The domestically driven economy as an engine provides an impetus for development no less powerful than the export-oriented economy. The engine of growth shifting from outward to inward by no means implies returning to the closed economy, but turning to the open economy at a higher level with higher efficiency.

18.3 The Adjustment of Pulling Forces from Investment Demand to Consumer Demand

The domestic demand to pull economic growth includes investment demand and consumer demand. For a long time, the existing growth pattern in developing countries, including China, has been greatly influenced by the Harrod–Domar Model, which aims at increasing GDP and driving economic growth through investment. The long existing rapid economic growth in China has been based fundamentally on heavy investments. Therefore, Chinese national income distribution has long been showing a pattern of high accumulation with low consumption. At the current stage of economic development, the mode of heavy deposits supporting heavy investments should not continue. Besides, the production overcapacity yielded by investment-driven production has led to an apparent decline in growth efficiency, and the drive of investment has even grown to be mainly responsible for the big economic fluctuations, which means the investment-driven economy in China has come to its end, unable to realize the goal of sustainable economic growth.

As China steps into the middle-income stage, an important aspect of transforming economic development modes is to shift its major driving forces from investment and export mainly adopted at the low-income stage to the coordinated efforts of consumption, investment, and export with a special focus on consumption. The significance of making this shift lies in increasing the contribution rate of consumption to economic growth, thus promoting the latter's efficiency and quality.

The economic growth driven by the expansion of consumer demand is essentially oriented toward increasing people's incomes and their consumption levels, which embodies the adjustment of the target of economic development from simply pursuing an increase in GDP to pursuing people's affluence and well-being. The purpose of socialist production to meet people's ever-increasing material and cultural needs to its maximum, which is always highlighted by the political economy theory, will be fully achieved in this consumption-driven economic growth.

Compared to investment demand, consumer demand in China at the present stage has more potential for increases. In terms of the scale of consumer demand, the population of more than 1.3 billion undoubtedly constitutes a tremendous potential, but there exists an even bigger potential in terms of the structure of consumer demand. First, with respect to the age structure, the aging society and the great proportion of children would both decrease deposits but might increase consumption. Second, with respect to the income structure, there will be a growing proportion of middle-income population with vigorous demands, especially for products and services provided by upgraded industries. Third, compared to the markets in developed countries, the consumer demand in the emerging markets would be stronger. For instance, in China, the demand for cars, housing, and information services has grown from scratch explosively.

The precondition of consumption-driven economic growth is to drive consumption and the primary task is fostering consumption capacity. The factors affecting consumption capacity are income, employment, and social security system. For the purpose of socialist production, the fundamental ways to raise people's consumption capacity are as follows: increasing the residents' income; maintaining high employment rate; full coverage of social security; increasing the consumption ratio in macro-distribution of national revenue and changing the condition of high accumulation with low consumption; enlarging and expanding to the majority the proportion of middle-income population. Consequently, economic growth will be fueled by the increase of residents' consumption level.

At the present stage, innovation in consumption formats has made a remarkable effect on stimulating consumption and consumption growth. Especially when China steps into the middle-income stage and its middle-income population has reached 0.3 billion, the mid- and high-level consumption arising from that will become a new driver for development. For instance, such new consumption formats as information consumption, green consumption, housing, tourism and leisure, education, cultural activities and sports, elderly care, healthcare, and household services grow obviously faster than the traditional ones. Especially with the aid of the internet-plus platform, the internet consumption and the sharing economy are expanding consumption fields both in width and depth. Consuming is becoming smarter, greener, healthier, and safer, which embodies the optimization of consumption mode and meanwhile motivates the optimization of production mode.

The development in service industry is pushing for an increase in consumer demand. Service and consumption are mutually dependent. The expansion of service consumption can help upgrade the consumption structure. IT application, standardization, and intensification in service industry can not only expand consumer demand, but also promote consumption level.

Of course, the shift from investment-driven to consumption-driven growth by no means substitutes consumption for investment. Turning to consumption is a goal, but it needs time because the investment-driven economy still has sustaining power. Especially when the macroeconomy is going downhill, the economy still needs investments as a driving force to rebound in the short term.

18.4 Shift of Reform Focus from the Demand Side to the Supply Side

China's economic development requires the coordinated contributions of the demand side and the supply side. The degree of their contributions is related to their systems, and reform provides impetus for them to realize their potential. The market-oriented reform in China since 1978 has in effect been a demand side reform, involving the elimination of the mandatory plan and the shift to the market economy. The stimulated demand side impetuses thus stimulated include micro and macro ones. The micro impetus mainly refers to the pressures from market selection, including market demand and market competition. The macro impetus refers to the economic growth driven by consumption, investment, and export in coordination and the fiscal and monetary policy adopted by the state in macroeconomic control, be it tight, expansionary, or neutral, which would influence the total amount of demands. After 40 years of reform, the demand side needs to perfect the management of demand. Based on this, China's economic reform should shift its focus from the demand side to the supply side.

The problems of the supply side are usually problems with the structure, which is a common weakness in developing countries. Problems of the supply side that involve structure, technology, and efficiency have long existed in developing countries and can be solved neither by turning to the market economy automatically, nor by adjusting the demand side. The structural problems of the supple side in China are symptomized by the coexistence of the insufficiency of effective supply and the excess of ineffective capacity. This structural contradiction of supply side is the feature of a particular stage of economic development: supply cannot adjust itself to the updated consumer demand at the new middle-income stage. At this new stage, on the one hand, the residents' basic living needs are satisfied and the consumer demands are transformed and upgraded to healthier, safer, cleaner, and higher level; on the other hand, the supply of products and services still remain at the low-income stage, characterized by the pursuit of quantities at the expense of qualities and the production for its own sake. The above-mentioned structural problems need to be solved through reforming the supply side.

The supply side structural reform involves cutting overcapacity, reducing excess inventory, deleveraging, lowering costs, and strengthening areas of weakness. The reform is aimed at increasing the efforts of structural reform, modifying factor allocation, expanding effective supply, strengthening the adaptability and flexibility of supply structure, and increasing total factor productivity. Specifically speaking, there are three reform targets.

First, seek the driving force of economic growth on the supply side. The supply factors influencing the potential economic growth rate include investment, technology, structure, efficiency, and so on. The present-stage recession of the supply side drivers only refers to the recession of supply capacity on the part of material resources and low-cost labor, while there are other potential supply side drivers, such as innovation, structural adjustment, and efficiency promotion, all being driving forces of economic growth. There is enormous room for increasing total factor productivity in particular.

Second, establish a long-term mechanism for effective supply. The insufficiency of effective supply is actually a structural shortage, as the present supply structure involving both product structure and supply quality cannot adapt to demand. Meanwhile, low-level and ineffective capacity takes up resources and results in inventory and overstock. Establishing a long-term mechanism for effective supply involves cultivating entrepreneurship to promote industrial optimization and upgrade, raising the technological level of products through scientific innovation, fostering craftsmanship, establishing refined governance system and culture, strengthening quality control and remodeling delicacy culture, keeping order in the market, strengthening and improving the market regulatory system, adopting severe penalties for serious violations, strengthening the construction of credit system, and creating trustworthy brands.

Third, liberate enterprise vitality. One crucial principle of socialist political economy with Chinese characteristics is to keep all participants motivated, which should also be a major principle for supply side structural reform. At present, enterprises in the real economy are shouldered with "three mountains": high taxes and fees, high interests, and heavy burdens. The enterprises have capacities but no benefits, and so many of them become "zombie enterprises". Reform is actually to handle in the process of national income allocation the interests among the state, enterprises, and workers with a focus on the interests of enterprises for they are the primary economic cells. On one hand, workers should share both the benefits of enterprise development and the risks of business. If an enterprise closes or cuts down employment due to the employment burdens beyond its affordability, it is still the workers who pay the price in the end. On the other hand, government should share part of its national profits with enterprises for one must first give in order to take. If the burden on the enterprises is eased, then the economic cells will be activated and the national income increased. Therefore, while in previous times, the governmental reform focuses on eliminating authority approval, at present it should focus on eliminating and reducing various taxes and fees imposed on enterprises.

After more than two years of supply side reform that focus mainly on cutting overcapacity and reducing excess inventory, China should deepen the supply side structural reform by giving priority to improving the quality of supply system and fostering new driving forces of growth, i.e., fostering new growth points and growth drivers in the areas of medium-high end consumption, innovation, green and low-carbon economy, sharing economy, modern supply chains, and human capital services.

18.5 Change of Principles for Growth from Efficient Growth to Inclusive Growth

In development theories, growth principles involve pursuit of equity and efficiency, embodied in distribution of growth achievements since the two aspects can only be balanced but not simultaneously achieved. There thus comes the issue of priority. At the low-income stage, China released a major policy to give priority to efficiency for economic growth, proposing to permit a part of people to get rich first and emphasizing distribution according to the contributions of production factors. This efficiency growth mode, consistent with investment-driven economic growth mode at the period, made a positive and apparent effect on increasing efficiency and motivating development factors, but meanwhile had another increasingly distinct effect, i.e., inevitable inequity in distribution based on efficiency principle.

After China stepped into middle-income stage, efficiency growth and its according major policies should not continue for the following reasons. First, the expansion of income gap resulting from more than 30 years of efficiency growth has reached the summit of Kuznets inverse U-shaped curve. Second, income gap can promote efficiency, but once the gap expands to a certain extent, it may damage efficiency. Economic growth is likely to encounter resistance from a large low-income community. Third, if stuck in "middle-income trap", China will most probably be faced with social contradictions resulting from increasingly expanding income gap. Under such circumstances, efficiency growth can no longer support the further increase of efficiency while inclusive growth might make it.

General Secretary Xi Jinping proposed the vision of inclusive growth in globalization at the G20 Hangzhou Summit with an intention to establish the awareness of building a community for all humankind with shared future, to reduce inequality and imbalance in global development, and to make people in all countries equally share the benefits of the world economic growth. It is evident that inclusive growth has extensive connotations, including sustainable development and collective development.

Its essential connotation is to share economic growth equally and reasonably and to narrow income distribution gap. In China, a socialist country, inclusive growth has to meet the requirement of promoting social equity and justice. After implementing more than 30 years the major policies to permit a part of people to get rich first, China needs to make the majority wealthy through the rich helping the poor so that people can equally and reasonably share the benefits of growth and thereby new driving forces of economic growth can be created.

The shift of focus from giving priority to efficiency with due consideration to equity to promoting social equity and justice is not intended to even income, but to keep fair in aspects of opportunities, rights, and rules in the growth process. It is especially important to address the problem of unfair distribution caused by unequal rights, which involves three aspects. First, handle the issue of abusing power for personal gains through adopting strict anti-corruption measures; second, handle the issue of seeking high income through monopoly positions; third, handle the issue of bigger income gap due to unfair distribution of assets.

Inclusive growth needs to target the issue of low-income particularly. At present, the number of low-income people is not small. Most of them have become middle-income and their consumer demand produces an enormous driving force for economic growth. The solution is to reform and improve the national income distribution system including the following aspects.

First, raise the proportion of labor pay in primary distribution. Since the reform, the first rich have generally been capital owners and enterprise operators depending on assets income and business income. Thereby, the gap between labor income and non-labor income has been distinctly growing. Given the increasingly growing income gap, primary distribution should not only highlight efficiency, but balance equity and efficiency as well. The proposal of raising the proportion of labor pay in primary distribution is made on the ground that labor-based earnings should be raised in step with increases in labor productivity.

Second, give more attention to equity in redistribution. The government takes inescapable responsibilities for fair distribution. The government can raise the proportion of residents' income in national income distribution through sharing part of its national benefits with the residents. Besides, it can promote equity and justice by improving the public fiscal system in the following two aspects. For one thing, government should ensure the equitable access to basic public services and bridge the huge gap between different regional areas and between the urban and the rural areas in terms of the basic public services such as basic medical care, primary education, public transportation, and public health with an emphasis on ensuring rural residents in underdeveloped areas the same access to the basic public services with urban residents in developed areas. For another, the government should refine the social security system covering both urban and rural residents. At present, there exists a big gap between urban and rural residents in terms of social security like medical care and elderly care. Farmers have no access to the social security enjoyed by urban residents. Especially when farmers lose their land for various reasons and consequently lose their land security, they will have more intense demand for social security. Building the social security system covering both urban and rural residents should give priority to finance.

At present, the major cause of growing income gap does not lie in labor income gap, but in property (non-labor production factor) gap resulting from all kinds of production factors participating in income distribution. The polarization of property distribution should be prevented in a socialist environment. It is impossible for inclusive growth to discourage production factors from participating in distribution in order to prevent property gap. Inclusive growth involves reforming the system of private property formation and handling the issue of unfair property distribution, including the following three aspects. First, construct an equity system of private property formation in aspects like opportunities, rights and rules; second, create conditions for residents to earn more property income from real estate (i.e., housing) and personal properties (i.e., stock shares), and create more opportunities for residents to earn properties through their own efforts fairly, such as making innovations and starting businesses; third, residents' properties and incomes should be protected by the law.

Obviously, the turn to inclusive growth embodies the promotion of China's economic development capacity and finding new driving forces for China's economic development at a new level. People support development on the condition of sharing its fruits, and social harmony, based on equity, can reduce social friction in the process of development.

18.6 Change of Growth Path from Depending on the Investments of Material Resources to Being Driven by Innovation

China's economic development has long remained at the factor-driven and investment-driven stage, characterized by mainly depending on the investments of material resources to drive economic growth, the same with the economic growth model in development economics. In this model, economic growth is the function of investment factors like capital, labor, and land. Though technology is included later on, it only functions as an exogenous variable and residual value. Only when a new economy and its corresponding growth theory occurred in the United States in the 1980s did there appear a theory of endogenous growth dependent on knowledge capital and human capital.

China has long relied on investments of material resources to drive economic growth, but once it enters the middle-income stage, the contradictions will soon become prominent in the following two aspects. First, in terms of factors as driving forces, the under-investment of material resources has been approaching its ceiling, and the supply of cheap labor force coming from agricultural surplus labor has evidently decreased. Second, in terms of investments as driving forces, it is based on high accumulation and low consumption. Entering the middle-income stage, Chinese people are not likely to bear low incomes in the long-term. The fundamental solution to this contradiction is to turn to an innovation-driven stage.

The concept of innovation is rarely used in existing development economics, but in modern times, without adopting the concept and theory of scientific and technological innovation, it is difficult to summarize the characteristics of modern economic growth, especially the characteristics of scientific and technological innovation reflected by the combination of knowledge innovation and technological innovation. The original technological progress took enterprise innovation as its primary source for technological innovation. Basically, enterprises proposed innovation needs and programs according to market orientation, so technological innovation was led by enterprises. The new scientific and technological revolution starting from the end of the 20th century and the new economy and knowledge economy resulting from it are characterized by the speed-up transfer from new technology to real productivity. The new scientific findings directly promote technological progress, and, in particular, the new scientific and technological breakthroughs directly promote innovation in industries like new materials, biotech, and new energy. This mode of scientific and technological progress takes scientific findings as its primary source. Against this background, the essence of innovation-driven economic growth is transferring scientific and technological achievements into productivity.

The turn to innovation for driving economic growth should avoid the following-up theory prevailing in developing countries, which believes that developing countries lag behind developed countries in science, technology, and economy, and they cannot step onto the same starting line with their developed counterparts in technological progress, so they have to adopt follow-up strategies to develop their high technology and new industries through imitation and introduction. This following-up theory is commonly seen in nearly all development economics textbooks. The pattern of technological progress promoted through following developed countries mainly involves original equipment manufacturer (OEM) processing and technological imitation, which is virtually a radiation of foreign innovative technology into China with its source of innovation abroad. The new technologies adopted are actually mature ones abroad with core and crucial technology outside China. So, the introduction of innovation can at best bridge the international gap but cannot change the status of lagging behind.

As the world's second largest economy, China should and can innovate its pattern of technological progress. In the past, China missed several industrial revolutions due to the low development level and so on, but at present, the world is flat, and due to the interaction between economic globalization and scientific globalization, network, and IT application ensures every country an equitable access to new science and technology as well as industrial revolution. Especially after the 2008 global financial crisis, the world will greet new science and technology and industrial revolution. China shall never miss this opportunity.

As a large world economy, China has already qualified itself for standing on the same starting line of innovation with other developed countries. China has obtained the same opportunity with its counterparts to develop new industries. For one thing, the international gaps in scientific research at the present stage are smaller than those in scientific and technological industries and besides, science and knowledge travels across the globe faster than technology. Therefore, the interaction and combination between science and technology as well as the innovation through the joint efforts of enterprises, universities, and research institutes can be promoted in various fields by the latest science and technology in the world, and meanwhile, the translation from science and technology into productivity can also be speeded up. For another, a large economy can achieve great missions by focusing on certain priorities. China can take advantage of the "whole nation" system, thus being capable of making major breakthroughs in certain fields through focused mass investments. Under such circumstances, the route of advancing Chinese science and technology can turn from the pattern of following-up to the pattern of leading. Some key fields can even make big transitions and other fields catch up with and even go ahead of the international level, thus occupying the commanding point of the world science and technology, especially through the deep integration of the internet, big data, artificial intelligence, and real economy.

Innovation as a driving force has become both a route for economic growth and an objective for transforming economic growth mode. The present prevailing economic growth mode is changing from extensive to intensive. The intensive growth mode basically means intensively using material factor and increasing the efficiency of factor use. Although the intensive economic growth mode involves the effect of technological progress, it is still stuck with the framework of promoting economic growth through material factor. Innovation-driven growth mode is different. According to its definition, it not only handles the issue of efficiency, but more importantly, utilizes intangible factors to make new combinations among all factors. It is the application and spread of scientific and technological advances to production and business for the first time, thus creating new growth factors. Consequently, innovation-driven growth mode is of higher standards and of higher level than intensive growth mode and can best reflect the characteristics of economic development at a new stage.

18.7 Change of Development Strategy from Imbalance to Balance

There is a division between balance strategy and imbalance strategy in development economics. The balance strategy believes that developing countries are not well equipped with capital and other resources to promote growth in all aspects when faced with structural constraints in economic development, so it is impossible for them to achieve a balanced development. Therefore, investment has to be made into some of the selected sectors and areas while other sectors and areas have to gradually develop by themselves by taking advantage of the external economy and connecting effects brought by growth in the above selected sectors and areas. In reality, the strategy is reflected by the imbalanced investments in industries and areas.

Since the reform and opening up, China has virtually adopted the imbalance strategy to permit a part of people to get rich first so as to fully mobilize the development potential in advantaged areas and industries in collaboration with marketization. First, China promotes urbanization and industrialization by prioritizing urban development and industrialization over the rural areas and agriculture. Second, China implements various regional development strategies, like coastal development strategy. Third, China adopts some preferential tax policies for some enterprises. All these strategies and policies are successful in bringing out fully the development potential in all aspects, breaking the ceiling of development in a rather short time and realizing a leaping development. Nevertheless, when this imbalance has developed to a certain point, problems of serious imbalance occur and its weaknesses show up. These include: the coexistence of overcapacity and the lack of effective supply in terms of the industrial structure; the lagging behind of agricultural modernization in terms of industrial and agricultural relations; the lagging behind of rural development in terms of urban–rural relations; the prominent issues of poverty in the central and western regions in terms of the regional structure; and the severe ecological damages in terms of the relations between growth and ecology; the lagging behind of social development in terms of the relationship between economic development and social development.

Stepping into the middle-income stage, China, faced with the imbalance of national economy, needs to turn to coordinated development in time. The imbalance strategy adopted at the low-income stage should not be allowed to continue, and besides, the balance strategy should be implemented to make up for the weaknesses. Otherwise, it is difficult to build an all-round moderately prosperous society, let alone step into a high-income stage.

The Marxist social reproduction theory can be concluded as a coordinated development theory. The two categories of balance strategies demand proportionate development based on overall coordination among sectors. The path of modernization with Chinese characteristics created by China's economic development is a path of balanced development integrating industrialization, IT application, urbanization, and agricultural modernization. The all-round moderately prosperous society should benefit all people and involve the coordinated development among economy, society, culture, politics, and ecology.

A balanced strategy should be implemented based on the vision for coordinated development, achieving balance among industrial structure, urban and rural structure, regional structure, and the relevant development strategy. This includes the coordinated efforts for economic growth made by the three driving forces: consumption, investment, and exports and the three industries. Aiming at the existing unbalanced economic development, China should address weaknesses based on the idea of coordinated development from the following three aspects. First, address the weakness in agricultural modernization to promote for the simultaneous developments of new industrialization, informatization, urbanization, and agricultural modernization; second, address the weakness of regional poverty to promote a coordinated development of urban and rural regions; third, address the weakness in social development to promote coordinated economic and social development; fourth, address the weakness in ecological civilization to promote sustainable development.

18.8 Modernization of the Dual Structure: From Non-agricultural Support to Direct Target with Respect to the Development of Agriculture, Rural Areas, and Farmers

The traditional route to avoid the dual structure is pointed out by the Lewis model: a large quantity of agricultural surplus labor transfers to modern industry while the latter expands its capital accumulation until all the agricultural surplus labor is transferred; then at this turning point, industry should support agriculture for its technological transformation. According to the Lewis model, agricultural modernization can be realized on the condition that its surplus labor is assimilated into modern industry and industry, in turn, supports agricultural technological transformation. In other words, agriculture is modernized through industrialization.

Since the 1980s, China has kept supporting rural enterprises to promote industrialization and urbanization in rural areas, creating a path that drives the development of agriculture, rural areas, and farmers with non-agricultural support, i.e., addressing problems in rural regions through de-agriculturalization, urbanization, and labor transfer. The effects are evident in the following three aspects. First, industrialization was speeded up and China has transformed itself from an agricultural country to a rising industrial one; second, urbanization has accelerated and China has entered the middle stage of urbanization; third, the development of agriculture, rural areas, and farmers are at a much higher level. However, the development of agriculture, rural areas, and farmers are simply driven by non-agricultural developments and they cannot catch up with the latter's speed, so the gaps between the urban and the rural and between industry and agriculture are not narrowed, but instead enlarged.

Modernization with a priority to industrialization cannot avoid the consequence of a relative lagging behind of agricultural modernization. Now, the developments of agriculture, rural areas, and farmers are the weakness of the integrated development of industrialization, IT application, urbanization, and agricultural modernization. As General Secretary Xi Jinping points out, even though the ratio of urbanization reaches over 70%, there are still 400–500 million people in rural areas, so the rural areas should never become bleak or left-behind places or hometowns in memory. Agricultural modernization and the construction of new rural areas should go hand in hand with urbanization, so that they can reinforce each other. The developments of agriculture, rural areas, and farmers represented by agricultural modernization should be strengthened in order to achieve the first centenary goals.[2] Therefore, the path in terms of the developments of agriculture, rural areas, and farmers should turn from non-agricultural support to direct target. The developments of agriculture, rural areas, and farmers should be the object and emphasis of modernization.

Agricultural modernization, namely developing modern agriculture, involves the following three aspects. First, the old mode of production and business operation should be fundamentally reformed to increase the productivity of labor, capital, land, and total factor so as to raise farmers' income. Second, agriculture is the base of national economy, so its modernization should meet the increasing demand for increasing the quantity and quality of farm products in the process of social modernization. Third,

[2]There are two centenary goals. The first refers to completing the building of an all-round moderately prosperous society by the time the Communist Party of China celebrates its centenary in 2021, and the second refers to turning the People's Republic of China into a modern socialist country that is prosperous, strong, democratic, culturally advanced, and harmonious by the time it celebrates its centenary in 2049. (Translator's note).

innovation in agricultural system should be carried out, involving reforming the agricultural operation system, strengthening agricultural systematization, reforming the rural land system, the distribution system of farm products, and so on.

Modernization of farmers is aimed at training professional farmers of new kinds. According to Theodore W. Schultz's theory, the existing production factors in agriculture have been effectively used, so new production factors need to be introduced for reform. The factors needed are science, technology, and human resources. Developing modern agriculture should not simply rely on farmers, mainly consisting of women and elderly people left behind in rural areas, but on a new breed of professional farmers trained through the investment of human capital. The farmers engaging in agriculture should receive education of modern culture and embrace the atmosphere of modern market economy. The realization of agricultural modernization should rely on knowledgeable and innovative farmers, qualified scientific researchers and technicians, and insightful public administrators and entrepreneurs.

The dual urban and rural structure refers to the coexistence of modern cities and underdeveloped rural areas, consistent with weak agriculture. The large and disperse rural areas are underdeveloped in terms of infrastructure, education, culture, and medical treatment facilities, and farmers in rural areas have no access to modern lifestyle and civilization enjoyed by inhabitants in the city. The basic path to overcome the dual urban and rural structure is by achieving urbanization. The path of urbanization created through practice in China refers to agricultural labor force entering cities and towns, while the present urbanization reverses the previous one in extending the impetus and factors of city development first to towns and in turn to rural areas, fundamentally changing the underdeveloped situation of rural areas. This is the urbanization of city factors. The past urbanization required rural workers to come into cities while the present urbanization requires the urban development factors to go outside of cities. The city factors and lifestyles extend to rural areas, which can be taken as a way of integrated development of urban and rural areas.

The integrated development of urban and rural areas is not intended to eliminate the latter, nor to eliminate agriculture, but to achieve an integrated development of the urban and rural areas while retaining their respective characteristics. It is not intended to lower the status of the urban areas to adapt to the rural situation, but to raise the status of the rural, to bridge the gap between the urban and the rural in terms of economic and social development, to remove the structural barriers against the flow of factors, and to form industrial divisions and distributions based on the inherent characteristics of the industries in both urban and rural areas. The urban and rural areas are on equal footing and in mutual permeation and integration in terms of economic, social, and cultural development. The integrated development of urban and rural areas involves the integrated development in five aspects: city and countryside planning, employment services, social security, public services, and city management.

The integrated development of urban and rural areas needs to transform towns into cities, i.e., to make them function as cities, with the implication to strengthen the functions of industrial development, public services, employment and population aggregation in small and medium cities and small towns.

People are at the core of urbanization. That is to say, farmers become city residents and enjoy urban amenities. There are two paths to realize it. First, speed up the reform of the household registration system, take well-ordered steps to make people moving out of rural areas city residents, and try to make basic urban public services accessible to all permanent residents. Second, make opportunities and facilities provided for city residents accessible to rural areas and towns, expand the opportunities of employment in towns, institute high-quality education, culture, and medical facilities in rural areas and towns, and increase supplies of public products and facilities for rural areas, and especially for towns. As a result, farmers can share various rights with city residents without moving to the cities.

In conclusion, agricultural modernization should give priority to the modernization of the quality of agricultural products based on scientific and technological progress; the modernization of rural areas should focus on the modernization of rural life and rural living environment based on the integrated urban–rural development; the modernization of farmers should emphasize on making farmers city residents on the basis of urbanization. To promote the modernization of agriculture, rural areas and farmers on this high-level, new types of industry-agriculture and urban–rural relations should be built based on the promotion of agriculture by industry, the support of rural development by urban areas, the reciprocity between agriculture and industry, and the integration between the urban and the rural.

18.9 Change of China's Status in Globalization: From Merging in with Comparative Advantages to Taking the Lead with Competitive Advantage

In the past 40 years of reform and opening up, China actually integrated itself into globalization with its comparative advantage in resource endowments. The effects were evident in the way that foreign-invested enterprises brought in the global value chains of high-tech products. On the chains, China's labor cost, land cost, and infrastructure were combined with foreign capital, technology, and management so that it rapidly integrated itself into global network of production, becoming a factory and low-cost manufacturing base for the world. Although Chinese enterprises were at the low-end of the global value chain with high outputs but low profits, they did share the benefits of economic globalization, the biggest of which was undertaking the transfer of advanced manufacturing through the global value chains. Chinese enterprises have notably improved their own science, technology, and industrialization through learning-by-doing, imitation and innovation, and digestion, absorption, and re-innovation.

After 40 years of open economy in China, today, when it comes to the opening up strategies, one should both acknowledge the benefits of the comparative advantage in resource endowments embedded into the global value chains and prevent the potential risk of being stuck in the trap of low-end comparative advantage. Participating in international division of labor and trade based on the comparative advantage in resources endowment and attracting foreign investment by making use of labor, land, and environment resources would certainly help gain a certain amount of benefits in trade and investment, but it can't change China's dependence on the economy and technology and market of the developed countries, nor can it narrow the gap in the economic technology between China and the developed countries.

Based on the analysis of the additional value of comparative advantage, it is believed that China's gross manufacturing products rank first in the world, but a large number of industries still remain at the medium and low-end of the global value chains and the parts of high-tech products manufactured in China stay at the low-end of value chains. Most of the core technologies and key technological links do not belong to China.

There are few creations from China and most of the brands are imported from foreign countries. There is a big gap of additional value between low-end manufacturing (processing and assembling) and medium and high-end manufacturing. China's role in the global value chains that relies on comparative advantage can no longer match the overall status its economy has achieved.

Based on the analysis of resource endowments, it is believed that comparative advantage in them no longer exists. The additional value achieved at the low-end value chain is essentially low, much lower in recent years when there arise new circumstances such as the short supply of labor and land, the significant increase of cost and the stricter environmental standards. This means that labor, resources, and environment no longer have the comparative advantages. As the price of labor and land increases, the additional value would further decrease. Besides, the advantage of scale at the medium and low-end of the global value chains no longer exists; i.e., no matter how much labor is poured into the low-end links, scale economy could not be achieved. This is the situation where hard work brings no affluence and high outputs bring low profits.

Based on the analysis of international competitiveness of manufacturing products, it is believed that China has become a large world manufacturing country, but among its manufacturing products, few are created domestically. The comparative advantage in labor and natural resources is based on low prices, but with the decreasing abundance of these factors, the relative labor price and productivity will no longer have a comparative advantage, nor will the relative land price and productivity. If China intends to transform itself from a large world economy to a great world economy, it should seek trade benefits not simply by relying on the comparative advantage in labor and natural resources, but by bringing capital and technology into full play at a higher level in a larger scope so as to quickly bridge the technological gap with the developed countries.

Based on the situational analysis of globalization, the past globalization was dominated by developed American and European countries, which reaped the most benefits from it. Since the 2008 world financial crisis and the subsequent American and European sovereign debt crisis, American and European economies have long remained in recession and stagnation and consequently slowed down the overall world economic growth. Alongside the economic recession, these countries represented by the United States promote reindustrialization and protectionism, especially the US preferential investment and trade policy implemented by the Trump administration. These policies are essentially anti-globalization. Conversely, China, as the world's second largest economy, takes the successive role of promoting globalization. In the past, China embedded itself into globalization with its comparative advantage in resource endowments, while at present it promotes globalization through participation in the global economic governance, which means participating in and taking the lead in the formulation and refinement of international economic regulations.

China's opening up strategy needs to change from comparative advantage to competitive advantage due to its changing status in economic globalization. Why competitive advantage? What are its differences from comparative advantages? The differences are as follows. First, the theory of comparative advantage, believed by people for over a century, is essentially a guidance for enterprises to participate in national trade and division of labor. However, under the circumstances of today's economic globalization, the theory of competitive advantage raises the concept of comparative advantage to the national level, taking nation as an economic unit. Competitive advantage refers mainly to national opening-up strategies without rejecting enterprise participation in international competition with their comparative advantage. Second, traditional theories of trade tend to take cost and product differences as conditions of trade, highlighting the comparative advantage of developing countries in labor and natural resources, while the theory of competitive advantage tends to give priority to technological progress and innovation, focusing on fostering a new advantage with core competitiveness in technology, trademark, quality, and services. Third, the traditional theory of comparative advantage is based on the condition of national resource endowments while the theory of competitive advantage is based on the question of whether the industry of a nation possesses competitive advantage over its competitors. Fourth, the role of a country's industries in the global value chains embodies its scientific and industrial competitiveness. China's science and technology in the past remained at a developing stage, following developed countries, and consequently at the low-end of the global value chains. In contrast, at present, China's scientific and technological innovation steps into the stage of keeping pace with the developed countries and even taking the lead. Accordingly, Chinese enterprises have promoted their role in the global value chains with an attempt to take the lead by means of expanding to the upper-stream parts of the industry chain like R&D and design, extending to the lower-stream parts of the chain like logistics, brands, sales channel, and updating the low-end processing and assembling link to the component manufacturing link with higher demand of technology and quality and higher additional value.

Consequently, the essential path to seeking competitive advantage is to promote the upgrading of domestic industrial structures by means of scientific and technological innovation with a special focus on developing emerging industries at the same level with the developed countries, thus forming industrial structures with competitive advantage over world-class competitors. This embodies the endogenous characteristic of growth and the driving characteristic of innovation. On the surface, it looks like the turn from exogenous pull to endogenous development, but actually international competitiveness of Chinese industries is promoted through scientific and industrial innovation, an endogenous innovation that supports opening up.

An innovation-driven economy in pursuit of competitive advantage does not exclude an open economy for it needs opening up to support innovation. Today's international economy is led by the flow of factors, especially that of innovation factors, which cannot be gained domestically but can be obtained from abroad through opening up to the world. Due to historic reasons and different development levels, advanced innovation resources are still mainly located in developed countries. Therefore, the open economy at a new stage should give priority to the introduction of the innovation factor. Growth as the focus of development in the past was essentially promoted by capital while other factors like technology and management basically followed capital, so accordingly, the open economy took advantage of international resources (foreign advanced technology and management) by introducing foreign capital. Nowadays, the priority of development is given to innovation, all various innovation factors follow talents, so accordingly, it is necessary to introduce high-end innovative talents and thus take advantage of other international innovation factors in order to develop innovation-driven economy.

In conclusion, China, as a large world economy, has made innovations in its economic development theory, which indicates that it intends to perfect itself rather than seek hegemony. As the world's second largest economy, China should adapt to the transformation and further free people's minds instead of adhering to the old patterns of thinking. It should think over the path of development for a great world economy from the historical starting point of a large world economy and find development strategies to transform itself from a large economy to a great economy, so as to realize the dream of the Chinese nation to build a powerful country.

Bibliography

洪银兴:《学好用好中国特色社会主义政治经济学》, 江苏人民出版社 2017 年版. Hong Yinxing. *Learn and Use Socialist Political Economy with Chinese Characteristics*. Nanjing: Jiangsu People's Publishing House, 2017.

习近平,《习近平总书记系列重要讲话读本 (2016 年版)》, 学习出版社 2016 年版. Xi Jinping. *Guiding Principles from the General Secretary Xi Jinping's Major Speeches (2016)*. Beijing: Xuexi Chubanshe, 2016.

Chapter 19

Conclusion: Reflections on the Construction of Socialist Political Economy with Chinese Characteristics in the New Era

Xi Jinping's thought on socialism with Chinese characteristics for a new era is the latest development in this field. The economic development since the 18th National Congress of the Communist Party of China (CPC) has proven that Xi Jinping's thought not only guided China's economic development into the new era, but also opened up new horizons for contemporary Marxist political economy. It is of great importance to further study the theoretical system and discourse system of socialist political economy with Chinese characteristics in accordance with Xi Jinping's thought.

19.1 Major Developmental Issues in the New Era as Orientation

The adherence to problem-orientation is a striking characteristic of Marxism. This fundamentally means listening to the voice of the era, answering the call of the era, and meticulously seeking solutions to urgent key problems to find out the law of development and promote theoretical innovation. In constructing socialist political economy with Chinese characteristics, such an approach basically requires being oriented toward the problems of the era. As the new era has its own characteristics, socialist political economy with Chinese characteristics is by no means the product of the socialist part of the past political economy, although there are a few similarities.

The starting point of socialist political economy with Chinese characteristics is the primary stage of socialism, in which China has remained for a long period of time. It is a lasting historical period that can still be divided into several sub-stages. The primary stage of socialism with Chinese characteristics has already gone through two periods successively: the period of "standing up" and the period of "growing rich". Now it is progressing to another period of "becoming strong". The overarching tasks for upholding and developing socialism with Chinese characteristics in the new era are to realize socialist modernization as well as the great national rejuvenation. These tasks should also be the overarching tasks for constructing socialist political economy with Chinese characteristics in the new era. In light of this, socialist political economy with Chinese characteristics in the new era must answer, both systematically and from the perspective of political economy, what kind of socialism with Chinese characteristics should be upheld and developed, as well as how to do so. This involves fundamental economic issues like the overarching objectives, tasks, plans, strategies, modes, driving force, as well as the strategic steps.

As socialism with Chinese characteristics has entered a new era, China's economic development has also entered the new era and has progressed from low-income stage to middle-income stage. It is now confronted with a number of major developmental problems, such as the unsustainability of high-speed growth caused by the decline of traditional impetus to development, and the exceedingly challenging "middle-income trap". In the face of the "new normal" phase of economic development, General Secretary Xi Jinping has pointed out that we are still in an important period of strategic opportunities for China's development. We need to enhance confidence, adapt ourselves to the "new normal" phase by acting in light of features of economic development at the current stage, and keep a calm, composed attitude. If the "new normal" phase is observed in consideration of the period of strategic opportunities and judged in a scientific way, it cannot be simply understood as the slowdown of economic growth but rather, as the entry of economic development into the new era through a scientific judgment. It is a period of time when economic development changes from high-speed growth to high-quality growth. High-quality growth is not naturally formed, but requires the crossing of three barriers, i.e., transformation of the developmental mode, optimization of economic structure, and change of growth impetus. Therefore, reflecting the mission of transformation of the political economy, socialist political economy with Chinese characteristics needs to shift its focus to the realization of high-quality development and target the barriers in need of removal so as to establish the political economy for the period of "becoming strong".

19.2 Putting People First as Disciplinary Nature

The core issue in upholding the guidance of Marxism is to address the question of for whom. Socialism with Chinese characteristics in the new era embodies the idea of putting people first. It also serves as the guiding principle for constructing a socialist political economy with Chinese characteristics in the new era. All economic theories that touch upon economic interests have this class feature. In the new era of socialism with Chinese characteristics, the class feature of political economy that we often mention refers to its representation of all the people's interests rather than being taken by one specific interest group. Therefore, the construction of theoretical system of socialist political economy with Chinese characteristics should aim at the realization of the overall interests of the people.

Political economy that puts people first is reflected in the scientific definition for the goal for economic development. Compared with the long existing developmental mode of "production for production's sake", political economy with Chinese characteristics has made clear that consumption plays a fundamental role in economic development. In this way, meeting the demand of people should be regarded as the goal of development. In the old socialist political economy, the developmental goal was to meet the ever-growing material and cultural demands of the people as much as possible. When it comes to the new era, the goal has been upgraded to meeting the needs of the people so as to lead to better lives. This method guarantees the rights and interests of the people in terms of economy, politics, culture, and ecology, and enables them to gain a stronger sense of contentment, further showing the progress that socialist political economy with Chinese characteristics is making in the new era.

According to the blueprint for modernization in the new era released in the 19th National Congress of the CPC, the idea of putting people first in socialist political economy with Chinese characteristics is embodied in four aspects. First, the improvement of people's well-being. On the basis of the living standards in an all-round, moderately prosperous society, people will live a richer life at the stage of realizing modernization by and large, and then enjoy much more happiness and peace at the stage of realizing modernization in all areas. Second, the all-round development of human beings, or in other words, the modernization of human beings. Third, the realization of common prosperity. At the stage of realizing modernization by and large, the gaps in regional development and living standards between urban and rural areas will have been narrowed significantly, and equal access to basic public services will have been basically realized. Entering the stage of realizing modernization in all areas, China plans to basically materialize the common prosperity of its entire population. Four, the achievement of harmony between human and nature. This modernization allows people to genuinely feel happy and enjoy fresh air, clean water, and green food.

19.3 Principal Social Contradiction in the New Era as Main Line

The analysis of basic social contradiction is the fundamental norm of Marxist political economy. However, subject to the need to overthrow capitalism, political economy that focuses on capitalist economy mainly analyzes the relations of production that fail to accommodate the development of productive forces. Socialist political economy with Chinese characteristics, on the other hand, not only continues with the norm of analyzing basic social contradictions but it also serves the need of constructing a new society by examining both the economic system that involves production relations as well as the economic development that involves productive forces. This is to say: the issue of economic development has become a research object of socialist political economy with Chinese characteristics.

The judgment concerning principal social contradiction imposes direct influence upon the direction and focus of social and economic development. The Third Plenary Session of the 11th Central Committee of the CPC concluded the thinking of taking class struggle as the key link and claimed that China's principal contradiction in the society was the contradiction between the people's ever-growing material and cultural need, and backward production. With this in mind, the political economy that used to guide people to get rich has is now focused on the major aspects of this contradiction since the reform and opening up. Today, with China entering the new era, the principal contradiction has transformed to the contradiction between unbalanced and inadequate development and the people's ever-growing needs for a better life. On one hand, China has progressed from low-income stage to middle-income stage, and people's living standards have been significantly improved. The people not only care about their "ever-growing material and cultural need", but also become more concerned with growing needs for a better life in terms of democracy, law, fairness, justice, security, and environment. On the other hand, due to the development since the reform and opening up, China's productive forces have been clearly enhanced, and its capacity of social production has ranked among the top in the world in many aspects. The statement of "the backward production" in the past principal contradiction no longer summarizes the real situation of China's economic and social development. The new contradiction is the restrictions of unbalanced and inadequate development on people's ever-growing needs for a better life.

The change of China's principal social contradiction is a historical change of overall significance. The analysis of this contradiction is the main line of social political economy with Chinese characteristics in the new era. China's long period at the primary stage of socialism is fundamentally caused by its lower level of productive forces than that of the developed capitalist countries. Accordingly, Comrade Deng Xiaoping pointed out that the essence of socialism is to liberate and develop productive forces, eliminate exploitation and polarization, and gradually achieve common prosperity. Later, General Secretary Xi Jinping noted that the idea that preserving the ecological environment is preserving productive forces, and improving the ecological environment as developing productive forces should be firmly established. Accordingly, determined by the basic features of the primary stage of socialism, the construction of the theoretical system of socialist political economy with Chinese characteristics aims to build a systematic economic theory covering the liberation, development, and preservation of productive forces.

According to the latest statement of principal social contradiction in the new era, socialist political economy with Chinese characteristics should adopt the analytic approaches of the two-point theory and focal-point theory to study the representation of the principal contradiction in the process of economic development as well as its corresponding solutions. The focal-point theory requires the analysis of the principal contradiction to be more focused on the major issues involved. For example, in face of the old principal, contradiction between the peoples' ever-growing material and cultural need and backward production, political economy previously focused on changing the backwardness of production. This being said, taking the principal contradiction in the new era as the main line, socialist political economy with Chinese characteristics should focus on the solution to the problem of unbalanced and inadequate development, including issues with efficiency and structure on the supply side. It is of utmost importance to increase total factor productivity through reforms on quality, efficiency, and impetus as well as the optimization of economic structure in the aspects of industries, regions, and urban and rural areas. These significantly enrich the thinking of socialist political economy with Chinese characteristics.

19.4 New Vision of Development

Political economy studies the economic laws. In the conference of the Political Bureau of the CPC Central Committee on July 29, 2014, General Secretary Xi Jinping pointed out that development should be scientific, sustainable, and inclusive by following the laws of economy, nature, and society. This statement is the theorization of the understandings regarding the regularity of economic development and the scientific grasp of its new characteristics and new trends at China's "new normal" phase of economy. We should obey the objective laws of the new era to form the concept of innovative, coordinated, green, open, and shared development. In this phase, innovative development focuses on solving the problem of development impetus and serves as the primary driving force for development; coordinated development aims at solving the problem of unbalanced development with an emphasis on shoring up weak spots; green development is concerned with the issue of harmony between man and nature, which stresses the construction of ecological civilization; open development aims to realize development that is both domestic- and external-oriented and to promote the establishment of a community of common destiny for all mankind; shared development refers to the issue of social fairness and justice, suggesting the realization of common prosperity. Generally speaking, a systematic elaboration of the new vision of development has become the basic content of socialist political economy with Chinese characteristics.

The new vision of development is a scientific conclusion on the practical experiences of China's economic development. Xi Jinping's thought on Socialism with Chinese characteristics for a New Era mainly embraces scientific guidance for the construction of China's socialist economy in the new era. It opens up new horizons for socialist political economy with Chinese characteristics. The new vision is a guide for development and reform in the new era. According to the report of the 19th National Congress of the CPC, socialist political economy with Chinese characteristics needs to further uphold and improve the reform and opening up so as to gradually generate important theories. In this way, China must uphold and improve its basic socialist economic system with no irresolution about working to consolidate and develop the public sector and no irresolution about working to encourage, support, and guide the development of the non-public sector. We must let the market play the decisive role and the government a better role in resource allocation to improve the socialist market economy structure. To improve its basic socialist distribution system, China must adhere to the principle of distribution according to work while improving the systems and mechanisms of distribution according to factors, aiming at promoting a more reasonable and orderly income distribution. Moreover, a modernized economic system should be built to advance new industrialization, IT application, urbanization, and agricultural modernization. Last but not least, China should take the initiative to take part in and promote economic globalization so that the system of opening up can be improved. All these constitute the contents of socialist political economy based on the new vision of development.

The logical system of a socialist political economy should consider the entry of China's economic development into the new era as the starting point. Four related aspects are scrutinized as follows: First, the analysis of the economic system must consider the goal of improving the socialist market economy, including the basic economic system, basic distribution system, and so on. Second, the analysis of economic operation should be directed by the improvement of efficiency and quality of economic operation, including market, enterprises, and macro control involved in operational system. Third, the analysis of economic development should be led by the socialist modernization, including economic development mode, economic structure, and impetus to economic growth with special attention paid toward modernized economic system. Fourth, the analysis of China's economic relations with foreign countries should be guided by the goal of establishing a community through common destiny for all mankind under the terms of the new trend of economic globalization as well as the new environment and system of opening up to the outside world. Together, these form the logic system of socialist political economy with Chinese characteristics under the guidance of the new vision of development.

19.5 Discourse System and Theoretical Resources

General Secretary Xi Jinping pointed out that philosophy and social sciences with Chinese characteristics should optimize three kinds of resources. The first resource is Marxism, including the basic principles of Marxism and the achievements and cultural forms of Sinicization of Marxism. The second resource is the fine traditional Chinese culture, which contains precious, rare resources gained during the development of philosophy and social sciences with Chinese characteristics. The third resource is foreign philosophy and social sciences, including the positive achievements of philosophy and social sciences in all countries throughout the world since they are beneficial to philosophy and social sciences with Chinese characteristics. In this way, socialist political economy with Chinese characteristics also needs the help of these theoretical resources to analyze China's contemporary economic issues.

Socialist political economy with Chinese characteristics is Marxism in contemporary China. Marxist political economy has not only offered the world outlook and methodology to socialist political economy with Chinese characteristics, but also laid the foundation for its discourse system. *Capital*, for example, is of particular importance with the systematic categorization of economics and methods established in it, the prediction of and prescription for future society, and the elaboration of basic principles of market economy. Many things in socialist political economy with Chinese characteristics can be explained by Marxist standpoints and methods included in the book. Socialist political economy with Chinese characteristics tells the story of China. As socialist economic practices with Chinese characteristics appear richer and more varied, the corresponding discourse system of political economy needs continual innovation in practice. New practice needs innovation-oriented discourse to tell the Chinese story. It also needs new theoretical generalization and a new category of economics to reflect Chinese wisdom. For instance, the new vision of development and the socialist modernization in the way of integrating the development of industrialization, IT application, urbanization, and agricultural modernization are not only the creation of China's practice, but also the theoretical innovation of socialist political economy with Chinese characteristics.

In an open world, socialist political economy with Chinese characteristics features openness rather than closure, including openness to Western economics. Contemporary Chinese economics and Western economics share the same economic background. In particular, if China expects to participate and play a leading role in the governance of global economy in economic globalization, it needs to adopt a common discourse to foster its economy to "go global". The common discourse can be obtained in a market economy as well as among developing countries eager to seek development. Knowledge is borderless. Therefore, socialist political economy with Chinese characteristics needs to critically absorb the well-established economic theories worldwide. The selective learning of Western economics in terms of theories and categories is based on China's full confidence in theory, path, and system with the adherence to the core socialist values as a presupposition. Major Western economic theories that socialist political economy with Chinese characteristics has used for reference so far include those concerning resource allocation, dual structure, middle-income trap, total factor productivity, sustainable development, knowledge economy, national innovation system, economic globalization, and so on. Of course, when entering the socialist political economy with Chinese characteristics, these Western categories and principles need to be absorbed critically and combined with Chinese reality. In particular, they need to be adapted to China's institutional characteristics and basic conditions.

In general, socialist political economy with Chinese characteristics in the new era is Marxist political economy in contemporary China. The construction of its theoretical system must always combine Marxist theories with China's practice in the new era. It must go with the times and target the principal social contradiction in the new era. It must also address China's challenges in growing stronger, or in other words, modernization.

Index

N

O

P

Lightning Source UK Ltd.
Milton Keynes UK
UKHW021242190122
397359UK00003B/253

9 789811 241529